Join Together

Join Together

Forty Years of the Rock Music Festival

★ ★ ★ ★ ★

Marley Brant

Backbeat Books

An Imprint of Hal Leonard Corporation
New York

Published in 2008 by Backbeat Books
An Imprint of Hal Leonard Corporation
19 West 21st Street, New York, NY 10010

Printed in the United States of America

Book design by Snow Creative Services

Library of Congress Cataloging-in-Publication Data is available upon request.

ISBN 978-0-87930-926-8

www.backbeatbooks.com

For my family…

Mom and Dad, Dave, Tim, Willie, Kathie, Carol, John, Jen, Will, Jeanie-weenie,

Fancy-face, Ubie, the Big A, Auntie Vera, Uncle "Sess," Ralph, Jocelyn, Megan,

Ralphie, John, Rosie, Luke, Julie, Jo, George, Beth, my forty-six first cousins,

Heather, Jasmine, Ava, the Fanster, and Cha

Contents

Preface

Join Together: Forty Years of the Rock Music Festival has been an extraordinary and enjoyable project. Being a child of the sixties, I remember the impact that "Monterey Pop" and "Woodstock" had on my generation. It was amazing to us that such gatherings would reflect *our* society, *our* politics, and *our* hopes for the future. And the music that we were exposed to because of the success of those festivals was pure magic. While watching Live 8 on television in 2005, I realized that the music festival has not only come full circle but is now often a worldwide experience. Music festivals of the 1960s reflected the "flower children" movement, but they continue to give voice to the young people of today. As music artists are introduced to new audiences, fans can follow their musical tastes by attending festivals that cater to their specific preferences or sample new music through a wide variety of performances, and people can gather together for the sheer joy of celebrating each other and savoring the music itself. Festivals come in many flavors now: local, destination, traveling shows, and globally televised political and sociological events—each with their individual stamp on the rock music landscape.

The idea of exploring the topic of the evolution of the rock festival appealed to me—I found the subject fascinating. I was excited to learn that so many others in the music industry thought so, too. Over ninety music artists have contributed their memories and insights to this book, offering their unique perspectives as both performers and music fans. Through their participation we are able to look through their eyes at the various elements and components of the major rock festivals and experience what it was actually like to be there.

Join Together: Forty Years of the Rock Music Festival is a presentation of many unique and important moments in rock history. Among the festivals featured are Monterey Pop, the Woodstock festivals, Isle of Wight, Knebworth, US Festival I & II, Altamont, Lollapalooza, Live Aid, Ozzfest, the Vans Warped Tour, the Coachella Valley Music and Arts Festivals, Live 8, Bonnaroo, Live Earth, and many other popular festival events. (I apologize if your favorite festival isn't included—there are many regional festivals that qualify as significant moments in music history and no doubt mean a lot to the people who attended them, but I've only been able to include a handful due to time and space constraints.) We'll look at the impact of the rock festival and how each of the major festivals reflected the music and society of its time. We'll see how each event was conceived, some of the mechanics involved in securing the sites and artist participation, the day(s) of the event, the music components of the festival as told through the words of the performers and attendees, and each festival's ultimate significance to rock music and to society. Previously unpublished stories and personal accounts by those who were there will allow us a unique perspective as we travel through time to experience these sometimes wonderful, sometimes dreadful, but always extraordinary and captivating moments in rock history. I had a great time researching the festivals and gathering the commentary. The artists involved enjoyed telling their stories and sharing their distinctive points of view. I hope you enjoy reading about the festivals as much as we enjoyed relating each story.

Marley Brant

Introduction

Although popular music has changed and evolved through the years, one aspect of the music scene is now a fact: the rock festival, past and present, is a musical and cultural phenomenon. The components change, the performers vary, the politics are updated and refocused, the outlets expand, the fans come, and the world watches with curiosity and fascination. Sometimes the music is standard and predictable, and other times innovative and electrifying. In a world where anything goes, controversy is common—and anticipated. The music festival is a community of those who love music and who love a good time listening or playing music. There's something in it for most who attend a rock festival, although many times it may not be what's expected.

The original rock festival—Monterey Pop—was created out of a desire to showcase emerging rock artists and draw together the growing hippie population of the San Francisco area into a syncopated federation of those involved in the sixties youth movement. While the popularity of the rock festival has ebbed and flowed over the years, the international success of the Live 8 and Live Earth festivals with broadcasts to focus attention on the issues of global poverty and the environment, and the 2007 Vans Warped Tour—featuring over 200 interchangeable bands—illustrate the continued attraction of this extraordinary congregation of music artists and their fans. The rock festival, in its various incarnations, is very much alive and very much a fundamental element of the presentation and enjoyment of popular music. Sometimes dismissed by those who don't see the attraction, or view festivals as a chaotic, hedonistic assault on the senses, the rock festival is validated by its popularity, evolution, and endurance. When it's all said and done, the rock festival is significant not only as a key element in the history of rock music but to the future of rock music itself.

The evolution of the rock festival abounds with weird and wonderful stories that define not only the music but our society—from the first laid-back "happening" to the massive experiences where body surfing and moshing are prevalent to the socially relevant events staged today. In 1967, musician Michael Bloomfield's words from the stage of the Monterey Pop festival defined a new phenomenon: "This is our generation, man. All you people, man, all together, man, it's groovy. Dig yourselves, 'cause it's really groovy."

Rock festivals appeal mostly to the young (or the young-at-heart) and celebrate both the community of man and the community of music. There is almost nowhere else that young people can congregate among their own to enjoy a society of like-minded individuals and music that appeals mostly to those under twenty-five. That isn't to say that rock festivals have no appeal to older music fans or families. It is not uncommon today to see the younger generation sharing the experience with those who were there at the beginning of this phenomenon. But the festivals aren't without their drawbacks—where else would you be willing to stand in line over an hour to use the Porta-Potties? Usually held during the summer months, festivals are hot, water is at a premium, and food is expensive. But the music . . . the music makes it worth any inconvenience that must be endured. Offering either a cross-section of subgenre rock or dedicated to a particular type of music such as heavy metal or up-to-the-minute alternative, or indie-rock, the music festival offers a veritable menu of fit-to-taste artists and bands. New music is introduced to those who may not have heard it and popular music is played by those who have built enormous fan bases, which sometimes have been developed through festival appearances.

Each rock festival is different and each one is special—sometimes offering the attendee a positive experience and sometimes not. The elements of the rock festival are varied and many. Many are destination-oriented, others traveling enterprises, and some are even televised worldwide. Some include presentations of art and information on alternative approaches to the ecology, technology, or everyday lifestyles. The music festival allows society the opportunity to observe upcoming generations in their own atmosphere: ready to take on the world through music and their individual and group identity. From Monterey Pop to Live Earth, the rock festival has come full circle, beginning with the love and peace movements, to the "me" generation, to the current atmosphere of activism. The rock festival endures to define our evolving society.

The Monterey International Pop Music Festival was the brainchild of musicians John Phillips, Cass Elliot, Paul McCartney, producer Lou Adler, and music promoter Alan Pariser, who dedicated their finances, resources, and industry connections to create a tremendous opportunity to prominently feature rock music in a festival set-ting. The Monterey Pop Festival offered rock fans their first occasion to experience three days of exceptional music and an opportunity to encounter, firsthand, the flower power movement that was defining the late sixties. Not only did Monterey Pop enjoy the status of being the first rock 'n' roll festival, but it was also the first rock benefit—the revenue of Monterey Pop was donated to a variety of area charities.

Many San Francisco-area musicians who viewed themselves as strong and important advocates of individualism (while at the same time enjoying the new communal feelings of "brotherhood and love" found in the Haight–Ashbury district) were set against capitalism and government aggression. The racially integrated list of performers who appeared at Monterey Pop, which included a variety of new-to-the-scene acts and a handful of rock's elite, played for both the exposure and the enjoyment. Monterey Pop was designed as an experience that would honor the music—a concept much appreciated by the performers who were asked to play and the fans who turned out to listen. The Monterey Pop festival marked the first major American appearance by Jimi Hendrix and Janis Joplin, artists who would go on to define the new rock music. Although it certainly was not without its problems, squabbling, and ego-tripping, John Phillips and his group's adventure was an overwhelming success.

There isn't a rock aficionado alive who hasn't heard of the commemoration of youth that took place on Max Yasgur's farm in tiny Bethel, New York in August, 1969. Hundreds of thousands of music lovers and flower children gathered to listen to contemporary bands, form a viable community, and "make peace not war." That festival, of course, was known as Woodstock. Woodstock made its mark in music history primarily due to the enormous size of its crowd: the festival had been planned for an unheard of audience of 200,000, but by the end of the festivities the attendance had soared to over 500,000. To almost everyone involved, Woodstock was quite an experience, and likely one that they never forgot. Despite the logistical nightmares and vast amounts of rain and mud, the magic that was Woodstock included memorable moments such as Jimi Hendrix anointing the dawn with a searing guitar assault on the national anthem, the debut of the honey-voiced quartet of Crosby, Stills, Nash & Young, and Country Joe and the Fish leading a cheer which defined the developing strength of the anti-war movement. In retrospect, often the most interesting aspects of the event were what happened offstage. Despite its problems, or maybe because of them, the event that was originally advertised as "A Gathering of the Tribes" and a "celebration of music and love" would come to represent a massive sociological transformation and define a generation.

On the other side of the ocean, on the Isle of Wight, the largest music festival ever held in the United Kingdom commenced one week later. This festival was headlined by Bob Dylan, marking the artist's first public appearance since a motorcycle accident that had sent him into seclusion. The festival was enjoyed by 250,000 people, yet it wasn't until 1970 that the Isle of Wight Festival was considered a major event. The 1970 festival marked the beginning of a downward spiral of disrespect and entitlement. The artists ran the gamut—there were over fifty of them performing during the three-day event: Joan Baez singing the Beatles' "Let It Be"; the Doors performing in darkness because Jim Morrison didn't want to be filmed by the event's documentarians; the second public appearance of the super group Emerson, Lake & Palmer; stellar sets by Supertramp and Free; and a closing performance by Richie Havens, the man who had opened at Woodstock. A class war broke out on the hill overlooking the festival grounds when people demanded to be let into the festival free of charge because they believed that the music "belonged to the people." The shows were interrupted several times by people jumping onstage to make inflammatory political statements. Sly and the Family Stone were pelted by beer cans and the audience was made to endure the appearance of Tiny Tim singing "God Save the Queen." When Joni Mitchell had an unexpected on-stage activist removed, the crowd turned sour, and she was brought to tears. The festival ended with promoter Ricki Farr encouraging everyone to join hands and to sing with him a bittersweet "Amazing Grace" and hope for a better tomorrow.

There were now "good" festivals and "not-so-good" festivals taking place throughout the United States and Great Britain. The feel-good vibe wasn't always within reach. At the Newport '69 festival near Los Angeles the music was first class, but the event included the unexpected: Jimi Hendrix cussed out the rowdy crowd and abruptly left the stage. A large-sized group of concert-goers expanded the festival on the third day by roaming the commercial area around the festival grounds in great numbers. The disorderly group broke windows, looted businesses, and provided adequate cause for the appearance of hundreds of "L.A.'s finest."

By this time it was clear that regardless of the appeal of music festivals, promoters needed to become better organized, security needed to be improved, and the concept of the rock festival needed to be simplified. In 1973, the Summer Jam at Watkins Glen drew over 600,000 people to hear music that emanated from only three bands: the Allman Brothers Band, the Grateful Dead, and The Band.

Music-based gatherings of large groups of people became a familiar opportunity all over the country and eventually throughout the world during the seventies. These festivals became historical checkpoints whereby current musical, political, and sociological trends could be measured and studied. Throughout the years, popular assemblies offered a variety of musical styles, genres, and artists. There were simple celebrations of music such as Bill Graham's "Day On the Green" in San Francisco. There were bigger, and ostensibly better, festivals such as California Jam, which was viewed as one of the last of the "peace and love" festivals but with a twist: there were no arrangements to film the concert or release a film as there had been with Monterey Pop and Woodstock, but portions of the Jam would be broadcast live on ABC television, which was a sponsor of the festival. "Flower Power" meet "The Man"—up close and personal. Through another corporate agreement, Los Angeles FM radio stations were allowed to use an innovative simulcast to broadcast the music for the first time, which allowed millions of those unable to attend the opportunity to enjoy the festival. The rock festival had been hitched up a notch.

Over in England, the 1974 Knebworth Festival offered a "Bucolic Frolic." The festival would be a fixture at Knebworth for the next four years, during which time the Rolling Stones, Led Zeppelin, Pink Floyd, Elton John, Paul McCartney, and Queen would appear. The crowd at Knebworth apparently enjoyed this festival's atmosphere as incidents of aggressiveness and disorder were kept to a minimum. The Knebworth Festival, although on a slightly smaller scale than its American counterparts, demonstrated how the rock festival *could* come off when the audience was treated with forethought and respect. For festival promoters everywhere it was an opportunity to live and learn.

The festival atmosphere changed enormously with the arrival of MTV. On Labor Day weekend 1982, a public party thrown by Steve Wozniak of Apple Computer featured a wide variety of artists including the Ramones, Talking Heads, the Police, Dave Edmunds, the Cars, Fleetwood Mac, and the granddaddy of all communal gathering bands, the Grateful Dead. The festival took the experience to the next level when it was broadcast live on MTV from a huge state-of-the-art stage in San Bernardino, California. Included in the experience was the US Festival Technology Exposition, which featured cutting-edge computers, software, and electronic music devices. The event was an enjoyable experience for those who attended but also reflected a subtle shift to the emerging trend of rock's elite to align themselves with the money of corporate America.

And the bands played on. The tradition of multi-artist carnivals continued through the 1980s, but the festival experience wasn't all it had been and attendance dropped off. In 1990, Perry Farrell attended "A Gathering of the Tribes," a music festival organized by promoter Bill Graham and the Cult's lead singer Ian Astbury.

The bill featured an interesting, diverse, mix of artists including Joan Baez, Indigo Girls, Lenny Kravitz, Soundgarden, Iggy Pop, and Public Enemy. Farrell's band, Jane's Addiction, had run its course and the group had decided to disband. Farrell thought headlining a similarly diverse festival would be a great send off for the band. Remembering the use of the term "lollapalooza"—which Farrell interpreted from an old movie by the Three Stooges to mean something unusual and outstanding—he organized a bill that included Nine Inch Nails, Butthole Surfers, Ice T with Body Count, Siouxsie & the Banshees, Living Colour, and the Rollins Band for the first Lollapalooza festival. Unlike music festivals of the past, Lollapalooza would be a touring festival, drawing participants from the counterculture and fans of alternative music from all areas of the United States and Canada. Farrell thought that by including diverse genres of music a strong statement would be made against what he (and many of the bands' fans and fellow musicians) viewed as the corporate takeover of rock music. This festival would also include features that were non-musical in presentation such as the Jim Rose Circus, virtual realty games, political and environmental information tables, and visual art. Lollapalooza would be a music-based "culture festival."

By 1992, the annual Lollapalooza festival showcased emerging alternative, grunge, and punk acts. Crowd surfing and mosh pits were not discouraged. The "cultural" aspects of the festival now included body piercing and tattoo booths, jungle gyms, and areas where televisions could be smashed to bits. Like any other large venture, Lollapalooza did experience problems. When Metallica appeared on the bill for Lollapalooza '96, many fans thought that the festival had lost its edge. That band was considered mainstream and the booking of Metallica had people calling foul to the original indie-alt concept of the festival. By 1998, Lollapalooza was unable to find an appropriate headliner and was cancelled. In 2003, Jane's Addiction reformed and Farrell once again launched the festival. Complaints about high ticket prices and corporate sponsorship caused a severe decrease in attendance and the festival was again cancelled due to poor ticket sales in 2004. But by 2005, Lollapalooza was back with seventy acts on five stages. Attracting over 65,000 people, this time the festival was considered a success.

Woodstock '94 was a festival held to celebrate the twenty-fifth anniversary of the original Woodstock. The "rules" this time were reflective of the changes in music presentation and the American community in general. Banned substances included drugs, alcohol, cameras, food, and . . . children. Although the list of performers included some of those who had appeared at the original festival such as Crosby,

Stills & Nash (without Young), The Band, Santana, Country Joe McDonald, Joe Cocker, and John Sebastian, the acts this time had a more contemporary edge. In an effort to make the gathering a true event, the promoters attempted to offer more than just a look back. Nine Inch Nails fans turned out in the thousands, as did fans of Aerosmith, Metallica, and the Red Hot Chili Peppers, who performed in light bulb costumes. Whereas the first Woodstock was "power to the people," this time the festival was sponsored by the people's soft drink: Pepsi.

In 1996 a festival for heavy metal called Ozzfest was launched with just a handful of acts, but that would change the following year. Headlined and promoted by metal rocker Ozzy Osbourne and his wife Sharon, the festival would produce many interesting and controversial experiences and stories. By 2004, MTV got into the act, broadcasting Ozzfest from the stage of the festival.

In 1999 a second attempt to return to the spirit of the first Woodstock resulted in a further corruption of the original festival's good vibes. Reflecting the violent and hedonistic society of the 1990s, this Woodstock would be defined by fistfights, destruction, and sexual assaults. Over 215,000 people came together for music and concluded the festival either participating in, or running from, an explosive audience outburst during which fences and looted concession stands were destroyed and used as fuel for bonfires. The unsettled mood of the crowd was immediately established by the ticket prices and location: $150 for the three-day event, which was held on an Air Force base. The lack of planning for effective sanitation was deplorable and there was little free water to stave off the effects of the high temperatures of summer. In their effort to turn a profit, promoters denied the request of several vendors to sell their food and drink at cost to offer relief. By the end of the festival a rampage by dissatisfied attendees resulted in a number of booths, portable toilets, trailers, and a small bus being set aflame. Not a good day for peace and love.

While attendance continued to be high for most of the rock festival events, television broadcasts allowed for millions more to participate and enjoy the music. Live Aid was an international festival unlike anything that preceded it. Bob Geldof of the Boomtown Rats, and Midge Ure, of Thin Lizzy and Ultravox, decided that the issue of famine in Ethiopia was not receiving enough attention and needed to be addressed. An international concert and festival was planned to raise awareness. The efforts of Live Aid, through a commitment from a variety of major recording artists, resulted in millions of dollars in donation money being raised for the people of Ethiopia. Live Aid was held on July 13, 1985 and set at Wembley Stadium in London, JFK Stadium in Philadelphia, and smaller venues in Sydney and Moscow. The rock festival had once again been redefined. Combining a high caliber of artists, performances that would be recorded in rock and roll history, and a humanitarian effort unlike any other in music history, Live Aid accomplished all that it had set out to do. Over 175,000 people attended the shows in the four venues, but the event was not as much noted for its in-person audience as for the fact that a reported 1.5 billion viewers from over 100 countries watched the broadcast live via one of the largest-scale, satellite and television broadcasts of all time.

Twenty years later, in July 2005, Geldof, Ure, and their friends once again reached out to the global community. This time the music and social interaction was not to raise money, but awareness for another world crisis: poverty. The goal of Live 8 was to increase and improve aid to those in need, encourage world leaders to drop debt, and negotiate more favorable rules of trade for the most impoverished countries. Over 1,000 music artists performed at the ten concerts, which were held in ten international cities: Philadelphia, London, Rome, Paris, Berlin, Edinburgh, Barrie (Canada), Johannesburg, Moscow, and Tokyo. The performers were both legendary and contemporary, and presenters included Bill Gates, Kofi Annan, Nelson Mandela, David Beckman, Bono, Richard Gere, Will Smith, and Brad Pitt. The festival was broadcast on 182 television stations and 2,000 radio stations. The BBC featured extensive coverage of the event, including many of the performances. Yet if anyone doubted that broadcasting the event cast a commercial element on the festival, the American stations themselves confirmed this aspect when vee jays misidentified the production as "Live Aid 8" and constantly cut away from music in progress—including an historical performance by Pink Floyd—to go to commercials or simply to yak at viewers. When critics later complained that MTV and VH1 did not broadcast the festival but rather "covered" it, both stations aired six hours of the events from the stage, commercial-free. The people's voice was heard.

The Vans Warped Tour debuted as a combination of music and extreme sports in 1994. The festival grew, went international, and artists anxious to expose their music signed on in great numbers to participate in festival-sponsored discounted CDs and DVDs that gave the bands additional exposure. By 2006, 200 interchangeable, independent bands were featured and different bands appeared in a variety of cities over the course of the summer. Attendance rose to over 500,000 in a year. Vans Warped Tour was audience-friendly, offering festival tickets at a price far less than Lollapalooza and Ozzfest. Even so, during a show in Houston in 1998, the members of the band NOFX threw $5,000—their fee for that night's performance—into the crowd, one dollar bill at a time, to demonstrate their displeasure at the price their audience had to pay for refreshments. Today, in addition to the cutting-edge music, the Vans Warped Tour is also viewed as a political outlet and an opportunity for the fans to display their personal identities.

The Coachella Valley Music and Arts Festival (held in Southern California) and Bonnaroo (held on a farm in Tennessee) feature a potpourri of music and offer a return to the spirit of Monterey Pop and Woodstock. Individuals, families, and those who yearn for a return to the days of non-threatening communal gatherings listen to a variety of artists and enjoy the summer weather. Bonnaroo and Coachella offer a mellow experience and have become the most popular destination festivals in the country. Still, many see today's festivals as too expensive and too hot, with too many performers and too many people.

From Monterey Pop to Lollapalooza, the Vans Warped Tour and Bonnaroo, music artists have performed and the rock festival continues to be experienced and enjoyed. The debate over the social relevance of music festivals may be intense and complicated, but the fact that the festival has made a significant contribution to the society it serves, and to rock and roll specifically, cannot be denied. All about the music, all about the youthful souls who embrace it, the rock festival is a concept that—regardless of changing definition—seems destined to remain a unique and important component of not only our music but of our culture. Rock on.

Join Together

1967
Groovin'

In U.S. news

10,000 people march against the Vietnam war in San Francisco; Muhammad Ali refuses to enter military service; race riots take place in Tampa, Buffalo, Newark, and Detroit; murders in Massachusetts are attributed to the "Boston Strangler"; Thurgood Marshall is nominated as the first black Supreme Court Justice; and June brings the "Summer of Love."

In world news

The Six Day War results in a victory for Israel; the Soviet Union ratifies a treaty with the U.S. and U.K. banning nuclear weapons in outer space; Moshe Dayan becomes Israel's Secretary of Defense; the People's Republic of China tests its first nuclear bomb; and the Biafran War begins.

In music news

The Beatles film a music video for "Strawberry Fields"; Keith Richards is busted for drugs; 3,000 people riot at an Animals concert; the Beatles drop acid; "All You Need Is Love" is broadcast live by satellite; and the first issue of *Rolling Stone* magazine is published.

Some of the year's most notable albums

The Beatles: *Sgt. Pepper's Lonely Hearts Club Band*; Jefferson Airplane: *Surrealistic Pillow*, Buffalo Springfield: *Buffalo Springfield*; Jimi Hendrix: *Are You Experienced?*; the Moody Blues: *Days of Future Passed*.

Rock's most popular songs

"Mellow Yellow"—Donovan; "Gimme Some Lovin"—Spencer Davis Group; "For What It's Worth"—Buffalo Springfield; "Respect"—Aretha Franklin; "Somebody to Love"—Jefferson Airplane; "San Francisco"—Scott MacKenzie; "Light My Fire"—the Doors; "White Rabbit"—Jefferson Airplane; "All You Need Is Love"—the Beatles.

The Monterey International Pop Music Festival
June 16–18, 1967

"It was a certain period of time where all we had to do was play music."
— Jack Casady, Jefferson Airplane

"There was a big shifting of gears. We were off into our new life and Monterey marked the beginning of that."
— Sam Andrew, Big Brother and the Holding Company

By the middle of the 1960s, attitudes about music had certainly changed. Mainstream America continued to enjoy romantic ballads and frothy pop music, but a harder edge was immerging as young people began to experiment with the more lyrically and musically intricate rock music. The rock 'n' roll of the fifties and early sixties—the time of "I Want to Hold Your Hand" and "The Lion Sleeps Tonight"—was evolving into a hard-driven and socially significant music form both in live presentation and on the airwaves. The teenage rebellion that had begun with the Beatles and their unique haircuts was just a warning shot. The need for young people to identify themselves far and away from their parent's generation was becoming increasingly popular and it was fast becoming an innovative lifestyle. The simple slogans ("See ya later, alligator!") and easy-listening lyrics of the past had given way to musical anthems and catch-phrases ("Peace, brother") which united youth across the country and throughout the world. First there was the music of "them" and now there was the music of "us." It didn't take long for the younger generation to realize that as well as being entertained by lyrics you could remember and music "you could dance to," a song could be used to represent a collective state of mind. It wasn't just your father's world anymore. There would be no more meek acquiescence to "my way or the highway" as many of America's youth would take their parents at their word and set out for what they considered a better, more independent life. Rebellious young men hit the road but also a movement was underway to bring women to the forefront of American society to become more involved in social issues and to enjoy the freedom outside of standard societal rules and expectations. This was a generation that wanted to find the balance between pleasure and social responsibility. Music was one way to accomplish that complicated symmetry. The more popular songs of the day dealt with love and marriage but more often with independence and social consciousness. It was a new world and the music of the late sixties was the perfect vehicle for expressing the transformation of America's youth.

The idea of music festivals wasn't anything new. The three-day Newport Jazz Festival had been popular since it first debuted in 1954. The music at that annual event had featured legendary performances by artists such as Thelonious Monk, Duke Ellington, Ray Charles, Count Basie, John Coltrane, Miles Davis, and Billie Holiday. A "sister" event to the Jazz Festival was begun by artists Pete Seeger, Theodore Bikel, Oscar Brand, and promoters George Wein and Albert Grossman in 1959. The Newport Folk Festival is notable for introducing artists such as Bob Dylan and Joan Baez, two musicians who would lead the revitalized sixties folk movement. The emphasis on "folk" music also included what we would today describe as country, with appearances over the years by artists such as Johnny Cash, Doc Watson, and Maybelle Carter; and blues with performances by such famed bluesmen as Howlin' Wolf, John Lee Hooker, Mississippi John Hurt, Sonny Terry, and Brownie McGee. The 1965 Newport Folk Festival included a controversial performance by Bob Dylan when he attempted to merge folk with blues and rock 'n' roll as he performed his first live electric set. This act introduced rock music to the festival crowd and it was only a matter of time before a festival devoted to the new music, and a new way of thinking, was set into motion.

Modeled after the Newport festival, folk and jazz festivals also became popular on the West Coast, in particular in the small city of Monterey, California. Monterey was known as a community of artists and was home to painters, writers, dancers, and musicians. This society was aware of, and involved with, the emerging San Francisco "counterculture," an artistic and humanitarian-based effort that declared a new approach to living and offered a physical location—San Francisco—where one could demonstrate and affect the changes envisioned by a society of youth. Yet it wasn't so much the need to gather with like-minded people that brought about the first rock festival, but rather a desire on the part of the organizers to validate the music that the young people of America were creating and enjoying.

Cass Elliot, the melodic and sweet voice of the popular group the Mamas and the Papas, was both well-known and popular on the Southern California music scene. Elliot's parties were legendary and her attempts to introduce local musicians to those new to the scene from places such as New York and England brought an exciting element to her numerous soirées. Elliot possessed an earth mother quality and loved to entertain at her lovely house on Woodrow Wilson Drive in the hills of

Laurel Canyon. Those involved with the local scene often gathered to "hang out" and participate in impromptu jams, sometimes with people they were meeting for the first time. On any given night friends such as Graham Nash, Eric Clapton, David Crosby, and Joni Mitchell would sit outside gazing at the twinkling lights of Los Angeles and play and create melodious, and sometimes socially significant, music.

One evening in late winter of 1967, Elliot, Papa John Phillips, Paul McCartney and Dunhill Records record producer Lou Adler were congregated at Elliot's house discussing the state of rock 'n' roll. The fact that the rock 'n' roll of the fifties had not disappeared as "a fad," which was the prediction of music industry professionals, but had instead thrived and grown to become a significant element in the continuation of the youth movement, was something these four people knew intimately. Paul McCartney—and his friends—had seen first-hand the power and influence his music held over teenagers. Lou Adler would recall that it also bothered the quartet of musicians that rock music was not considered to be an art form, unlike the more traditional blues or jazz. Rock music in general was moving away from the rhyming pop tunes of the past few years and developing into a more serious, sophisticated and intricate music. Rock music had played a major role in the lives of all four of these people and they began exchanging ideas on what they could personally do to "legitimize" the genre. It was decided that the idea of showcasing an assembly of rock acts for a charitable event was worth serious consideration.

Meanwhile, Los Angeles-based music promoter Alan Pariser had attended the 1966 Monterey Jazz Festival and was thinking of the possibilities for a similar sharing of rock music. An heir to the Sweetheart paper business, Pariser was a man familiar with thinking big. Pariser approached Benny Shapiro, another music promoter, with his idea. Shapiro had a popular club on the Sunset Strip called Club Renaissance (the House of Blues now stands on the site). Shapiro thought Pariser's idea was a good one and agreed to partner with him to make it happen. They would use the Renaissance as their headquarters. Pariser also brought in his friend Derek Taylor, who served as the Beatles' press agent and was their close friend.

Pariser and Taylor contacted John Phillips and Lou Adler to discuss the possibility of having the Mamas and the Papas headline a rock festival in Northern California. The Mamas and the Papas were extremely popular but in Northern California, where the seeds of a strong cultural revolution were beginning to sprout; there was also a strong base of more exploratory rock and roll. It was suggested that the Mamas and the Papas might want to expand their fan base and become a greater part of that new music. Pariser suggested that Phillips and Adler become involved with putting on a one-day concert at the site of the Monterey Jazz Festival. Adler and Phillips thought it would be an excellent way to "validate" rock, especially if the festival was to become genuinely involved with the community and serve as a music-driven charitable event. When Benny Shapiro decided that he had gone as far with the project as he wanted to go (perhaps because a charitable festival was going to be considerable work for no financial gain), Adler and Phillips stepped in to help out with the finances along with their friends record producer Terry Melcher and recording artists Johnny Rivers and Paul Simon. (It was reported that Shapiro had asked that he receive $10,000 for his share of the festival.)

Initially, John Phillips and his group the Mamas and the Papas, Lou Adler, Paul McCartney and the Beatles, Alan Pariser and Phillips' friends the Beach Boys would serve as the executive committee along with assistance from Melcher, Simon, Rivers and Rolling Stones' manager Andrew Loog Oldham. The event would be primarily financed by those on the committee.

With financial involvement came the opportunity to have a say in who might be placed on the bill. John Phillips, Lou Adler and Paul McCartney had a lot of contacts within the music industry, but they decided that "corporate" music would be limited in its involvement in their festival. Certainly there would be a place for artist development executives to have input but the focus was to obtain the talent at a grassroots level. Because the festival was perceived as a charity event, and the fact that if the festival was a success the exposure would benefit the acts, popular rock bands and artists from both southern and northern California were invited to perform without pay at the Monterey County Fairgrounds in Monterey, California.

John Phillips would remember that nearly every local artist, band manager or agent called him attempting to secure a spot on the bill, to the extent that the festival office was eventually forced to obtain an unlisted number. Phillips felt a bit guilty for changing the number as that was not in keeping with the spirit of the festival as its organizers had defined it, but so many calls were coming in that the business of actually mounting and delivering the festival was being compromised. Derek Taylor would later say that of all the artists who were approached to become a part of the event, no one said no. Taylor claimed that there is a sense of guilt among those who have succeeded in living their dream of playing music for a living and the idea of a charitable, inclusive event was appealing to many. Whether this is true or not, those who were approached liked the idea of a community festival where there would be little commercialism and a lot of great music. There had certainly never been an opportunity for a celebration of rock music on such a large scale as the festival offered. Traveling rock and roll concerts had been popular in the early development of rock 'n' roll thanks to people such as Alan Freed and Dick Clark, but that had been for profit. Monterey Pop would not be focused on that aspect of the music industry—at least not during the days it would actually be happening. Instead it would be a fellowship of people coming together purely for the music in the spirit of love and peace.

If the artists were to perform without pay, Adler and the others felt it was their obligation to at least provide them with the best of facilities, eating and hotel accommodations, transportation, and sound equipment. Adler had become very familiar with the backstage areas of clubs while serving as a manager for Jan & Dean and as producer of the Mamas and the Papas and Johnny Rivers, and of course the majority of the others on the committee were artists themselves. Although future artists would dictate their personal requirements down to the color of the M&Ms, at this point in time, most rock musicians were unaccustomed to having their needs and comfort even considered.

When Phillips, Adler et al put out feelers to the community of performing artists, they were pleased by the overwhelming positive response and the fact that the festival would represent a cross-section of artists and some of rock's most exciting, emerging new acts. In an effort to demonstrate that rock music could stand as its own entity alongside other, more accepted, genres of music, the organizers decided to expand the bill to feature rock 'n' roll, the new psychedelic rock, pop, blues, soul, jazz, and to introduce to a live American audience the music of the sitar. Artists would come from all over the world to demonstrate that music truly creates a community of man. "It was a gathering of all different types of music, from the East and West," says Jefferson Airplane's Jack Casady. "Ravi Shankar and Otis Redding, who were from very different places, were playing to people that hadn't heard their music before. There was such a variety of acts on the bill that it was different and thrilling. The music was from everywhere."

All of the artists agreed to perform for free and any profit that was made from the festival would be donated to the Monterey Pop Festival charity, although initially it was unclear who specifically would benefit from that charity. The sole exception to this rule was sitar guru Ravi Shankar, who was paid $3,000 to perform for almost five hours. It had been Alan Pariser's idea that Shankar perform on Sunday afternoon to "open the minds" of those in attendance. Shankar had already been offered a performance fee before the decision was made that none of the artists be paid, and Pariser wanted to honor that agreement.

By now the "British Invasion" had passed but several popular British bands needed to be included if the festival was going to represent the worldwide rock movement. With Paul McCartney involved, the question was obvious: would the Beatles appear at the festival? That monumental event was doubtful because the Beatles had decided that they would no longer tour and the possibility of their performing live was seemingly out of the question. (Hope sprang eternal, however, as rumors of a surprise Beatles performance were whispered throughout the festival by those in attendance. There was also a rumor that the Rolling Stones may drop in to play a few songs. What many didn't realize was that due to the recent legal problems of Keith Richards and Mick Jagger [they had been arrested for British drug violations], the Stones were lying low and their travel was restricted for the time being. Those who gathered for the festival would need to be satisfied with the English bands the Who and the Animals.)

Pop music would be represented by bands such as the Association (who would open the festival), and the Mamas and the Papas (who would close it); solo artists Johnny Rivers, Laura Nyro, Scott McKenzie; the duo of Simon & Garfunkel; and an anonymous appearance by the Group with No Name. Soul music was featured through the performances of Lou Rawls, Booker T. and the MGs, and Otis Redding; and r & b by the Butterfield Blues Band, Canned Heat, Al Kooper, and the Blues Project. In addition to the two British acts, rock music was represented by the Paupers, the Byrds, and Buffalo Springfield. Hugh Masekela would represent jazz, and Ravi Shankar world music. An entire contingent of San Francisco bands would be on hand to introduce their sound to a larger audience: Big Brother and the Holding Company, Country Joe & the Fish, Quicksilver Messenger Service, the Steve Miller Band, Moby Grape, the Electric Flag, Jefferson Airplane, and the Grateful Dead. There was also a young man who had begun to draw some attention in England. Paul McCartney insisted that an American guitar player named Jimi Hendrix be added to the bill. When the diverse line-up was revealed to the public, those who decided to attend the festival had no idea what they were in for but they innately sensed it would be good.

As popular as the idea of this festival was within the community of music artists and those in the "Flower Power" movement, the community of Monterey understandably looked at such a venture with apprehension. The Monterey Jazz and Monterey Folk festivals had been fairly mellow, but with rock 'n' roll . . . John Phillips and Lou Adler visited the small city several times to assure those in charge that every letter of the law would be followed and extra policemen would be hired, not that they would be needed but simply to ensure that nothing got out of hand. (Ironically Phillips later recalled how he was at his most persuasive with the officials of Monterey while he was tripping on LSD.)

The promoters stayed true to their pledge that they would provide only the best for those musicians who would so graciously donate their time and talent. Lou Adler remembered bringing in a construction crew to establish a musicians' "camp". A communications center would be vital to the success of the event, and crews with walkie-talkies would spread throughout the fairgrounds. It would be easy for everyone to get around as the transportation operation included cars and drivers for the talent; and bicycles, scooters, and even motorcycles to enable a quick response and expedience should the need arise. Clean-up crews would be well-manned. There was an arts committee to manage booths where people would sell flowers, tie-dyed clothing, beads, and art, and face-painting would be available (Country Joe MacDonald had *his* face painted there for his stage appearance.) One of the booths would be operated by Paul Beaver and Bernie Krause. It was Beaver and Krause who decided that the Monterey Pop Festival would be a terrific opportunity to demonstrate the music synthesizer developed by Robert Moog. They had been impressed with the synthesizer and had been attempting to interest musicians to use the new technique. After the festival several bands decided to include use of the Moog in their music and the careers of Beaver and Krause were launched.

Local football players were hired as bodyguards, and Sam Karas was appointed head of security for the Citizens Committee for Monterey Pop Festival. Karas later remembered the festival as hardly needing any security at all. Because marijuana was becoming such an integral part of the youth culture, those in charge knew that there would undoubtedly be a lot of "weed" in the audience and likely in use by the performers. It was agreed by the promoters, Citizens Committee, and local police that unless there was a problem with someone being seriously stoned and out of control, or a danger to themselves or those around them, arrests for the use of marijuana would not be made.

An artist-friendly stage was constructed and the organizers realized in advance that since the concert would feature huge amounts of amplification there would need to be a very special sound system. And that sound system was meant to impress. Audio engineer Abe Jacobs was brought in to oversee this important aspect of the concert. Jacobs was known for the excellent job he did providing live sound for the various bands in the San Francisco area and it was agreed he would design and build a state-of-the-art system for the festival. Speaker systems were built on site. (Jacobs would continue to design inventive sound systems for the New York stage productions of "Hair" and "Jesus Christ Superstar.") The Beatles, although not in a position to join the bill, donated additional equipment.

So much attention was taken to ensure that the artists were well cared for that funds began to run low. San Francisco rock promoter Bill Graham contributed $10,000 to the cause. Graham, who was an integral force in San Francisco rock music, was involved in almost everything in that music scene (with the exception of those events promoted by his rival Chet Helms) and it seems odd that he would not be invited to be more involved. But as respected as Bill Graham was, he was sometimes difficult, and the promoters of the festival may have not wanted to have a domineering promoter too involved. Everything was in place and set to go: artists, the stage, the sound system, operations, and booths. On June 16, 1967 the first rock music festival would open at the Monterey County Fairgrounds in Monterey, California and continue over June 17th and 18th.

Although dozens of bands and solo artists thought the idea of launching a rock festival was indicative of that exciting time in rock music, not all who were asked (or wanted to appear) were available. The Beach Boys had initially agreed to perform but cancelled. Many "in the know" speculated that the laid-back Southern California band were afraid that they may look dated and out of sync with the evolving youth culture if they appeared alongside the more cutting-edge and contemporary bands from San Francisco. But the reason for their cancellation was more likely due to the falling-out between leader Brian Wilson and the rest of the band when Wilson became obsessed with their current project "Smile." The Rolling Stones, of course, were up to their ears in their own problems due to their drug busts, and the innovative Donovan was refused entry into the United States because of his drug-related arrest in Britain. The newly-formed Captain Beefheart & the Magic Band were asked to appear on the bill, but their guitarist Ry Cooder didn't feel they were ready to face a large audience and so they passed.

The promoters were taking a huge gamble in hoping that the fan bases of the bands would actually show up, but also that those who were beginning to catch on to the love and peace movement would attend. Many Americans had a hard time discerning between "hippies" and those who would later become known as "flower children"—a debate that continues to this day.

It may be said that while hippies were anti-society, flower children created their own society. While both the hippie and flower children movements were based in the ideology of "make peace, not war," the San Francisco hippies were actually living a hand-to-mouth lifestyle that could prohibit them from going to Monterey to enjoy the music. Hippies evolved from the beatniks and bohemians of earlier generations of white Americans and were concerned with shedding the mantel of traditional society and promoting themselves as people who rejected the established political institutions to form their own insular society predominately in communes or small hovels off the street. Their ideology embraced independence and the Monterey Festival may have been viewed as another type of organized exploitation of their new-found music and brotherhood.

Those who would later be dubbed "flower children," on the other hand, were sometimes "weekend warriors"—mostly teenagers and young twenty-year-olds who dressed in pretty clothes and grew their hair long to be in style rather than from a need to rebel. In fact, most of the males in this category didn't have long hair at this time. The genesis of the "Flower Power" movement also had its roots in San Francisco, mostly through young people who traveled to that city on their summer vacation to investigate the new hippie way of thinking. While in agreement that professing love and peace was an admirable way to live, these people weren't quite ready to shed their comfortable lifestyles to live on the street and participate in anti-establishment discussions. In fact, the flower children at this point were only a handful, and wouldn't come into their own until April, 1969 when a group of people gathered in Berkeley, California to plant flowers, shrubs, and trees in a "Peoples Park." (The park was destroyed by authorities because the gathering of young people had created something without a permit and was therefore outside the law—the flowers represented a symbol of peaceful resistance.)

There was no *Rolling Stone* magazine (that would come later in November, 1967), or *Spin* magazine (founded in 1985), so word of the festival was spread mostly by word of mouth. Popular art director Tom Wilkes was hired to design and create a logo that could be used in advertisements and on posters to entice people to attend. Wilkes created a woodcut of Greek mythology's God of Nature wearing a psychedelic necktie while playing the panpipes—a figure that was used to celebrate the uniqueness of the event. (Wilkes also designed a 70-page program book.) The telegraph of young voices can be strong indeed and Monterey Pop was one of the first beneficiaries of the new collective consciousness. On the first day of the festival, thousands of kindred spirits appeared at the fairgrounds ready to listen to great music, commune with nature, and make some new friends. At least 50,000 participants appeared each day of the festival, and during the three days of the festival, over 200,000 people would attend. The air was fragrant with flowers and marijuana, but also with goodwill and fellowship.

The release two weeks earlier of the Beatles' avant-garde record *Sgt. Pepper's Lonely Hearts Club Band* sounded a warning shot that popular music was about to change. During preparations for the festival, John Phillips was talking to one of his friends, musician Scott McKenzie, and told him that he'd like to somehow get the word out that the event was intended as a peaceful gathering whereby the new society of youth could demonstrate that they were perfectly capable of enjoying rock music without disturbances and conflict. McKenzie suggested that Phillips should compose a song that would reflect the way the organizers of the festival wanted it to be perceived. The two began noodling on their guitars and Phillips soon had the first words of the song that would be recorded by McKenzie and would become the anthem to the "Summer of Love." "San Francisco (Be Sure to Wear Flowers in Your Hair)" represented all that Phillips and his cohorts on the organizing committee were trying to convey. The song invited people from all over the country to travel west and experience the atmosphere of peace, and communal living, and to participate in a massive "love in."

And come they did. Although the fairgrounds were set-up to accommodate five thousand people for each show, those arriving early far surpassed that number. Roads were blocked and tents were pitched. Sleeping bags and blankets soon littered the ground. The area was quickly at capacity and the organizers knew they were in trouble. Counting on the generosity and "good vibes" that they had been expounding, Phillips, Adler, Pariser, and their staff asked the citizens of Monterey to help, out of "brotherhood," with the inundation of bodies. Nobody could have expected what happened next. Soon the good people of Monterey were allowing the young people to camp out on their lawns and the Board of Education allowed the use of the high school football fields as campsites. Somehow, someway, all those who had come to Monterey to express the philosophy of a kinder, gentler nation, were being accommodated.

Although it had been decided to defray costs that a minimal admittance fee would be charged, many felt that was somehow unfair and people began to be admitted free. The master of ceremonies, Chip Monck, decided to play music over the p.a. between sets to keep the audience entertained and to allow crews to set up for the next band or artist. Everything about the festival—even the down time—was designed to be entertaining and enjoyable.

The bands and solo artists were undoubtedly as excited as those in the audience. But some were so laid back (or stoned) that it would have been hard to tell. Many of the musicians had traveled to Monterey on a PSA flight out of San Francisco. Those waiting to board that flight were not secretive about what they had been smoking and the revelry that had begun at the airport carried over to the flight itself. Harvey Kornspan, manager of the Steve Miller Band, remembered the pilot announced that the airplane would be flying at 12,000 feet but that based on reports from his crew, he was aware that many of those on board were "cruising considerably higher." Those who traveled from overseas to participate in the festival had similar experiences. Eric Burdon remembered going through customs with Brian Jones of the Rolling Stones. The pair didn't want to be caught with their abundance of marijuana and pharmaceuticals, so they ducked into the bathroom first, where they ingested as much of it as possible. They somehow made it to their hotel, where they spent hours riding up and down on the elevator and having, well, a high time. All of the artists were thrilled that they would each have their own motel room while at the festival.

The use of drugs was starting to be a defining factor of the music scene. The hippies of Haight-Ashbury in San Francisco were also no strangers to marijuana, pills of various descriptions and effect, as well as that new glory of choice: LSD. It was certainly an era of new-found freedom and experimentation and many believed there was no better way to push the boundaries and set yourself apart from society than to avail yourself of the opportunity to expand your consciousness. Owsley Stanley, the soundman for the San Francisco-based band the Grateful Dead, was a familiar "chemist" on the scene. Owsley had the "best" acid and freely disseminated his wares to anyone who was interested in trying the newly popular drug. Synthesized in 1938 at the Sandoz Lab in Switzerland by Dr. Albert Hoffman as an agent to address issues involved in psychotherapy, the properties of LSD are conducive to feelings of ecstasy and an open-to-anything mindset. Conversely, bad "trips" as they are called, can cause the user to feel as if they are completely severed from reality. This aspect of the drug was, of course, downplayed as young people attempted to open their perspectives and see their world in a new way. Owsley Stanley was happy to assist in the LSD adventure and was introducing his latest version of the drug at the Monterey Pop Festival. Pete Townshend of the Who claims that he took some of Owsley's LSD during the festival and never took another drug for eighteen years. Also evident during the first day of the festival was the stronger "windowpane" LSD, which usually caused those who took it to be paranoid and completely off-the-wall. Whether it came from Owsley, or someone else, LSD and its counterpart, marijuana, were very much evident backstage. (Although many in the audience no doubt imbibed, had the prevalent drug *there* been LSD, it's likely that the event may not have been as serene. As it was, a handful of drug users beat on trash cans and set lawn furniture on fire. (But the incidents were contained and those with less than honorable intentions taken aside.) Michelle Phillips later claimed that John Phillips had assured everyone during a planning meeting that there would be no drugs (likely while he was *on* drugs).

Those who had traveled to Monterey knew that the music was going to be special but they didn't realize at the time *how* special. The weather was pleasant, there were none of society's "rules" to follow, and everyone in attendance was there for the same purpose: to enjoy themselves. Lou Adler had even flown in orchids from Hawaii to place on the chairs up front. The gathering of music artists, from the well-known to the undiscovered, and performances that would become legendary, were ready to begin.

Most of the artists scheduled to appear at the fairly small fairgrounds, while already experiencing a degree of popularity through recent radio play, were ready to launch on a larger scale and many would become legendary rock icons. The Monterey International Pop Festival kicked off at 9 p.m. on Friday, June 16, 1967 with the well-liked band the Association. It was interesting that the organizers of the event, founded to mainstream rock music, would begin the concert with the performance of such a mellow, pop-oriented entity. The Association had enjoyed a hit the previous year with the love song "Cherished," but was perhaps better known for their first release, "Along Comes Mary." There had been controversy when the record first received airplay in early 1966. Radio stations were swamped with telephone calls of protest that the song was obviously about marijuana (sometimes called Mary Jane), a substance that was currently threatening the status quo. The band laughingly denied any such veiled reference to the drug, but the song continued to be popular with young people who believed that they were in on the joke. Perhaps this comradery, real or imagined, is why the Association was chosen as the act to kick off the festival. The band was attired in traditional coats and ties, looking nothing like most of the people in the audience, but their music seemed to be well received.

Number two on the bill that first night was the Canadian rock group the Paupers. The band had only a moderate Canadian hit with their single "If I Call You by Some

Name," but was known as an excellent live band that had opened for the likes of Jefferson Airplane, Wilson Pickett, and the Lovin' Spoonful. It probably didn't hurt that the Paupers were also managed by Bob Dylan's manager Albert Grossman.

They were followed by the soulful vocals of Lou Rawls, who had released a jazz album the previous year, yet he had also opened for the Beatles in Cincinnati during their 1966 American tour and so he was well-known to many of those who loved rock 'n' roll. Rawls was recognized as an electric performer and his album *Live!*, with its hit r & b single "Love is a Hurtin' Thing," garnered him many fans. He was a proven entity to represent jazz, r & b, and soul. Respected British folk artist Beverly [Martyn], who had been added to the bill at the suggestion of her old friend and fan Paul Simon, followed Rawls.

Johnny Rivers was next to perform. Rivers had opened Elmer Valentine's Whiskey a Go Go on Los Angeles' Sunset Strip with a one-year contract in 1966. Rivers proved a popular entertainer and Valentine's partner Lou Adler released Johnny Rivers' album *Live at the Whiskey A Go Go* that year. Opening with the single "Memphis," a cover of the Chuck Berry song that would rise to number two on the pop charts, the album itself would prove tremendously popular and reach number twelve on the Billboard chart. Hit records "Maybelline," "Midnight Special," "Mountain of Love," "Seventh Son," "Poor Side of Town," and "Secret Agent Man" showed Rivers' career had legs. In addition to being a close friend of his producer Lou Adler, Rivers' success had shown that his being placed on the bill was certainly not a show of cronyism. But some of those in the audience didn't see it that way for some reason. Perhaps they were put off by Rivers' obvious attempt to fit in. He now had a Beatles style haircut and he walked on stage with a Sonny Bono-esque fur vest. Rivers opened his set with the Beatles' "Help" and was rewarded with boos and catcalls. Many got up from their seats and found something to do elsewhere. Maybe if Rivers would have stuck with playing the songs for which he was known then the audience would have been more accepting. The reaction to Rivers was uncharacteristic of the festival audience. Maybe they just needed to stretch their legs and were a bit irritable.

Eric Burdon and the Animals followed Rivers. The Animals, featuring the bluesy voice of front man Burdon, had a huge hit with "House of the Rising Sun" in 1964. Although seemingly a part of the British Invasion, the group wasn't as pop-oriented as many of their contemporaries in that movement. The Animals played more blues, as evidenced by their hit records "Don't Let Me Be Misunderstood," "Boom Boom," "We Got to Get Out of This Place," "It's My Life," and "Don't Bring Me Down."

The original Animals were history by 1967, but Burdon and a new group of colleagues later that year cut "San Francisco Nights" as Burdon embraced the new psychedelic culture. Eric Burdon would remember his time at the Monterey Pop Festival as a singular defining moment of the 1960s. He would later call it the only true pop music festival. He and the Animals were lauded for their appearance, but Burdon felt their music that night was only "all right." They opened with a soulful violin intro to "Paint it Black" but Burdon felt it was the performance of "Gin House Blues" that captured most of the audience's attention.

The first night of the festival ended with the last act: Simon & Garfunkel. Paul Simon had been enjoying the festival and felt it was in the spirit of a "jubilee." The intense duo, who had met in elementary school during a production of "Alice in Wonderland" where Garfunkel had played the White Rabbit and Simon the Cheshire Cat, were known primarily for their hit singles "Sounds of Silence," "Scarborough Fair," "Homeward Bound," and "Cloudy." Art Garfunkel would later remember Monterey as an opportunity for artists to show that they were making music for the spirit of it, rather than for commercial gain. Simon's poetic, intellectual melodies coupled with Garfunkel's melodic vocals (although some in the crowd looked bored by the acoustic set), would close the first night of the festival leaving everyone. . . "feeling groovy."

Looking back over the first day of the festival left those who had worked so hard to bring about a serene and relaxing day of music, art, and fellowship feeling satisfied. Things had gone well. The people of Monterey and their city fathers had been skeptical but even they agreed that they had been pleasantly surprised at the degree of organization and the general absence of rowdiness.

The communal group the Merry Pranksters had traveled down in their dayglow bus to join in the fun. Rumors of disguised Beatles and a performance by the Rolling Stones continued to drift through the audience. The crowd was exuberant and was itself a social statement with beautiful eclectic clothing that included capes, hoods, boots, caftans, vests, slogan buttons, and headbands. Any air of security was almost a nonissue. David Wheeler served as a festival liaison with the local police and everything ran smoothly. There had been some concern from the police that the Hell's Angels and area radicals would show up to cause some trouble. Although there were some Angels in the audience, the fears of the authorities went unfounded. Some Monterey police officers even allowed flowers to be placed in their hats (some wore riot helmets), tucked into their shirtfronts, or placed on their motorcycles by those in attendance. People were happy and peaceful, and obviously dedicated to having a good time. There were flags, kites, dancing, and even pets. The police smiled. This new generation might not be so bad after all.

As the evening came to a close, the festival, so far at least, was deemed a success. Granted, there was an abundance of drug use and that in and of itself made for an unpredictable atmosphere. But in spite of a few incidents, the drugs didn't appear to interfere with the genial mood. The organizers had been very careful to factor in drug use among those in attendance and they were ready for any problems that might arise. A first-aid clinic in a teepee, run by Dr. Bowersocks of Monterey, had been constructed onsite to provide medical assistance should it be needed. According to Lou Adler, the purpose was two-fold: those in need could be tended to and they would also not interfere with the music or disturb others.

Saturday, although much the same in attitude, brought a different, more exciting group of musical performances. Whereas Friday night is usually perceived as a more tranquil, end-of-the-week return to one's personal life, Saturday night is for letting loose and enjoying yourself and those at the festival were ready. On June 17, the boogie band Canned Heat opened the festivities. Canned Heat was considered L.A.'s answer to the popular northern California ensemble the Paul Butterfield Band. They had yet to release their debut album but the bluesy and upbeat tunes, fronted by the pleasurable vocals of Bob "The Bear" Hite, were lively yet relaxing. Canned Heat's performance of a genre of rock that was still primarily known to black audiences was quite an eye-opening experience for many of the white kids from the suburbs who were exposed to this type of music for the first time.

Very few could have predicted what happened next. Big Brother and the Holding Company were a San Francisco band who had appeared on the scene and captured the attention of the hippies and flower children by playing their "hurricane blues." The group had formed in 1965 and, at the suggestion of San Francisco concert promoter Chet Helms, added singer Janis Joplin to the group with her debut on June 10, 1966. The band would play as the "house band" at Helm's popular Avalon Ballroom. Few outside the San Francisco scene knew who Big Brother and the Holding Company were. That was all about to change.

"Monterey was a watershed event for Big Brother and the Holding Company and, indeed, for the entire San Francisco counterculture," remembered Big Brother's guitarist and songwriter Sam Andrew. "We had a clear idea about what was going to happen there when we signed up for the Festival. Monterey was John Phillips deciding that he was going to package that crude San Francisco sound and sell it 'Los Angeles-style' to the world. He wrote the theme song to the event and Scott McKenzie sang it. This is a typical story. Two people who had nothing to do with San Francisco writing a sugary tune that was not experimental, new, energetic, or revolutionary about a scene that was all of these. Am I glad that Monterey happened? Oh, yes. Thank you, John."

Big Brother and the Holding Company's set was pretty loose and not, by their standards, one of their better sets. "I had a lot of fun playing at Monterey, but I must note that the two sets we played there were not the best we ever played," says Andrew. "That's the way it is, I am sure, for many bands. A band will play a startlingly innovative and flawless set one night in front of twenty-five people and that night will disappear into oblivion, while the next night, played in front of thousands and at a significant occasion for everyone, will feature a set that, shall we say, is not deathless art. C'est la vie. I just wish our set could have gone a little better for that momentous occasion. That people heard our band for the first time because of documentaries of Monterey is very scary to me, and goes far to explain the critical reception of Big Brother. We had moments where we were flying high, breaking new ground, and playing music that was not written in any book, but those moments did not happen at Monterey."

The innovative band had become known for their originality and fervor, but perhaps playing outside in the heat of the day wasn't conducive to Big Brother and the Holding Company's approach to music. Regardless, they found a groove and demanded notice by the crowd. Some of that attention had to do with Janis Joplin. She shrieked, she moaned, she stamped her feet. Joplin wasn't just all about the music; she was all about the blues. Mouths dropped and people moved closer to the stage. Who *was* this woman? The audience sat stunned by Joplin's performance but once the shock wore off they decided that they loved her. John Phillips remembered Joplin's first performance as fierce and claimed she had the audience under her spell quickly. Michelle Phillips said that Janis caught the crowd's attention because not only was she talented but no one had ever seen a white woman sing black music like that.

"Of course the big story for us was the introduction of Janis to the big world and that went well enough," remembered Sam Andrew. "People who had never heard or seen her understood suddenly what she was about. Some of those big time Los Angeles professionals suddenly knew that they were in deep water when they heard Janis sing 'Ball and Chain.' This was no 'wear flowers in your hair' song."

Janis Joplin would end up as Monterey's belle of the ball, but her Saturday afternoon performance with Big Brother and the Holding Company was relatively brief. Observing the crowd's enthusiastic reception of Janis and Big Brother, John Phillips asked her to perform again during the evening when more people would get the opportunity to see her. Joplin was surprised and appreciative. She cried. Janis Joplin was definitely someone who should be experienced in the dark.

It was a difficult task following Big Brother and the Holding Company but nobody had predicted what a showstopper that band would be. Country Joe & the Fish was another San Francisco band. Primarily comprised of singer and songwriter Country Joe MacDonald and guitarist Barry "The Fish" Melton, the entity was a progressive rock band that was featured often on San Francisco radio stations KSAN and KMPX. Country Joe & the Fish were popular at places like the Avalon Ballroom and Fillmore Auditorium, where their music was significant for its anti-war content. The band's performance during Saturday afternoon wasn't its tightest, most musically proficient. Joe himself seemed almost too stoned to perform and, by accounts, the bass guitar was functioning oddly. David Cohen remembered popping acid in front of 10,000 people during his "Acid Commercial" ditty. (In an ironic happenstance, during one of the anti-war songs a huge jet airplane came in for a landing at nearby Monterey Airport, drowning out the music.) Regardless of any problems County Joe & the Fish were having, the audience enjoyed the band and it's safe to say that Country Joe & the Fish made many new fans that day. (Joe McDonald would later remark that his band felt that they weren't respected by those from Los Angeles. He also said he just assumed that he and his band were going to get paid for their appearance.)

"The Monterey Pop Festival was not only the launching pad for Country Joe & the Fish, it also launched the professional careers of the other San Francisco Bay area bands, and many of the other performers who played there," says Barry Melton. "Monterey was the first of the great rock festivals. But more than anything else, Monterey is the first of the great benefit festivals—a beginning to a tradition of social responsibility that has become a hallmark of the modern music industry."

Al Kooper is an innovative musician, songwriter, and producer, who had been instrumental on the organ for the ground-breaking performance of Bob Dylan at the 1965 Newport Folk Festival. (Kooper's Hammond organ is noteworthy on Dylan's recording of "Like a Rolling Stone.") In 1967, Kooper co-founded the Blues Project out of Greenwich Village, New York. The band was noted for its long jams and, now playing in the West, was said to be the East Coast's answer to San Francisco's the

Grateful Dead. Kooper had quit the band prior to their appearance at Monterey Pop and had been instrumental in the founding of Blood, Sweat & Tears. He performed on his own Saturday afternoon, and also played with the band from which he had recently departed, the Blues Project. Roy Blumenfeld remembered the band's playing to be a little tighter than most of the West Coast bands, but bassist Andy Kulberg thought that he and his bandmates were uptight and unhappy because they didn't feel that they fit in with the other bands.

In a further nod of appreciation to the influence of blues to rock music, the Butterfield Blues Band performed next. The group featured Paul Butterfield (an ace on harmonica and vocals) and guitarists Elvin Bishop and Michael Bloomfield. The Butterfield Blues Band closed Dylan's controversial Newport Folk Festival appearance (although without Butterfield) and their album *East-West* introduced many to the harmonious instruments from India, featuring the sitar. The group was exceptionally talented and would be the genesis of several essential future blues bands and artist collaborations.

The psychedelic jam band Quicksilver Messenger Silver, another San Francisco scene staple, performed next. They would later personify the drug-induced euphoria of the times with their hit single "Fresh Air." "We were scared," remembered guitarist Gary Duncan. "I was scared. I had never been in front of that many people in my life. The whole set went by in a flash and it was finished."

The Steve Miller Band, another unsigned San Francisco band that would become immensely popular with their future releases "The Joker," "Fly Like and Eagle," and "Take the Money and Run," followed Quicksilver. According to their then-manager Harvey Kornspan, the band didn't know if they were going to be invited to participate at the festival because they were certainly not among San Francisco's elite. Kornspan showed up at Phillip's office to make his pitch anyway but Phillips had already heard the band and invited them to come on board.

Michael Bloomfield's latest entity the Electric Flag (which included vocalist and drummer Buddy Miles) closed the Saturday afternoon segment of the festival. Bloomfield created the band to offer what he called "American Music" and the group featured several genres including blues, rock, r & b, and soul. The Electric Flag had something for everybody.

The performers set for Saturday evening were also a mix of genres: psychedelic rock, jazz, blues, pop, r & b, and soul. If the audience didn't care for one type of music, the next band would feature something else. From the performers' point of view, the way the bill was constructed offered a fantastic opportunity for those who represented each genre to gain exposure for both themselves and their unique niche to a broader audience. Moby Grape opened and was a perfect representation of that mind-set. The group was a fusion of country and blues with an apparent jazz influence. Coming together from bands such as Jefferson Airplane (original drummer Skip Spense), the Cornells (which was a band primarily consisting of celebrity's sons), and the Frantics, the musician make-up of the band was qualified and effective. Their psychedelic leanings didn't hurt their San Francisco appeal either. The band was not only good but different from many other bands: all five members of Moby Grape wrote music and sang.

The music of the next artist, South African horn player Hugh Masekela, was a revelation for many in the audience. Masekela had been ousted from his home country as part of that government's campaign of anti-apartheid in 1961. While the elements of anti-apartheid were a few years from being the focus of international social activists, this was certainly an issue the new generation of global thinkers sought to understand and address. Masekela had appeared at the Whiskey a Go Go in L.A. to great acclaim and the year following the festival he had a major hit single with "Grazing in the Grass." The light show that played behind the musicians drew the crowd into Masekela's tribal rhythms and soulful horns.

It was time for a Southern California band to take the stage and the music of Los Angeles was perfectly represented with the Byrds. The band, which was formed in 1964, had by this time been through various incarnations and music styles from folk, to country, to rock, to psychedelic. They had hit records with "Mr. Tambourine Man," "Turn, Turn, Turn," "Eight Miles High," and "So You Want to Be a Rock and Roll Star" (which included a brass appearance by Hugh Masekela). The San Francisco bands welcomed their counterparts from the south as Californian brothers but at the time of the festival tensions within the band were at an all-time high. Roger McGuinn and Chris Hillman were having issues with David Crosby's ego. Matters were made worse at the festival when Crosby insisted on talking politics between songs and championing the cause of LSD, insisting that it would be a good thing for the country to have every man, woman, and child drop acid.

The frail-looking Laura Nyro was better known for her songwriting than as a singer, although she was a favorite among musicians. Nyro had at one time been considered for the lead vocalist of Blood, Sweat & Tears, and had written their hit "And When I Die." She also had written hits for Three Dog Night ("Eli's Coming"),

The Fifth Dimension ("Stoned Soul Picnic" and "Wedding Bell Blues"), and Barbra Streisand ("Stoney End"). Nervous and on-edge, Nyro was unhappy with her appearance at the festival and left the stage nearly in tears. Michelle Phillips took Nyro for a car ride around the area to offer her some sisterly comfort. The performers at the festival were, after all, one big family.

Jefferson Airplane was a hugely popular San Francisco band who was already signed to a record label and was realizing national success with their single "White Rabbit" from their hit sophomore album *Surrealistic Pillow*. The band hadn't experienced an extensive tour at the time of the festival and was happy to perform in front of such a large audience. "We didn't have festival experience so we didn't know what to expect," says bass player Jack Casady. Regardless of their festival inexperience, the band played well and Grace Slick caught people's attention as the female singer in a masculine, guitar-dominated band. Jorma Kaukonen felt that with the exception of maybe Canned Heat, the other bands were more professional than his band at that time. Even so, Jefferson Airplane's exposure at the festival, and through the consequent concert film, was instrumental in launching them on a national basis.

"It benefited us enormously," reflected Casady. "People who had never heard of us got a chance to hear us. They [also] didn't really know who the Who or Jimi Hendrix was. Those who played represented so many points of music. The nature of music was a competitive spirit and it was a great opportunity to play a festival for people who hadn't had a chance to hear us and hear all the other music you wanted to hear."

Because of the relative smallness of the festival and the gentle mood of the audience, "The musicians could interact with the crowd and with each other," says Casady.

The camaraderie backstage was appreciated by the performers in attendance. "Backstage was like magic to me," says Gary Duncan. "Brick pathways with bars and restaurants for the artists only. I was sitting in a small restaurant, eating a burger and looked up to see Otis Redding, Duck Dunn, Steve Cropper, and the entire Memphis crew eating burgers, looking at me and smiling. They were my heroes and I was there eating with them. That's what I remember the most."

Booker T. and the MGs was always a thrill for fans and musicians alike to watch perform. The crème de la crème of soul musicians, the band featured keyboardist Booker T. Jones, virtuoso guitarist Steve Cropper, and legendary bass man Donald "Duck" Dunn. Based out of Memphis, the band had gained popularity on radio with their instrumental "Green Onions" and in various incarnations on such hits singles as Rufus Thomas' "Walkin' the Dog," Sam and Dave's "Hold On (I'm Comin')" and "Soul Man," Otis Redding's "Try a Little Tenderness," and Wilson Pickett's "In the Midnight Hour," among a host of other popular records. The band's festival performance featured The Mar-keys, which was Cropper and Dunn's "other" band.

But it was Booker T. and the MGs' friend and collaborator Otis Redding who was chosen to close Saturday night's show. And what a closing it was. The audience was on their feet from the first song and didn't sit down until Redding's set had ended. Otis Redding was from the small town of Macon, Georgia, and had been "discovered" by promoter Phil Walden, who encouraged Redding to travel to Memphis to record for the legendary Stax Records. Redding enjoyed hit singles with "I've Been Loving You Too Long" and "Try A Little Tenderness," but was relatively unknown to the crowd at Monterey Pop. It didn't take long for Redding to win over the predominately white flower children and immerse them in his unique brand of Southern soul. But his first song "Shake" caused the police chief to threaten John Phillips with shutting everything down because the audience was acting so wild. Phillips yelled to Redding to take it down a notch and Redding soon had had the audience eating out of his hand as he affectionately dubbed them the "love crowd" and told them that they better be loving their seats or they would lose the electricity.

"I knew the whole Stax/Volt recording scene and who played on what long before Monterey," says Sam Andrew. "So to see all these players up close and to feel the energy that came out of Otis Redding, who was so quiet and gentle offstage, was electrifying."

The other musicians playing the festival were also in awe of Redding's ability to so capture the audience. "It was a real thrill for me to see Otis," says Jack Casady. "And Booker T. and the MGs. . . all of them." (In retrospect, it's interesting that the audience, while certainly into each of the performances including the more assertive acts, usually remained seated and politely cheered or applauded.) Redding established a fabulous rapport with the crowd, a true give and take, and they loved him for it. The crowd didn't want to let Redding end his set and he returned for four encores, telling those in the crowd that he didn't *want* to go, he *had* to go. There would be no looking back for Otis Redding; after Monterey he was a star. (Redding paid tribute to his Monterey experience by returning to Georgia and writing "(Sittin' On) The Dock of the Bay." Unfortunately, the twenty-six-year-old singer was killed along with six others just three days after recording the song when their airplane crashed into Lake Monona in Madison, Wisconsin. "Dock of the Bay," released posthumously, would be Redding's first number one hit single. *Rolling Stone* would later rank Redding at number twenty-one on their list of "Greatest Performers of All Time.")

Sunday afternoon arrived and, oddly, Ravi Shankar was the only artist scheduled to perform. Shankar later said that he had been asked to play during the evening but had requested that he play in the afternoon when people wouldn't be otherwise distracted. Perhaps the other musicians were sleeping off the events, both on- and offstage, from the night before. Regardless, Shankar would play for several hours as the audience enjoyed the sun and the good vibes. Shankar and his musicians, particularly his drummer, whose hypnotic beat truly mesmerized the audience, genuinely enjoyed themselves. (It is interesting to note that there were many in the audience of Indian descent, a presence that no doubt helped bring a global feel to all those in attendance.) By 1967, sitar music had been employed successfully by artists such as George Harrison and the Beatles, and Brian Jones and the Rolling Stones. Shankar is a sitar guru and as he played hypnotically it was easy to experience the attraction of the instrument. Many in the crowd had never been exposed to the instrument and did not fully understand the music of the sitar. (Many applauded after Shankar took a long time to tune his instrument.) But the audience—with musicians Mickey Dolenz and Michael Bloomfield in attendance—sat mesmerized. Shankar had asked that no tobacco or drugs be used during his performance (yeah, right), because he wanted to present a spiritual experience.

"After the mayhem and chaos of the previous night, after taking acid with Hendrix and jamming for what seemed like years, to listen to Ravi Shankar drifting across the audience was an experience I cannot describe," remembers Quicksilver's Gary Duncan. "All the electric music, all the lights, all the drugs, was nowhere close to the intensity and meaning of his music." The audience loved the music and rewarded Shankar and his players with a long, standing ovation.

Sunday night brought another well-received appearance by the Blues Project, and then Big Brother and the Holding Company and Janis Joplin returned to the stage. John Phillips remembered that Joplin was extremely nervous but as soon as she got on the stage, she stomped her foot and "got Texas." Cass Elliot sat in the audience in open-mouthed astonishment over Joplin's performance.

The Monterey Pop Festival, despite its anti-establishment premise, had been launched by successful music industry insiders. In the early days of preparation for the event, as they began to see what was taking shape, it became unwise for record labels not to plan to attend. The label "suits" had begun to hear rumblings of a rock music "movement" and of course didn't want to lose out on any revenue the new music may potentially bring to their companies. They showed up in stealth mode, seen on the periphery of the festival, talking to artists and to each other, competing to sign several of the talented acts they had watched blow the audience out of its socks. Their trips from Los Angeles and New York were well rewarded. One of the first artists signed to a record deal was Janis Joplin. The Electric Flag, Big Brother and the Holding Company, and Jimi Hendrix received recording contracts because of their appearance at the festival. "Everything changed for the scene at large and for Big Brother in particular at Monterey," reflects Sam Andrew. "We acquired Albert Grossman as manager, Columbia Records for a recording company, and we began to live in New York and Los Angeles at this point. There was a big shifting of gears. We were off into our new life and Monterey marked the beginning of that."

Folk musician Cyrus Faryar led an anonymous band of musicians—dubbed the Group with No Name—through a short set, and then Southern California favorites Buffalo Springfield took the stage. One of the Springfield's major players—Neil Young—had left the group right before their festival appearance and the band's friend David Crosby returned to the stage to fill in Young's spot.

Representative of the second wave of British power bands was the Who, formed in 1964. The band had released two albums in England and was appearing on American stages for the first time as part of their first U.S. tour. Their song "My Generation" perfectly fit the mood of the festival. Roger Daltry would later say that he enjoyed a few bands like Moby Grape, but he wasn't that impressed with most of the bands. The Who's leader, guitarist and songwriter Pete Townshend, enjoyed the experience of listening to the American bands. But the Who came with their signature attitude. The buzz at the festival was all about an American-born guitar sensation that had been placed on the bill by Paul McCartney: Jimi Hendrix. There was an uncomfortable moment backstage when Pete Townshend tried to discuss the order of the bill with the Jimi Hendrix Experience and there was a debate over which group should go on first. According to Townshend, both were going to introduce "guitar pyrotechnics" to the American audience. The group that went on first might make that premise less exciting for the act to follow. Hendrix said he would go on first, but Townshend apparently told Hendrix that he had a problem with that because he thought that Hendrix was a great artist and Townshend didn't think that he, himself, was. There was a remark made backstage that Townshend just wanted to be the first to smash a guitar and it was suggested that a coin be flipped to decide the order of appearance.

(John Phillips later said he flipped the coin, but Townshend remembers it being tossed by Brian Jones.) Hendrix would take the stage after the Who. Townshend may have been respectful of Hendrix's talent, but he was also determined that his band be noticed and not upstaged by Hendrix.

Since the bands were all playing for free, the Who were provided with only their first class plane tickets and accommodations. Bassist John Entwistle was annoyed that the group was not allowed to bring their own amplifiers without cost. Consequently the band had to use equipment that they felt was not up to their usual standards. Entwistle would later say that he felt that the equipment hampered the band's performance. As the Who began their last song, "My Generation," Townshend told the audience "This is where it all ends." With Keith Moon flailing madly behind a somewhat bored-looking Roger Daltry, Townshend swiped at a microphone with his guitar and then proceeded to theatrically smash the instrument all over the stage. Those in the crowd were astonished and many were shocked. They had never seen a band behave this way. The band may have been representing their defiant public posturing with their violent signature of smashing their instruments but such behavior certainly wasn't conducive to the mellow, peace-loving atmosphere of the past few days. Townshend had wanted the Yanks to notice his band and he had achieved his goal. Ravi Shankar, for one, wasn't impressed: he later said the destruction was so upsetting to him that he had to leave the festival. Others found the action exciting.

San Francisco's favorites, the Grateful Dead, mellowed out the atmosphere created by the Who as they mounted a stage laid waste by those who went before them. In protest to what they perceived as commercialism by the Los Angeles-based promoters, the Dead had also outfitted a stage in a campground at Monterey Peninsula College with borrowed equipment, where they played with Jimi Hendrix, Eric Burdon, and some of the other San Francisco groups the night before. Some of the bands—those not making a lot of money at that time—didn't mind the money being spent to entice them to perform. "It was evident that someone spent a lot of money to put it all together," reflects Gary Duncan. "Every band had a new set of Fender amps, which immediately went into our own trucks and we kept them along with Hammond Organs and whatever else we could 'liberate' from the stage after our set. There was a new back-line for every act and nobody seemed to care where the other stuff went. There is a lot of gear that just 'disappeared.' The cost of that gear alone should be an indication of the gravity of the event."

Then it was time for Jimi Hendrix, the artist who had generated the most festival buzz but who had not yet been heard in concert by such a large audience. Previously known as Jimmy James, the guitarist had played clubs in Greenwich Village in New York City but was now primarily based in London, where he formed the Jimi Hendrix Experience with Noel Redding and Mitch Mitchell. Paul McCartney and Mick Jagger were entranced by Hendrix and insisted that he be placed on the bill. Rolling Stone Brian Jones, who had been wandering through the festival looking quite beautiful and quite stoned (and who was dubbed the "King of the Festival"), introduced Hendrix. If those in the audience thought they had been surprised by the antics of the Who, they were about to be shocked even further. Having enjoyed Owlsey's LSD perhaps a few times too many, Hendrix nonetheless played his Fender Stratocaster with incredible proficiency. Like the Who, Hendrix was no stranger to theatrics. He simulated sex with his guitar, with the amps, with himself. He finally abandoned himself completely to his pagan celebration by kneeling before his guitar, lighting it on fire, beckoning the fire to reach higher with his fingers, and dancing around the instrument in worship. Drummer Mitch Mitchell and bass player Noel Redding were pretty damn good, too. The Who and the Jimi Hendrix Experience had accomplished what other performers in the festival had shied away from: a battle of the bands.

The performance by Jimi Hendrix was astonishing to the audience for a variety of reasons. Hendrix engaged the audience while at the same time indulging himself and even showing off by playing his guitar behind his back. At first the audience didn't seem to be that into the act but they quickly decided that whatever it was this guy was doing, they liked it. For anyone who attended that night, Hendrix's performance was all they could talk about. "I was with Jimi Hendrix in Monterey," remembers Sam Andrew. "Being up close to him was a big thrill. I was one of the few people in San Francisco who had heard his [English] album before he arrived and I was intensely curious to see whether he could duplicate that onstage. Of course he went on to eclipse that album totally in his live performance. Jimi talked to me about what scales he was using. He was a real scholar, a real musician."

Eric Burdon would later say that it was Hendrix's best night, but also his worst. Hendrix grabbed the attention of a vast audience through his appearance but future audiences would now expect to see the outrageous theatrics every time he played. Burdon felt that Hendrix's music was now compromised and he said that Hendrix agreed. There were others who were offended by Hendrix's style of playing, including

Ravi Shankar who later said that he got angry when Hendrix used his instrument obscenely and felt it was sacrilegious when Hendrix destroyed his guitar.

Although John Phillips had to be aware of the power of a Hendrix performance, he scheduled Scott McKenzie to follow. McKenzie, who according to Phillips was now the "Guru of Flower Power," had no experience playing to such a large audience as the song "San Francisco" was only his first recording. Singing the song that he and Phillips had written as an invitation to come to the festival in peace, sunlight, and good will, McKenzie lulled the audience back into their drug-induced euphoria. After all, the song had been written to encourage those who attended to wear flowers and behave. ("San Francisco" had become an instant Top 10 hit in the United States and was truly influential in bringing tens of thousands of young people west to the San Francisco area and launching the "Summer of Love.")

Phillips' band the Mamas and the Papas were then brought out to close the festival. Even though Phillips' activities and responsibilities to the festival had kept his group from properly rehearsing, the Mamas and the Papas were in their groove and ready to live up to their reputation of fine harmonies and memorable songs. The four singers were likely tired from all of the festivities at that point, however, and sometimes had difficulty staying in tune.

But many of the musicians were not ready for the Hendrix vibe to end. They jammed underneath the stage—Jimi on guitar, Buddy Miles playing a bottle, Eric Burdon on tambourine—until promoter Bill Graham asked them to knock it off as they were drowning out the Mamas and the Papas. (Jimi had earlier asked to play backstage in the area reserved for those guests who didn't have overnight accommodations. Eric Burdon remembers him shimmying up a nearby pole to plug in his small amplifier.)

The event ended on a positive note. There were no major problems, no deaths, no riots, and no arrests, none of the things that the "establishment" had predicted. "I have many memories of the Monterey Pop Festival," says Barry Melton of Country Joe & the Fish. "And those memories have remained etched in my consciousness long after memories of other events of that time have faded. I will never forget the spectacle of Jimi Hendrix setting his guitar on fire. And Otis Redding put us all to shame with the solidity of his backbeat. But most of all, the Monterey Pop Festival was a time of hope and optimism, and it was perhaps the high point of sixties counterculture. People were happy, the world was new, and the overwhelming majority of the musicians were gathered to play for free, for charitable causes. There was no violence, there were no arrests, and there was no trouble. We really thought we could change the world. And for a moment, in Monterey, it looked like all things were possible."

Documentary filmmaker D.A. Pennebaker had been asked to film the Monterey Pop Festival to preserve the weekend's events for posterity. Pennebaker had seen *Endless Summer,* a film about California surfing, and had become aware of that state's attraction to youth from all over the country. He said a sense of freedom was in the air and he was anxious to explore it. Pennebaker wasn't prepared for a venue that was largely a livestock pen but he was a creative man and he could visualize it. Wally Heider, whose mobile studio had provided the sound for many live San Francisco band performances, recorded the music and sounds of the festival on an eight-track tape he borrowed from Brian Wilson and San Francisco's lighting guru Chip Monck set the lights. (Although Chip Monck would let Pennebaker down a bit by allegedly dropping acid while doing his job and messing up some of the stage lighting.) Pennebaker filmed with state-of-the-art, portable 16mm color cameras that were equipped to record synchronized sound. He later decided that the best way to express the spirit of the festival was as a musical experience without any narration. The resulting film *Monterey Pop* is a classic. After expenses, the film would garner money for various Monterey Pop Festival charities that were represented by the Monterey Pop Foundation. [Contractual arguments kept some of the bands from signing releases (some simply didn't trust the "corporateness" of the project and didn't want to be included) and kept the planned festival album from being released until 1992.] Pennebaker's film would eventually gross over $2 million dollars. It's also interesting to note that after people saw Jimi Hendrix's performance for the first time in the film, sales of guitars in the United States tripled. Eric Burdon would memorialize the atmosphere of the festival with his song "Monterey," in which he mentions the various acts appearing at the festival while in the background, the instruments recreate the various styles of performances.

Those who couldn't (or didn't) make it to perform at the festival were likely regretful. Although it was probably to the Beach Boys advantage that they didn't appear as the crowd didn't seem to want to embrace the bubblegum music of the past few years. (Had the Beach Boys performed, they might have included their recent song "Good Vibrations" and won over the crowd with its captivating ethereal quality.) Even though other L.A. bands were represented in the Northern California setting, it was those bands that were considered hip and happening. Residents of Northern and Southern California have never really gotten on well, with each side believing that their portion of the Golden State is the more socially relevant. During this time, the flower children of Northern California were anxious to become affiliated with the hippie movement to cast off traditionalism and contribute to the new order; while many in Southern California still conformed to the surfer-stoner lifestyle with love, peace, and beads thrown into the midst of their art of "hanging out." Despite whatever philosophical differences the audience may have had, the musicians who played at the festival could unite in spirit. "Records then were regional," says Jack Casady. "You had people recording in the East, in the West, in the South. It was a friendly rivalry between San Francisco and L.A. It was a point in time when L.A. was not the only place where music was being played and recorded. The L.A. bands were fabulous and professional and clean and clear."

When those in attendance returned home from the festival they were too keyed up with what they had experienced to let it go. They had seen too much. Fashion, recreational drugs, and most of all the communal, youth-oriented mini-society that they had been involved with during the weekend, made a huge impression. It was perhaps in that moment that, as Lou Adler so succinctly put it, a moment became a movement. The achievement of the event was incredible and certainly worth contemplating. Journalist Robert Christgau would write that the success of the festival was so unprecedented that it took everyone by surprise. The "love crowd" not only existed but it *got along*. People showed that they were open to accepting rock music as a legitimate force in its own right, as the organizers of the event had hoped, but also that this new generation remained open to more traditional forms of music as well. This wasn't a divided group of individuals focused on how they might individually benefit. This was a new *society*, open to everything life had to offer.

Even so, the portrayal of those who went to the festival— alongside the hippie and flower children of the Haight—was seen as naive by some. Jerry Garcia felt that the media portrayal of these people was a joke because it all wasn't as innocent as it was sometimes depicted. Regardless, what had been experienced in Monterey on that June weekend was surprising and glorious. But it was also a threat to those who held the power. After the peaceful, no-problem Monterey Festival, the State Fair Board of California passed a proposal that would prevent any event (without explicit permission from the city) that would possibly attract more than 2,000 people.

Presented as a non-profit event (in addition to the success of Pennebaker's film), the festival raised over $200,000 by selling rights to some of the footage to ABC television. (Lou Adler said that the deal with ABC was probably sealed when they saw footage of Hendrix humping his guitar, although of that particular moment they said not on *our* network.) One of the main recipients of the charity was Haight-Ashbury's Free Clinic. The Monterey Pop Festival Foundation is still in existence today.

All was not sunshine and roses, however. Pennebaker and the organizers found themselves $75,000 in the hole. A large amount of money vanished from the festival coffers, along with the woman who served as bookkeeper. Some of the organizers of the festival wanted to finance another version of the festival in 1968, but this loss of money seems to have been the central reason for putting the kibosh on that idea.

When it was all said and done, the Monterey Pop Festival was a groundbreaking event, both musically and sociologically. The event was multicultural in tone, a veritable delight of music genres, racially integrated, a charity benefit featuring groundbreaking acts and performances by musicians who were poised to become legendary. . . and *nothing bad happened!* Grace Slick thought that the festival was the best of all time for both musicians and the audiences because it was easy to get food, use the portable toilets, and the festival itself wasn't too big. More importantly, Lou Adler would call Monterey Pop a "blueprint" for future music festivals. Adler also noted that the event brought something new to the table for the music industry: Promoters learned that by showing respect to the artists who performed for them, providing them with decent accommodations, and the freedom of creativity they deserved, it would benefit the music industry and the music itself.

Haight-Ashbury was all over the media as the hippie movement drew attention to their new alternative lifestyle. As the first of its kind, the Monterey Pop Festival was featured by massive amounts of media attention so it could demonstrate to the world at large that rock music fans were not out of control or focused on anarchy but rather were mostly peaceful, open-minded youths who embraced diversity. Twenty-five hours of music and fifty thousand people had an impact on America—and on the world—that was never expected. Most people in mainstream society didn't even realize any such movement existed. The "love crowd" was just beginning to make themselves known.

"It was a certain period of time where all we had to do was play music," remembers Jack Casady. "[The festival] was small by today's standards. Security was in its infancy as a security business but people weren't pushy. It was a peaceful affair. It was relaxing and enjoyable. It was a large group of people that didn't have seat numbers."

"Before Monterey there were no large venue festivals, as people referred to them," says Gary Duncan. "After Monterey there were many, but Monterey was the Alpha and Omega of them all. Not because of the size of the show. . . I suppose it was the "cosmic timing" of the event which gave it gravity. It was the first time a show of that magnitude had been attempted and I'm sure the first time that much money had been invested in a musical event. Woodstock is famous for its size. Altamont was infamous for obvious reasons. At the age of sixty-one, I have played music at more than a hundred "festivals" but Monterey was, what can I say? It was Monterey. It was the first and last, which is probably as it should be."

Festival of the Flower Children
August 26–28, 1967

> *"Peace and love? Maybe if you were sitting in a field, stoned out of your head, oblivious to all but one's immediate company and drug supply."*
> —Brian Godding, Blossom Toes

In England, those associated with rock music that had observed the new movement evident in the success of the Monterey Pop Festival didn't want to be left behind. The music of the youth "revolution" had apparently been launched by the Beatles' *Sgt. Pepper's Lonely Hearts Club Band* album and the Beatles were, after all, British. It was now officially the "Summer of Love" in the United States. Although many in England thought "flower power" was a bit simple and inane, there were others who thought that thinking of peace and love was certainly a step forward from the tumultuous, not-so-distant period of World War II and Britain's recovery from that war. England had been in the doldrums until the arrival of the Beatles. The Beatles had lit a fire under the youth of the country and now were encouraging them, through innovative and experimental music, to take another step away from the mindset of their parents and the gravity of the previous two decades by indulging themselves and offering camaraderie with all mankind through a mutual love of the music but also by action and deed.

The Festival of the Flower Children was held on August 26-28, 1967 and would commemorate that global state of mind. The celebration was the first of its kind in Great Britain. The event was held at Woburn Abbey, home of the Duke and Duchess of Bedford. (It is interesting to note that the Duchess was away from home during the festival—she thought that it was literally a *flower* festival.) Advertised as the world's largest love-in, the festival bill was an entertaining mix of well-known and up-and-coming bands and artists including the Small Faces (who would headline Saturday night), Eric Burdon and the New Animals (headliners for Sunday night), the Jeff Beck Group (closing the festival Monday), the Bee Gees, Family, Al Stewart, Alan Price, Dantalion's Chariot (dressed all in white), Marmalade, Tomorrow, Blossom Toes, Zoot Money and the Big Roll Band, Tintern Abbey, and Breakthru. Jimi Hendrix is sometimes listed as being on the bill, but no one remembers seeing him there.

The Festival of the Flower Children was officially opened by an air balloon floating over the crowd and dropping hundreds of colorful flowers on those below. Although the attendance of the festival in total would eventually number approximately 14,000 young people (predominately male), many came only to see what the hoopla was all about and simply passed through in limited numbers for a brief period of time. "It was not particularly well attended, not on the day we were playing anyway," says Brian Godding of Blossom Toes. "If my memory is correct, those who were there were mainly local 'hillbillies' looking for a laugh and a bit of trouble. This was not uncommon then as the whole 'Flower Power' thing in the U.K. was treated with disdain and ridicule by most of the population, especially out in the 'sticks.'"

Constables walked the grounds and made their presence felt but few in the crowd felt threatened. Incidents were few and far between. When the audience got a little too excitable and crowded the stage, the show's emcee, disc jockey John Peel, requested that the crowd move further back from stage and the audience calmly complied. During Marmalade's set, someone threw sparklers into the crowd and without much thought to the possible consequence; the sparklers were thrown back at the band. The stage canopy caught fire but was quickly extinguished. Despite the number of people and the newness of such a gathering, the festival was a fairly relaxed and uncomplicated event. The greatest complaint from those who attended was the high cost of refreshments.

The music of the festival, while considered good, wasn't seen as particularly memorable. Press coverage would later state that the music, as well as the festival itself, was boring. One of the highlights was Eric Burdon singing a toast to Monterey Pop with his new song "San Franciscan Nights." England's answer to the Monterey Pop Festival was pleasant, but certainly did not have the impact of its Yankee counterpart. "As far as getting any 'vibe' from these sort of gatherings we, and most of the other bands, would not have hung around any longer than necessary!" says Brian Godding. "The 'vibe' would have been to get out of the compound and mud in one piece and with all our equipment intact! Peace and love? Maybe if you were sitting in a field, stoned out of your head, oblivious to all but one's immediate company and drug supply. But I personally would be very skeptical of any performer who claims to have had any enlightening or even pleasant experiences 'artistically' back then. Technicolor dream? Technicolor yawn! Not the most 'fave' of my career or life. But things could have been worse I suppose . . . could have been in the bloody army!"

Great Britain would go on to have exciting and legendary festivals, as would many countries in Europe. But although the Festival of the Flower Children was the first, it was certainly not the most successful or entertaining. Or remembered, evidently. Monterey Pop had planted the seed, but the international growing of the rock festival had yet to truly begin.

1968
Dance to the Music

In U.S. news

Thousands of war protesters march on Washington, D.C.; Carl B. Stokes is elected the first black mayor of a major U.S. city; LSD is declared illegal; Lyndon Johnson does not seek reelection; Martin Luther King, Jr., is assassinated; the Civil Rights Act of 1968 is signed; students take over the Columbia University administration building; anti-war protesters demonstrate at the Democratic Convention in Chicago; Neil Armstrong walks on the moon; and Manson's "family" commit the Tate–La Bianca murders.

In world news

Che Guevara is executed in Bolivia; pro-Communist riots break out in Hong Kong; the USS Pueblo is seized by North Korea; the Tet Offensive begins; the My Lai massacre takes place; 5,000 Russian tanks invade Czechoslovakia; and the peace-loving Maharisha Mahesh Yogi catches the public eye.

In music news

The Beatles' Apple Corp. is launched; the musical *Hair* debuts on Broadway; rock artists perform at Shea Stadium in a campaign benefit for Democratic Presidential candidate Eugene McCarthy; John Lennon and Yoko Ono release their album *Two Virgins*; and television airs the comeback special of Elvis Presley.

Some of the year's most notable albums

The Beatles: *White Album*; The Band: *Music from Big Pink*; the Rolling Stones: *Beggar's Banquet*; Blood, Sweat & Tears: *Child is Father to the Man*; Jimi Hendrix: *Electric Ladyland*; the Byrds: *Sweetheart of the Rodeo*.

Rock's most popular songs

"Born to be Wild"—Steppenwolf; "Hey Jude"—the Beatles; "Jumpin' Jack Flash"—the Rolling Stones; "Dock of the Bay"—Otis Redding; "Sunshine of Your Love"—Cream.

Denver Pop Festival
February 14, 1968

> *"Inside, safe from the smoke, I watched a cop taking a leak. He propped his gas mask up on his forehead, chuckled, smiled a big grin, said to the guy standing next to him, 'More fun than shootin' bunnies, ain't it?'"*
>
> —Lee Underwood

Given the volatile nature of American society, it would only be a matter of time before the tone set at Monterey Pop was altered to become a memory of times past. A lot had been happening, both in the United States and in the world. The elements of change and unrest among young people could no longer be denied. The Vietnam War had now been raging for nine years and America's youth was beginning to throw off the traditional patriotism of years past as they watched thousands of their own being sent off to serve the military—and die—for a complicated and dubious cause. The war didn't make sense to millions of people but rather than simply accept that the president and government of the United States knew what they were doing, many began to question that premise. In many ways the world was the same as it had always been— tumultuous and complex. Yet society was changing and many no longer felt the need to acquiesce to the dictates of a government they sometimes didn't understand or with whom they disagreed. Children had always rebelled against their parents but the rebellion taking place now was not the usual moodiness of teen angst but a true questioning of their elder's wisdom and actions. The older generation didn't comprehend this new mindset. It seemed disrespectful to them. Tempers flared as both generations refused to try to understand or accept the other. Tension was felt in homes and acted out in public. Clashes of opinion and disregard for standard American authority became more common. It didn't take long at all for the problems of society to reach the arena of the rock festival.

Colorado promoter Barry Fey became friends with San Francisco's rock impresario Chet Helms. Fey and Helms collaborated to open a club called Family Dog in Denver in 1967. Fey brought in San Francisco bands such as the Grateful Dead and Big Brother and the Holding Company to entertain the young people of the area who otherwise didn't have access to that caliber of music. This type of social gathering was foreign to the city establishment and Fey was forced to obtain an injunction against the police to stop them from hassling the performers and clientele. But Fey would not be deterred from introducing the new rock sound to the people of his city. He booked Jimi Hendrix to appear at the Regis College Field House on February 14, 1968. Hendrix drew 4,700 people and was extremely well received. (Fey would also book Hendrix in Tucson and Phoenix.)

The atmosphere of Denver, like most of the country, was beginning to change. On May 29 and 30, members of Clergy and Laymen Concerned About Vietnam gathered on the steps of Denver's Federal Customs House to read the names of the 33,000 young Americans who had thus far been killed in the war. At that time, Barry Fey was already deep into his preparations to stage a three-day festival of rock music.

Although they were wary about what could possibly happen during a large gathering of young people, Denver officials decided to work with Fey to ensure that the youth expected to flood the city from towns beyond Denver were properly accommodated so as not to encourage area instability and potential civil disobedience. The site of the event would be Mile High Stadium, home of the Denver Broncos football team. The Metro Denver Urban Coalition provided portable toilets and water trucks, and the city elders went so far as to allocate a campground for the visitors to their city. Shuttle buses would be used to ferry people to the stadium. Barry Fey brought in Bill Hanley, who had experience with the sound system at the Monterey Pop Festival, to take charge of the sound and Chip Monck was on hand to serve as "Master of Ceremonies." Tickets were set at six dollars per night, with a discount of fifteen dollars for the three-day event. The stage would be set up on the turf forty feet from the stands.

Fey decided that Jimi Hendrix should top the bill and scheduled Hendrix to appear on the final night of the festival. Rock would be represented by additional acts such as Iron Butterfly and Johnny Winter; pop rock by Three Dog Night and Creedence Clearwater Revival; country rock by Poco; jazz-rock by the Flock and Tim Buckley; and bluesy rock by Zephyr. Big Mama Thornton (the original singer of Elvis Presley's hit "Hound Dog" and Janis Joplin's "Ball and Chain") would open the show and the eclectic acts of Frank Zappa and the Mothers of Invention, and Rev. Cleophus Robinson were also included. Tommy Bolin, Aorta, and Aum would complete the bill. (The event had been planned to be the debut of Crosby, Stills, Nash & Young but the quartet's debut album had been delayed and Fey decided he didn't want to pay big bucks to a band without an album.)

The talent on the first day of the festival was well-received even though the bill for that day was a diverse mix of sounds. Big Mama Thornton seemed to be popular, although it's likely that most of the people in the audience who enjoyed her set didn't realize what an original she was. The Flock followed and they too introduced the crowd to unfamiliar arrangements. Three Dog Night pulled the crowd in with a set of their hits and took their performance a step further. "Three Dog Night set a smoke bomb type devise that filled a portion of the stage with smoke," remembers the band's Chuck Negron. "Cory Wells got on top of the Hammond Organ as the smoke engulfed him. The police attacked our roadie who was in charge of the effect and dragged him off the stage with the help of the stage crew. They thought we were starting a fire. Things were getting tense."

Then Frank Zappa and the Mothers of Invention hit the stage. "Frank Zappa got the crowd into a frenzy when he involved them in an audience participation that separated the left side of the crowd and the right side," recalls Negron. "He started with body sounds such as a fart and moved on to one side saying 'shit' and the other side saying 'fuck' or some word like it. It started off, left to right, and he directed them to get louder as he got to the middle of the crowd and then started the other portion of the crowd to softly start and end it as loud as they could get. Something like shi. . . Shi. . . SHI! SHIT!!! fuc. . . Fuc. . . FUCK!!! It was funny and amazing how he controlled the audience and had them almost totally in sync. I believe it was the start of the police fearing they were losing control of the festival because I noticed their reaction of fear while observing Zappa and his control over thousands of people. They were on alert after that."

Iron Butterfly finally took the stage to close the first day of the show with their less inventive hard rock. During the evening approximately 100 gatecrashers stormed the chain-link fence in an attempt to get into the festival for free. The private security guards handled them, but when a flying bottle hit a policeman's helmet, there was a temporary disruption as the cops chased the perpetrator through the crowd. All in all, however, the events of the first day went fairly well.

On the second day, the festival was opened by the inventive blues guitar of Johnny Winter. What Winter remembers most about the festival is that it was "wet and muddy." Regardless of his physical circumstances, Winter was prepared for the immensity of what he was seeing. "We knew that it was building into something big from the news we were getting on national TV on our way there," Winter remembers.

Winter was followed by Creedence Clearwater Revival, who had the crowd up and dancing. All was well on stage, but back at the entrance to the festival things were starting to get out of hand. This night between 300 to 500 people tried to climb the fence and get in for free. This crowd felt that the music was "theirs" and should be offered free of charge. (Barry Fey asked them why they thought the music belonged to them—he didn't ask to go to a movie theater for free.) Eight additional police officers reported to the festival, including Denver's Chief of Police. The officers tried to stop the young people from swarming the gate but were clearly outnumbered. The decision was quickly, and unwisely, made to contain the crowd through the use of tear gas. The cops threw the canisters and the crowd threw them back. The gas blew through the stadium and several people in the audience (including a child) were taken to the hospital.

Tim Buckley and guitarist Lee Underwood were on stage. "That afternoon, Tim and I stood on a stage, looking up at thousands of people, just the two of us playing our hearts out," remembers Underwood. "Suddenly, after only four songs, a great roar erupted from the crowd on our left. Wire fences crashed down. Hundreds of fans that had been denied entrance to the sold-out festival rushed in. People screamed, ran, fell, tried to get away. Cops in gas masks attacked the crowd with clubs. Other cops set off tear gas bombs. Smoke clouds billowed up into the stands and wafted out on the field. Tim and I heaved our guitars into cases and ran down the stairs at the side of the stage, out into right field. People coughed, screamed, yelled, and cried while cops attacked them wherever they could."

Barry Fey and Chip Monck jumped onstage and encouraged everyone to return to their seats.

"Tim and I got separated," recalls Underwood. "Whenever a wave of smoke came my way, I lay down on the grass, covered my head, buried my face in soil, then got up clutching my guitar and kept running for the restrooms, coughing, crying, eyes stinging, lungs hurting. Inside, safe from the smoke, I watched a cop taking a leak. He propped his gas mask up on his forehead, chuckled, smiled a big grin, said to the guy standing next to him, 'More fun than shootin' bunnies, ain't it?'"

Barry Fey would later say that he felt the trouble at the gate had less to do with getting in for free and more to do with baiting the police. The American Liberation Front had sent hundreds of its members to the festival to stir up emotions about the Vietnam War. To alleviate the trouble and return the festival to a semblance of order, Fey decided that it was best to open the gates and let everyone in for free. When Zephyr came onstage, lead singer Candy Owens told the crowd to lie down so they wouldn't get the tear gas in their eyes and advised them not to hassle the already upset police.

The next evening was calmer and all the bands were well-received. The event had returned to "just" another rock festival, so much so that some of the bands who performed that day barely remember it. "Poco was already booked into the Troubadour in Los Angeles, a popular folk club that had become our home base—trading rehearsal time for bookings at the club," remembers Richie Furay, who appeared at the Denver festival with his new band Poco. "We were working that week with none other than Steve Martin, who was just developing his act and making a name for himself. I'm not sure how all the details came together, but the plan was for us to catch a plane from L.A. to Denver, where two of the original band members were from, Saturday morning and perform that afternoon, and fly back in time to do the show at the Troubadour that night. It all looked good on paper, even the Lear Jet to get us back and forth. But as is so often the case, things bogged down somewhere on the ground or in the air. I don't even remember our performance because everything was so rushed. It was one of those 'get 'em on and get 'em off' so the next group can 'get on and off.' If you weren't the headliner on one of those events it could be a little stressful, but the publicity made it all worthwhile. It was a Barry Fey event and we looked at it as a career opportunity and publicity."

"I guess the most memorable thing about the whole 'event' wasn't so much the Pop Festival itself—mingling and meeting other artists and doing our set—but coming back to L.A. that night and Steve covering for us," Furay continues. "I think we were over an hour late for our first set. It was the first time I had ever seen the 'arrow through the head' routine, and as funny as it was, Steve was not a happy guy as I remember."

By this time, many of the bands were becoming accustomed to playing on multiple-act bills. A gig was a gig was a gig. "In the end, it was all over so fast and the details are a blur," says Furay. "I think it was fun, but who knows? It was a whirlwind event."

The Jimi Hendrix Experience went onstage at 10:30 that night, with Hendrix dressed in a red silk shirt, a blue bandana, and a flowered vest. He had stopped setting his guitar on fire during most of his performances by this time but that didn't mean he was any less controversial. Hendrix (as usual high on acid), told the crowd, "We've seen some tear gas. That's the start of the third world war. Just pick your side, that's all I say." During "Purple Haze" scores of people broke loose from the audience and jumped onto the field. Although those people were contained, the mood of the crowd seemed to be venturing back into unruliness. During "Voodoo Child" first Noel Redding, then Mitch Mitchell, quit playing and left the stage. Jimi kept playing. Finally some roadies came on stage, picked him up by his arms and legs and carried him off-stage, where he was put into a truck. People started rushing the truck but the band escaped injury. This was the last appearance of the Jimi Hendrix Experience.

The festival came to a close. A total of 58,000 people had attended the Denver Pop Festival. Fourteen policeman had been injured (and eight of their cars damaged), and there was an estimated $50,000 in damages. Alan Cunningham of the *Rocky Mountain News* would call the festival a "three-day orbit of screaming and wildly vibrating animal sounds."

If the American public had become aware of the beginnings of the youth movement, most probably thought it was just "kids being kids" and nothing to concern themselves with outside of the rebelliousness that may have been playing out at home. Because of the location of the Denver Pop Festival, it's likely that many outside of the area knew what had gone on there—good or bad. That type of exposure was all about to change.

Miami Pop Festivals
May 18, 1968
December 28–30, 1968

> *"I suppose they came for the experience."*
> —Leigh Stephens, Blue Cheer

The sunshine and flower people of California may have been the ones getting the attention but the appeal of being a flower child wasn't exclusive to the West. While many of the youth of the Southern United States thought that the peace movement was "just a bunch of hippies," many of them were excited by the music that originated from the West Coast. It was decided by a group of music promoters (which included Michael Lang), that a Florida version of the pop festival would be welcomed by those who had been unable to get to Monterey to experience it first hand. The location of the festival was to be at the Gulf Stream Race Track in Hollandale, Florida on May 18, 1968. This time there would be performances by different bands and artists, with the exception of including the one performer who had garnered quite a bit of excitement at that original pop festival: Jimi Hendrix. The scheduled two-day event included diverse acts such as Frank Zappa and the Mothers of Invention, the Crazy World of Arthur Brown, and a band called Blue Cheer.

The group Blue Cheer was known at the time for their hit remake of the fifties classic "Summertime Blues" and appeared with stacks of amps behind them. The band's Leigh Stephens says the festival wasn't memorable because of the audience but rather for what went on behind the scenes. "It was very hot," remembers Stephens. "So hot and humid that the hotel, the Castaways, air conditioners did not work. There was a limo shuttle service to and from the venue and we would just ride back and forth to stay cool because the limo air conditioner worked really well. I remember taking several trips back and forth with Jimmy Carl Black from the Mothers. It was also so hot that my Fuzz Face pedal batteries melted and I had to put the unit on ice on stage. I warned Hendrix of the problem because he had the same unit, but he went on later at night and it was a little cooler."

The varied show bill created different modes of excitement in the audience. Arthur Brown sang his signature song "Fire" with a burning headdress on his head. "The highlight of the evening was the Crazy World of Arthur Brown," remembers Stephens. "He had this hat he set on fire. People were very impressed with that."

Hendrix arrived by helicopter. He had interrupted his recording of the album *Electric Ladyland* to appear. Hendrix played two sets, one in the afternoon and one in the evening. The amps malfunctioned during his set but the performer was not deterred from giving the audience what they came to hear (and see). Hendrix was back to setting fire to his guitar and he smashed it to boot. The parts of the guitar somehow ended up being given to Frank Zappa.

After their performances, many of the artists relocated to a nearby bar where they could cool off. Others just tried to keep the heat at bay while trying to get a glimpse of the festival and its participants. "I hung out by myself when I wasn't riding the shuttle," recalls Leigh Stephens, "and [with] a girl I met there. I couldn't go down to the bar where everybody hung out in the evening because I was underage. Linda Eastman, who toured with us and took pictures, was there bleaching the tips of Hendrix's hair before the show."

In retrospect it was a good show and a fairly tame festival experience. "I suppose they came for the experience," says Stephens about the crowd. "The whole thing seemed really normal. Lots of people, well behaved."

A lot of the second day was rained out, but most of those who attended seem to leave the festival believing that they had a good time. Many couldn't wait for another festival. By the end of the year, they would get their wish.

The second Miami Pop Festival was held again at the Gulfstream Race Track December 28–30, 1968. This time over 100,000 people came to participate. Along with Jimi Hendrix and the Grateful Dead, the music included legendary performers and new-to-the-scene musicians such as Chuck Berry, Marvin Gaye, Steppenwolf, Fleetwood Mac, Joni Mitchell, Iron Butterfly, and Junior Walker & the All Stars. The Native American rock 'n' roll group Tiger Tiger (composed of Lee and Stephen Tiger of the Miccosukee Tribe of Florida, where their father served as Chief), was an interesting addition to the bill.

On the first day, Jose Feliciano, Country Joe & the Fish, Buffy Saint-Marie, Chuck Berry, the Infinite McCoys, John Mayall's Blues Breakers, Booker T. and the MGs, Dino Valente, and Fleetwood Mac performed. Day Two featured Junior Walker and the All Stars, the Butterfield Blues Band, Flatt & Scruggs, Marvin Gaye, Joni Mitchell (who had been gaining attention and attended the festival with Graham Nash), the Boxtops, Richie Havens, James Cotton, H.P. Lovecraft, and Steppenwolf.

Steppenwolf was fairly new to the scene and were pleased to be included. "When we arrived about an hour early it was chaotic backstage," remembers Steppenwolf's keyboard player Goldy McJohn. "The massive crowd was really just out to enjoy and no signs of misbehavin'. Just pure rock 'n' roll gratitude from the crowd. We missed Woodstock due to prior gigs, one being the Miami Pop Festival. Personally, it made me feel very humble to be there as a guy in a band playing for so many people."

Day Three of the festival included Canned Heat, the Turtles, Iron Butterfly, Joe Tex, Ian & Sylvia, the Grassroots, Pacific Gas & Electric (who signed a recording contract with Columbia Records after their appearance at the festival), the Charles Lloyd Quartet, the Sweet Inspirations, and the Grateful Dead.

There were things to enjoy in addition to the music at the festival billed as "A thousand wonders and a three-day collage of beautiful music." Featured were "Kaleidoscopic Elephants, Blue Meanies on Parade, Meditation Grove, Giant Ti-Leaf slide, and the World's first electronic sky divers."

Two stages had been set up with one in the middle of the racetrack to present bands such as Three Dog Night, and the other stage was in the meadow area featuring performances by Sweetwater, Junior Walker and the All Stars, the Grateful Dead, and others. The Grateful Dead were new to Southern audiences and after their performance they were the talk of the festival. It was close to 100 degrees each day but few seemed to care. This was *a happening*.

Those who performed were sometimes surprised at the reception they received from the crowd. "It was our first huge fest," remembers Sweetwater's Alex Del Zoppo. "Just before we began our set, Fred [Herrera] decided to keep Nancy [Nevins] offstage until we were well into the groove of "Motherless Child," letting us warm up with about a full two minutes of instrumental jamming. The audience, already noticeably intrigued by our unusual sound and instrumental line-up, seemed to go whack when Nancy stepped out and began to sing. As our set continued, they applauded louder for each new song, and then wouldn't let us leave. We had a number of encores. What a rush it was for us then. That audience didn't know who we were when we began to play, but *did* after we finished. From then on, we could do no wrong anywhere in Florida—and (thank God) we loved Florida!"

"In those days, bands didn't typically elicit encores, and because we did, perhaps the reviewers took notice," says Sweetwater's Fred Herrera. "By the time we finished with "My Crystal Spider" and "What's Wrong," they applauded until we had totally left the stage area. Someone quipped 'Sweetwater made Miami Pop!'"

"Three days of the best groups in the country and northern and eastern America's introduction to them," muses Three Dog Night's Chuck Negron. "Three Dog Night went from being an unknown group to having their first million selling record, 'One,' and becoming a headliner."

The music-hungry crowd was thrilled to be there. "At first, [what I saw was] the immense size of it all with people in bleachers very far from us and tons of people on the field filling up all the space from the bleachers to the stage," recalls Sweetwater's Alex Del Zoppo. "Secondly, the audience was all attentive, not as indifferent as the crowds in L.A. or San Francisco, who were more jaded and had seen it all. Harvey Gerst (an old friend, guru and our Acoustic Control Amp rep at the time), played electric guitar with us, becoming an infrequent, unofficial band member from then on."

If any of the performers were feeling overwhelmed by the immense size of the crowd, there were other artists with whom they could commiserate. "We met some friends backstage before going on—Charlie Allen from Pacific Gas & Electric, et cetera—and that made us feel immediately at home, so we were in a great mood when we took the stage," recalls Fred Herrera. "The sheer size of the audience was definitely a step up, but being that our first gig ever was at a 10,000 attendee Love-In, this gig was more exciting than frightening, so it only made us play better."

The adulation of the crowd wasn't all the performers received. "The most beautiful girls I had ever seen were at this festival and I had the time of my young life," says Chuck Negron. "I think I fell in love all three days with three different girls. Some of our innocent actions didn't end up without consequences and there were young girls left pregnant. I met my son ten years ago when he located me and informed me I was his father and his mother was a wonderful girl I had spent a lot of time with at the Miami Pop Festival. She never told me even though we spent time together when I would be in Miami years later. To give you an idea of the possibility that this happened to many girls, another member of Three Dog Night was taken to court and paid child support to a young girl he had spent time with at that festival."

Michael Allsop of Three Dog Night remembers being dosed (without his knowledge) with PCP by a pair of "hippie chicks." Psychedelic posters were handed out free at the gate. The kids in Miami weren't used to the long hair and bell bottoms yet, but they quickly adapted to the freedom of expression that those who played at the festival championed.

"A lot of festivals got a wee bit carried away [like] Altamont," says Goldy McJohn. "To quote Mr. John Lennon, 'Give Peace a Chance,' or Rodney King, 'Can't we all just get along?' Each generation has its good sides and bad. So much has changed in the world. Maybe the sixties music and its message helped. I, for one, certainly hope so. We were the 'new kids in town' but we always believed we'd make something of ourselves."

Elvis personified the rebellion of youth in the fifties and in the early sixties the music (and hair) of the Beatles unleashed yet another wave of commotion in households across America. As the ambiance of brotherhood expressed in the music heard at Monterey Pop spread north, south, and east it became clear that the carefree ideals of Flower Power were something that American youth could—and would—embrace. What happened at Monterey Pop would not only change what was heard on the radio but influence a cultural movement unlike any in American history.

Hyde Park Free Concerts
June 29, 1968

Jethro Tull, Tyrannosaurus Rex, Roy Harper, and Pink Floyd played a free festival at London's Hyde Park on June 29, 1968. An event at the park had taken place months earlier, but it was only a quasi-impromptu concert off the bed of a flatbed truck by musical artists seemingly unremembered. This time, Pink Floyd's Nick Mason remembered the event as more of a picnic in the park than any sort of Monterey Pop-type gathering. Tyrannosaurus Rex played while seated cross-legged on the floor of the stage, and Pink Floyd, appearing without founding member Syd Barrett, played only a brief handful of songs. Regardless of the scope of the event, a good time was had by all and those who organized the little festival event decided that the event should be repeated.

Hyde Park free concerts continued once a month for the remaining three months of the summer with Traffic, the Pretty Things, Fleetwood Mac, Ten Years After, Fairport Convention, and the Move, among some of the bands joining in the fun. The next year the festival series returned, this time including Blind Faith, Donovan, King Crimson, Al Stewart, and the Rolling Stones (with their new guitarist Mick Taylor).

The Hyde Park concerts would become a summertime staple. The concerts continue today with Hyde Park Calling, which features name acts over a weekend, but those under sixteen must be accompanied by an adult over twenty-one for admission. Guess that's one way to keep "the kids" out of trouble.

Milwaukee Summerfest
1968

In the midst of the national dissonance of 1967, Milwaukee, Wisconsin's Mayor Henry Maier decided to launch a festival that would not only bring people together, but revitalize the downtown area of the city. Maier appointed forty-one people to plan the event under the non-profit organization Milwaukee World Festival, Inc. The community gathering featured music and family entertainment held at thirty-five different locations around the city. A beauty pageant, boat race, ski show, film festival, air show, carnival rides, and a firework display were included in the festivities. In 1968 the festival returned and by 1969 sixty locations were designated as entertainment spots. Perhaps the event was overbooked, since the festival lost money that year. But the venture was saved with the help of three local businessmen and it was decided that one major venue would host what would now be dubbed Milwaukee Summerfest. The festival continued to grow in attendance but was not without its setbacks, including when riots broke out during concerts by Humble Pie, and the Blackberries, in

1970. The eighties brought artists such as Eric Clapton, Sting, and R.E.M. to the Summerfest stages. It was decided that a state-of-the-art amphitheater would be an asset and the Beach Boys opened the Marcus Amphitheater in 1987.

Over the years the Milwaukee Summerfest has become a much-anticipated event, held over eleven days, starting on the last Thursday in June and running until the Sunday after July 4th. The Guinness Book of Records states Summerfest is the "World's Largest Music Festival." The current promoters claim that nearly one million people attend the event annually, which is held on seventy-five acres along Lake Michigan at Henry W. Maier Festival Park in downtown Milwaukee.

The festival thrown by Mayor Maier has grown to include various types of music, a play area for children, comedians, demonstrations and amusement park rides. There is even the Skyride: a horizontal chairlift that offers views of the venue. By 2007, the fortieth anniversary of the festival, music was heard from eleven different stages by dozens of bands. A variety of headliners have appeared such as James Brown, Destiny's Child, Tom Petty & the Heartbreakers, INXS, Bon Jovi, B.B. King, Collective Soul, Brian McKnight, Daughtry, Peter Frampton, Umphrey's McGee, Rusted Root, and Dashboard Confessionals.

"Performing at 'The World's Largest Music Festival' was quite a surreal experience for me," says singer/songwriter Ari Herstand. "I grew up in Wisconsin, so I had been an audience member for many years before actually performing the festival. Being able to perform every day was mind-blowing. Knowing that at any given time, any one of the one hundred thousand people on the grounds could walk by my stage, get enticed, and become a new fan is incredible. I love building my base in a grassroots manner like that."

Appearing at a hometown festival, especially one of such large proportion, is sometimes a goal that bands and musicians set for themselves. "There was about six years between the first time I attended Summerfest and the first time we actually got to play," says Christian Schauf of Catchpenny. "I remember being in awe of how many great bands there were in such a small space and thought it'd be a dream to be a part of it all. After having a group I thought was Summerfest worthy, it still took us three years of begging to finally get invited to play. We were able to live out that dream this past July. Playing in 95 degree heat was tough, but the crowd was so big, and it was one of our more fun shows of the summer. Being voted Fan Favorites on the Emerging Artists Stage was simply the icing on the cake."

In recent years the festival has partnered with Country Music Television to broadcast some of the festival appearances by headliners such as Tim McGraw, Big & Rich, and Sugarland. The African World Festival group and a special event entitled "A Gospel Celebration" offer faith-based music. An abundant variety of food—everything from "gator on a stick" to chocolate dipped strawberries—is offered and bazaars are held in tents erected around the site. In 2007, there was even the Jimi Hendrix Red House, a mobile, interactive museum with displays focusing on the icon's music legacy.

Of course, like any music festival, problems arise. "My first year performing the festival, the summer of 2006, for my very first show I stepped on stage and started my very first song," remembers Herstand. "I began beat-boxing and the second I hit the loop pedal all the sound stopped. The sound guy looked at me and threw his arms up in bewilderment. I tried the mics and got nothing. The sound guy and stage managers came running at the stage, started plugging things in and out frantically, fidgeting with wires. Dumbfounded, I stood on the stage not knowing what to do. Then I looked up at the Skytram and saw that it wasn't moving either and everyone's legs were just dangling in midair. Then I noticed there was no sound coming from any of the other stages. We got word that the entire power had gone out on Day One of Summerfest! So, I jumped offstage, grabbed some musician friends of mine and, with an upright bass, three acoustic guitars, a snare drum, and a sax, we all played acoustically in front of the stage for about an hour, trading songs, jamming to covers we all knew and just having a great time. By the end of the hour, our area was packed, as we were the only place in all of Summerfest that had live music and that is the reason people come to the festival in the first place, right?"

Despite the problematic elements of technology and nature, appearing at a festival can result in memories worth their weight in gold for some musicians. "Summerfest, two years ago," muses Goran Kralj of the Gufs. "Our first Summerfest after a three-year hiatus. It was the talk of the town. The Gufs were coming back to Summerfest. The rock stage was filled and the crowd was ready for a great show. The only problem was that a massive storm was coming. All the festival stage managers were looking at the Weather Channel and it looked like the show was going to be rained out. We decided to go on and take our chances. All I remember is being on stage and seeing thousands of people singing along and dancing, while lightening kept on striking in the distance off Lake Michigan. The rain never came full force, and only at [one] time sprinkled a bit to cool off the crowd on what was a hot evening. It was the perfect effect that made the crowd, and the band, that much more into the show. It was a moment I will never forget."

Newport Pop Festival
August 4–5, 1968

If you were living in California, it was impossible to ignore the fact that change was in the air. Representing the new order were the hippies in Northern California and their counterparts on the Sunset Strip in Los Angeles, the flower children. The music emanating from the transistor radios of young people was getting a little more harder-edge than the Beatles' innocuous early-career singles. Teenagers in Middle America had yet to truly test the confines of their society on any meaningful scale, but teens in Southern California, many who didn't care about changing anything at all, wanted to party amid the sounds of the new rock music of their generation.

The Newport Pop Festival was held in Costa Mesa, California on August 4 and 5, 1968. Over 100,000 people came to hear the Byrds, Quicksilver Messenger Service, the Paul Butterfield Blues Band, Steppenwolf, Illinois Speed Press, the Chambers Brothers, Iron Butterfly, the James Cotton Blues Band and. . . Tiny Tim. There was little "festival" spirit at the event—it was more of a well-controlled, multi-act concert. But for those in Los Angeles and Orange Counties, it was a start.

Isle of Wight Festival
August 31, 1968

"We had to get through the technical aspects of it all."
—Jack Casady, Jefferson Airplane

In 1968, the United States was not the only place the hippie and flower children experience was breaking out. The ideology of the youth movement was now spreading throughout Europe as well. Carnaby Street and the "mod" ornamentation of British designers had caused those in London who had scoffed at flowery dress and peace signs to reconsider. The hip and cool of London had made a statement: they were just as "with it" as any of their American counterparts. The year 1968 brought the first of a series of festivals that would come to be well-attended and much-appreciated by rock music lovers in Great Britain: The Isle of Wight Festival.

The first Isle of Wight Festival really wasn't much in the scheme of things. It was held for only one day and evening at Hell Field, on the Ford Farm near Godshill, on the Isle of Wight on August 31. The event was attended by only 10,000 people.

The Isle of Wight was an interesting choice for a gathering of youth. The Isle was removed from some of the limitations that would have been present in areas closer to London. "They tended to pick places without city ordinances so they didn't have the type of problems that came with those restrictions," says Jefferson Airplane's Jack Casady.

The festival was organized by Rikki Farr (son of British Heavyweight Boxing champion Tommy Farr and brother to musician Gary Farr), and featured a variety of pop and rock acts, with Jefferson Airplane headlining as the only American act on the bill. There were rumors that the Beatles would attend and maybe sit in with some of the other groups scheduled to perform, but even that failed to elicit much excitement. Two trailers were coupled to create a stage and things were kept simple. The facilities weren't much but since the festival was only one day, people didn't seem to mind. The festival was based on the premise of those who liked rock music would gather for an afternoon and evening to be spent in the company of others with like taste. Even the performers agreed to keep it simple—their only accommodation was a small tent.

Local bands such as Halcyon Order took the stage before appearances by better-known bands such as the Pretty Things, Tyrannosaurus Rex, Smile (whose appearance at the festival would be their only live performance), the Move, Orange Bicycle, Blonde on Blonde, the Crazy World of Arthur Brown (who attempted to set *something* on fire during his song "Fire" but failed), Fairport Convention, and the Aynsley Dunbar Retaliation.

The air was frigid and windy, and many of those who attended were ill-equipped to stay warm and enjoy the show. The plastic designating the boundaries of the festival grounds was ripped off the fence and used to keep warm by many in the audience. At one point a toxic fire was started to stave off the cold. The show lasted into the night and ended the next morning at about 8 a.m.

The Jefferson Airplane, who were on the European leg of their tour, came to the festival with stage effects including a huge p.a. system and a liquid light show screen that they introduced to the British audience. Their gear was perhaps more impressive than the band's performance that night, but it wasn't necessarily the band's fault. Although their set lasted over ninety minutes, they continued to have problems with their sound, which resulted in the band having to stop often and retune. "It was windy that day," recalls Jack Casady. "We had to get through the technical aspects of it all. It was a tremendous chance for us to go over to England. We were breaking out of our home territory and moving around a lot at that time. It was an interesting time of new music and new artists."

Few minded the problems the musicians were having on the stage. The crowd was primarily there for the experience. This first Isle of Wight Festival was certainly far less than what it would become in the future. During the next two years, the Isle of Wight Festival would grow into something much bigger and much more newsworthy.

1969
Come Together

In U.S. news

Apollo 7 broadcasts from orbit; Richard Nixon is elected President and announces the first troop withdrawals from Vietnam; the Chicago Seven go on trial; Nixon gives his "Silent Majority" speech; Vice President Spiro Agnew calls the media "nattering nabobs of negativism"; Alcatraz is seized by a group of Native Americans; and the first U.S. draft lottery begins.

In world news

Tommy Smith and John Carlos raise their hands in the Black Power salute during the Mexico City Olympics; rioting occurs in North Ireland; Yasser Arafat becomes the head of the PLO; Golda Meir is the first female Prime Minister of Israel; and Salt I negotiations regarding nuclear weapons take place.

In music news

The Beatles perform for the last time; Jim Morrison is arrested for indecent exposure in Miami; Elvis appears in Las Vegas; John and Yoko stage a bed-in and record "Give Peace a Chance"; and Brian Jones is murdered.

Some of the year's most notable albums

The Beatles: *Abbey Road*; Neil Young: *Everybody Knows This is Nowhere*; Creedence Clearwater Revival: *Green River*; Janis Joplin: *I Got Dem Ol' Kozmic Blues Again Mama!*; Led Zeppelin: *Led Zeppelin*; the Who: *Tommy*.

Rock's most popular songs

"Aquarius/Let the Sunshine In"—the Fifth Demension; "Get Together"—the Youngbloods; "Give Peace a Chance"—Plastic Ono Band; "Honky Tonk Women"—the Rolling Stones; "Proud Mary"—Creedence Clearwater Revival; "Come Together"—the Beatles; "Suite: Judy Blue Eyes"—Crosby, Stills & Nash; "Suspicious Minds"—Elvis; "Whole Lotta Love"—Led Zeppelin.

Newport '69
June 20–22, 1969

"It was fairly disorganized and the crowds largely stoned."
—Fred Herrera, Sweetwater

By the start of the summer of 1969, young people who had been cooped up in classes or routine jobs were ready to get back out in the sun and celebrate their music and themselves. On June 20–22, a three-day music festival was planned for Newport, California. After problems arose, a site adjacent to San Fernando Valley State College in Northridge, California called Devonshire Downs was selected. Over 140,000 people would attend but the sense of entitlement that had reared its ugly head in Denver would once again present itself and threaten the enjoyment of those who came to the festival.

Appearing were Jimi Hendrix (billed as the Jimi Hendrix Experience), Spirit, Joe Cocker, the Ike & Tina Turner Revue, Taj Mahal, Albert King, Southwind, the Edwin Hawkins Singers, Creedence Clearwater Revival, Eric Burdon, Albert Collins, Lee Michaels, Steppenwolf, Friends of Distinction, Brenton Wood, Jethro Tull, Buffy Sainte-Marie, Love, the Rascals, the Chambers Brothers, Poco, Three Dog Night, Marvin Gaye, Sweetwater, Charity, Jerry Lauderdale, the Byrds, Johnny Winter, the Flock, and Mother Earth. By now, the record companies were taking out ads in the festival "program," which was one clear indication of how corporate the California festivals were becoming. The festival experience was also becoming less communal and peace-loving. People were attending in droves but the atmosphere of the events seemed to be more about getting wasted and saying you'd been there than in taking the time to meet new people and share collective views. Music continued to be a highlight of the festival experience and some truly memorable performances occurred, but the memories seemed more for the artists than for the audience. The act of appearing at a festival was not yet commonplace for some of the bands and festivals were a great way to see other artists perform.

"It took place about two months before Woodstock," remembers Fred Herrera of Sweetwater. "I remember the promoters had lost their original venue, actually in Newport, and had to hastily set up the stages at their new location in Devonshire Downs in the San Fernando Valley. Because of this, logistics were not too well worked out. It was fairly disorganized and the crowds largely stoned."

Singer Brenton Wood ("The Oogum Boogum Song" and "Gimme Little Sign") remembers the event as "a fun time in my life. It was a time everyone seemed to like one another. I got a chance to meet a lot of artists and had the opportunity to perform with some of the all-time greats of the industry. It was a great concert."

The backstage area was a mass of trailers and gear, and the security was so tight many of the musicians were hesitant about going out into the crowd lest they not be allowed to return. Those who came for the "experience" of it all sometimes wondered what that experience actually was.

But communing with the audience was sometimes fun for the performers. "In that era, we often invited people up onto the stage, as long as it didn't mess up our playing," says Sweetwater's Alex Del Zoppo. "That was part of our 'Join the Band' segment. We were scheduled in almost a headliner position, coming on very late, but then because of some sort of curfew, they flashed the lights and told us we had to quit—with the crowd unsatisfied. Well, they say, 'Leave 'em wanting more.'"

Although festivals were not truly commonplace yet, some of the artists who had appeared at more than one were becoming jaded or complacent. Jimi Hendrix was paid, according to reports, at least $100,000 to headline Saturday night. During his trip to the venue, he mentioned that the money he was receiving was more than Elvis had ever been paid. Yet Hendrix set that night was not a good one. Some people remember a few representatives of the college's Black Students Union trying to talk politics with Hendrix while he waited backstage, but Hendrix was more focused on what he had come there to do and there was some animosity. It was also said that someone had dosed Hendrix with acid and that was why his performance that night was sub-par. Hendrix was certainly no stranger to acid so that seems unlikely, but regardless of the reason why, Hendrix did not perform to the audience's expectation and there was some booing.

"Hendrix came on about an hour late and the crowd taunted him," remembers television producer Willie Olmstead, who was in the audience. "He said to one person, 'Hey, you in the white pants—Fuck off!' He told the crowd not to call out songs, but that made it worse." Calls for his "hits" annoyed Hendrix and he played some jarring renditions after yelling at the crowd that if they wanted hits, he'd give them "some fucking hits." He slammed into some nasty chords and bashed away at his guitar . . . and the audience. He eventually pulled the cable from his guitar and stormed off the stage.

It wasn't all Hendrix. The audience of over 60,000 was rowdy that night and there had already been some problems with crowd control. People once again decided that they should be admitted free and a large group scaled the chain-link fencing that surrounded the festival grounds, causing the fencing to collapse on those below it. Hells Angels were acting as security—whether hired to do so or taking it upon themselves—and began punching those they could catch. People were getting pushed and shoved, and the Los Angeles Police Department (not unfamiliar with the campus due to previous anti-war demonstrations), decided to let their presence be felt. The police battled back the mass of people and one of their helicopters hovered overhead, shining a light down on those who were attempting to push their way in.

"People were at the gate in masses," recalls Olmstead. "Many didn't have tickets and were trying to bully their way in for free. Several security people were standing in front of the gate. Then a few people threw gallon glass wine bottles at the guards. As glass started to break one guy from the crowd was yelling 'Quit throwing fuckin' shit!' As the crowd got uglier, the security people were told to get out of the way. The crowd tore down the fence and about a hundred people got in for free. As I approached the entrance, security had the gate back up again and only people with tickets were allowed in."

The damage wasn't over. A canvas draping caught fire and flames leaped through the air near the exit. As each band came off stage, they quickly moved away from the festival. There was no telling what would happen, but most of the raucous people had taken to the nearby streets of suburban Northridge to break windows and cause minor mayhem throughout the upscale business district. That was enough for the LAPD, who determined the event was a "riot" and thus took what they believed to be appropriate action.

By Sunday, a day that was hotter than expected, things had quieted down and the festival was allowed to continue, although it was down 20,000 in attendance. Hendrix returned during the afternoon to play again. He acknowledged to the crowd that he and they had "gotten off on the wrong foot" and played an inspired, bluesy set that culminated in a jam with members of Mother Earth, the Full Tilt Boogie Band, Eric Burdon, Lee Oskar, and Buddy Miles.

"This was nearly a 'hometown' gig for us, being L.A-adjacent and all," says Alex Del Zoppo. "It was a two-day event with a boatload of top acts and a record attendance to date. There were lots of clashes between attendees and the police. However, there were some great performances going on, including Hendrix with Buddy Miles for the first time."

At least the festival ended on a positive note. But the violence and anger troubled many. Festivals were supposed to be about peace and love, not antagonism and resentment. The festival crowd needed to step back and take a breath.

Bath Festival of Blues
June 28, 1969

"My only recollection is that the Bath Festival was just another gig."
—John Mayall

The British, meanwhile, seemed to be figuring out how to throw a successful festival party. The Bath Festival of Blues was organized and promoted by Freddie Bannister and held on June 28, 1969. The bill included Rory Gallagher's band Taste, John Mayall, Roy Harper, Fleetwood Mac, Ten Years After, Keef Hartley, the Nice, and Led Zeppelin. The setting was not the barren fields or fairgrounds to which many festivals had been relegated. This time a small stage had been erected not far from gothic residential buildings. A crowd of 12,000 people gathered to hear music offered in an almost intimate setting. This was Bannister's first festival and he pulled it off without incident.

The festival kicked off with the Liverpool Scene, who got the audience in the mood for some laid back but exhilarating performances. Who today would expect Led Zeppelin to kick back and play in the afternoon on a relatively small stage? The talent was exceptional and the setting engaging. Even so, to many of the artists who appeared the festival wasn't particularly notable. "My only recollection is that the Bath Festival was just another gig," says John Mayall. "At that time we were playing up to eight gigs a week, year-round in the sixties and early seventies."

But the music had an impact on those who came to listen. The festival certainly had the elements to make it an experience worth repeating. Over June 27–28 the following year, the Bath Festival of Blues and Alternative Music would rock.

Atlanta International Pop Festival
July 4, 1969

"It was hot and sticky. We always thrived on an audience response, so we poured on the steam and just made it happen."
—Alex Del Zoppo, Sweetwater

In 1969, the American South wasn't known for its new order of teenage society but promoter Alex Cooley certainly wasn't going to let an opportunity for a huge celebration of rock music pass him by. Cooley had attended the Miami Pop Festival and the peace, love, and music movement intrigued him. Miami had been successful, but Miami was a city unlike any other in the United States. It was less representative of the South and more known as a beach and party destination. Cooley felt the time was right to bring the festival experience to the Deep South, an area from which many of the young men of the region were fighting and dying in Vietnam, and specifically to Georgia, where segregationist Lester Maddox was currently in power as Governor. Cooley's intent was to do something where it could be demonstrated that hope was alive, new ideas were welcome, the South was not ideologically isolated from the rest of the country, and the social climate could—and would—change.

Cooley lined up a diverse group of performers led by "Mr. Rock 'n' Roll" himself, Chuck Berry. Popular acts like Blood, Sweat & Tears, Chicago Transit Authority, Creedence Clearwater Revival, and Johnny Rivers would appear alongside some of the artists who had been popular at the Monterey Pop Festival including Janis Joplin, the Paul Butterfield Blues Band, and Canned Heat. Al Kooper and Johnny Winter would be on hand, as well as some up-and-coming bands like Grand Funk Railroad, Led Zeppelin, Spirit, Pacific Gas & Electric, and Delaney & Bonnie & Friends. Sweetwater and Ten Wheel Drive would round out the bill, and the jazz music of Dave Brubeck was even tossed into the mix.

On the 4th of July weekend, 1969, over 100,000 people gathered at the Atlanta International Raceway in Hampton, Georgia, twenty-five miles south of Atlanta. The temperature was scorching, and despite the careful planning of the promoter, water and ice were at a premium. Cold beer was expensive and it was said there was no ice to be had in the four-county area surrounding the festival site for three days.

The music was brilliant and took the crowd's mind off the heat. "We were getting used to these festivals to the point where they sometimes became a blur, but by this time these folks treated us like royalty," says Sweetwater's Fred Herrera. "There were two posters printed for this event, one with only drawings of each band. That was the first thing they showed us before we went on . . . and there we were in effigy. We did really well there."

Janis Joplin was a large draw for the concert but she wasn't necessarily the star of the show. Writing for *Metro Beat*, Tim McCabe noted that Sweetwater, who were placed in the tenuous position of having to follow Joplin, received "more applause than 'Queen Janis.'"

Even the show itself sizzled. Grand Funk Railroad was so loud, it was said they could be heard on Peachtree Street in Atlanta—twenty miles away. Their amps were stacked fifteen feet high behind them. One of the highlights of the festival was Johnny Rivers' late night entrance. His band started, the spotlights crisscrossed the sky, and in came Rivers with his guitar around his neck, dangling from a helicopter ladder, from which he was slowly lowered onto the stage. During Led Zeppelin's set a naked man with a star wand jumped on stage to catch the attention of Robert Plant (as well as those in the audience). The crowd wasn't having it—a beer bottle was smashed over the guy's head and the show continued. There may have been flower children in the crowd, but the festival was one big Southern-style party.

"It was held at the International Speedway," remembers Sweetwater's Alex Del Zoppo. "It was hot and sticky. We always thrived on an audience response, so we poured on the steam and just made it happen. I also remember walking around later on the festival grounds and seeing a large circle of hippies holding hands, spinning around and singing, 'La-la-la-la' the melody from our 'Rondeau.' What a late sixties period scene that was!"

Although making money on the event was not paramount to what promoter Alex Cooley was hoping to accomplish, he would net $12,000 from the festival. But the experience that Cooley and the others who performed brought to those who loved music in the South was priceless. Cooley would go on to make good times through rock and roll his mission.

Atlantic City Pop Festival
August 1–3, 1969

In the North in New Jersey, over 110,000 people gathered for the Atlantic City Pop Festival just a few weeks later on August 1–3. The festival was well-organized and despite the heat, attendees enjoyed the variety of name acts. Because it was held in the city, the festival was more an extended concert, with those who attended free to enter, or exit, as their music taste dictated.

The bands were stellar and included a potpourri of rock styles with Little Richard representing bebop; B.B. King, Booker T. & the MGs, the Chambers Brothers, and Janis Joplin providing soul; Three Dog Night offering pop rock; and Joni Mitchell playing folk music. Santana and Canned Heat brought the rhythm, Dr. John the boogie woogie, Procol Harum their sophisticated English rock, and Jefferson Airplane, Arthur Brown, and Iron Butterfly played psychedelic rock.

As a concert event, the Atlantic City Pop Festival demonstrated that music celebrations didn't *have* to be held away from the populace and that young people *could* behave while they partied in the city. The mainstream city kids enjoyed their music but the counterculture youth were about to have their day. All eyes would soon be on a gathering so big, so important to American culture, that those parents who believed that if they just shut their eyes and waited that their kids would return to the fold and become productive members of their mother's and father's social order were in for a rude awakening. The social revolution was *on* and it would be fully demonstrated with a festival event called Woodstock.

The Woodstock Music and Art Fair
August 15–18, 1969

"The onstage bit was great fun as was the crowd, but the rest I think I could have passed on."

—Leo Lyons, Ten Years After

Joel Rosenman and John Roberts met on a golf course in 1966. Rosenman, the wealthy son of an orthodontist who owned a Long Island dental clinic, was a recent graduate from Yale Law School. Roberts enjoyed a multi-million dollar trust fund as heir to the Block Pharmaceutical family. The young men decided to share an apartment as each put his mind to deciding which path he might follow into the future. Rosenman and Roberts got along well. Each enjoyed music and other forms of popular culture. While relaxing at home one day, Rosenman and Roberts came up with an idea for a television sitcom that would mirror the relationship between the iconic characters of Lucy and Ethel, only this time the zaniness would be enacted by males. Plotlines based around the men getting involved in a variety of business situations appealed to Roberts and Rosenman. They decided to live the lives of their fictional characters, as just maybe they were simply bored and lacking focus on how they could make an important contribution to business or society. The two young men placed an ad in the *New York Times* and the *Wall Street Journal* with the heading "Young Men with Unlimited Capital looking for interesting, legitimate investment opportunities and business propositions." They received thousands of replies. Some were legitimate but uninspiring and others were off-the-wall and ridiculous. The classified ad was noticed by various people of power in the world of finance but nothing proposed really clicked with Roberts and Rosenman.

On the West Coast, music writer and producer Artie Kornfeld was enjoying his position as an energetic force in the new rock order as Vice President and Director of Rock Music at Capitol Records. Kornfeld had become friends with Cass Elliot when the two were students at American University and was likely plugged into Elliot's social scene. Kornfeld had initially made his mark through writing Jan and Dean's hit song "Dead Man's Curve" and co-writing, with Steve Duboff, other whimsical hits such as Crispian St. Peters' "Pied Piper" and the Cowsills' "The Rain, the Park and Other Things." One day a young man named Mike Lang appeared in Kornfeld's office without an appointment. Lang was a laid-back entrepreneur from Florida. Originally from Brooklyn, New York, he had left his studies at NYU to move south to Coconut Grove where he would open one of the South's first head shops. (Head shops were gaining popularity nationwide as the one-stop retail venues to buy bongs and wrappers, other drug paraphernalia, love beads, black lights, counterculture art, and hippie clothing.) Lang had been one of the promoters of the Miami Pop Festival in 1968. He was now living in the small community of Woodstock, New York, and was managing a rock band called Train, for whom he was attempting to land a recording contract. Lang had heard or read that Artie Kornfeld had also grown up in Bensonhurst, Brooklyn, and thought that was as good an introduction as he needed to one of the music industry brass.

When Kornfeld's secretary told him that the young man in the waiting room was from the old neighborhood, Kornfeld felt that was reason enough to at least see what Lang wanted. Kornfeld ended up agreeing to take Train into the studio (which he did to unsatisfactory results) and a personal friendship between Kornfeld and Lang developed. Late one night after a game of bumper pool, Kornfeld mentioned to Lang that he was only being exposed to mainstream commercial artists at Capitol Records and he wanted to see what else was out there in the "new" music scene. The pair started spinning an off-the-wall fantasy to rent a theater on Broadway to have a giant party for a group of friends and be entertained by artists whose music they enjoyed. Expanding on the idea, Lang said rather than Broadway they should have it in Woodstock—a lot of artists had relocated to that idyllic spot and it would make the perfect setting. In fact, thought Lang, they should open a recording studio there and really focus on new, more adventurous music. That idea appealed to Kornfeld and that was all fine and good, but the conversation kept returning to the idea of a big party featuring all kinds of eclectic artists playing their music. Lang had witnessed the appeal of Miami Pop and had noted how many people had ultimately shown up to enjoy the music. As Kornfeld and Lang talked, the numbers of those who might attend a similar event in Woodstock grew larger and larger. After a few months of visualizing their fictitious event, Kornfeld and Lang decided to make their festival a reality. They formed a company called Kornfeld Lang Adventures.

Kornfeld and Lang apparently had not seen the ad placed by Rosenman and Roberts, but Train's lawyer Miles Lourie was familiar with the pair's quest for an entertaining investment. After Rosenman, Roberts, Kornfeld, and Lang met to discuss the possibility of a festival, Rosenman and Roberts made the decision to invest at least $250,000 in the endeavor. Rosenman would later claim that the idea of the festival had been Roberts and Rosenman's after Lang and Kornfeld had approached them about opening a studio in Woodstock. Regardless of whose idea it was, Woodstock Ventures was formed with each of the four men serving as a partner in March, 1969.

Kornfeld was still working for Capitol Records at this time and his contract there prohibited signing agreements with any other entity. His stock in Woodstock Ventures had to be held by Lang, but eventually Kornfeld was so enthused with the festival idea he decided to leave his position at Capitol. Woodstock Ventures moved into an office on 57th Street in Manhattan. Kornfeld would work with the marketing and promotion staff there and Lang opened his own office to work with a production staff. Bill Hanley was brought on board to handle the sound system and Chip Monck would be on hand to oversee a variety of festival components.

After securing the money they needed for the proposed festival, one of the first things that needed to be accomplished was to set a theme for the event. It was important to Kornfeld and Lang that their "party" be much more than just a concert. It was to be a proper festival with arts and crafts, and a literal sense of youth community. To the promoters, it was important to include the words "Music and Art Fair" in the festival marketing. Artist Arnold Skolnik was hired to produce a logo. Skolnik presented the team with artwork that included the chosen words as well as a "dove" (which in fact was acknowledged by the artist to be a catbird) and guitar symbol.

Now it was time to select a site. Real estate agents began work on helping Woodstock Ventures find a place large enough to accommodate at least 50,000 people. Not much more could be planned until a site had been secured and when a 300-acre industrial park owned by a man named Howard Mills, Jr., in the town of Wallkill, New York was offered for $10,000, the decision was made. The site, zoned for industry, concerts, and cultural exhibitions, was not far off the New York State Thruway and electricity and water lines were already in place. But when Michael Lang heard about the pending deal he wasn't happy. He had pictured a back-to-the-land atmosphere, not an industrial park. His partners agreed to look for an alternative site, but in the meantime retained the lease in Wallkill.

When Woodstock Ventures approached the Wallkill town officials for their approval, they presented the festival as an event featuring folk singers and jazz bands. The promoters claimed that they expected no more than 50,000 people to attend. A well organized, casual weekend in the sun was portrayed.

The promoters in fact wanted to appeal to fans of rock music but also felt it important to present the festival as an exclusively youth-oriented congregation. While ads were placed in traditional publications like the *New York Times*, the fashionable underground press, represented by the new *Rolling Stone* magazine and the established *Village Voice*, were fed exclusive information to create a buzz. The slogan now was "Three Days of Peace and Music." The promoters felt that the use of the term "peace" would appeal to those who were becoming increasingly involved with the anti-war movement but would also set the tone for the festival, thus ensuring that those who attended would know in advance what type of behavior was expected from them.

The expense of putting on the event started to significantly rise when the artists were approached. Not many people knew who Kornfeld and Lang were and the event seemed a massive undertaking for such an untried entity. To prove their intent, Woodstock Ventures offered Jefferson Airplane $12,000, more than twice their usual performance fee. The Who would be among the highest paid and soon the talent budget rose to over $180,000.

In Wallkill, local residents were becoming a bit uncomfortable. Reports of the ads, with their emphasis on rock music and flower children, were discomforting to them. By this time drug use was rampant within the youth movement and the community didn't know what to expect if 50,000 "hippies" showed up. When people started to express their fears to Howard Mills, he spoke to the people at Woodstock Ventures. The festival organizers tried to reassure Mills that nothing bad would happen because they had hired Wes Pomeroy, a former Justice Department assistant, to head a security force. Reverend Donald Ganoung was hired to act as a liaison between the promoters and the townspeople. Stan Goldstein, a friend of Lang's who had been involved in the successful Miami Pop Festival, was also now on board.

The promoters set up shop in a barn on Mills' property, where they had radio and telephone hook-ups. Things were starting to move forward. Allan Markoff, the only local resident with any professional audio engineering experience, was hired to work with Bill Hanley on the festival sound. Kornfeld and Lang had been attempting to raise additional revenue by getting a major studio to commit to filming the event for later release as a feature film. They weren't having much luck. The film centered on the Monterey Pop Festival had not yet earned money for its distributors and there wasn't much interest from the Hollywood community in going down that road again. It would take someone involved in the independent film scene to bring the festival to theaters. Former neurology student Michael Wadleigh was just beginning to be recognized as an up-and-coming indie film producer through his documentaries about the recent activities of Martin Luther King, Jr., Bobby Kennedy, and George McGovern. Wadleigh thought that taking some footage of the festival may be interesting and he would consider it.

Town meetings were being held in Wallkill to address the issue of the festival and what may, or may not be, expected. Mills was now receiving anonymous death threats on the telephone. The message was plain and simple: the majority of the people of Wallkill did not want a rock festival in their backyard.

During promotion of the festival, it became essential that tickets for the event also include a pass for a camping space. With so many thousands expected, the area motels would in no way be able to handle those planning to participate in a three-day event. The organization of a campground was of paramount importance. The thought of young people showing up in Wallkill and just plunking down without direction was overwhelming. Stan Goldstein contacted a communal group called the Hog Farm of California to lend some guidance. Wavy Gravy, a beatnik comic whose real name is Hugh Romney, served as the ceremonial head of the group. The Hog Farm was composed of a group of young people who were "living off the land" and who often showed up en masse at music events. Goldstein thought that the Hog Farmers could demonstrate how it should be done to those who had never camped out before.

In early July, amid threats of hippies being shot on sight from some of the more radical of the town populace, the Wallkill Board of Supervisors passed an ordinance whereby a gathering of over 5,000 people was prohibited. On July 15th, the hammer fell on the festival when the Wallkill Zoning Board of Appeals decided that since the promoters were not well-enough organized, they would ban the festival from taking place in their town. The three-day gathering of peace and music would need to find a site elsewhere.

A man named Elliot Tiber heard about the problem and stepped forward. Tiber ran a resort hotel called the El Monaco in Bethel, New York, and he had a permit for a music festival already on hand. When Lang looked at the site—fifteen acres—he didn't feel it was large enough. Tiber suggested that his friend, a dairy farmer named Max Yasgur, may have some land available for the festival. Artie Kornfeld's cousin was friends with Yasgur's nephew and, simultaneously, also suggested that Yasgur be contacted. The word was that Yasgur needed some money to maintain his dairy enterprise.

Lang traveled to Bethel, about fifty miles from Woodstock in Sullivan County, and met Yasgur in an alfalfa field. Lang thought the site was perfect. He negotiated a deal with Yasgur, who figured up the costs of losing his present crop and re-seeding another with a pad and a pencil while the two men talked. (Yasgur was certainly not a "country bumpkin" unaccustomed to business dealings. He had attended New York University to study real estate law and had previously made the decision to continue his family's dairy enterprise, which he had moved from Maplewood to Bethel for expansion purposes. Yasgur's was, at this point, one of the largest milk producing enterprises in the county.) By the time the other members of Woodstock Ventures headed up to Bethel to check out the site that Lang had approved, Yasgur had reconsidered and upped his price to $75,000. The others involved agreed: even at that price, the lease was worth it. Because they didn't want a repeat of the Wallkill fiasco, the promoters decided to keep the new location to themselves until they could get things well in order and cause a minimum amount of panic among the locals. That plan, however, went down the drain when the promoters went to dinner at a nearby restaurant and were overheard talking about the deal. Before they had even left the restaurant, the festival was being discussed on the local radio.

Lang continued the Wallkill party line that the festival was probably only going to bring in 50,000 people, although he was hoping it would be much more (and later said to a film crew during the set-up of the festival facilities that his estimation was 200,000). He didn't want to scare the community, but the community was already on alert. Soon signs instructing residents to boycott Yasgur's product in order to convince him to stop his "hippie music festival" appeared all over town. Over 300 people attended a town meeting to voice their concerns. Behind their backs, one local resident offered to fix everything with the town folk if the promoters would quietly give him $10,000 in cash. (Whether this suggestion was agreed upon or not remains a controversial issue today.) Regardless, in July permits were approved by the building inspector. There was some dissent over the issuing of permits, but eventually the community was convinced that the revenue garnered from the festival would outweigh any problems and the town reluctantly backed off. It was time now for Woodstock Ventures to move on to the other elements of the festival.

The promoters returned to approaching and booking the talent. Of course local resident Bob Dylan was asked to perform but while Dylan was in negotiations to play at the festival his small son fell ill and he decided to drop out to be with his family. An invitation extended to Frank Zappa and his Mothers of Invention was declined. "The Mothers were asked to do Woodstock and Frank Zappa turned it down," says former Mother Jimmy Carl Black. "He said, 'It is only going to be a few hippies there and I am tired of playing for those dope heads.' That was a big mistake, in my opinion."

Since his appearance at Monterey Pop, Jimi Hendrix had become quite a draw. Hendrix had been making lots of money and if he was going to come onboard to headline this latest festival, he wanted $32,000. Lang agreed to Hendrix's demands and would tell the other acts that Hendrix was being paid for two sets. (Hendrix had only agreed to one set and also made the stipulation that no one would follow him, no doubt a knee-jerk response to the confrontation with the Who at Monterey.) John Lennon later told Artie Kornfeld that he had wanted to attend the festival but he was visiting in Canada and was denied a visa into the country. Lang and company decided that the opening bill for the first day of the festival would be mellow with folk artists performing. The weekend would be for rocking.

The people of Bethel were still not convinced that the festival would be any less than a takeover of their small settlement. Over 800 residents of the little town of less than 4,000 signed a petition to stop the festival once and for all. They were concerned with the roads becoming overburdened and frankly didn't know what to expect from the "longhairs." They were afraid that the hippie laissez-faire lifestyle would cause problems for which they were unprepared. Threats continued to be hurled at those residents who supported the festival. A lawsuit was filed when people became concerned that there wouldn't be enough portable toilets. The promoters promised to order more. Supporters argued that it was too late to stop the festival and suggested that those who were in opposition just accept the inevitable. In the end, the majority of the people of Bethel seemed resigned to the festival. Their thoughts now turned to how such a gathering might benefit their community. Life in the Catskills was not exactly prospering at this time. With people coming in for the festival who would need food, drink, and parking, maybe there were benefits to accepting the unavoidable.

Yasgur's pasture was mowed and prepared to act as an amphitheater. The stage was under construction when the promoters had an idea. Maybe the people of the town would be pacified if the goodwill of Woodstock Ventures was demonstrated upfront. They decided to send the Earthlight Theater and the band Quill to entertain them. Not a smart move. After the hometown crowd gathered to listen to Quill, the performance group stripped naked and presented their "theater"—a play called "Sex. Y'all come." It's a wonder the townspeople didn't go berserk and somehow manage to put a stop to the festival immediately. Everything they had been told was contrary to their suspicions, and now their fears seemed all too real. Inexplicitly, most shook their heads and wandered home with an apparent attitude of "Whatcha gonna do?"

Two days before the festival Artie Kornfeld had convinced Warner Bros. that for $100,000 to pay for film, they may record some terrific footage. Even if the festival was a bust there would at least be some good music. If it turned into what the townspeople feared, then there may be insurgence and that would also be interesting to have on film. Kornfeld signed a hand-written contract with the studio's Ted Ashley. Michael Wadleigh had some good ideas but not any real financing to sign a crew. He gathered about 100 people from New York who agreed to work on the basis that they would be paid double their fee if the film was a success. If it wasn't, they would at least have the experience and could enjoy listening to some "name" music while working. Wadleigh would eventually arrive on the site of the festival with over one thousand reels of film. (Martin Scorsese would serve on the crew as an editor and assistant director.)

By the time the dissenting group of townspeople came up with their last ditch idea of protesting the event by forming a human blockade across the road, it was too late. The small highways leading into Bethel were already jammed full of people with tickets to the festival. On the day before the festival, traffic on State Route 17B was bumper to bumper for over ten miles. Even festival organizer Artie Kornfeld had to abandon his limo and hitchhike with his wife into the festival.

Other than the growing traffic jam, things looked in control. The Hog Farmers had arrived by bus and built small kitchens and shelters around the site. People who looked like they may be dependable were recruited to serve as security and given an armband designating them as such. Stands were erected to house booths of arts, crafts, and the food concession "Food for Love." The Free Kitchen was set-up outside for those who didn't have food vouchers, which came with paid tickets. The Hog Farm and the Merry Pranksters had even put up their own stage that they had designated as a "free stage," and opened the floor to anyone who wanted to play music or jam.

By Friday the area was packed. Overnight, young people had arrived to camp out on people's yards and in their fields. Traffic was impossible to navigate. Because of the traffic jam the day before, the ticket booths had not been put into place. (Tickets were being sold in New York record stores and by mail order.) The inability to get the booths erected to meet the demand of those already arriving was not a good sign for the men financing the festival. When the ticket takers arrived in their orange jackets requesting that everyone who had entered the festival grounds for free go back and re-enter for a fee, it was decided that move was unreasonable. There was nothing left to do but take down the fence and allow people inside without charge. The promoters obviously weren't thrilled with this turn of events, but what could they do? Letting the kids in for free sure beat a full-scale riot.

The Youth International Party set up a site a short distance from the stage and christened it "Movement City." The leader of the group—activist Abbie Hoffman— had already threatened the promoters that unless they made a contribution to the group, the organization would do what they could to disrupt the festival. (They had already distributed fliers advising people not to pay admission.)

Before noon, buses containing over 100 of New York's finest pulled up at the site. Off-duty officers of the NYPD had volunteered to work at the festival for fifty dollars a day, but when they arrived a representative of New York's Police Department was waiting to tell them that if they participated they would be subject to censure by the department. Most got back in the bus and returned to the city. A few of them stayed to work under assumed names—as long as they were paid *ninety* dollars a day.

Meanwhile, things were not going well on the highway. The road jam was now miles longer. The brass of the New York State troopers had refused to work with the festival planners and it was said that they had secretly hoped the traffic problems would spell disaster for the event. They should have thought that through. Individual troopers tried to do what they could, but once the traffic jam started, little could be done to relieve it, especially after cars were left abandoned in the road as people tried to get out of the traffic and into the festival. Retrieving their vehicles would be a problem for another day.

People were now swarming in and the numbers grew *far beyond* 200,000. The promoters feared that they would run out of food if most of the people stayed for the three days of the event, but why wouldn't they if they had already invested this much time and effort? Roberts and Rosenman felt that maybe the site should be declared a state of emergency, but they reconsidered that position as such a move would give free reign to Governor Nelson Rockefeller to request that the National Guard come in and disperse the people already there. Such an action would not be welcome, but it didn't really matter: a statement was issued from Rockefeller's office that because the festival was not an act of God, no state of disaster existed. In the view of many in power, this observation reflected what they felt: the hippies, flower children, or whatever they were calling themselves, were not important. Regardless of any formal declaration of need, those coming in were already experiencing a lack of food. The promoters put out the word that they needed hundreds of thousands of sandwiches and the members of the Monticello Jewish Community Center commenced to making as many as they could. Food and supplies were now being flown in from nearby military installations as they became available. There was already all this hoopla, and other than the guitars being strummed from a handful of the amassed party-goers, not a premeditated music note had been sounded.

Security had been given the directive that if someone needed assistance they should help them but otherwise leave people to mind their own business. Drugs would not be a problem as far as law enforcement was concerned, since it was likely that there would be so much usage that there would be no way in hell it could be controlled. Besides, to some of the promoters' thinking, this was an event by and for the people. They shouldn't have to worry about such things as being busted for smoking a little weed or dropping a few tabs of acid. Promoter Bill Graham was at the event and he, on the other hand, stated that those in charge needed to have at least "some control."

The music had been scheduled to begin at four o'clock. Most of the performers, however, had not been able to get into the festival from their motels outside the area. Production assistants were scurrying to contract helicopters to fly the musicians onto the festival grounds.

The band Stillwater was to open the show. "I, personally, was under a mountain of pressure because I *needed* to get back to Riverside, California the following morning to attend the first day of my two-week USAF Reserves summer training (yes, I was still in the Air Force Reserves, believe it or not)," remembers Sweetwater's Alex Del Zoppo. "I had agreed to play Woodstock *only* if we could play *first*, on the *first* day, allowing me to leave immediately afterward, a decision that never quite panned out, and ultimately cost us a spot in the movie. When we were awakened at the Holiday

Inn in Liberty, New York (the default lodging for the acts, about fifteen miles from the festival site) that Friday morning, we were already surrounded by the ultimate traffic jam. We soon became aware that all the narrow roads leading to the site were literally becoming parking lots, as people anxious to get to Yasgur's farm were increasingly just abandoning their vehicles and walking. Already, the entire 100 miles of the New York throughway between NYC and Liberty was bumper-to-bumper. Things were congesting fast, and getting worse by the minute."

The crowd was more than ready to hear some music and Lang had to think fast. Sweetwater had been scheduled to open the show but they couldn't get to the stage. Since Richie Havens was backstage, and he required the shortest and least complicated set-up, Havens was asked to open the show. On August 15, 1969 at just after five o'clock, Havens strummed his guitar and the music of the Woodstock Festival began. As Havens played . . . and played . . . and played (over two and one-half hours and several encores), starting with "High Flyin' Bird," and ending with an improvised song he called "Freedom," the other acts were still unable to get backstage.

Swami Satchidananda came onstage to talk to those gathered about the spirit of love as late-arriving performers were still being led backstage. The order of opening artists had long been abandoned. Chick Monck, serving as the Master of Ceremonies, grabbed Country Joe McDonald. McDonald wasn't ready to perform but managed at least a short set of five songs that engaged the crowd. McDonald ended his time on stage with the infamous "Fish cheer" ("Gimme an F . . . ") and a rousing audience-participation of his "Fixin' to Die Rag." John Sebastian, who was formally of the Lovin' Spoonful and launching a solo career, didn't feel he was ready with his solo music and had made the decision to not play at the festival, but when Monck asked him to play he bravely took the stage (in his own words) "too whacked [on drugs] to say no." Amazingly, as high as Sebastian was, he managed to wind his way through five songs including "Darlin' Be Home Soon," "Younger Generation," and, in the end, did a pretty good job entertaining the crowd. While drugs were front and center at the festival, contrary to appearances, not everyone was participating in that scene. Some people found the drugs self-indulgent and chose to experience the music in its most purist form.

Something had to be done to get the acts to the stage. It was after all a *music* festival. Finally, a U.S. Army helicopter arrived with some artists. (One may wonder if when they discovered the underlying tone of the event—a gathering of peace with a majority who protested the war—the Army brass didn't regret their decision to help.

Richie Havens would later point out that those participating were anti-war, not anti-soldier. The Army would also later help by flying in a medical team.)

"We got a little more than halfway there, when all the lanes ahead were filled with parked, locked, cars," continues Del Zoppo. "Our festival guide had a walkie-talkie and promptly called for a helicopter. As we flew over the last hill, as far as the eye could see in any direction, there was a blanket of colors covering all the ground below. I remember asking the helicopter pilot what kind of crops we were looking at, thinking they were wild fields of colorful flowers or something. He snarled, 'Them's all *people*, man!' With our mouths agape, we realized that he was right. One of us said, 'Damn, they *are* people . . . and lots of 'em.' We knew that was the biggest event *ever* and we were about to try and entertain them all!"

It was finally time to have the artists who had been intended to open the show take the stage. The psychedelic fusion band Sweetwater was prepared for their set and they came on next. The band had been touring with the Doors and was just emerging as one of the more melodious rock bands. Their songs ran from the time relevant "What's Wrong" to their signature song "Motherless Child."

"Arriving late, they told us that Richie Havens had been thrown on in our place," remembers Del Zoppo. "As soon as we landed, we were whisked toward the stage. When we began to play, we heard our voices bouncing back at us a few seconds later from the gentle hill hundreds of yards in front of us. We soon realized that we had *no* monitors. Who needed drugs with this set-up? Despite Albert [Moore, the band's flute player] going nearly berserk throughout (brown acid?), and with us being separated a good distance from the audience making it difficult to play off of them, it took a lot of work to get that vast audience to focus completely on what we were doing. We eventually got our musical bearings and threw in a medley of song snippets from some new pop tunes (something we occasionally did, simply to 'blow the audience's minds'), eventually getting our standing ovation by the end of the set."

"Since we were the first electric band on, and they were still getting their sound system together, with no monitor speakers, the earlier numbers of our set were a bit spacey," remembers Sweetwater's Fred Herrera. "That also meant that our stuff didn't get recorded as well as the acts that followed us. In effect, we were the 'sound check' for the rest of the bands at that festival. Rushed in, and not having things together made that a fairly piss-poor set compared to our usually strong ones. Yes, we eventually reached a workable medium with the sound, but more than half the set was over by then, and some of us were in a bad mood because of it. The biggest gig ever, and we had the worst playing conditions—not an optimal situation."

Sweetwater was followed by the Incredible String Band with songs that included "When You Find Out Who You Are." Next Bert Sommer entertained with songs "Jennifer" and "Smile." Sommer's rendition of Paul Simon's "America" showcased lyrics that perfectly fit the tone of the festival.

Michael Wadleigh had contributed $50,000 of his own money, as well as his independent film company funds to pay Kodak for film, and by this time he was running around attempting to get the music and the atmosphere of the festival on film. (Wadleigh had just come from filming a documentary of mountain climbing in Wyoming.) It was his decision, along with the promoters, to at the very least capture the anti-war songs of each act because filming the entire performance of each band or solo artist would take a lot of film, which was in limited supply. Wadleigh would need to go with the flow and see what his cameras were able to capture.

The weather had always been a concern of the promoters. It was summer and with summer came sudden showers and storms. Many of those at the festival had come equipped with tarps, umbrellas, or ponchos should the weather be problematic. Normally, those items would have been all that was needed and for many it was. What was at issue was the fact that the sheer number of people in attendance may cause additional problems if the skies should open up . . . and open up they did.

As Tim Hardin performed a set that included "If I Were a Carpenter" and "Misty Roses" it started to rain. Ravi Shankar wasn't deterred and played his five-song ragas throughout the intermittent showers. Melanie came on to sing two songs, including "Beautiful People," a song that the assembled crowd took to mean as them. Arlo Guthrie engaged the crowd with marijuana references in his song "Coming into Los Angeles" and ended his set with "Amazing Grace." Joan Baez took the stage for a long set including "I Shall Be Released" and two Gram Parsons songs: "Drug Store Truck Driving Man" and the haunting "Hickory Wind." Baez ended the music portion of the day with "We Shall Overcome."

The crowd, however peaceful, demanded that the music continue despite anything nature might throw their way. It had been planned that the music would begin at seven in the evening on Saturday but with all that was going on that strategy had to be abandoned and rethought. The promoters decided that, if at all possible, there should now be no interruption in music and, if they could get all the acts to cooperate, the bands would go on later and play through the night.

During the soggy day, people had been cleaning up their personal spaces as best they could. Most were unaware that during the early morning a tragedy had occurred. Seventeen-year-old Ray Mizak had been asleep encased in his sleeping bag when the driver of a tractor towing a tank to empty the portable toilets failed to see the young man and ran over him. Mizak was dead before he could be airlifted to a hospital. He probably never even woke up.

The festival grounds were beginning to look—and smell—like a medieval encampment but the spirits of those who had come to celebrate music and themselves were high. During the rain the previous night the crowd had been encouraged to help each other out and most seemed to rise to the challenge. The Hog Farmers had secured grain, vegetables, and soy sauce, and were now cooking natural food for thousands. The medical tents were treating people with feet cut by stepping on refuse, and a few cases of exposure. There were also more than a few dozen bad acid trips that the forty-five doctors in attendance (most working without pay), needed to treat. The mood remained, for the most part, mellow. Yoga was being taught from the stage and in small groups throughout the grounds. Even though there was still no declaration of disaster, a National Guard helicopter began dropping in food and dry clothes. Everyone was trying to make the best of things, passing around marijuana, sharing wine, enjoying each other's company, and waiting for the next music act to hit the stage.

But there was still a problem with the music. Because of the change in plan for the Saturday night show, the managers of some of the acts now felt they had carte blanche to refuse that their bands take the stage unless they were paid in advance. John Roberts asked the manager of the Sullivan County National Bank to help him accomplish this. Roberts assured the banker that he could pay him back from his New York City bank account and offered a personal check (the reported amount varies from either $50,000 or $100,000). The bank manager finally agreed and made his way to the bank to collect the cash. He needn't have worried about having enough cash to fill Roberts' request. Overnight, the people of the town had deposited bags of revenue collected from those who had bought food or services before supplies started to run low. Even so, although the townspeople may have made some money indirectly from the festival, most of the people lost money due to their big hearts. Many of the people of Bethel had supplies and simply gave whatever food they had on hand to the young people who had none. Some set up a soup kitchen in one of the abandoned buildings in town. Of course not everyone was so accommodating. There were a lot of curses thrown at the kids and some of the people made a buck off the needy youth in whatever way they could without regard to any humanitarian efforts. But there were now thousands eating food provided by a "sharing of the loaves" made possible by the Hog Farm. It had been their intent that everyone share what they had and thus encourage a community of one. The idea was actually working.

The band Quill kicked off the music at 12:15 on Saturday with a forty-minute set consisting of only three songs and ending with a jam. The Keef Hartley Band, which featured a mix of jazz, blues, and rock, followed with everything from "Spanish Fly" to "Half-breed." Santana had the crowd boogying with "Waiting," "Jingo," and "Fried Neckbones," among other songs.

Canned Heat continued Santana's vibe, beginning their set with "A Change is Gonna Come," their hit "Going Up the Country," and ending their set with a song they called "The Woodstock Boogie." Earlier in the day, as they tried to make their way to the festival site, Canned Heat had been pushed aside by a news crew when they attempted to board a helicopter. Lead singer Bob "The Bear" Hite asked what the team thought they were doing and they replied that they were going to report the news. Bear put it in perspective when he responded "Fuck you. We're going to *make* the news." Drummer Fito De La Para felt that the crowd was with the band all the way. Certainly one man was when he jumped on stage and gave Bear a big hug. After security removed the man, who was handled compassionately by Bear, Bear turned to Fito and noted that if the band wanted to, they could start a revolution "right now."

Mountain performed an hour-long set including songs such as "Stormy Monday," "Dreams of Milk and Honey," and a song that they would later title "For Yasgur's Farm." Janis Joplin was a big hit with songs like "Summertime," "To Love Somebody," and "Kosmic Blues," and was called back for two encores. Joplin sang "Piece of My Heart" and then "Ball and Chain." Sly and the Family Stone went on at 1:30 in the morning and had everybody on their feet with "Dance to the Music," "I Want to Take You Higher," and "Stand!"

The Grateful Dead came on next, although maybe they should have passed on the opportunity. The band tried to entertain with songs like "Mama Tried" and "Turn on Your Love Light," but their equipment was so heavy that it finally broke one of the rotating pallets and had to be set up all over again. Jerry Garcia admitted to being "plumb atrocious" that day. He was zonked on Czechoslovakian acid and remembered that while the rain poured down on him he feared being electrocuted. There were also unfounded shouts that the stage was collapsing. The members of the Grateful Dead were the first to admit that it wasn't the band's greatest performance.

Creedence Clearwater Revival followed the Dead. Creedence had been one of the first bands to sign on to perform at the festival. John Fogarty was apprehensive by the time Creedence took the stage: it was after 2 a.m. and he felt that the Dead had put everyone to sleep. When Fogarty attempted to get some audience feedback, he was rewarded with a lone man lighting his Bic lighter and yelling that the crowd was with him, man. Fogerty said he played the rest of the set for that one guy. The band tried to get things back on track with many of the songs they would become legendary for performing, beginning with "Born on the Bayou" in a set that included "Green River," "Bad Moon Rising," "Proud Mary," and ended with "Suzy Q." Bass player Stu Cook would later say that while the band played some classic Creedence, many people still don't realize they were at the festival. (Creedence was ultimately unhappy with the set and decided they didn't want to have it included in the *Woodstock* movie.)

At sometime after 3 a.m. the Who took the stage. It was rumored that the Who almost didn't perform their set as there was some sort of argument over their pay for the event. Although the band would later note that while Pete Townshend felt completely in sync with the altruistic goals of the festival, Roger Daltry just gave those ideals lip service, John Entwhistle apparently ignored any such beliefs, and Keith Moon outright hated all the lofty premises of the "hippies." The Who's set opened with "Heaven and Hell" and "I Can't Explain," and segued into "It's a Boy," which introduced their new rock opera *Tommy*. After the *Tommy* songs the band performed "Shakin' All Over," "My Generation," and "Naked Eye." The set included twenty-five songs in total.

But an event occurred in the middle of the Who's set that remains controversial even today. After the band had completed "Pinball Wizard" and Pete Townshend stood tuning his guitar for the next number, political activist Abbie Hoffman took the microphone and began railing about the injustices done to "political prisoner" John Sinclair. "I think this is a pile of shit. . . ." Hoffman began to rant. Townshend turned around abruptly and soon Hoffman was tumbling off the stage. Hoffman later claimed that Townshend accidentally bumped into him, but most people who saw what had happened said that Townshend deliberately hit the unwelcome Yuppie leader with his guitar and screamed at him "Get off my fucking stage!"

Peter Townshend later said that it was the most political thing that he had ever done. One way or another, Hoffman was off the stage and the Who continued their set. The sun rose as singer Roger Daltry sang the closing song chorus "See me, feel me . . . ." The words were somehow appropriate. At the end of the set, Townshend pounded his guitar into the stage and then threw it into the audience in another dramatic ending for the theatrical band. Roger Daltry would later remember the performance as not being on a par with their usual high standards and as one of the worst the band ever played.

Jefferson Airplane ended the music with a set that kicked off at 8 a.m. The San Francisco band opened with "Volunteers," included "Somebody to Love," "Plastic Fantastic Lover," "Uncle Sam's Blues," and ended with "White Rabbit."

"A lot had happened in our career between Monterey and Woodstock," says Jack Casady. "We were making more music, more albums. We were on tour so it was just another show for us. We had many shows at that time. We got in a day earlier and checked into the hotel. We watched all the traffic problems and all of that on TV so we knew what it was like. We had to travel in through a cow pasture—helicopter in. We had been scheduled to go on the night before and we didn't go on until [early] in the morning. The time was running behind. It was an exposed stage and because of the rain and mud, people had to be aware of electrical elements. For me it was terrific. It was like you were inside a rushing steam locomotive at the time. Looking back, it was the sum of its parts and we were one of the parts."

By Sunday afternoon, everyone was pretty well settled into the festival, rain or shine, or rain. It's interesting to note that over time, although the size of the festival has been its most noteworthy element, not everyone agreed on the number of people attending the event. Even so, there can be no doubt that it *was* the biggest event of its kind, regardless of accurate numbers. Reports of "half a million" were heard from the stage, but the New York State troopers estimated 450,000. Others said that if you looked at aerial photos, you could clearly see there were no more than 150,000. While that may have been the number of people in front of the stage, that wasn't counting all the people spread throughout the campgrounds, fields and forests, and on the roads. Some even thought the numbers were higher than half a million, including Bethel historian Bert Feldman who estimated it was closer to 700,000. The important thing, at least to Mike Lang, was that everyone was "pulling together."

By Sunday afternoon, three babies had been delivered in nearby Monticello Hospital, and two young men were dead from drug overdoses. As John Sebastian noted from the stage after a report of one of the babies being born on the festival grounds, the Woodstock festival was a "true city."

Sunday would feature another stellar bill: Joe Cocker, Country Joe & the Fish, Ten Years After, The Band, Johnny Winter, Crosby, Stills, Nash & Young, and Jimi

Hendrix. Considering the trials and tribulations of actually making it to the stage, each act shined.

"I recall the [*Woodstock*] movie probably more than the gig," says Ten Years After bass player Leo Lyons. "It sounds strange, but my biggest recollection at the time was how long we'd traveled to get there with no food and no sleep. We arrived from St. Louis, Missouri on the day of the gig. The hotels were full and there was nowhere to rest but in the back of a U-Haul truck. I remember the rain and the mud. The onstage bit was great fun, as was the crowd, but the rest I think I could have passed on."

Joe Cocker kicked off Sunday's music at 2 p.m. with "Delta Lady," but after his set, which ended with the event-fitting "With A Little Help from My Friends," another sudden storm caused the music to be put on hold for several hours. Scores of people felt that maybe now was a good time to start making their way home. Most, however, hunkered down, ready to wait out the storm and be ready for the music to resume. It was suggested that the crowd was big enough that if they put their minds together and think hard to stop the rain that they could do it. A chant of "No More Rain" went up but, alas, to little result. Many people decided to indulge themselves in nature and stripped down, and slid and played in the mud amid the sounds of make-shift music in the crowd. To one young man, however, the rain was evil: he suggested that the helicopters and planes flying overhead had "seeded" the clouds and caused the rain to doom the gathering.

Country Joe, this time with "the Fish" and their band, resumed the show at 6 p.m. McDonald reprised his "Fish Cheer," "Fixin' to Die Rag," and the band performed several other songs.

Ten Years After followed, opening with "Good Morning Little Schoolgirl" and closing with "I'm Going Home." "[I remember] the downpour and seeing the steam rising from the audience," remembers Leo Lyons. "We felt a great connection with the people there. I liked that. The playing was, as always, enjoyable."

The Band came on to provide a strong, eleven-song set that included "I Shall Be Released," "This Wheels on Fire," "Don't Do It," and "The Weight." Blood, Sweat & Tears began their set with "More and More" near midnight, included their hit "Spinning Wheel," and ended with "Something's Coming On."

Johnny Winter was scheduled to perform that night. "We flew in by helicopter and got there Sunday morning. We hung out backstage in the food area and just listened to bands until it was our turn," remembers Winter. "Jimi [Hendrix] was there and many others, just hanging around. All our equipment was there and we played a great set."

Appearing with his brother Edgar for "I Can't Stand It" and "Tobacco Road," Johnny ripped through a hot set including "Mean Mistreater" and "Leland Mississippi Blues." But there was one moment during the festival that stands out in Winter's mind. "[It was] playing Sunday night and the rain stopping right around the time we started, around twelve-thirty at night I think. The crowd was huge."

Crosby, Stills, Nash & Young began an acoustic set at 3 a.m. with "Suite: Judy Blue Eyes" and included their now-signature songs "Helplessly Hoping," "Guinevere," and the Buffalo Springfield classic "Mr. Soul." The quartet then segued into an electric set including "Long Time Gone," "Bluebird," and "Wooden Ships." David Crosby would later say that the group was "scared shitless" as this was only their second appearance as a music entity. Another reason they might have been nervous was that the helicopter carrying Graham Nash and drummer Dallas Taylor to the event had nearly crashed.

The Paul Butterfield Blues Band was next with songs such as "Everything's Gonna Be Alright" and "Born Under a Bad Sign." Sha Na Na brought good old-fashioned rock 'n' roll with songs "Teen Angel," "Wipe Out," "Duke of Earl," and "At the Hop." Although he remembers "wanting to be alone in a crowd of 500,000," drummer Jocko Marcellino feels his group's appearance at the festival was important. "I was the youngest performer at Woodstock at eighteen," says Marcellino. "It was our eighth gig. We stayed all weekend and finally got on second to last before Jimi Hendrix. But luckily we made the film, which gave us a world-wide stage and kicked off our career. We got paid three hundred and fifty dollars, but the check bounced."

Jimi Hendrix was to close the show with a set that was scheduled for midnight. Due to the long delay caused by the storm and the enthusiasm of the bands performing, Hendrix did not take the stage until nine a.m. Monday morning. By that time most of the people were finding their way back to their real life and Hendrix only played to a crowd of about 80,000. His set lasted two hours, which was the longest of his career to date, and included "Foxy Lady," "Fire," "Voodoo Child," "the Star Spangled Banner," "Purple Haze," and ended with "Hey Joe."

Despite the outrageously good quality of the bands who played (even if some of them weren't up to par during this particular performance), there were still others who wanted to perform but for some reason were unable to make it to Woodstock. The Jeff Beck Group was scheduled to play, but the band broke up the week before the festival. Joni Mitchell's manager encouraged her to forego the festival to appear on the "Dick Cavett Show," where she would be seen by more people. Iron Butterfly was stuck at the airport and when they demanded that a helicopter be flown in to fly them directly to the site, the promoters said no, an appearance by the band wasn't a priority as they had other things on their mind. Lighthouse changed their minds thinking that it wasn't the kind of atmosphere they preferred. Guitarist Ethan Brown had been scheduled to sit in for a few numbers but he had been arrested on drug charges three days earlier. John Lennon was asked by Artie Kornfeld to encourage the Beatles to play. Lennon didn't think he could do that if he even wanted to, but offered his Plastic Ono Band. Somebody "passed" on Lennon's offer. Led Zeppelin almost committed but then was offered a gig at higher pay so decided to play elsewhere. The Doors were asked but Jim Morrison didn't like outdoor venues. Jethro Tull thought it would be a waste of their time. Bob Dylan entertained the idea of appearing, but eventually declined saying he couldn't do it because his son was ill. The Mothers of Invention and the Moody Blues also dismissed the idea of performing at Woodstock. One can only imagine what it would have been like to pick and choose the performers if all who were asked to play were available.

When Hendrix ended his set, most people were trudging their way home through the quagmire and the mess. By this time, the festival grounds were not a pretty site. The promoters would pay over $100,000 to clean up the accumulated garbage and waste. A huge hole was dug and everything left on the ground was bulldozed in and set on fire.

The party that had taken about nine months to prepare was over. No one could have predicted all that would take place in those three days. A report by the New York State Health Department would later state eight miscarriages had been reported and over 750 people were treated for problems pertaining to drugs. As Max Yasgur noted earlier from the stage "a half-a-million young people" proved they could "get together and have fun and music and have nothing but fun and music."

For most of those who performed at Woodstock, the festival was a memorable experience in their lives. Johnny Winter considers his experience there "very positive." Winter recalls that "even though it kind of ran itself after awhile, the people were very calm and friendly. [The festival] gets music to the fans on a grander scale, and sometimes they make a mark, like Woodstock."

"It was mid-summer, and even though it was way up in the boonies, there are an awful lot of people living on the East Coast," reflects Stillwater's Alex Del Zoppo. "Never having had their own fest, I believe they spontaneously felt it was their duty to attend one only 100 miles from NYC. And, of course, everyone was looking for something to do to get their minds off of the Vietnam War. [Woodstock] was the first really enormous festival and it created such a buzz (even the major press covered different stories about it for weeks afterward) that the 'corporate establishment' soon took serious notice (possibly for the first time) of what people that age had to say. We believe it changed everything. To this day, Woodstock is the benchmark all other events are measured against. We even heard a newscaster comparing the worldwide Live Earth events to Woodstock—nearly forty years later. The best part of it all was the fact that it was never planned to be such a monster fest, witnessed by the cheesy fences they put up, and tickets for Friday, Saturday, and Sunday sold separately, as if they could herd out the people who didn't pay for Saturday. The whole thing was a complete fluke—it just 'happened.' Originally billed as 'a few days of 'peace' in the mountains,' they had no major corporate sponsorship, a last-minute venue change, and minimal advertising (considering the amount of folks that attended), and extremely nasty weather. Yet with a half of million people there, there were no fights or major problems. Everyone behaved themselves . . . because they felt they were part of something much bigger than themselves. Indeed, many of the attendees (and us included) felt reborn, having gone through that once-in-a-lifetime experience. Even with the Air Force thing hanging over me, I was buoyed mightily by that event."

Leo Lyons of Ten Years After remembers Woodstock as a defining moment for rock music in a way that may have not been expected. "The festival was positive in the way that it showed the world there was a generation of people who genuinely wanted to change things for the better," he says. Lyons sees the subsequent *Woodstock* film as having had a huge impact on the music industry. "The movie changed the music business forever. After *Woodstock*, the marketing and media people moved in for the big bucks and that's what the business is today. The film certainly escalated Ten Years After's profile and Alvin Lee's in particular. I think today there's too much media hype, but who knows? Things go round in circles. I see lots of new bands out there playing real music."

"Woodstock turned out to be almost an anti-war rally, even though it wasn't billed, or planned, as such, but every young person attending just *knew* that war we were in was completely bogus," says Stillwater's Fred Herrera. "Notable too is the fact that there were another two hundred thousand people trying to get there from Canada, most stuck at the border. After that, the 'powers that be' at that time started to take youth more seriously, probably noting their potential 'clout,' economic and otherwise."

"We were arriving at the end of a decade that gave us the Civil Rights Movement, the assassinations of Jack Kennedy, Bobby Kennedy, and Dr. King, the Summer of Love, the sixty-eight Chicago Convention," says Sha Na Na's Jocko Marcellino. "There was a social explosion: the women's movement, civil unrest, the anti-war movement against the war in Vietnam. From the campuses of Berkeley, Columbia, Kent State, the Sorbonne, and everywhere in between. It was a daring and volatile time. Woodstock became the decade's last great fling. It would prove to be not only a turning point for Sha Na Na, but it would be ear-marked as the greatest pop concert in history and a landmark for the sixties counterculture."

"At least for our generation, it was a time of proving your self-worth," says Jefferson Airplane's Jack Casady. "It was an eclectic gathering that tried to offer some hope for the future of mankind. It maybe wasn't going to change the world, but it was going to change *our* world. You didn't know if it was going to happen again or if it would be a one time thing. It was a positive aspect of a time when there were a lot of negative aspects. People embraced the music as one of the ways to share the human condition. You were awed by the enormity of it."

Country Joe & the Fish's Barry Melton places another perspective on the festival. "It's odd that Woodstock has left such a giant footprint on our cultural memory, save that in many ways it marks the end of an era," Melton muses. "By the time of the Woodstock festival, much of the hope and optimism that gave birth to the counter-culture had faded. We'd been through the riots in Chicago, the assassinations of Dr. King and Bobby Kennedy, and the Tet Offensive. The violence of the era was even carried to the stage, as will be forever memorialized by the confrontation between Pete Townshend and Abbie Hoffman. The festival itself was a logistical nightmare. And more than any other single factor, it was the Woodstock festival that drove large-scale rock concerts into stadiums where the dynamics of assigned seating, and the logistical advantage in managing large crowds, ensured there would never again be such large unstructured festival[s]."

The elements of the music festival had indeed changed since Monterey Pop. Whereas that festival had been mostly about the music and enjoying the company of others, Woodstock would encompass so much more. Whether or not the Woodstock festival was a positive thing is subjective at best. "The elements of the festival had changed due to the nature of the beast," says Jack Casady. "People now wanted to promote their own agendas. There were now political elements, of course, and that affected the festival and took it to where the festival became harder to manage. You had places where people wanted to get in for free, like [later] at the Isle of Wight. There became other elements in play."

Social evolution and changes in music presentation aside, it was now time for Woodstock Ventures to pay the piper. Artie Kornfeld had called the event a "financial disaster" and that it was. Although Kornfeld felt that the festival had little to do with "money or tangible things" and was, in fact about "life lessons," there were financial people involved who needed to settle their bills. Woodstock Ventures owed $1.3 million alone on John Roberts' letters of credit. Marketing costs were more than double their projections and production costs ran around $2 million. While the figures being bandied about showed over one million dollars in ticket sales, the total cost of the festival was well over two-and-one-half million dollars. Checks were bouncing and people stood with their hands out looking for their money. By Thursday, Roberts and his family made a deal with the Sullivan County Bank to pay off the debt owed there. It was later determined that the promoters would also have to refund money taken for tickets that couldn't be used because the people who bought them couldn't get into, or even near, the festival. Several weeks later, Kornfeld and Lang were bought out of Woodstock Ventures for approximately $32,000 by Roberts and Rosenman. Through subsequent record sales and movie profits, the Woodstock festival would become profitable for only some of those involved.

Drugs had obviously been a major element of the festival and their consequences continued to be a concern to the people of Bethel. During the festival the Hog Farmers had comforted those experiencing bad trips and problems that arose from various other pharmaceuticals, but drug busts had been made. By late August, Bethel Town Justice Stanley Liese was hearing over 175 legal cases, involving mostly drug possession and drug dealing.

The film based on the event, simply titled *Woodstock*, would go on to enjoy great success. Released in 1970, it would win the Academy Award for Best Documentary Feature. The Woodstock festival not only made a mark on American culture but also became known throughout the world. A few years after the festival, Max Yasgur had the opportunity to meet Israel Prime Minister David Ben-Gurion. When he introduced himself and where he was from, Ben-Gurion remembered that Bethel was the site of "Woodstock."

The legacy of Woodstock continues to affect the lives of those who were there. "Before we had a name, our band had gone together to see, not play, the first decent-sized festival, Monterey Pop," says Fred Herrera. "That excursion changed our lives. We decided that *that* was what we should be striving for. A little over a year later, we were on our way to becoming a must-have festival act. Having successfully played all of those pop fests in what Alex likes to call the 'Golden Age of Pop Fests,' was an experience that can never be duplicated again—mainly because *then*, things were actually run by people who had a sense of community, and they were trying to help it all come together, even though they sometimes had little experience or financial structure and did everything by the seat of their pants. My God, Woodstock tickets were only $7 bucks for a day, $21 for the whole weekend. And on top of that, the vast majority of people attending saw it all for *free*, because the fences came down the first day before any acts played! *Now*, every big music event is completely well-planned out and totally organized, aimed at making massive fortunes. Bottles of water now cost more than Woodstock tickets did! Every event is now sponsored by beer or cigarette companies, or something akin to that. Flash forward to today, and when people hear the name Sweetwater, they almost immediately mention Woodstock. There's not a year when, as August 15 comes around, we are not inundated by news people asking what it was like then and fans commemorating the event, saluting us."

"Our lives changed personally after having gone through all of those huge communal events and especially Woodstock," says Alex Del Zoppo. "It really felt that everyone attending was in one big family of man, and indeed, everyone made an effort to live up to that ethic. It was a truly wonderful time to be alive, and even with the possibility of the Air Force individually 'activating' me, and most likely sending me to Nam, I still felt at complete peace at these events. It was simply amazing while it lasted. Professionally, it changed our lives as well. Even today, a mere mention of the fact that we played the great grand-daddy of all fests, always immediately grants us the esteem we had back then."

Del Zoppo also sees the changes festivals such as Woodstock brought to a band's performance presentation. "Acts started to think bigger, began to take how they looked and moved more seriously," he reflects. "After all, when acts are playing to the 'cheap seats' at a giant festival they've got to really work that crowd to get the attention of *all* of 'em! Acts began to gear themselves for just such events. We, in fact, wrote "Join the Band" because of those open, outdoor fests that always had people coming on stage with us, and "Just For You," keeping in mind how it would play live at other big events like that."

"These fests were significant to the music *business*, that's for sure," adds Fred Herrera. "Observe advertising from the early sixties and you'll notice that it was all geared toward middle-aged people, the ones with money at that time. However, after seeing such large crowds attend these events, and especially Woodstock, suddenly record companies, radio stations, promoters, and other previously estranged businesses suddenly looked at young people as an important *market* for their products, and only *then* began to increasingly aim their advertising toward youth. Today, virtually everything advertised is aimed at young people."

The Woodstock festival was not only reflective of the developing youth society but a factor in the development of American society in general. "The sense of community that we all felt at those events cannot be denied," says Del Zoppo. "We had all felt as if no adults took us seriously before [festivals such as Woodstock] and we were helpless. The military draft hung over all our heads, the war was grinding up our friends weekly, yet *we* had no say in the matter. When we were at these festivals though, they were all about *us*, for *us* and gave us a sense of belonging that was sorely needed in society at that time. Because of these festivals, we knew what peace could accomplish. We saw it work over and over again. They were the playgrounds that us kids were allowed to play in, to mingle in, and discuss what goals *we* had and what *we'd* do if we had the reins. Look at who most consumer items are aimed at today."

"Even though many young people at that time embraced 'free love' and cursed like sailors ('Gimme an F!'), we still were kind to one another, respectful of life and other's feelings, much like the 'do unto others' passage,'" adds Fred Herrera. "We were not the ones waging war for profit (or who knows what) then. When we grew up to become today's leaders, most of us took with us that strong ethic. We have to thank those playgrounds for our chance to sort it all out."

Although not the first music festival, Woodstock would be the most remembered. The rock festival was now not just the providence of those who were fortunate to be at the right place at the right time but an entity known by people everywhere. There were several positive festivals still to come, but as Bob Dylan sang, the times they were indeed "a-changin'."

Texas International Pop Festival
August 30–September 1, 1969

"This was another fest held at a monstrous-sized racetrack, with the bleachers and infield crammed with people, but hot and dusty!"

—Alex Del Zoppo, Sweetwater

Angus Wynne III, whose father created Six Flags Over Texas Amusement Park in Arlington, Texas had been to the Atlanta Pop Festival and liked what he saw. Wynne and his Showco production partner Jack Calmes joined forces with Alex Cooley, the promoter who brought the Atlanta festival to life, to form Interpop Superfest. They decided to throw a little party of their own at the newly-opened Dallas International Motor Speedway in Lewisville, north of Dallas. The festival would be held over Labor Day weekend, August 30–September 1, 1969.

The music bill was large with artists (many of them Texans) from several different genres. Those who attended the festival were treated to legendary performers such as B.B. King, and Sam and Dave; funk performances from Sly and the Family Stone, Tony Joe White, and Delaney & Bonnie & Friends; boogie from Canned Heat; and the music of diverse entertainers such as the Chicago Transit Authority, Herbie Mann, Santana, and the Incredible String Band. There would be blues from James Cotton and Freddie King; rock and roll from Ramon and Ramon and the Four Daddios, and Grand Funk Railroad; soul from Rotary Connection; psychedelic rock from Johnny Winter, Texas Band Space Opera, Nazz, Shiva's Headband, Spirit (who smashed and destroyed their guitars at the end of their set), Sweetwater, Ten Years After, and Led Zeppelin. Texan Janis Joplin would appear in a triumphant homecoming. (It was said that Joplin was extremely nervous about appearing in front of her home crowd.)

"This was another fest held at a monstrous-sized racetrack, with the bleachers and infield crammed with people, but hot and dusty," remembers Sweetwater's Alex Del Zoppo. "We absolutely loved that festival. There were a number of acts we had played with before, and especially the West-coasters, Spirit, Janis, Santana, and Sly, made us feel at home. I think it was the first major U.S. stop for Led Zep, as well."

The performers were brought backstage by either limousine or, after the highway became congested with cars, by helicopter. The festival was well-organized and the show ran smoothly. The stage had been set seven feet off the ground so people could see the acts and security would not be a major problem. The press was stationed in front of the stage before a decorative wooden fence. "It was my first festival," recalls Tony Joe White. "My drummer and I steamed it up, which one hundred degrees will do. The thing I remember also was the whole place running out of water and big trucks bringing it in later—wild."

"It took place exactly two weeks after Woodstock, and we were still in high spirits from that monumental event," remembers Fred Herrera of Sweetwater. "As hot as it was, we did great, getting them on their feet by the end of our set."

Nearby Lee Park was a popular hangout of the peace and love crowd, but attendees were encouraged to camp instead at Lake Lewisville (a popular skinny-dipping spot). The Merry Pranksters provided a free stage on the campground and featured unsigned Texas bands. Several times those who had appeared on the festival's main stage, but weren't quite ready to call it a day, would play on the free stage. The Hog Farm was once again present to provide free food, security, and a medical tent for those who found themselves, or their friends, on "bad trips."

Although residents of conservative Lewisville were initially quite nervous about what the festival may bring to their town (and an editorial in the local paper told them to expect the worse), the festival went off with few glitches. At one point the chief of police walked onstage to praise those in attendance for their good behavior. Over 150,000 people attended and almost everyone got along. A baby was born and the only misadventure was when one of the participants died from heat stroke. The event was dubbed by the press as "The Best Little Woodstock in Texas."

Isle of Wight Festival
August 31, 1969

"You are the body beautiful."
—Rikki Farr

The Isle of Wight Festival of 1968 had been fairly successful and in 1969 that festival grew even more popular. American artists such as Bob Dylan, the Band, and Tom Paxton were scheduled to appear and the British were well-represented with Joe Crocker, the Moody Blues, and the Who among the two dozen performers who would perform over three days. The amount spent on the performers was high and a better-than-average stage was erected.

Attendance exploded with over 150,000 people coming to the festival this year—only 10,000 had participated in the first Isle of Wight Festival. Ron and Ray Foulk promoted the festival through their Fiery Creations enterprise. The promoters promised a festival where poetry and film would be part of the festivities, and there was even a large tent where people were encouraged to "do their own thing," whatever that was.

People pitched tents and slept, or visited on sleeping bags. Dormitory tents were available for the first time. The facilities weren't much, though. Some water taps were installed but food supplies were fairly meager. Fortunately, many people brought their own supplies.

"The overall impression is that [Isle of Wight festivals] were pretty loose affairs," says Pentangle's John Renbourne. "Variations in levels of chaos is what comes back mostly. Also that they were big occasions for running into a lot of old acquaintances as well as a lot of other acts all at one time. Real gatherings, but consistently humorous from the confusion angle. The two biggies were, I suppose, the Isle of Wight festivals for sheer size and intensity. Just getting across to the little suburban island in conservative Southern England on the dinky passenger ferry literally loaded to the gunwales with ravers was an event in itself. And that wasn't even the beginning; things had been building up for months. As soon as word was out, people wanted to tag along for the ride with assorted parties setting out and gathering momentum, every vehicle crammed with riders. The main drift was, after all, a massed show of alternativity—to vastly outnumber the authorities and have a good time. Dope had reached a zenith by then."

Despite the close quarters, those who attended behaved in a civilized manner and there were no major problems or incidents to report. Over 150 Isle of Wight police officers, who had their leave cancelled due to the numbers expected at the festival, took a stance of minimal "presence."

Producer Rikki Farr was serving as emcee and told the assembled crowd that they were a "blessed generation." "You are the body beautiful," Farr declared.

The main attraction was Bob Dylan. His performance was well anticipated as the music icon had not made a major appearance in several years. As the evening progressed, Dylan kept his audience waiting. Just as the crowd began to get restless and things threatened to get out of hand with beer cans being lobbed toward the stage, Dylan appeared. His ensuing set was well-received, but some felt it was not long enough. Dylan played for a little over one hour and when the crowd demanded more he gave a ten-minute encore. The audience was less than sated but the emcee explained (in typical British manner) that "Bob Dylan came here to do what he had to do and he's done, and I'm afraid that's the end."

"Dylan was practically a disaster at the Isle of Wight festival," remembers John Renbourne of Pentangle. "Last on and playing to a crowd pretty much wiped out after days of getting wrecked. The white suit and relatively low-key electric set seemed to elicit mild disbelief. What they were waiting for was a retro sixties savior to beam them up. Tom Paxton hit the spot though. Blue jeans and anti-war songs. I was standing to the side of the stage as he came off. You could really feel the huge natural high. That must have been a great occasion for him."

Whether or not those involved enjoyed the festival amid the "haze," most seem to have had some kind of a lasting experience. "That's not to say I didn't have a good time," says Renbourne. "I may well have. I'd have to ask the roadies. Those guys usually made the most of most situations. A couple of great characters were looking after Pentangle at the Isle of Wight festivals—Bargee Bob and Pikey Bill, both Bermondsey dockers for whom the word 'authority' had no meaning. But then neither did 'star sign' or 'peace, man.' At the time of Dylan's arrival at the site there was a big security drive. No one was allowed out, roads were closed, and there was a lot of hoopla that hyped the anticipation. Word was that he was being taken to a secret and impenetrable location. We were all standing around in the beer tent waiting to leave. Bobby and Billy finally walked in. 'Where have you been?' someone asked. 'Having a drink with the other fella,' they replied. 'Bob Wozznane . . . he was all right, he was getting it down.'"

In the end, those involved with the 1969 festival were pleased with their success. Their problems had been minimal: press accommodations and litter were their only real concern. Unlike what had been problematic in the United States, this festival was not only musically successful, but audience accommodations seemed to work.

Toronto Rock and Roll Revival
September 13, 1969

> *"We've never done this number before—best of luck."*
> —John Lennon

The music festival was continuing its alignment with the peace movement, if even peripherally. Yet people in the music business were beginning to feel that musicians in the rock genre were developing entitled attitudes about their "art." Larger sums were being demanded to perform and audiences expected more name acts to play at the larger gatherings. Promoters of an event in Toronto, Canada made the decision to draw as large a crowd as possible and decided to invite artists from the more inclusive world of good ole rock 'n' roll to join them. The Toronto Rock and Roll Revival would have a little of everything. What better way to combine the two, if sometimes indistinct, world of rock 'n' roll with the newer revolutionary hard rock than with the involvement of the guru of the peace movement: John Lennon. But the festival didn't start out with that high of a profile.

Produced by John Bower and Ken Walker, the concert was scheduled at Varsity Stadium in Toronto for September 13, 1969. Local bands such as Whiskey Howl, Milkwood, and Nucleus would perform and the bill would feature old school titans of rock and roll such as Chuck Berry, Jerry Lee Lewis, Bo Diddley, Little Richard, and Gene Vincent. Junior Walker and the All Stars would provide some funk; Doug Kershaw some cajun fiddle; Cat Mother & the All Night Newsboys some pop; Tony Joe White a little country blues; and Screaming Lord Sutch . . . whatever. Rock would be represented by Chicago Transit Authority, a new band called the Alice Cooper Group, and the harder-edged sound would be provided by Ten Years After and the Doors.

D.A. Pennebaker and his Leacock Pennebaker Productions had been hired to film the event. Pennebaker was only informed of the concert nine days before it was scheduled to happen. When Pennebaker was first approached, he was concerned that his efforts would be extensive but with little professional reward since he had already "done" an excellent festival and concert film with *Monterey Pop*. But perhaps if there was less focus on the heavier bands that had come to prominence over the past couple of years and more time spent on the legends of rock n' roll, then such a film may be interesting. Ultimately money was the deciding factor. Leacock Pennebaker would be less involved in the marketing and distribution of the film and more concerned with the filming of the documentary itself. Of course, as undertakings of this sort tend to do, financial involvement became more complicated.

Pennebaker was relying on the expertise of Chip Monck and hoped his least concern would be the lighting, but when Monck was unable to get a visa due to drug problems in the States, lightning became Pennebaker's biggest obstacle. While Pennebaker addressed the lighting problem and other various sundry issues involved with filming at the last minute, he was approached by lawyers informing him that unless certain financial aspects of the concert production were settled immediately, Pennebaker would not be allowed to film. Contracts and performance fees were quickly dealt with and the preparations continued.

The stage stood under a huge blue-and-white canopy and was surrounded by snow fences. Los Angeles avant-garde personality Kim Fowley was tagged to emcee. The bands involved were definitely crowd pleasers. The Alice Cooper Group backed Gene Vincent during Vincent's electrifying set. "Alice" (whose real name is Vincent Furnier) played harmonica and the band so clicked with Gene Vincent that he invited them to back him up for a couple of studio demos. The Alice Cooper Group's appearance at the festival was more straight-ahead rock than the theatrical performances for which they would become known.

Tony Joe White, backed only by drums and a bass guitar, was riding the success of his hit "Polk Salad Annie" and the crowd seemed to enjoy him. "I remember how cool it was of the crowd to make me feel like I was playing to a real swampy crowd," remembers White.

Leo Lyons of Ten Years After remembers the festival but doesn't feel it played a large part in his music career or as a moment of any particular achievement. "To be honest, we flew in, did the gig and left," says Lyons. "I enjoyed the gig and have some home movie footage, but the whole of the late sixties–early seventies was an exhilarating time for me."

Screaming Lord Sutch was an interesting addition to the bill. Known for both his oddball horror music and his political involvement through his self-invented National Teenage Party, David Edward Sutch gave an animated performance. (His 1968 album *Lord Sutch and Heavy Friends* was considered an appalling effort despite appearances by John Bonham, Jeff Beck, Jimmy Page, Noel Redding, and Nicky Hopkins. Sutch committed suicide by hanging himself in 1999.)

Chuck Berry gave a great show, with his legendary duck walks and mugging to both the audience and the cameras. Berry introduced a new song that he called "My Ding-a-Ling" and encouraged the crowd to sing along. The crude but catchy tune was a big hit. Berry stayed on stage over an hour, finishing as the sun went down. Berry was known for his workmanlike approach to performing, but at this event he seemed to actually be having a good time.

As the lights of the stadium came on the audience rejected the "football" atmosphere of their glare. Fowley attempted to explain that the lights were needed for the film crew but the crowd wasn't having it. Cans and bottles began to fly and a few scuffles broke out. Finally, to cheers from the crowd, the lights were dimmed and the show continued. The lights would go off and on the remainder of the night but by that time the audience was drawn more into the performances and no ugly incidents occurred.

Jerry Lee Lewis attacked his piano with a vengeance and gave the crowd exactly what they had come looking for, as did Bo Diddley with his soulful backup singers. Junior Walker and the All Stars engaged the audience with their funky numbers. Little Richard, in his dazzling white mirrored suit, was as self-indulgent as ever and had the crowd on their feet. (Richard had warned the people controlling the lights that he would only appear in a single spotlight.)

The Doors were riding their chart-topping single "Touch Me" at the time of the Toronto Rock and Roll Revival. While his band mates enjoyed watching the acts of their boyhood heroes together, Jim Morrison stood alone at the back steps of the stage through several performances. When it came time for their band to perform, Morrison was ready to make his presence felt and the Doors performed admirably, making the audience wait for their giant hit "Light My Fire."

The music of Doug Kershaw was new to some in the audience and was not as well-received as the legendary fiddle player deserved. Even so, Kershaw braved some catcalls and played a lively set in spite of them. But Kershaw no doubt made many new fans that day.

Kim Fowley had been teasing the audience about John Lennon flying in to make an appearance but few in the crowd actually believed him. It was almost standard by now for any festival or large gathering to include rumors such as this or, even better yet, that the entire band of Beatles were showing up to play. But this time it was for real.

The Beatles hadn't taken the stage as an entity for three years. John Lennon had appeared with the Rolling Stones for their documentary *The Rolling Stones Rock and Roll Circus* and he had also made an appearance at Cambridge with Yoko Ono, but Lennon had not performed before a large group of people in a very long time and never alone. When the Toronto organizers called to invite Lennon to participate, just days before the event, the Beatle misunderstood what it was they wanted. They had been thinking that Lennon could come and serve as "a presence" but Lennon mistook them to be inviting him to perform. On a whim, he said he would play at the concert, but he first had to round up a band to back him. (Some accounts have Lennon *asking* to perform.)

Lennon's long-time friend Klaus Voorman (who had befriended the Beatles while they lived and performed in Hamburg, Germany, and who later had been a member of the Manfred Mann group) committed to play bass guitar and ex-Alan Price drummer Alan White would provide percussion. Lennon decided that only Eric Clapton would do for lead guitar but he was unable to get in touch with Clapton. That wasn't the only problem. There was also the issue of obtaining a visa to enable Lennon to enter Canada, which John Bower was finally able to arrange with the Canadian Department of Immigration. As the rest of the newly-formed "band," gathered at the airport to leave (minus Clapton), Lennon called his roadie Mal Evans to tell him it was all off—without Clapton he wouldn't play. As it turned out, Clapton had actually been at home in bed but he didn't hear the telephone ring. George Harrison's assistant Tony Dorman had a telegram delivered to Clapton, which was received by Clapton's gardener. Once Clapton was awoken and handed the telegram, he called Lennon to say he would be happy to go to Canada and play. A later flight was booked and the performance was back on. Dan and Jill Richter had been filming documentary footage for Lennon and Ono, and they accompanied the pair to Toronto to get this important event in the life of John Lennon on film. (Beatle manager Allen Klein also made provisions for recording the event on film.)

The group of friends, calling themselves the Plastic Ono Band, was now bound for Canada but had yet to decide on what songs would be performed, and they certainly did not have time to rehearse. They had never taken the stage together before making their commitment to appear at the festival. The four men—and Yoko—went to the back of the airplane to sort through some sheet music and talk about possible numbers or songs that each of them knew well enough to play live to an audience. They came up with about eight tunes but when they tried to run through them the noise from the plane was so loud they couldn't hear each other. (They didn't have amps for their guitars onboard.)

Eventually the band arrived backstage, after being escorted from the airport by over eighty members of the Toronto Vagabonds Motorcycle Club (the club also escorted the Doors). When they were shown their dressing room area, Lennon smirked at the dinginess of his surroundings and happily said to Yoko "Welcome to rock 'n' roll." The band quickly breezed through some bits of the songs they had decided on—songs that consisted primarily of the basic twelve bars found in guitar renditions that any musician would know. Lennon later said that he was "sick from nerves" and threw up for hours until it was time for him to take the stage. He would later amend that statement to include that he was also "full of junk." Klaus Voorman later confirmed Lennon's nervousness, but said that he himself wasn't nervous as he didn't see that it mattered whether the hastily put together band was "good or bad."

Before the new Plastic Ono Band took the stage, Kim Fowley had the lights dimmed and encouraged the audience to light a match, which they did. The effect was dazzling. Lennon later said that it was the first time he'd ever heard about an audience doing something like that. "It was fantastic," he said.

The band came onstage and set up in the old Beatle formation. Lennon told the audience they were going to play some songs they all knew because they'd never played together before this. They tore into "Blue Suede Shoes," "Money," "Dizzy Miss Lizzy," and "Yer Blues" with vocals by Lennon. Eric Clapton thought it was "refreshing" to perform the songs, stating that was the type of music that both he and Lennon really loved. Then Lennon announced, "We've never done this number before—best of luck" and he began the cacophonic guitar of "Cold Turkey," a new Lennon composition that had yet to be recorded. Ironically, while singing about going cold turkey, a popular term for drug withdrawal, Lennon almost vomited from the drugs in his system.

After the intensity of "Cold Turkey," which left the audience somewhat stunned, Lennon returned them to the more familiar, more relaxed Lennon vibe by saying "This is what we came for really, so sing along." He couldn't quite remember all the words to "Give Peace a Chance," but the chorus was one they could all sing. The crowd put their arms into the air and swayed together to the music.

The audience was in no way prepared for what came next. Lennon announced "Now Yoko is going to do her thing—all over you." Yoko had been on the stage throughout the set, hidden in a white bag, and emerged every now and then to hold lyric sheets for Lennon. She "performed" "Don't Worry Kyoko" (which Lennon called "half rock and half madness"), and then "Oh John (Let's Hope for Peace)" complete with the guitar feedback of Lennon, Clapton, and Voorman as they backed off the stage and left their guitars bleeding into their amplifiers. Lennon later called the number "completely freaky." The audience was, surprisingly, relatively tolerant of Ono's extraordinary musical vision and likely accepted her as Lennon's partner, if not a unique artist. Little Richard said later that people threw bottles at her and she had to run off the stage, although that doesn't seem to have been the case. Ronnie Hawkins later said that some in the audience remember a handful of people yelling for her to "get the fuck off the stage." But Lennon remembered it differently. He said that out of the massive amount of people there, "maybe fifteen didn't like it" and he didn't hear any booing. After it was over, the Plastic Ono Band left the stage. Lennon later remarked that he couldn't remember when he had such a good time.

Others on the bill found Ono's performance interesting as well. "I agreed to close the show for the festival so I put together a helluva band to go with me, knowing it was going to be a major music event," remembers Doug Kershaw. "I asked Charlie Daniels to come along as a band member, and he said he'd be happy to. This is before his explosion as a recording artist. We kept hearing rumors at the festival that John Lennon might appear, but nobody knew for sure. I was backstage half-listening to some of the bands playing when the promoter brought the word that Lennon had arrived. 'And he plans on playing.' the promoter added. I just assumed that a former Beatle would close the show instead of me, but I was told that Lennon had no intentions of grabbing my closing slot. I was stunned. No way am I gonna close for John Lennon, I told the promoter. I thought he would pass out. But I meant it. Not that I was afraid of following John, even though I knew he was a god to the audience, it was out of respect for Lennon, for the Beatles, for the history. When John himself came and talked to me about it, I explained my position. He didn't say much, but I could tell he understood. At least he agreed to close. After I finished my portion of the show, Charlie Daniels and I found a good spot on the sidelines so we could watch John Lennon perform. The guy was electrifying. So much pure, natural talent. But then, everything became confusing on stage. I could hear the audience whispering, and some fans were pointing. That's when I noticed a blanket bunched up in a small mound back by the drums. It looked as if somebody had forgotten to remove a pile of drum covers. At least that's what I thought until, all of a sudden, Charlie and I noticed the damn thing was moving. Very slowly it inched and humped its way all around the stage. We were so distracted by the moving blanket that we couldn't concentrate on John Lennon's music. 'What the hell is that?' I finally whispered to Charlie. He hunched shoulders. 'Damned if I know,' he said. We tried to listen to John's next song, but the blanket seemed to be getting more energetic. And it was inching closer and closer to Lennon as he sang. 'What the hell is that?' I whispered again to Charlie. 'Damned if I know,' he said again. And so it went, until John Lennon finally finished his show. That's when he turned and acknowledged the blanket. 'My wife, Yoko Ono,' he announced. The blanket then stood up, and Yoko appeared from beneath it. She stepped up to the microphone to sing a duet with her husband. Charlie Daniels and I almost died. We weren't even making any musical judgments. It was just the damnedest thing we ever saw. That was Yoko Ono moving all around in that damn blanket, I kept thinking. Talk about a show-stealing scene."

"The thing that sticks in my mind to this very day is John's white suit, which he nearly vomited on," says Klaus Voormann. "His shaky knees when we were marching out there up on stage. The rest you all know. A band that doesn't know itself, straight from an intercontinental flight in to the stadium, no rehearsal, no sound check. Up on stage with Yoko. John's first appearance after the Beatles. Out there waiting for him, an impatient, curious audience expecting John to top the Beatles! Now you tell me, does that sound like fun?"

The concert ended at 1:45 in the morning and it was on to the next thing. The festival, the Pennebaker film titled *Sweet Toronto* was well-received, several of those who also appeared later released their performances on the DVD, and the Plastic Ono Band released the album *Live Peace in Toronto, 1969*. Lennon claimed that his label, Capitol Records, didn't want to release the album due to the involvement of Ono, but the Lennons finally persuaded them to do so. The album went gold the next day.

Spending over $100,000 on talent and realizing revenue of $150,000, the event was apparently a success. Because of the involvement of John Lennon, the event would be forever remembered as the "Toronto Peace Festival" rather than as the Toronto Rock and Roll Revival, but remembered it would be.

Altamont
December 6, 1969

"The crowd doesn't reason."
—Jack Casady, Jefferson Airplane

John Lennon always claimed that, at the beginning of their career, almost everything the Rolling Stones did that was perceived as innovative was merely a carbon copy of something the Beatles had already done. The Stones had not (other than Brian Jones' appearance at the Monterey Pop Festival to introduce the Jimi Hendrix Experience), participated in any of the peace and love festivals with the exception of an evening at Hyde Park. Maybe Lennon having his day in the sun in Toronto was the catalyst for Mick Jagger to decide that an appearance by the Stones at an American festival was long overdue. The Stones were just completing a tour of America and decided that a free concert at the culmination of the tour, where they would "give back" to their fans (whatever that meant), would ensure that they were important participants in the current youth movement.

The Stones' American tour was closing December 6, 1969. The first choice for a festival location was Golden Gate Park, in the city of San Francisco, where the hippie and flower children movement had all begun. Permits to use the park for such an event were pending when Mick Jagger and the Rolling Stones held a press conference to announce that the Stones would play . . . for free. City officials were aghast. They knew what had happened at Woodstock and surely the numbers would be equally as large as that historic festival if the Rolling Stones were the headlining band. Many of those involved suspected that Jagger made the announcement to actually ensure that the number of those attending would be as great as Woodstock and that the Rolling Stones would be at front and center of the subsequent publicity. A film of the event was already being planned. Over 100,000 were now expected and there were concerns that the park facility, as well as the various public services of the city of San Francisco, would be extremely challenged should that many people actually come to the festival. After San Francisco public officials voiced their concern and disapproval to the Stones' organization, the site of the concert was moved to Sears Point Raceway in Sonoma, a small town north of San Francisco.

As the date of the festival drew near, problems arose with the Sears Point location over something having to do with film distribution rights. At the very last minute, local businessman Dick Carter stepped in to offer the Altamont Raceway, a venue southeast of San Francisco located between the towns of Livermore and Tracy. The contract was signed the day before the festival was to take place. As the organizers hurried to make the necessary changes to their plans, the logistics concerning portable toilets and medical facilities were low on their list of priorities. They were more concerned with their plans for the sound system that would definitely need to be adjusted. The day was forecasted as hot and muggy, and the site was mostly dirt and barren without trees for shade. It was hard to coordinate food and drink concessions at the last minute and there was a dearth of refreshment franchises (but not, as it would turn out, for dealers of pot and various other drugs). These problems would prove to be the least of the organizers' concerns.

The Hells Angels, a motorcycle club based in California since 1948, had been acting as security at some of the dates for the Grateful Dead. The Angels enjoyed the Dead's music and were available to serve as security for the Altamont festival for a small fee. The rough appearance and menacing behavior of many of the Angels traditionally kept the more naïve flower children in line. Still, the Angels as an entity claimed that they would not be attending the Altamont festival to serve as crowd control, but to enjoy the music. There hadn't been anything notable about the Angels' involvement serving in a loosely-based security capacity up to this point, but that was about to drastically change.

On the recommendation of the Grateful Dead organization, Rolling Stones tour manager Sam Cutler hired the Hells Angels to guard the band's equipment. The Stones had used the London chapter of the club as security during their free concert in Hyde Park. But there was certainly a difference between the British and the American chapters of the organization. The London Angels, at that time, were more often than not mere posers, looking tough but with little bite. The American Hells Angels took themselves very seriously. Unfortunately, Cutler didn't know how seriously. From Cutler's standpoint, the Angels would be stationed near the backstage area and that would be that.

Several artists had already committed to support the Stones. Santana had been popular at previous festivals and they would open. The Flying Burrito Brothers were added to the bill at the request of Burrito member Gram Parsons, who was a close friend of Rolling Stone Keith Richards. Crosby, Stills, Nash & Young had enjoyed Woodstock and were happy to play at a California festival. Jefferson Airplane and the Grateful Dead would represent the now extremely popular San Francisco music scene.

Albert and David Maysles signed on to produce a documentary film about the event and captured all the last-minute preparations (and problems) on film. The day before the concert, 5,000 people had already gathered, ready to party. By the day of the festival, which was being dubbed "Woodstock West," over 300,000 had arrived. In a gross miscalculation, the stage stood only three to four feet above the ground, which not only created a security problem but restricted viewing the bands for those near the back of the crowd. For the thousands who were sitting far from the stage much of the music would be inaudible and the performers would appear ant-sized.

"Altamont was a really strange thing," remembers rock music fan Jim Ratledge, who was there that day. "We had to park about three-quarters of a mile from the race track and walk the rest of the way through some really dirty fields. The crowd started from the stage [which was elbow-to-elbow] and worked its way up the little depression and the surrounding knolls. There were a lot of people that were selling their product and some were giving it away. As the crowd got bigger so did the intensity of the people."

Despite any problems that may have occurred offstage, Santana performed a tight, inspired set. Their debut album (*Santana*) had just been released and songs taken from the album were huge crowd-pleasers. As the band played, the audience grew. People in the crowd followed the natural tendency to move closer to the stage and the Angels used pool cues to "encourage" them to move back. (They sometimes accomplished their goal by throwing full cans of beer.) Santana stopped playing at least twice, unsure of what was going on around them. When a few motorcycles were knocked over (likely accidentally), the owners of the bikes became enraged. "Most people couldn't really see what was going on in front of the stage," says Jack Casady. "They couldn't understand why the music was stopping. People couldn't see. The hasty construction of the stage didn't help. And the sound system was weak."

The Hells Angels may have been enjoying the music but many of them seemed to be enjoying their power of intimidation more. It wasn't just the "hippies" that were indulging in drugs and alcohol. The Angels' drug of choice was mostly "reds" a term used for amphetamines, which often produced paranoia and aggression in those who imbibed. There was alcohol, marijuana, and LSD thrown into the mix as well.

Sam Cutler felt threatened by the closeness of the audience to the stage and moved the Angels he had hired to the edge of the stage. Noting the antagonism between the Angels and the crowd up front, Cutler also apparently had the idea that if the Angels' beer was moved to that location it would serve to contain the Angels in a single area. He paid them $500 for the beer they brought and set up the beer off to the side of the stage.

The situation on the festival grounds wasn't that stable either. People started getting hungry and thirsty, and obtaining food and drink was nearly impossible for those enveloped in the heat and humanity. There just wasn't enough to go around. When a snack truck appeared on-site, it was quickly surrounded by dozens of people who pushed aside the man inside and grabbed handfuls of food until the truck was empty.

"Location, location, location, as they say in the real estate business," reflects Jack Casady. "[The problem] was a lack of shelter. Lack of physical comfort had a lot to do with it. Basically there were a lot of elements involved."

During the Jefferson Airplane's set, singer Marty Balin got into an argument with some of the Angels when he tried to keep them from beating up a young man in the audience. A scuffle ensued and Balin was punched in the face. He fell into the area in front of the stage. Although Balin was briefly unconscious, the music continued. "At the time, we didn't even realize Marty was gone from the stage," says Jack Casady. "You had to keep the beat going. It wouldn't have helped Marty to stop the beat. When you see crowds and the crowd mentality that gets people pushing and shoving like that, it's very scary. The crowd doesn't reason. Things happen when people crowd like that."

Guitarist Paul Kantner told the crowd what had happened and how the Hells Angels had knocked out Marty Balin. One of the Angels grabbed the microphone and threatened Kantner. Putting an end to the show would have likely resulted in a riot. "I don't think people knew what was going on down in front," says Casady. "There were no video cameras or cell phones then."

After the Grateful Dead witnessed the lack of respect allotted the bands by the Angels, they decided that they didn't want to put themselves in that position. And who could blame them?

"As the sun started going down, and the helicopter brought the Stones in—that's when things started to get busy," recalls Jim Ratledge. "The aroma and smoke from pot was starting to look like a cloud over the crowd. People were dancing around like they didn't have a care in the world (some were really out of this world). Mind-altering drugs abounded, you had your pick. As the music started you saw a strange blue cloud starting down by the stage and it worked its way up one side of the little depression over to the other side, and by the time it got to where I was seated, it looked even stranger (like small blue dots) only to realize that it was made up of thousands of small blue Frisbees that people kept throwing. The funny thing about it was the direction that they all seemed to move (as one large group). Everyone was throwing them in the same direction."

The arrival of the Rolling Stones to the stage seemed to take forever, even though most of the Stones had been at the site most of the day. (It was reported that bass player Bill Wyman had trouble getting to the event, although it is unclear why.) The music from the last band ended at 4 p.m. Mick Jagger had been wandering in and out of his trailer playing "rock god," but he wanted a dramatic entrance for the Stones and decided to wait until nightfall to have the band take the stage.

The appearance of the Rolling Stones didn't deter the attention of those who were in a mood to fight. Small scuffles continued throughout the Stones' set. One was serious enough to catch Jagger's eye as he pranced on the stage and attempted to give the people a good show. Jagger stopped the band and pleaded with the crowd to "be cool." He didn't understand why they would chose to fight and not get along (even as he sang "Sympathy for the Devil," a song that Jagger admitted always started trouble). Both Jagger and Richards vowed to stop playing and leave the stage if the violence didn't stop. Yet they couldn't stop playing, or there certainly would have been a violent reaction. The Stones, visibly upset (especially Mick Jagger), had no choice but to continue their performance. (It was later determined that many of the Hells Angels who had caused problems that day were "prospects," meaning that they had not been fully initiated into the brotherhood and perhaps it was to impress the Angels that they showed their more aggressive side.) Most of the people far from the stage were only aware of "some kind of scuffle" and had no idea the extent of the violence happening until much later.

Four deaths occurred that fateful day: Richard Savloy and Mark Feiger were killed when a car drove through their campsite and failed to see them and one young man somehow drowned in an irrigation ditch. The most dramatic death was that of Meredith Hunter. Words were exchanged between Hunter and a few of the Hells Angels while the Stones sang "Under My Thumb." As Hunter's girlfriend Patty Bredahoff attempted to draw Hunter away from the confrontation, Hunter evidently decided this was one fight where he didn't want to walk away. Hunter drew a gun. One of the Angels leaped over the backs of those involved with Hunter, drew a long knife, grabbed Hunter's hand (presumably with the gun in it), and stabbed him in the shoulder. The live-footage in the film *Gimme Shelter* shows that Hunter was stabbed twice more as he was dragged to the ground. Hunter was stabbed multiple times in the back, neck, and head. The Angels formed a tight circle and removed Hunter from the area while the man who stabbed him disappeared into the crowd. Hunter was taken to be airlifted to a hospital, but it is likely that he was dead before the helicopter ever left the ground. The incident was recorded on film by the Maysles brothers and the entire sequence of events regarding Hunter's death plays out, frame by frame on film. (Initially the filmmakers withheld their documentation from the press as they feared they would be in danger from the Angels.)

"As the Rolling Stones got going with 'Sympathy for the Devil' all hell broke loose," recalls Ratledge. "All the action that was going on down by the stage (the stabbing), the music, the Frisbees, the altitude of peoples' awareness (higher than a kite) got really spooky. People started freaking out a little and there was talk of people seeing very large rats (but I think that it was some bad acid—too much strychnine)."

While the Stones' Keith Richard later laid the blame for the violence on the presence of "ten or twenty" Hell's Angels, he saw the incident as more of an "American thing." Richards pointed out that when the Stones performed for free in Hyde Park there was no trouble. He found the difference between England and the United

States to be a factor. Richards claimed that "you can put half a million English people together and they won't start killing each other." Mick Jagger remarked that he "didn't want it to be like this." Bill Graham likened the event to a holocaust, saying that the police should have stepped in, twisted Jagger's arms behind his back, put him in front of the radio, and told him to call it off.

Jefferson Airplane's Jack Casady looks at what happened more pragmatically. "Horrible things happen every day," says Casady. "Are you going to insert yourself into that? You can pick any country and you can be right there and you can feel the world is in trouble. But I don't know that [the mood at Altamont] had anything to do with any change in society. Everybody who writes about it sees it in a different way." (But his experiences at Altamont haven't persuaded Casady to stop participating in festivals. He says "I look forward to every stage I get on.")

"After the Stones were done and every one started going back to their camp sites, things started to mellow out," says Jim Ratledge. "But some people had way too much fun and overdid their consumption on everything. People started to build camp fires and crash out. The fire that was close to where I was staying (along with my brother and friends) had about ten people sitting around it. (It was built right at the t-bone section of two dirt roads). People were just b.s.-ing about the concert and we had just left the fire, when a car sped right into the crowd and camp fire. It trapped several people under the car and two died. The driver of the car jumped out of the car and took off running out into the fields. I don't know if he was ever caught, but we all tried to help the ones we could, but the two that were trapped under the car lost their lives that night."

There were also said to have been four births connected with the festival but those received much less publicity. The media—while sympathetic to the fact that a man had been killed—seemed to love the notoriety of what happened at Altamont. They quickly dubbed the festival "the end of the Woodstock Nation" and used the event to put their nail in the coffin of the peace and love movement.

Alan Passaro, who was held accountable for the fatal stabbing, was acquitted of the crime when the jury ruled self defense because Hunter pointed a gun. (Hunter's mother, Alta Mae Anderson, would later request that the area where her son was stabbed be turned into a park. That didn't happen but future rock concerts were banned and even the car races would now be limited to crowds of only 3,000 people.) Rock Scully, the manager of the Grateful Dead, summed it up when he said that the Stones "wrote the script. They got what they paid for."

1970
Power to the People

In U.S. news

The Chicago Seven are found not guilty; cigarette ads are banned from television; the National Guard opens fire on student war protesters at Kent State University igniting student demonstrations on campuses across the country; the U.S. voting age is lowered to eighteen; and American troops withdraw from Cambodia.

In world news

The Nuclear Non-Proliferation Treaty goes into effect; and John Lennon pays £1,344 in fines for ninety-six people who protested against the South African rugby team playing in Scotland.

In music news

The Beatles announce their break-up; Jefferson Airplane and Janis Joplin are fined for using profanity during a concert; Jim Morrison is found guilty of profanity and indecent exposure; John Lennon is fined for indecent art display; and "The Long and Winding Road" is the last U.S. number one hit for the Beatles.

Some of the year's most notable albums

Guess Who: *American Woman*; Pink Floyd: *Atom Heart Mother*; Crosby, Stills, Nash & Young: *Déjà vu*; Three Dog Night: *It Ain't Easy*; Derek & the Dominos: *Layla and Other Assorted Love Songs*; the Beatles: *Let It Be*; Black Sabbath: *Paranoid*; James Taylor: *Sweet Baby James*.

Rock's most popular songs

"All Right Now"—Free; "Black Magic Woman"—Santana; "Fire and Rain"—James Taylor; "Iron Man"—Black Sabbath; "Maybe I'm Amazed"—Paul McCartney; "Let It Be"—the Beatles; "Love the One You're With"—Stephen Stills; "My Sweet Lord"—George Harrison; "Ohio" and "Teach Your Children"—Crosby, Stills, Nash & Young; "Whole Lotta Love"—Led Zeppelin; "War"—Edwin Starr.

Bath Festival of Blues and Progressive Music
June 27–28, 1970

"When you tour as much as we did, after a while one show becomes like the next."
                                                                —Johnny Winter

After the events at Altamont the festival scene was hurting, but not altogether dead. Those involved with music in the United States may have been pondering the state of communal gatherings but things were fine overseas. That's not to say that things remained the same. In 1970 the two-day Bath Festival would be expanded to include "alternative music" and the traditional festival would not come free of controversy. This year the festival was billed as England's answer to Woodstock yet the attendance numbers wouldn't be quite as high. Many of the situations that occurred at Woodstock, in particular long lines, sanitation problems, and food shortage, remained a constant of the music festival but the mood concerning the musical possibilities at Bath were fairly upbeat despite potential problems that threatened to turn the festival into quite a mess. Local townspeople reserved judgment before forming an opinion about the strangers in their midst and, in general, seemed to be okay with it all.

The bill was massive: popular British bands Led Zeppelin, Pink Floyd, Moody Blues, Fairport Convention, and Coliseum; American bands the Byrds, Jefferson Airplane, Frank Zappa and the Mothers of Invention, Santana, Steppenwolf, It's A Beautiful Day, Canned Heat, Hot Tuna, and the Flock; and artists including Country Joe, Johnny Winter, John Mayall, John Peel, Donovan, Dr. John, Keef Hartley, Maynard Ferguson, and Joe Jammer rounded out the list of performers.

The requisite traffic jam did occur and police presence was increased, but the police in general got along well with those in attendance and the respect shown one another at the festival seems to have included the cops. By now business enterprises catering to youth were anxious to become aligned with the festivals. Tower Records and Unicorn Books, which sold or gave away copies of alternative press, were represented by booths.

The music portion of the festival—surely why most people came although many said they were there to experience a "community of brotherhood"—didn't get off to a great start. Traffic problems caused delays in setting up and the bands themselves were often left waiting. Like it had been at Woodstock, the order of appearance had to be reconfigured several times and it was several hours before the "official" first notes rang out. (Joe Jammer and his colleagues served as the "festival band" and took

Jimi Hendrix, Monterey Pop Festival, 1967

Country Joe MacDonald, Woodstock, 1969

Bob Dylan, Isle of Wight, 1969

Mick and Tina, Live Aid, 1985

Tommy Guidon, Halifax, Warped Tour, 2005

Photo courtesy Tommy Guidon

Molson Canadian Rocks for Toronto, 2003

Photo courtesy Stuart Chatwood

Jane's Addiction, Lollapalooza, 2003

Ozzy Osbourne, Ozzfest, 2000

Photo by Joe Giron/Corbis

the stage between those scheduled to appear but not yet present or ready. The audience grew tired of them but the band soldiered on, trying to provide at least some entertainment.)

Drugs were, of course, in abundance and were made easily available. A public service organization called Release assisted with medical problems and situations, and tended to those who needed help. An anti-establishment attitude was once again on tap: Country Joe gave his "Fish" cheer at least five times, as he played in the rain.

By Saturday, the problems of who was where on the bill continued. Pink Floyd welcomed the dawn from the stage. Canned Heat performed next and the dancing and stomping of Bear Hite made the stage shake. They quickly had people on their feet dancing. The acts that had been scheduled to end Saturday night finally came to a close.

There was a long delay as the Sunday show was again late in launching. The crowd grew restless. Donovan, who had not been scheduled to appear but told the organizers he would be attending the festival and be available if the need arose, came onstage to play for two hours. Little had been seen of the popular minstrel recently. His set was enjoyed and the crowd mellowed. Other crowd pleasers included Frank Zappa and the Mothers of Invention who, in usual form, played mostly for themselves and didn't let any of the technical problems of the festival bother them. John Mayall and his band were perhaps a bit loose but certainly acceptable. Johnny Winter provided an entertaining set, but he doesn't necessarily remember the festival. "They all have their special moments," says Winter. "But when you tour as much as we did, after a while one show becomes like the next."

The Hell's Angels were present once again and took up their usual bouncer stances, whether employed to do so or not. Many of the Angels were given backstage passes by Fairport Convention, who had been carried to the stage on the biker's motorcycles. Certainly the events of the Altamont festival were known to most of those present and decisions were no doubt made to not invoke the ire of the Angels in any way. Only a handful of relatively small incidents broke out. The Angels, down at the front of the stage, were in their element when Steppenwolf came on and played "Born to be Wild."

About this time the Moody Blues arrived but when they heard it would likely be hours before they could take the stage they decided that they didn't want to wait so didn't perform. Pink Floyd played only a few very long numbers. (As strange as it is to imagine today, they had been playing quite a bit locally and weren't the main attraction of the festival.)

As the afternoon wore on and evening came, the weather turned cold. The crowd, however, had waited for Led Zeppelin, and Jefferson Airplane, and the majority of the people had stuck around to hear them. The Flock was on stage ahead of Led Zeppelin and the crowd seemed to be enjoying their eclectic music. (One ambiguous story has assertive Led Zep manager Peter Grant pulling the plug on the Flock so his band could take the stage.) Over 200,000 people enjoyed Led Zeppelin as they played for over two and one-half hours. The long set was extremely well-received and many people think it was one of the best Led Zeppelin sets of all time. Others found it pretentious and overblown.

Hot Tuna delivered a searing set accompanied by naked dancers (which hadn't been in the game plan but were enjoyed nonetheless). By the time Jefferson Airplane reached the stage a strong wind was blowing and made it difficult for the band to perform up to their usual standard. When rain started coming down in torrents and lightning appeared, Paul Kantner received a jolt from his microphone. It was all part of the festival experience. Things happened and they were handled. Although many elements remained the same, off-the-wall things did happen at different festivals. Promoters and performers alike were learning to deal with whatever complication arose. As for the circumstances at Bath, Jack Casady says, "The only difference is there were a bunch of English people there. People build on what happens at other festivals and things should get better by the next one."

The Byrds came out shortly after Jefferson Airplane and played a crowd-pleasing, improvised acoustic set. It was the first such set of their current incarnation with Clarence White and Gene Parsons, but because of the weather the band was forced to forego their planned electric set. Nonetheless, the Byrds were called back for almost a dozen encores. Finally the master of ceremonies had to take to the stage to ask for pity on the group—they were worn out. Dr. John eventually took the stage and closed the festival. Another day, another festival.

Atlanta International Pop Festival
July 3–5, 1970

"Roll a joint and share with your brothers and sisters."

—A remark from the stage

Alex Cooley had been so pleased with the Atlanta Pop Festival that he decided to bring it back for a second year. This time the festival would be held at the Peach County Raceway in Byron, Georgia. The festival was promoted as "Three Days of Peace, Love and Music" and included performances by local music heroes the Allman Brothers; American bands such as Grand Funk Railroad, Captain Beefhart, and Spirit; and English bands Jethro Tull, Ten Years After, and Procol Harum. B.B. King, Terry Reid, John Sebastian, and Johnny Winter were also available and ready to perform. Jimi Hendrix, with less than three months to live (although he of course didn't know it), headlined.

Cooley had been expecting only about 100,000 people. It was evident before the first act had taken the stage that the promoter's estimate was wa-a-ay off. Traffic on the main highway was backed up nearly all the way to Atlanta, which was about ninety miles away. The first festival had been popular but this scene was something else. Somewhere between 350,000 and 500,000 people occupied the small town of Byron. Police Chief James Barbour would claim that there were so many people that the alligators and water moccasins were run out of nearby Echeconnee Creek.

It was a hot, humid Southern summer day that included (as is usual in Georgia) periodic rain showers that would sometimes interrupt the music. Drinking water was at a premium. (Although not in the nearby creek where people cooled themselves off clad only in their birthday suits.) Bags of ice sold for five dollars. Lack of adequate supplies was not the only way that the large numbers would be a challenge for the festival, or for the town. Governor Lester Maddox threatened to send in the State Police to deal with the drug offenders but that didn't happen. There was only one full-time police officer in Byron and, although a few part-time officers were called to duty, it was quickly decided that unless something occurred that was a major problem it was best to just let those at the festival have their weekend fun. (No arrests were made that weekend—a tribute to Southern hospitality.)

The Lighthouse Family enlisted help from medical personnel based at Atlanta's Grady Hospital and set up the traditional tent for drug overdoses, heat-related problems, and bad acid trips. Brown rice from a free kitchen was given to those who were hungry and without money. Fire engines came to hose down people and cool them off.

The Allman Brothers, in their original formation, played intermittent searing sets that included a version of "Whipping Post" that apparently lasted ninety minutes. As the sun rose on Sunday morning Richie Havens played "Here Comes the Sun," creating a magical moment.

While that moment was unplanned, premeditated entertainment of another kind would occur later that night. Cooley had arranged for fireworks to light the sky at midnight on July 4 while Jimi Hendrix played his version of "The Star Spangled Banner." Hendrix had agreed to the special effects but apparently forgot about them because he jumped into the air when the firework display surprised him.

A nearby jam stage had been set up and was well-used and much-enjoyed throughout the weekend. The music was the better part of the festival experience. Since the police had decided that drugs would not be an issue, vendors not only freely sold illegal pharmaceuticals but advertised them through the use of menus and hat-check girls. There was a suggestion from someone on the stage to "roll a joint and share with your brothers and sisters."

Those at the festival were a mixed bunch of flower children, rednecks, blacks, whites, liberals, and conservatives—the entire variety of Georgia's society. Everybody got along, accepting each other that day as equals. Few had a problem with the rampant nakedness as people battled the extreme heat in the most natural way possible. Motorcycle clubs continued to be a part of the unscripted "security" and stood with menacing looks at the admission gate. This time it was mostly the Outlaws, which were a tad tamer than the Angels. When the bikers started to take their roles too seriously by the final day, the festival was evidently declared to be "free."

The festival was fun for some, a headache for others, but all-in-all was not a Woodstock-type moment in time. "[The festivals] were two different types of crowds and atmospheres," says Johnny Winter.

Cooley decided not to throw a third festival. That wasn't the end of the line for Cooley, though. He would continue his music promotion career as the region's premier presenter of music as well as many years later establishing Atlanta's popular Music Midtown festival.

Goose Lake International Music Festival
August 7–9, 1970

It was just a matter of time before a massive music festival hit the Midwest. Jackson, Michigan would host almost 200,000 for a festival with a large and inclusive bill. The event was organized by Russ Gibb, who had brought rock music to the ears of millions of aficionados through his work as a radio personality and his ownership of Detroit's

Grande Ballroom. (Gibb was also the innovator of call-in radio and the deejay who launched the infamous "Paul is Dead" Beatles controversy.)

It was no surprise to the organizers when the city fathers of Leoni Township adamantly opposed the festival and threatened litigation. The actions of the townspeople were ineffective but set a dark mood for the celebration. Once inside the razor-wire fences of the festival, attendees were forbidden to re-enter the grounds. Helicopter patrols circled over the festival but local police made the decision to only intervene if necessary as they feared a riot if they were to make drug arrests. Drugs were rampant and the police state of the festival caused a certain degree of animosity that couldn't help but sour the mood of those who came to hear the music.

Performing were some of the (by now) almost expected festival-act bands such as Jethro Tull, Ten Years After, John Sebastian, Mountain, and Chicago. Rod Stewart was a special guest as were the Flying Burrito Brothers. John Drake Shake, RAM, Litter, Flock 3, Mighty Quick, Power, and Suite Charity played, but it was the exciting "local" bands such as Bob Seger and the Silver Bullet Band, SRC, Savage Grace, the James Gang, Iggy Pop and the Stooges, and Brownsville Station that stole the show. (Joe Cocker, Savoy Brown, and Alice Cooper had been scheduled to perform but did not.) The acts were exciting, but probably the most interesting—if perplexing—moment of the festival from the stage was provided by Iggy Pop. Pop and his Stooges gave their usual distinctive performance but that performance went on . . . and on . . . and on. A rotating stage was being used so that the next act could set up while the first act was playing, and a decision was made to "ride" the Stooges off and introduce Mountain, who waited patiently for the Stooges' set to end. As Mountain began to play, Pop flew out of the wings, jumped on Mountain guitarist Leslie West's back, and hit him repeatedly in the head. West, a large man, responded by shaking Pop, a scrawny man, off his back and beating him with his guitar. Pop ran offstage and Mountain's set continued. It was just another day at a festival.

Isle of Wight Festival
August 26–29, 1970

"You're acting like tourists. Give us some respect!"
—Joni Mitchell

A new wave of rockers was coming through the festival gate but some of those people by now seemed infested with hard drugs and a bad attitude. The mellow, everyone-is-equal, atmosphere had begun to deteriorate into a paranoid sense of entitlement. Those who attended festivals began to catch on that many of the musicians who performed for them were asking for—and receiving—large sums of money for just showing up. They began to grumble that too many of the performers were arriving at the shows so high on drugs that they didn't deliver a good show. It was one thing for the spectators to be high and loose, but they weren't being paid the big bucks. A "show me" attitude began to develop and many times that mind-set was well-embedded even before anyone took the stage. The bands that appeared at festivals grew apprehensive. They liked playing to a crowd that was just there to enjoy the music and didn't put them on notice that they had better produce. Those who attended the festivals, on the other hand, now felt that they shouldn't have to pay for any of the music, that if the musicians truly felt in sync with them as a people, they shouldn't expect to be paid but would want to play for the love of the music and the festival experience alone. The collective festival attitude was beginning to turn ominous and resentful.

The 1970 Isle of Wight Festival at Afton Down would become known as Woodstock—U.K. and was the largest British festival to date. It was "the biggest gathering of humanity I ever fucking saw," says Shawn Phillips, who performed.

The Foulk brothers' Fiery Creations, along with promoter Rikki Farr, had enjoyed the success of their previous festivals and decided that it was time to expand. On August 26-29, 1970 approximately 500,000 people gathered at East Afton Farm. Many notable bands and artists were scheduled to perform including Jimi Hendrix, the Doors, the Moody Blues, Jethro Tull, Joni Mitchell, Joan Baez, and the Who. The super band of Emerson, Lake & Palmer would make its large-audience debut. The band had played only once before in a club. But the significance of their appearance did not seem to make a notable impression on at least one of the band members: Keith Emerson remembers it this way. "I got in and I got out as quickly as possible. I was home sleeping peacefully in my small London bedsit by the time the Who went onstage at around 2 a.m."

The local people of the Isle had thus far been cooperative, even though they were more than a little anxious when the numbers of the revelers continued to increase. They worried that the reputation of the family-friendly resort had been compromised by the sometimes unclean, unsanitary, naked "hippies." But by September 1969, the citizens of the Isle were up in arms. A fourteen-person committee was appointed by the Isle of Wight County Council to address the issue of pop festivals in general. The report they made, based on the data and experiences of the previous year's festival, was not complementary. Alderman Mark Woodnutt, who represented the island, wanted to see legislation enacted by Parliament that would place restrictions on pop festivals. Ray Foulks was at a meeting sponsored by the Wootton and Fairlee Ratepayers and Residents Association to represent the proposed 1970 festival. The people at the meeting, including some politicians and many residents, were vocal about their distaste for yet another large gathering of untamed youth. Woodnutt claimed that the lack of sanitation at such events was a health risk to residents and suggested legislation that would limit a gathering of people to 500 with only fifty being allowed to camp overnight. Ray Foulk, who was called on the carpet for the previous festival's road congestion, sanitation problems, and loud music, acquiesced and suggested to the crowd that if the residents of the Isle of Wight did not want another festival, the promoters could go somewhere else. Foulk made it clear, however, that the promoters were looking for a bigger, more appropriate site on the island that would handle the numbers expected and hey, hadn't the previous festival brought in money for the area's economy? Finally, the committee asked that a compromise be reached. They would cease complaint if the promoters agreed to an appropriate plan to address the issues raised. Some of the residents threw half-baked death threats and continued to make a lot of noise, but the plans for the festival continued.

The Foulks scouted around but couldn't find an acceptable site. They began to look at a location on the other side of the island. A site in East Afton was selected but the Foulks' decision was immediately met with complaints from the National Farmers Union. The promoters agreed to a one million pound bond to cover damage to farm property and finally, after weeks and weeks of confrontation, discussion, and compromise (including an agreement to supply additional sanitation facilities, security, fencing, with local representation and bonding), the site was secured. All this was only the beginning of the Foulks' problems.

There was also a clamor from others who had taken an interest in the event. There was the huge element of those who thought that music festivals—for the people, by the people—should be free. They protested. The Hell's Angels, who had been providing security for most of the festival events in Britain weren't happy that they were being denied access to this latest celebration. They protested. The White Panthers, representing their new order, thought the festival would be an opportune time to voice their agenda. They protested. Activists from Germany, France, and the United States demanded their right to be heard. They chimed in. Even the bands were creating controversy. Their liberal inclusiveness had put them in a dominant public position and many festival devotees were beginning to think the bands were getting a little too big for their britches. Some people felt the artists weren't respecting the fans by refusing to play for free, and more often. The underground press blasted the promoters for wanting to make a profit. Everyone seemed to have something to say.

The site chosen for the festival was not the best. A hill overlooked the stage and those who chose not to pay admittance could easily hear—if not see—the music. Once the droves of celebrants began to arrive, many set up tents along the top of the hill, which was dubbed "Desolation Row." The usually gloomy English weather was surprisingly favorable but it was no surprise that a number of people who showed up to participate hadn't bought tickets. Security, along with their guard dogs, covered the gates and fencing to discourage free entry. There was a lot of pushing and shoving.

On Wednesday, August 26, 1970 the first music of the festival was finally, after months of complicated planning, reaching the ears of the audience. The entertainment, like the mood of the festival, was exceptional. "From the point of view of actually performing, the bands that got across were generally the most demonstrative," remembers Pentangle's John Renbourne. "It paid to play loud and work in big gestures. The sight of the audience spanning out as far as the eye could see added to the general unreality. Sound checks were minimal and sound crews embraced the good-time spirit along with everybody else. So the actual playing was really a low spot. More a case of having got through it, or imagining so."

Judas Jump opened the festival. Also performing that day were Mighty Baby, Kathy Smith (who later became known for supplying John Belushi with his fatal drug overdose), and Rosalie Sorrels, who played with David Bromberg as her guitarist. Bromberg would then play his own, unscheduled set. Howl and Redbone performed. Kris Kristofferson had a bad moment when the crowd booed the bad sound (which was later set right) and Kristofferson left the stage in disgust part-way through "Me and Bobbie McGee." (He would return for a better set on Sunday.)

On Thursday, August 27, Gilberto Gil had the crowd dancing with his Tropicalia music. Black Widow, Andy Roberts Everyone, Terry Reid, Howl, Gary Farr, and Supertramp also took the stage. To many who came to the festival, Supertramp was a new band to them as it was before their massively successful album *Breakfast in America*.

The Groundhogs also played that day. But they already had an education in the variables of music festivals. "I remember being driven to the ferry and telling our driver to step on it, as I thought we were going to miss the one we were booked on," the band's Tony McPhee remembers. "We did make it okay, and on the boat was the guy who was drumming for Blodwyn Pig at the time and who we knew quite well. At the site we were met by Rikki Farr, Gary's brother, who was stage managing and organizing all the band's onstage times. At the time when Blodwyn Pig was due to go on, Rikki was told that their drummer hadn't arrived yet (which we knew was a fib!). So we were asked to go on instead, earlier than when we were originally told. Just two weeks before, on August 15, we had arrived at Krumlin to play the ill-fated Yorkshire Folk, Jazz, and Blues Festival (a day late owing to our then-manager's uselessness), and were told they would let us play *if* they could fit us in. [Musician] Jo Ann Kelly came to see us as soon as we arrived and told us we probably wouldn't get paid as there were a load of forged tickets and one of the promoters had disappeared across the moors. So there was a large audience, they expected 50,000; sitting in the most miserable conditions, the site was a quagmire owing to heavy rainfall, looking at an empty stage as nobody wanted to go until they got paid. Our attitude was that we traveled all that way, we were going to play, paid or not. So we went on and entertained a very appreciative audience. The photos taken at that festival were used for *Split*, our biggest selling album. So we were determined never to get involved in backstage politics at festivals and it worked for us later."

Friday August 28 would feature Tony Joe White, the Voices of East Harlem (a children's choral group who had the crowd on their feet through two standing ovations), Lighthouse (who would play again the following day), Arrival, Family, Cactus, and Fairfield Parlour (formally known as Kaleidoscope). "It was a happening," says Tony Joe White. "Over six hundred thousand people in this big valley and every singer and musician that I liked were there. I was gonna play alone, but Cozy Powell, Jeff Beck's drummer, joined me onstage and we rocked."

Taste was on the bill, but they would soon part ways, allowing Rory Gallagher to pursue a satisfactory solo career. Also performing were Procol Harem, and Chicago, who closed the show amid roaring approval.

Throughout the days of the festival plainclothes policemen, dressed in hippie garb, cruised the site. Evidently their directive was to only intervene if there was a problem (similar to many other festivals), so drugs were freely available and liberally ingested. But by the weekend, seventy-three arrests had been made. That figure actually wasn't bad for a crowd of such size. "Situations" arose when Hells Angels and Skinheads were told they could not bring weapons into the festival and balked when their shivs and clubs were to be relinquished before they could board the ferry carrying people to the festival. On a more positive note, small gatherings of religious factions were present to help anyone in need, and medical tents were available for first aid and drug-related problems.

In the meantime, the bands were being paid in cash as they took the stage. Rikki Farr claimed that was an expected element of the unstable nature of a music festival. "A recurring sub-theme was money—getting paid," says John Renbourne. "From what I heard, most festival promoters pulled a flanker of some kind, and it might be interesting to find out just how many bands got what they thought they had coming to them. The Isle of Wight boys called themselves something like 'Fiery Creations' and apparently lived up to it by burning a bunch of acts."

When it came to paying the talent at festivals, this situation was evidently not the worst. "The Crumlin festival was the classic," recalls Renbourne. "Ludicrously situated way out in the moors somewhere, bands and equipment stranded, and the promoter [was] caught legging it out across the tundra with the proceeds. Reportedly 'suffering from amnesia.'"

Up on the hill, over 5,000 watched as a hot air balloon advertising the *Daily Express* glided over the festival. The promoters weren't happy with the "free" music these people were enjoying. Security drifted through the crowd asking for "donations." Perhaps they received some, but the festival mood was changing. The political rabble-rousers were doing their job and doing it well. The crowd in front of the stage was watching a terrific show but the politicos were wandering the festival stirring up trouble. A number of "plants" urged those who had not paid to demand their right to a free concert. They shouted, they yelled, they name-called—whatever it took to get the attention of both the crowd and the organizers of the event. (At one point a frustrated Rikki Farr yelled from the stage that they could all "go to hell!")

Opening the show on Saturday, August 29 was the duo Good News. Saturday would bring another diverse roster of talent from solo artists Shawn Phillips, Leonard Cohen, Donovan, and Joni Mitchell. As Mitchell sang "Woodstock," a scruffy hippie named Yogi Joe wiggled on stage to "talk" to Mitchell and make her and the audience aware of the situation on Desolation Row. In a more traditional music setting Yogi Joe would have been thrown off the stage by security, but this time security first tried to "persuade" him to leave the stage. When that didn't work, the stage crew hauled him off as the crowd jeered. The incident left Mitchell shaken. She admonished the crowd that they were "acting like tourists. Give us some respect!"

John Sebastian took the stage and played for nearly eighty minutes. His set included a surprise appearance by his former Lovin' Spoonful guitarist Zal Yanovsky.

Shawn Phillips followed Sebastian, although Phillips originally was not even on the bill. "I was living in Italy at the time and had just come up to London to give my new songs to my then-publisher Dick James," recalls Phillips. "Somebody asked me if I wanted to go to a festival and I said sure. We got into a private single-engine aircraft and arrived there. I was never actually booked or scheduled to officially play. During the second day, somehow or other, one of the bands or artists had to cancel, or couldn't be found, and they had to find someone to fill in. I don't even remember who came to me to ask if I wanted to play, but I said yes, of course. I got up there and did a set of tunes that I was familiar with at the time, which was actually most of *2nd Contribution*. I remember the crowd giving me standing ovations in the middle of the set and an ovation after the set that lasted almost eight minutes. You can imagine the energy from that 650,000-strong crowd, but I have to be honest and tell you that [the festival] made no difference to my career professionally. Ironically enough, I was the only person who wasn't filmed at that festival."

There were performances by jazz entities like Miles Davis and Lighthouse. "When Miles Davis took the stage I was standing behind one of the amps on stage," remembers Shawn Phillips. "I remember being totally flabbergasted by the fact that what they were playing was being created on the spot. It was the single most amazing improvisation I have ever heard, even to this day. The flow of ideas between the players that led to incredible sections of interacting rhythms, and jamming, and then Miles would play a single note and the entire piece would shift dramatically into another mood. *Nobody* plays like that anymore. It was, simply, an extraordinary moment in musical history. I did understand that it was so advanced that ninety percent of the crowd didn't know what the fuck had just happened."

One of the powerhouse bands that played was the Who, and they played throughout the night and were, as usual, a crowd-pleaser. The majority of those at the festival seemed to agree with the lyrics of their song "Young Man Blues," which postured youth as having "nothin' in the world these days."

The crowd was interested to hear the music of the Doors. Singer Jim Morrison, looking tired and drunk but making an effort to stay in tune, had refused those making a film the opportunity to spotlight him, and his decision caused the band's set to be performed in virtual darkness. The Doors seemed out of place.

Emerson, Lake & Palmer were playing together as a band for only the second time. They were more theatrics than music, with Keith Emerson dressed in flashy clothes and playing his organ while suspended upside down.

Ten Years After delivered their usual entertaining set. "Woodstock was considered the event of the century and everyone was wondering if the Isle of Wight would be another Woodstock," remembers bass player Leo Lyons. "That was never going to be possible, particularly after the [*Woodstock*] movie. I think Woodstock had more of a political overtone. America was in an unpopular war. I think people wanted to change things. The Isle of Wight, aside from a group of political gatecrashers demanding that all festivals should be free, seemed more relaxed. Maybe I felt that way because I'm English. I enjoyed both gigs tremendously. I had more time to see other bands at the Isle of Wight."

And there was Tiny Tim, singing "There'll Always be an England" with the audience engaged in a robust sing-along. Tiny was excited about appearing at the festival but found "that terrible marijuana" distasteful. He wasn't the only one. The undercover officers asked Rikki Farr to make an announcement that they would offer "amnesty" to any one under the age of seventeen who handed in their drugs. It is doubtful there were any takers.

Outside the festival grounds, Hawkwind (who played intermittent sets from Thursday through Monday) and the Pink Fairies (who played during the weekend), performed on a second platform called Canvas City. The concerts were free, but the bands collected spare change to feed those at the festival who had run out of money.

In the meantime, things were heating up on Desolation Row. The fence that had been erected in order to appease the citizens of the Isle of Wight was a major bone of contention. The activists urged the people to tear it down in protest. Rikki Farr claimed that the fence had been erected to also protect the people inside the festival, but many in the crowd weren't having that. The promoters gave a group of people over 300 gallons of paint and told them to "paint the fence invisible." What they painted were anti-establishment slogans, swastikas, and four-letter expletives. When activists tried to yell down the organizers, claiming that festivals were just another way for "the man" to exploit the masses, tempers began to flare. And so did the stage when a spotlight exploded that evening and the stage was briefly set afire.

Sunday, August 30, the last day of the festival was ushered in with the melodies of Melanie. The folk-pop artist had been made to wait quite awhile before performing and didn't know when—or if—she was actually going to take the stage. She had left the festival site but was persuaded to return as the Who's set went on and on. . . and on. Upon Melanie's arrival backstage, she was briefly entertained by Keith Moon (a person unknown to her at the time), who attempted to raise her spirits.

After Melanie finally was allowed to perform, Sly and the Family Stone roused the crowd with their infectious dance and boogie tunes. Yet even they were subjected to a difficult time. Before they could come back for their encore, someone jumped on the stage to harangue the audience about politics. The crowd booed the intruder but someone threw a beer can that hit Freddie Stone. Sly and Family decided they'd had enough and left.

Joan Baez and Leonard Cohen performed, although both artists seemed better suited to a coffeehouse. (In regard to the debate over admission, Baez claimed that for some, "If I charged fifteen cents that would be too much.")

The show continued with musicians being brought to the stage by any means possible. "The seemingly simple logistics of arrival and departure became a major consideration and a matter of one-upmanship among the ranks of performers," says John Renbourne. "The straggling aftermath of a big festival is something along the lines of Napoleon's retreat from Moscow. Once is enough. Vans just didn't do it. But helicopters did. John Paul Jones takes credit for that brilliant idea. It was the answer all right. Just great for those bands coming in and going out. Not so great for those stuck on stage knocking it out amidst the din."

Ralph McTell was well-received by the audience, but his manager berated the promoters when McTell was asked to leave the stage before his encore so that Donovan could set up for his set. Pentangle was interrupted by yet another political trouble-maker. Good News, Heaven, and Donovan, playing both an acoustic and electric set, performed.

Free was very popular at the time and their set was well-received. "When Paul Rodgers and Free played I was out front in the audience, maybe a hundred yards from the front of the stage," remembers Shawn Phillips. "The day was fading fast and the skies were turning a deep orange when they went into the song 'All right Now.' At the precise moment they sang the chorus 'All right now, baby its'a all right now,' a huge purple-and-yellow air balloon rose up from behind the stage and majestically floated away in the distance, over a crowd of humanity that was literally spread out further than the eye could see, until it disappeared. A wonderful ecstatic moment."

The Moody Blues were there. The intricate melodies of the eclectic band should have been hard to pull off, and probably were, but they sounded very close to their studio recordings. Especially appreciated was a heart-felt version of "Knights in White Satin."

An incident peripherally involving Jethro Tull had broken out earlier in the day. In an effort to stem their increasing hemorrhage of money loss, the promoters wanted those in the area down front to leave and re-enter so as to discourage and disperse those who had snuck in for free. Naturally, those who didn't pay were not going to leave and abandon their coveted spot near the stage. One of the organizers admonished people that if they didn't leave, Jethro Tull couldn't do their sound check and thus wouldn't be able to perform. Tull's manager Terry Ellis was livid that it was being implied that Tull would not play unless they had been paid. "Don't blame it on the artist," Ellis firmly entreated. "There are a thousand different things to pay for. Don't tell our public we're holding out for bread." Ellis and the members of Tull were not amused as they had said no such thing. When Tull took the stage that night, front man Ian Anderson called the statement "crap." Jethro Tull then played a spirited and entertaining set.

Sections of the stage had by now been pulled down as well as the fences. The rabble rousers, many of them American, had received what they wanted: a disruption of the festival. Yet in the end the music won out. For most of the people in attendance, the quality and abundance of the music had been worth the problems and interruptions.

Jimi Hendrix had thought the festival would be "a drag." He now thought festivals were a joke. Little did he know that this festival would be his last public appearance as he didn't have long to live.

"My first experience of Jimi Hendrix," remembers John Renbourne. "Something that has stayed in the mind. With all the festivals, the knack is to get in and get out as smoothly as possible. I remember we were heading out early to beat the mass exodus and congratulating ourselves just when Hendrix started. The van was parked up on a rise with a clear view down to the arena. And that was that—all totally immobilized for the duration, and stuck in the queue again."

An extremely thin Hendrix had some problems with the sound system but gave a laudable performance, opening with "God Save the Queen." When he continued to have technical problems, he advised the crowd to "go buy some hot dogs."

On August 31 Richie Havens, who had been pushed onstage early to open the Woodstock festival, played "Here Comes the Sun" as the sun rose over the Isle of Wight and closed the festival.

Rikki Farr walked onstage to tell those still in attendance that the promoters had "lost everything" but that wasn't what mattered to them. Farr said all the problems were worth the end result, which was to bring music to those who wanted to listen and to come together. "Go home with some love and some peace," he encouraged the crowd. Farr asked everyone present to join hands and, while a lone guitar played "Amazing Grace," he held up his hands in peace signs that were reflected back at him from the front of the audience. Tears came to Farr's eyes as he said "thank you" and the crowd roared its approval of what the organizers had accomplished.

For reasons both positive and negative many of those who performed that weekend remember that year's Isle of Wight Festival. Yet for some, performing in front of the masses that weekend wouldn't be a defining moment in their personal lives. At least not for Shawn Phillips. "For years I thought that moment was a driving force in my creation of music, but shortly after certifying as a National Registry Emergency Medical Technician (EMT) from a fourteen-month course, I was lead on a call involving an elderly lady who had stepped out of bed too hard and fractured her pelvis," recalls Phillips. "I took great pains to keep her from suffering, with a scoop stretcher and so forth, and when I handed her over to the staff at the ER and told her she was in good hands she grabbed my arm and looked in my eyes and said 'Thank you so much for taking care of me.' And the Isle of Wight disappeared into the distances of my mind."

The festival was over, but many of those who had enjoyed the five days of music and sun didn't want to go home. Many didn't know how they were going to *get home*. An emergency committee was set up on-site, coordinated by Rev. Robert Bowyer, to enlist people to help with the clean-up in order to earn money that would enable them to make their way back to their real lives. Some of those who were leaving and without concern donated leftover food and spare change. The Hampshire Police Department advanced money to young people whose parent's guaranteed payment back to their hometown police departments.

Mark Woodnutt was back in the newspapers saying that he wasn't happy with the public displays of affection and "fornication," and once again stumped for his anti-pop festival legislation. By Monday morning, Ron Foulk (who would later retire on the Isle of Wight) was saying that the Foulk brothers' festival dream had "become a monster" and that the 1970 Isle of Wight Festival would be their last. Rikki Farr called it "The last great event."

The 1970 Isle of Wight *would* be the last substantially-sized festival for some time. "You must remember, at that time the fledgling music industry had not taken control of the radio," explains Shawn Phillips. "The manipulation of the creativity of the musicians for the maximization of profit and the creation of 'formula' music [hadn't taken hold]. The music that was being heard was because of its quality and the very uniqueness of the composers. It was an industry that was not being fueled by the raging hormones of adolescent teenagers and the accessibility to their parents' money. The music was complex and required you to actually listen, and the lyrics reflected the confusion of an entire generation that didn't understand the political forces that were driving the world toward an unethical war that had nothing to do with freedom, or democracy, but was secretly trying to maintain a profitable opium trade in the Golden triangle. The Isle of Wight was a coming together of a huge group of people that basically said 'Hey, let's listen to this amazing music and see if we can't figure out why we're living in a society that is based on 'you be good and we'll reward you, you be bad or contest us and we'll bust your ass.' And above all, you *absolutely have to be a consumer and we're going to exhort and manipulate you to be as competitive as you can possibly be against your neighbor.'* They didn't understand that then, as well as now, the world is controlled by maybe 3,000 people and their singular aim is to make a profit. *Nothing else matters to them!*"

"As to the social implications," says John Renbourne, "the 'significance of the spiritual renaissance,' the 'rise of the consciousness revolution,' and such like, the festivals seem just as likely to have been the result of the combination of two rather basic ingredients. Having been targeted heavily for some time by the record companies to the point that 'underground' music had eventually become commercial, the freaks were ready to fly the flag. To which promoters reacted with a time-honored attitude: lots of punters equals lots of dosh. Maybe some of that sounds a bit jaded, but it is what comes back."

Tony McPhee has seen both the good and bad in festivals. "The early festivals, especially the two Isle of Wight Festivals, mattered because there were some pretty crappy things going on in the world," says McPhee. "Nothing's changed much. They were a way for a diverse audience to find common ground in music. To play in front of a huge crowd as at the Isle of Wight was the easiest and quickest way to increase your fans, so our professional and personal lives were enriched. I think it was a well-run festival. We only stayed for the day, as we had other gigs for that weekend, so I can't really comment about the rest of that festival. I can only admire people that organize festivals. They must be saints, or crazy, or both!"

Vortex I
August 28–September 3, 1970

Festival promoters had experienced both the very good and the very bad by this time. It took a lot of money to launch a festival and many promoters who had climbed aboard the initial festival bandwagon were growing leery of the double threat of townspeople and audiences. Most Americans didn't trust those who attended festivals to behave, and many times with good reason. Yet young people were continuing to make their presence known—loudly and visibly—in the United States and that presence couldn't be ignored. Something was about to take place in the West that would once again validate the music festival.

The Vortex I Festival is not one of the most remembered in rock history but it bears the distinction of being the only rock festival sponsored by a state Governor. In August, 1970 when President Richard Nixon announced that he would be appearing at the American Legion convention in Portland, Oregon to discuss the ongoing Vietnam War, he drew the attention of people other than the Legionnaires. The theme of the convention was "Victory in Vietnam." To demonstrate against the war, the People's Army Jamboree planned an anti-war rally to be held on the same day as Nixon's appearance at the convention. There were over 25,000 Legionnaires expected and the city officials estimated another 50,000 war protesters were on their way into the city to participate in counteraction.

Protests lasting seven days at Portland State College had resulted in dozens of injuries the previous May. The U.S. Department of Justice claimed that Portland had the highest risk of violence in the country that summer and warned the city and state officials that a gathering on the scope and intensity of the Chicago Democratic Convention protest was not only possible but likely. Governor Tom McCall decided to step-in to divert a major clash between the two political factions involved in this latest gathering of opposites. McCall asked the People's Army Jamboree to reschedule their assembly. The organization claimed that they were publicly asking that the workshops and demonstrations that they had planned be held in peace and refused to reschedule. McCall and his advisors put their heads together to think of a way to counter the perceived threat of aggressive protest. They arranged with civic leaders to schedule a rock festival that would be held that week at Milo McIver State Park, near the city of Estacada, Oregon.

The event would be called Vortex I: A Biodegradable Festival of Life. Although it would be rumored that headliners such as Jefferson Airplane, Deep Purple, Jimi Hendrix, and the Grateful Dead would appear, the event featured mostly local bands. Even though rock superstars didn't appear to entertain, the mass of people who showed up to hear music enjoyed themselves. The usual displays of the love and peace generation, such as nudity and hazy contemplation resulting from copious amount of feel-good drugs, were once again present but the festival was primarily one of peace and brotherhood.

In the end, Nixon cancelled his appearance at the last moment, the American Legion enjoyed their parade through the downtown streets of Portland, the Peoples Army Jamboree accomplished their education goals, and the festival went off without incident. And, by the way, Governor McCall was reelected.

1972
Bang a Gong

In U.S. news

Shirley Chisolm is elected the first black Congresswoman; Alabama Governor George Wallace is shot; political burglars break into the Watergate offices; the first Libertarian Party National C.onvention is held; the Supreme Court rules that the death penalty is unconstitutional; actress Jane Fonda tours North Vietnam; and comedian George Carlin is arrested in Milwaukee for reciting "Seven Words You Can Never Say on Television."

In world news

Bloody Sunday occurs in Northern Ireland; Nixon travels to China; and Nixon and Brezhnev sign the SALT I and Anti-Ballistic Treaties.

In music news

A Led Zeppelin concert is cancelled in Singapore when officials won't let the band off the plane because of their long hair; John and Yoko co-host mainstream America's *Mike Douglas Show*; New York Mayor John Lindsay says he'll support Lennon in his bid to remain in the U.S.; and Billy Preston is the first rock act to play Radio City Music Hall.

Some of the year's most notable albums

Mott the Hoople: *All the Young Dudes*; the Eagles: *The Eagles*; the Rolling Stones: *Exile on Main Street*; Yes: *Fragile*; Neil Young: *Harvest*; David Bowie: *The Rise and Fall of Ziggy Stardust and the Spiders from Mars*.

Rock's most popular songs

"Horse with No Name"—America; "All the Young Dudes"—Mott the Hoople; "American Pie"—Don McLean; "Heart of Gold"—Neil Young; "Layla"—Derek & the Dominos; "Nights in White Satin"—Moody Blues; "Rock and Roll Parts 1 & 2"—Gary Glitter; "School's Out"—Alice Cooper; "Take it Easy"—the Eagles.

Mount Pocono Festival
July 8–9, 1972

> *"Many of the acts had other concerts to get to the following day so everyone was trying to get on stage as soon as possible and then try to get all their equipment and crews out of this total mess called the Pocono's Festival."*
>
> —Chuck Negron, Three Dog Night

The Mount Pocono Festival remains in the minds of many who attended as a really lousy couple of days. The festival was held on July 8–9, 1972 in Long Pond, Pennsylvania and featured important bands such as Emerson, Lake & Palmer, J. Geils Band, Badfinger, Humble Pie, Three Dog Night, Rod Stewart, Edgar Winter, and the Groundhogs. While over 200,000 people ultimately attended, the festival doesn't seem to remain high on anyone's list of meaningful experiences. The first day was cold, torrential rain followed, and the by the next day it was *really* cold . . . and wet . . . and muddy.

It was one of those festivals where lots of people were there, but outside of the weather, few remember the details of the festival. "We still detested backstage politics when we played the Pocono Festival in 1972," remembers Tony McPhee of the Groundhogs. "We weren't surprised when we went on early in the day, just after Claire Hamill. As we came off stage after our final number, 'Cherry Red' of course, I felt a spot of rain on my face. That turned into torrential rain until about 6 p.m. We were shown on national TV as they turned up to cover the whole festival, but the rain [changed the broadcast]."

"We were the headliners for that festival and due to rain and delays we had to wait all night long before we could get on stage," remembers Three Dog Night's Chuck Negron. "Many of the acts had other concerts to get to the following day so everyone was trying to get on stage as soon as possible, and then try to get all their equipment and crews out of this total mess called the Poconos Festival. Emerson Lake & Palmer's roadies and the Rod Stewart management and crew tried to get on the stage at the same time, which resulted in an all-out fist fight on stage."

The music may—or may not—have been good, but trying to enjoy the total festival experience was difficult for those who attended. They would have to either travel, or wait for another festival to come to town.

Erie Canal Soda Pop Festival
September, Labor Day Weekend, 1972

"The place looked like Woodstock, only wetter."
—Tommy Chong

The wait for the next festival wasn't long. The summer of 1972 would conclude with a large event in Illinois. The perception of music festivals by the general public was now more a consensus than the opinion of a few: music festivals brought too many people, too many drugs, and too many problems. On the other hand, if you didn't mind getting wet, facing the hostility of the locals, and being exposed to people near you being stoned or tripping, the music was usually pretty good and you could have a decent time. Still, the excitement of the music festival just wasn't what it once was. It was somewhere to go and hear bands you might not otherwise have the opportunity to hear but getting through the event could be a pain in the ass.

The promoters hung in there, through mountains of permits and legal work and complaints from residents and fans alike. The music festival seemed to be a challenge to those in that business. Where others had failed to make a profit, the gamble to pull it all off was intriguing. Like moths to the flame, promoters would continue to give it a shot.

Tom Duncan and Bob Alexander were next to step up. The two promoters had organized a small, successful music festival in Evansville, Indiana featuring Ike and Tina Turner, Johnny Winter, and the New Riders of the Purple Sage at the start of the summer. Duncan and Alexander were excited to repeat the experience, only this time the plan was to include more performers. They anticipated maybe 50,000 or so would attend. The Erie Canal Soda Pop Festival was to take place in Chandler, just a hop, skip, and a jump from Evansville. But the people of Chandler had been hearing about the current state of music festivals and they wanted nothing to do with Duncan and Alexander's plan. Being successful where other outraged locals had been stymied, a demand by those in the area to ban the festival from taking place reached the courts and resulted in the temporary barring of large festivals anywhere in Indiana. The festival site was moved to Bull Island, a 900-acre piece of land not far from Griffin, Indiana that was technically east of the state line, on the Wabash River in Illinois near the small city of Carmi. The quick change of location prohibited the people of that small town from gathering the necessary steam to prevent the festival and plans moved forward.

The complicated location of the site allowed a place for the promoters to have their festival but caused massive problems with transportation. There were only two roads into the area and by the opening day of the festival, traffic was backed up nearly twenty miles. Because the island bordered both Indiana and Illinois, law enforcement was not only minimal but uncoordinated. By the time over 200,000 people arrived at the festival (with an estimate of 100,000 more to come), the only police presence was three White County deputy sheriffs.

The promoters sold thousands of tickets based on an advertised bill that included the Eagles, Black Sabbath, the Allman Brothers, Nazareth, Fleetwood Mac, Bob Seger, and many other name performers. Because the final location wasn't decided on until the last minute, many of the bands who initially committed pulled out. There was so much confusion that perhaps they doubted whether anything good could come of their participation. When Joe Cocker's management showed up at the site and saw what was going on, his performance fee was allegedly doubled. The promoters refused to pay and Cocker did not appear. In the end, only a handful of bands even showed up to perform: Black Oak Arkansas (who provided the sun-beaten crowd with sun visors which were dropped from a helicopter before the band took the stage); the Eagles (who were just beginning their radio dynasty); Gentle Giant (who left the stage soon after taking it, claiming that the sound was wrong and the organ that they relied on was out of tune); Brownsville Station; Canned Heat; Foghat; Albert King; Cheech and Chong; Fanny; Birtha; and Flash Cadillac & the Continental Kids. Although thousands of tickets had been sold in advance, Sunday morning the ticket booth was shoved over and the festival was declared what else? "Free." Ravi Shankar played during the morning of the third day and asked, as he had at Monterey Pop, that the already high-flying crowd abstain from using drugs during his performance.

To some the festival was noteworthy for reasons other than the music. "The one thing I remember was the five or six hours we spent driving, trying to get to the stage so we could perform," recalls Tommy Chong. "The van we were in crawled along so slow that people were walking faster than we were driving. It had been raining off and on during the whole event. The place looked like Woodstock, only wetter. When we finally got to the stage we found the cash trailer (the trailer where bands were paid) and collected our fee. Then we went on stage and watched the all-girl group Fanny perform. They were great looking, and great sounding, females. They could rock out.

Another rain squall hit while they were on and the plastic sheets covering the stage filled up with rainwater right over the center stage. The tarp filled up until it was over-flowing with a waterfall coming directly center stage in front of the singers. I got a little worried because there was a lot of electricity on that stage and I was afraid someone was going to be hurt. But the Gods of Rock were taking care of their own that night and no one was even scratched. The [back] stage resembled a mini-concert with all the roadies and other band guys mingling with the sound crew and their girlfriends."

People were disappointed that the rain was ruining their good time. As the summer downpour turned the ground into mud, and food and water started to run short, the mood of the festival turned dismal. The abundance of drugs didn't help. Lack of food became a serious problem until the Salvation Army appeared to dole out free soup. When a truck carrying food onto the festival grounds was spotted, the drivers were yanked out of their cab, the contents of the truck off-loaded and looted, and the truck itself burned in protest.

The festival sagas of life and death remained true. A young woman was flown out by helicopter to deliver a baby at nearby Welborn Baptist Hospital, but a young man drowned in the nearby river. Another person was run over while asleep in his sleeping bag. Cheech Marin announced that people should "be careful" and told the audience about the fatality, but they thought it was part of Cheech & Chong's comedy routine.

"When Cheech and I finally took the stage, it was about ten at night and the rain suddenly stopped, the huge crowd listened while we went through our routines, laughing at the right time and howling at all the pot jokes," remembers Tommy Chong. "I believe Cheech did make some announcements about swimming in the river but I don't remember his exact words. We only performed for about a half-hour, if I remember, because it was very hard to gauge the response, so it was on and off like 'wham bam thank you ma'am.' You know, I don't remember how we got out of there. Apparently we were supposed to have a helicopter at our disposal; however, I think it was being used for a coke run. . . as in Coca Cola. You know, for as much drugs there was at that event, neither Cheech nor I got high at that gig. I remember wanting to be sharp and alert that night because of the enormous challenge it was entertaining 30,000 or so stoned folks. We had to be sober to carry that one off."

The crowd had been entertained but still was not happy. When the last act finished playing, a group of people set fire to the stage. It was an unhappy ending to an unsatisfied weekend of "festivities." *Evansville Courier* reporter David M. Berry described those leaving the festival as looking similar to a line of refugees from a "war-torn country." These migrants were "tired, dirty, disillusioned, hungover, drugged," according to Berry.

By the time it was all said and done, the promoters of the Erie Canal Soda Pop Festival found themselves facing lawsuits from various local and state entities, vendors, the IRS, and the owner of the island itself. Damages were reported from corporate sponsors including Coca-Cola, Hertz, and local ice and food concessioners. The promoters were made responsible for a $52,000 lien by the IRS. Over fifty land owners in Posey County filed suit. The era of Peace and Love appeared over.

1973-1976
Dream On

In U.S. news

Nixon is elected president; Atari video games debut; Frank Serpico exposes corruption in the New York City Police Department; representatives of the American Indian Movement occupy Wounded Knee; the first hand held cell phone is manufactured; the DEA is established; the Watergate scandal rocks the country and Nixon resigns.

In world news

The Olympic athletes massacre occurs in Munich; International Human Rights Day is proclaimed by the United Nations; the Paris Peace Accords ends U.S. involvement in Vietnam; the first release of POWs from Vietnam takes place; Brezhnev and Nixon meet to talk; and the oil embargo crisis occurs.

In music news

Elvis appears via satellite in the "Aloha from Hawaii" special; the Rolling Stones headline a benefit concert for Nicaraguan earthquake victims; and Lou Reed is bitten by a fan during a concert.

Some of the year's most notable albums

Pink Floyd: *Dark Side of the Moon;* the Eagles: *Desperado;* Elton John: *Don't Shoot Me I'm Only the Piano Player*; Bruce Springsteen: *Greetings from Asbury Park, NJ;* Led Zeppelin: *Houses of the Holy;* Stevie Wonder: *Innervisions;* New York Dolls: *New York Dolls;* Lynyrd Skynyrd: *Pronounced Leh'-nerd Skin'-nerd;* the Who: *Quadrophenia;* Queen: *Queen*; Black Sabbath: *Sabbath Bloody Sabbath.*

Rock's most popular songs

"Bad, Bad Leroy Brown"—Jim Croce; "Ballroom Blitz"—the Sweet; "Frankenstein"—Edgar Winter; "Money"—Pink Floyd; "Radar Love"—Golden Earring; "Ramblin Man"—Allman Brothers Band; "Angie"—the Rolling Stones; "Crocodile Rock"—Elton John.

Watkins Glen Summer Jam
July 28, 1973

It had been almost a year since the debacle that was the Erie Canal Soda Pop Festival. Promoters Shelly Finkel and Jim Kopnik had organized a Grateful Dead concert at Roosevelt Stadium in New Jersey but decided it was time to bring the large music festival back home to the state of New York by staging an event on July 28, 1973, in Watkins Glen. Woodstock was still remembered fondly among the community of music and young people, but four years had passed since that glorious event. The Vietnam War was slowly ending and the youth of America seemed weary of their political activism. Young people were ready to party again and a festival seemed the perfect outlet for the dark days of the past few years. Watkins Glen, located on Seneca Lake, one of New York's Finger Lakes, seemed an appropriate entertainment venue as it was the site of the annual Watkins Glen Grand Prix.

Where Woodstock had been a diverse bill of music artists, rock subgenres, and was a three-day festival, Watkins Glen would feature only three bands: the Grateful Dead, The Band, and the Allman Brothers Band, who would each perform over the course of one day. The bands chosen to appear were all established acts with extremely loyal fans. The plan was to charge an admittance of $10. When the promoters announced the bill, they said that they expected 75,000 people to attend. After the various permits were issued the number rose to 150,000.

People liked the idea of another New York music festival and thousands headed to Watkins Glen. By Tuesday, July 24, there were so many people gathered that the decision was made to open the ticket gates and let people in to enjoy makeshift camps and "hang out." By Wednesday there were 50,000 people, by Thursday 100,000, and by Friday over 250,000 people were in attendance to enjoy the festival. While 150,000 tickets were initially sold, the festival would follow in the footsteps of previous enterprises and later be declared "free." By the day of the festival over 600,000 people were there: the largest gathering for a music festival—or anything else for that matter—in the history of the United States to date (according to the Guinness Book of Records).

The traffic situation was once again a grave concern. On Friday, New York State troopers closed the roads to thru traffic and actually tried to turn away even those with tickets. Traffic was backed up at first over fifty, and then one hundred miles. The State troopers set up roadblocks and signs were placed on the New York Thruway that the festival was sold out in hopes that people would (somehow) turn back. Cars were left abandoned on the highway as people tried to walk to the site. Watkins Glen

Police Chief A.T. Elsworth claimed that the "kids" weren't coming for the music, but rather in an attempt to create another Woodstock.

As always, security continued to be a problem but although there were some arrests for altercations, overt drug use, and destruction of property, there was nothing particularly bad to act on. State and County Police were able to do their jobs without interference from the mass of people and the mood of the crowd remained fairly composed. The Village of Watkins Glen, on the other hand, was left without such important amenities as mail delivery or police protection.

Bill Graham provided twelve sizable amplifiers for the stage. (It has been said Graham "donated" the amps but Graham wasn't one known for actually *donating* equipment so this seems questionable.) The bands involved obviously wanted to check their sound and the day before the concert those gathered were treated to The Band as well as the Allman Brothers Band actually playing a few numbers, and then the Grateful Dead took the stage for a long improvised set. At nightfall, amid an unseasonable frost, campfires were seen across the ninety-five acres of the festival site. (According to *Rolling Stone* magazine, one of the roadies present thought it looked like a scene from the Civil War.)

On the day of the festival, the bands certainly gave those who braved the traffic and inconveniences a good return on their investment in the event. It had been raining on and off all day but that didn't stop people from dancing to the gypsy music of the Grateful Dead, who came on at noon. The Dead played for five hours.

The Band took the stage at 6 p.m. but were interrupted for thirty minutes by a thunderstorm. They returned to play over three hours (during the rain and subsequent interruption Garth Hudson continued to play his organ to the delight of the crowd).

The Allman Brothers Band closed the show with a four-hour set. But wait: there's more. Members of all three bands gathered on stage to jam on "Johnny B. Goode," "Not Fade Away," and Duane and Gregg Allman's (who wrote the song along with Donavan) "Mountain Jam."

While the music was top-notch, the jam aspects of the acts created an entertaining but somewhat monotonous music atmosphere. Long instrument solos and intermittent song lyrics were hypnotic, if not sleep-inducing. Much of the crowd was probably stoned anyway and thousands of them couldn't even see the stage, let alone the musicians.

The mud, drugs, and nudity that seem to be a cornerstone of music festivals were very much a presence and lines for food, drink, and toilets stretched for quite some length. (The portable toilets were overflowing before the concert had even begun.)

There was only one death at Watkin's Glen and it was extraordinary. Willard Smith of Syracuse, New York was a noted skydiver who intended to make an impression on those at the festival by flying through the sky over the audience in a shower of pyrotechnics. Smith had an artillery simulator tucked into the band of his vest that was supposed to ignite at a predetermined point of his dive and create an impressive display. The device went off prematurely and exploded, causing Smith's chest to be impacted. Smith was engulfed in flames and was dead by the time he reached the ground.

A pirate radio station (CFR AM/FM out of Hartford, Connecticut) operated for twelve hours from the site of the festival and broadcast the events as they happened. In exchange for food, those involved with the station agreed to also broadcast information from the State troopers about the roads and highway every thirty minutes. CBS shot footage of the festival and, while the bands had arranged for their sets to be recorded, the Grateful Dead refused to release their images or music without their direct control of content. Since the network refused to honor such an agreement, a proposed album and film documenting the event was scraped.

The aftermath of the festival was not pretty. Tons of garbage was left (which was eventually picked up by members of two large communes who performed the work in exchange for a small amount of money). Area hospitals had treated approximately fifty injuries of those at the festival. Three months later, the promoters would be sued by dozens of area residents claiming that they experienced damage to their property and livestock. (One group of people had been arrested for butchering a farmer's pig in an attempt to have a barbeque.) Settlements were made out of court. Watkins Glen Summer Jam, the largest gathering of young people ever, left a lingering and unforgettable memory in the minds of many.

Ozark Music Festival
July 19–21, 1974

"A lot of us missed Woodstock, including some who were there. The 1974 Sedalia concert sounded like it was going to recapture that show's legendary vibe . . . just like the big time, only . . . smaller."

—John McEuen, Nitty Gritty Dirt Band

With a motto of "No Hassles Guranteed," Musical Productions Inc., out of Kansas City, Missouri organized what they claimed (to state and local officials) would be a bluegrass and pop event entitled the Ozark Music Festival. On the weekend of July 19–21 the festival was held at the Missouri State Fairgrounds in Sedalia, Missouri. The promoters told those concerned that probably no more than 50,000 people or so would show up, which wasn't much more than usually came to the Missouri State Fair (which was also held on the grounds during the summer). They were wrong.

"A lot of us missed Woodstock, including some who were there," says John McEuen of the Nitty Gritty Dirt Band. "The premise of the 1974 Sedalia concert was to recapture that show's legendary vibe . . . just like the big time, only . . . smaller. Well, it started that way, 'smaller.' The word was that although it was doubtful the hyped for 40,000 people would show up, it could still be a great time, like we'd all heard that Woodstock was for many . . . only this time there was money in it for all. Then it grew."

By Friday morning, so many people had arrived in the small town that traffic was so backed up and tangled that driving to work or leaving the city was nearly impossible for those who lived there. Teenaged bodies sat or sprawled on neighborhood lawns and curbs, awaiting the opening of the fairgrounds. The people of Sedalia were horrified.

"First it was finding out a week or so before that yes, there were 50,000 ticket buyers *so far* . . . " remembers McEuen. "Tickets were selling faster as it grew close. Then, finding out people were there, showing up mid-week already, and the three-day show hadn't started yet. By mid-week of the show over seventy-five thousand sold, half of them were there, and already there was nowhere to park in the little town, so they parked everywhere. VWs with hippie signage, pickups, buses, campers—anything that would easily classify as a rolling party showed up."

By Saturday morning the festival had grown to over 150,000 people. "Then *another* twenty-five, fifty thousand showed up the first show day, in addition to the pre-sold," continues McKuen. "Then McDonald's closed because it ran out of food. This closing shook up even the hippies, like the Navy running out of sailors would an admiral. The very basis of one's existence—food—was compromised, and it made one subliminally uneasy with the rest of the day. (McDonald's run out of food? Wow . . . cool. Really? Hmmm . . . How are we gonna eat? What does this mean? Well, cool . . . We'll find food.) Remember this was when people didn't complain about McDonald's, but felt lucky to find one. As they say, 'back in the day.' Back when people said things like 'I really got fried last night,' before they said, as they do now, 'I can't eat that, it's fried.' The official count on Saturday of 184,00 people was a shock to all."

For its part, the music portion of the festival was well-organized. Two stages rotated so that changeovers were quick and the performers, flown in by helicopters, went on as scheduled. "It became a mandatory chopper-to-stage gig if you wanted to get to work," remembers McEuen. "Even the politically protesting music hippies started to appreciate the Vietnam vet [pilots] in a way they never imagined (as street traffic made it impossible to drive to the stage)—their only way to rock and roll was to fly in low. Like a M.A.S.H. run, bands picked up at the hotel were ferried to the backstage landing spot, then they'd take back the band that just finished back to the hotel for a different R & R . . . and S . . . and D. The *good* news on the Saturday we played was that the Hell's Angels had taken over backstage security . . . and were doing a fine job."

Midwestern Hell's Angels were on hand to act as festival security. Even so, incidents of violence were minimal and many others thought the Angels were doing a good job. (The Angels also reportedly set up "brothels" on various buses that encircled the grounds.)

Wolfman Jack served as emcee to a bill that included some of the most popular acts of the day: the Eagles (who dedicated their song "Already Gone" to Richard Nixon as the crowd cheered); Bachman-Turner Overdrive; Jefferson Starship; Aerosmith; Lynyrd Skynyrd; Bob Seger & the Silver Bullet Band; Joe Walsh and Barnstorm; the Souther Hillman Furay Band; the Marshall Tucker Band; America; REO Speedwagon; Leo Kottke; the Ozark Mountain Daredevils; the Amboy Dukes; the Nitty Gritty Dirt Band; and a guy named Bruce Springsteen. At the height of the music, there were estimates of a total number of 300,000 or more in attendance.

The festival conditions provided, as usual, a challenge for the performers. "We were preceded by guitar great Leo Kottke, so when he finished we were to set up—while the Ozark Mountain Daredevils played on the other half of the stage," recalls John McEuen. "I arrived early, well before Leo went on, and decided to go out and be 'with the people' I had just flown over. I wanted to see what it was like in the middle of 184,000 people who, from the stage, looked like a field of basketballs with hair on top. I swam out to the sound scaffolding and surveyed the sea of hair, all crammed on to the fairgrounds racetrack as Kottke started playing. I was wondering why Leo had covered his guitars with towels, thinking that must help the sound on this huge stage . . . or maybe he was sweating too much. I was to find out soon why."

The sound system that had been established for a good-sized audience suddenly wasn't efficient. "Wolfman Jack, America's D.J. at the time, was introducing the next act," remembers McEuen. "We had known Jack a while, done his TV show ("Midnight Special") many times, and I wanted to see what it was like to see him in front of a live audience. Well . . . from the sound stacks he was about one inch tall and that basso saw blade voice of his sounded like it was coming from someone's car speakers across the field. The sound was set up for 50,000 or so people, but there were now three and a half times that many . . . but it was okay once the bands kicked in."

While a lasting memory for some, the Ozark Music Festival was for others, well, a festival. "I don't remember much about the Sedalia gig, other than the fact that they told me we played it," says Mike "Supe" Granda of the Ozark Mountain Daredevils. "At that point in time, we had only been together a few years and only had one album out. We were the new kids on the bill. I was on Cloud 9,999,999. We'd heard about those festivals in Atlanta, Miami, and Dallas. When we got asked to play one at the fairgrounds in Sedalia, Missouri, we jumped at the chance. We only had to drive two and a half hours."

Another component of the music festival was also very much present. "Like I said, I don't remember much about it, other than it being a hillbilly version of all of the above," continues Granda. "I do know that no matter how stoned those people in Atlanta, Miami, and Dallas got, they didn't come close to how stoned the people in Sedalia got—performers as well as crowd members. We are very proud of marijuana. It makes us dance and sing. I think this, along with playing music in the sun, is *always* a good idea. Like they say, 'If you remember the '60s, you weren't there.' If you remember Sedalia, you weren't there."

The organizers of the festival were taking care of business. The Missouri National Guard kept an eye on things, although not with any imposing presence. The Guard even used their helicopters to fly those who had overdosed on drugs to area hospitals.

The bill was a powerhouse mix that afforded the bands the opportunity to play with other artists that they may have only known by reputation or from the radio. "As the N.G. Dirt Band had three recent Top Forty hits ('Mr. Bojangles,' 'House at Pooh Corner,' and 'Some of Shelley's Blues') and the *Circle* album had recently been released, we were anxious to do our set," says McEuen. "This was one place, Missouri, where we knew we could hold our own up against the others like REO, Skynyrd, the Tucker boys, and the Eagles. I headed back to get my stuff set up and felt like I was preparing to get on the *Titanic* knowing what I know now. It was an 'edgy' feeling, knowing there were simply too many fish in the bowl. We started off with 'Shelley's Blues,' a banjo-led song, and being the first banjo on this hot stage in the heart of the baking Ozarks helped get some new heat from this sweltering audience. Our set was hot all the way through, and this was truly one of our best shows of that year."

The Midwestern heat was one thing, but the temperature felt onstage was another. "Did I say it was hot?" asks McEuen. "This region was, after all, where most of the training for Vietnam was going on. It was reportedly 104 degrees onstage—that was the air that was moving—the reflected heat from all the metal light trusses, added to the plywood stage heat reflection, made it feel like we were in a giant chicken rotisserie and about 115 degrees. The third song, 'Cosmic Cowboy,' I played my lap steel guitar. I vividly remember picking up the sun-drenched metal slide bar and dropping it as fast as I could—it was about 140 degrees. I poured water on it to cool it enough to hold on to it, then made the mistake of putting my lap steel on my lap and touching the strings. *Now that* was hotter! It had been absorbing the direct sun and well . . . the song was going to start so I took a bottle of water and dumped it on it, and was glad it still worked. I understood Kottke now."

Even adverse circumstances didn't effect some of the bands and they were able to enjoy the music. "The cosmic long-hairs' anthem started and brought the biggest hoot we had ever heard (the lyric: 'I just want to ride and rope and hoo-o-o . . . t') right on cue," continues McEuen. "Closing with 'Battle of New Orleans,' we had won the battle to stay alive, and left to a standing ovation from the 183,000 people. It's good for 'ego reality' to keep in mind that they were standing all day long, though—it wasn't possible to sit down in that crowd. I think the cumulative weight the band lost in our hour was about twenty-eight pounds, and we left a couple of choppers later. Had to catch REO first. They were great. Overall, reflecting back over the NGDB's forty years on the road, Sedalia was one of the top ten for us. Maybe it had something to do with the previous time we played the fairgrounds [1967] when we opened for the Jackson 5. This Sedalia show was, in spite of heated adjectives above, a lot cooler."

"Apple, Coke, and MCI hadn't entered the picture yet," says Supe Granda. "This was music, for the sake of making music and no other reason. I can't remember what I did, but I had the time of my life. I'm still having the time of my life. I'm one of the lucky ones. It beats working at Home Depot."

The estimate of the damage to the town and fairground was reported to be over $100,000, which was big money in 1974. The grounds had to be cleaned up quickly to make way for the scheduled Missouri State Fair. As in festivals past, the sanitation wasn't all it could be. After the festival was over, State-hired helicopters sprayed lime over the area as a precaution against an outbreak of disease. The State Fair took place and the people of Sedalia went back to their lives.

Knebworth
July 20, 1974

> *"I remember looking out and seeing all kinds of flags and pennants flapping in the breeze and thinking it looked sort of medieval—it was Britain after all."*
>　　　　　　　　　　　　　　　　—Patrick Simmons, the Doobie Brothers

Possibly in an effort to bring back some of the "dignity" of the music festival, the Knebworth Concert was launched in 1974. The site of the festival this time would not be a vacant field or farmland but rather a historical and beautiful estate in Herforshire, England that featured a Gothic Tudor manor adorned with gargoyles and griffins and beautiful gardens. The estate had been the home of the Lytton family since 1490. Sir Robert Lytton fought with future king Henry Tudor at the Battle of Bosworth and eventually became his aide. The history of the Lytton family is the stuff of English legacy: Edward Bulwer-Lytton, statesman and author (*The Last Days of Pompeii*), was an associate of Charles Dickens, who often visited the estate. Bulwer-Lytton's son Robert was Viceroy of India and later Ambassador to France. Suffragette Lady Constance Lytton was also family and Winston Churchill was a visitor to the estate. With its rich British history, the Knebworth House was quite an unusual setting for a pop festival.

On July 26, 1974, the grounds would be open to host Freddie Bannister's "Bucolic Frolic," a festival featuring Tim Buckley, the Sensational Alex Harvey Band, Van Morrison, the Mahavishnu Orchestra, and the Doobie Brothers. Headlining the bill would be the Allman Brothers Band. The 60,000-watt sound system would be matched by the number of those in attendance. The small town was reasonably concerned about the problems that would arise with thousands of young people descending and Chief Superintendent Tom Oliver of the local police believed that the festival would be "a good exercise for the men" under his employ. Yet the festival ran remarkably well and the only cause for alarm came when a grouping of portable toilets (with people inside) sank into a sewage ravine.

"My specific recollections are of seeing John McFee, Huey Lewis, and their band Clover backstage and being amazed at a bunch of American hippies having transplanted themselves there in England," says Doobie Brother Pat Simmons. "I remember looking out and seeing all kinds of flags and pennants flapping in the breeze and thinking it looked sort of medieval—it was Britain after all. We did play the festival with Van Morrison. I remember him being great, backed by some local British lads, who I hung out with after the show. Went to the home of one of the band members somewhere in Wembley, I think it was. Had a great time and stayed there until the wee hours drinking, smoking, and telling stories. A wonderful memory for me. I love the U.K."

The festival at Knebworth House would prove so successful that a yearly gathering would become an English tradition. In 1975 the attendance rose to 100,000 people who came to hear Pink Floyd, Roy Harper, Captain Beefheart and His Magic Band, Linda Lewis, and the Steve Miller Band.

"My experience was when I was playing in Captain Beefheart and His Magic Band," recalls Jimmy Carl Black. "In my forty-nine years as a professional musician, I have never played for that many people in my life. There were 250,000 bodies there and we were on an eighty-foot platform. All I could see from behind the drums was a sea of color. That bill was the Steve Miller Band, The Fairport Convention, Captain Beefheart, and the headliner was Pink Floyd. What a bill! Beefheart is immensely popular in England so we were right under the Floyd. I had a lot of fun at that gig and the whole tour. [Beefheart] had forgotten the words to his songs (how he did that is a mystery to everyone in the band) before we went to England so his wife Jan made up these huge cue cards with all the lyrics on them. When he finished a song he would sling it off the eighty-foot platform and it would take quite a few minutes to float down to some lucky fan in the audience. There are some people that have great memories of that show and the reason I know is they have come up to me over the years that I have been touring in England and said 'Man, I have one of those cards that the good Captain threw away that afternoon.'"

The only unpleasantness this year was only unpleasant to some. A fence was torn down to allow hundreds, if not thousands, onto the grounds without paying.

In 1976, the festival continued to grow. This time 120,000 people would gather to see Lynyrd Skynyrd, 10cc, Hot Tuna, the Don Harrison Band, Todd Rundgren, and headliners the Rolling Stones. Even members of the Royal Family came to the party.

As the popularity of the music festival dipped in the late seventies, the Knebworth Festival saw its numbers decrease. The attendance for the 1978 concert was down to

60,000—the number of those who attended the very first festival. That year the bill featured Jefferson Starship, Devo, Tom Petty & the Heartbreakers, Brand X, Atlanta Rhythm Section, and Genesis. Attendance dipped further in 1979 when only 45,000 showed up to listen to Frank Zappa and the Mothers, Peter Gabriel, the Boomtown Rats, the Tubes, Dave Edmunds, Wilco Johnson, and Nick Lowe. Yet by the following year the numbers were once again on the rise. When it was decided that the event would be held over two weekends, 200,000 people showed up to hear Todd Rundgren, the New Barbarians, Southside Johnny, Commander Cody, Chas & Dave, the Marshall Tucker Band, Fairport Convention, and Led Zeppelin.

The increase in numbers brought an increase in problems. The sets were longer than expected, causing the shows to run overtime, and the theft of sound equipment and the destruction of trolleys were not appreciated by those who tried to bring off the festival without trouble. The festival—and the organizers—were given a second chance by the townspeople and the following year (an event the Beach Boys headlined), the festival was better organized. The success of that year's festival, though, may have been primarily due to the fact that the Beach Boys were not a tremendous draw at that time and only 45,000 people attended.

For the next two years the Knebworth festival would be devoted to jazz, classic rock 'n' roll, and big band music, and was represented by diverse artists such as Chuck Berry, Benny Goodman, Muddy Waters, and Dizzy Gillespie, among others. The following two years were devoted to four-day Christian events known as the Green Belt Festivals. But rock music was back at Knebworth by 1985 and headlined by the newly reformed Deep Purple. Rain caused mud problems and the crowd was a little more irritable than usual, but the festival was allowed to continue the following year with a bill featuring Queen, which would be the band's very last concert appearance. That year would mark the first fatality at the festival when a man was stabbed. The crowd was so thick that the ambulance was unable to reach the victim until it was too late to save him.

The Knebworth festival didn't return until four years later, in 1990. With the return of the music came big changes. Gone was the "community" feel of the concert. The arrival of "corporate rock" was demonstrated by the festival being broadcast worldwide by MTV, the cost of the tickets, the somewhat upscale audience, and the heaviness of the bill. Dubbed the "Dinosaurs of Rock Concert," the bill featured no less than Paul McCartney, Eric Clapton, Elton John, Robert Plant, Jimmy Page, Pink Floyd, Genesis, Cliff Richard, Status Quo, and Tears for Fears. That show was a hard act to follow and it wasn't even attempted until 1992 when Genesis headlined a bill sponsored by Volkswagen. The atmosphere of a "festival for the people" had definitely changed. The costs for putting on a concert had risen to the extent that ticket prices prohibited many young people from attending. It wasn't really the progressive music of their generation anyway, but things were about to change once again.

In 1996, the Knebworth Festival was back but with an entirely different perspective. A sold-out crowd of over 250,000 people attended the two-day festival to hear cutting-edge bands such as Oasis, the Charlatans, Chemical Brothers, Prodigy, and others. Knebworth's current resident Henry Lytton-Cobbold even enjoyed the concert. It would become the biggest rock event in British music history to date.

Robbie Williams would headline a concert at Knebworth in 2003 that would surpass the previous attendance record. An estimated 130,000 cars attempted to reach the venue, causing a massive traffic jam. Today's Knebworth Festival is done on a much smaller scale and includes a variety of music genres, arts, and crafts.

Nambassa
1976

Rock music festivals were not restricted to the United States and the United Kingdom. Festivals were catching on all over the world. One noteworthy international festival was Nambassa, which focused on music, art, and environmentally diverse lifestyles. It was held on farms around Waikino and Waihi, New Zealand in 1976. Booths featured holistic health, energy alternatives, microbiotics, alternative medicine, and workshops were conducted. The music included homegrown bands such as Split Enz; Australia's Little River Band; jazz great Dizzy Gillespie; blues legends Sonny Terry and Brownie McGhee; pop's Barry McGuire; and country's Charlie Daniels. A charitable trust operates in conjunction with the festival, which continues to be both entertaining and educational.

1978

Runnin' with the Devil

In U.S. news

Volkswagen becomes the first non-American car company to open a plant in the U.S.; the first Unabomber attack occurs at Northwestern University; a federal emergency is declared at Love Canal; and San Francisco's Mayor George Moscone and City Supervisor Harvey Milk are killed by former Supervisor Dan White.

In world news

China lifts ban on Shakespeare; conflict continues in Ethiopia, Somalia, Rhodesia, and Zambia; Israel invades Lebanon; Bob Marley's The One Love Peace Concert is held in Kingston (reuniting opposing political leaders); Louise Brown is the first baby born via in-vitro fertilization; the Camp David Peace talks between Begin and Sadat bring peace to Israel and Egypt; Vietnam attacks Cambodia; and Jim Jones calls for mass suicide at his Peoples Temple.

In music news

The Blues Brothers appear on *Saturday Night Live*; the first Canada Jam Fest is held in Ontario; and the Rutles spoof "All You Need is Cash" on BBC.

Some of the year's most notable albums

The Cars: *The Cars*; Dire Straits: *Dire Straits*; Peter Gabriel: *Peter Gabriel*; Toto: *Toto*; Van Halen: *Van Halen*; *Saturday Night Fever* soundtrack.

Rock's most popular songs

"How Deep is Your Love"—Bee Gees; "Hollywood Nights"—Bob Seger & the Silver Bullet Band; "I'm Every Woman"—Chaka Khan; "My Best Friend's Girl"—the Cars; "Paradise by the Dashboard Light"—Meat Loaf; "Renegade"—Styx; "Runnin with the Devil"—Van Halen; "Sultans of Swing"—Dire Straits; "Werewolves of London"—Warren Zevon; "YMCA"—Village People.

California Jam II
March 18, 1978

> *"Live and learn."*
> —Frank Marino, Mahogany Rush

The first California Jam was held at the Ontario Speedway in Southern California in April, 1974. The festival attracted over 200,000 people and featured appearances by the Eagles, Black Sabbath, Earth, Wind & Fire, Black Oak Arkansas, Deep Purple, Rare Earth, Seals & Croft, and Emerson, Lake and Palmer. The Jam was viewed as one of the last of the peace and love festivals, with portions of the Jam broadcast live on ABC television, a sponsor of the festival. Through another corporate agreement, Los Angeles FM radio stations were allowed to employ the recently innovative simulcast to broadcast the music for the first time.

On March 18, 1978 California Jam returned to the Ontario Motor Speedway and was even more successful than the first concert festival. This time 300,000 people gathered to hear Aerosmith, Ted Nugent, Foreigner, Heart, Santana, Mahogany Rush, Rubicon, Bob Welch, and Dave Mason. Once again, the festival was well-organized and executed, and the day ran pretty much according to plan. The promoters grossed over three million dollars.

The artists on the bill this time were an interesting mix. Santana, Bob Welch, and Dave Mason were festival veterans from the early days. Mahogany Rush had also played their share of outdoor events. Some of the more experienced musicians looked at the evolution of the festival in an entirely different way than less-knowledgeable, new artists who found themselves on festival bills. Frank Marino remembers his experience at California Jam II well. "I had minimally interacted with many of these artists on other shows, so we were not perfect strangers to one another," says Marino. "But I wasn't the sort of artist that ever made it my business to go and hang out a lot. I didn't feel like I really had anything in common with many of them and, in fact, felt a bit like an interloper of sorts because I knew that I didn't believe as many of my contemporaries did. I could feel that I was not really 'one of the gang,' so to speak, and at many of these shows most other artists would not interact with me, for many years prior. This was no different, really. In retrospect, I wish I had interacted with one particular artist, because he was, in my mind, true to his roots and true to my beginnings, and true to the music. That was Carlos Santana. But I actually was way too shy to go and talk to him, because I knew of him from my early days and knew he was the "real deal." I wish I had gone to meet him, now that I'm older and more mature. Likewise, I felt the same about Dave Mason. But I met neither of them there. I played a few gigs with Santana, other than Cal Jam II, and I still didn't muster up the nerve to go and meet him. Live and learn."

Marino says he remembers the band's appearance at California Jam II "quite specifically because, as is well-known by my fans, I was one artist who was not particularly enamored by the whole experience, for a variety of reasons." Marino feels he has an opinion that may differ from others in regard to music festivals. "I came from a generation that revered music and message as important, a kind of art form. That generation is known today as the "Woodstock Generation," for lack of a better term. But as you probably know full well, the term "Woodstock Generation" isn't really meant to pertain to the Festival itself, nor even the music at the Festival. It really means that there was a generation of people, which included musicians and fans alike, that had a type of common interest in things social, and the music provided by the artists of that generation became part-and-parcel of the message of the generation. Now, some say that this message was simply love, or peace . . . or even drugs. But that's not entirely accurate."

"These festivals of the late sixties were, in fact, very significant to social development and to political awareness," Marino continues. "At least that's how it began. But, like most things, it changed drastically because it became financially successful for many, artists and promoters alike. As soon as monetary success was added into the mix, many promoters and artists tried to re-capture and 'sell' this ideology. But there are only so many artists out there with that genuine ideological message and, when there were not enough to 'fill a bill' the industry began to manufacture them, to create 'imposters,' if you will. This really began to happen during the early to mid-seventies. Artists and managers alike wanted to taste a bit of what was true during the preceding generation and to profit from it. So, it became fashionable to build acts that would partake in the new 'movement.' But they had the wrong idea, in many cases, of what this constituted. They thought it simply meant the presentation. Consequently, the seventies became a slow drive towards greater and greater excessiveness in presentation. At first, music was still a part of it. But gradually, it began to take a back seat to the presentation. What used to be called 'concerts' became known as 'shows.' And the shows became spectacles. As all of this brought in more revenue for the promoters, more and more of them were put together. Bands began to fashion their art, their albums, even their clothing and demeanor with the express purpose of being included in this free-for-all. And so the music began to suffer, the message began to disappear, even be derided by some. The very idea of 'musical message,' or social change through music and art became something to be joked about or laughed at behind the scenes in many quarters, which I personally witnessed."

Corporate sponsorship *was* expanding within the music industry. The purpose of that industry was, after all, to make money. Artists could posture themselves as anti-establishment but if they wanted to make a career out of their music they were forced to intimately interact with the establishment as represented by the record companies. Record companies intent on positioning their artists as a little bit different or absolutely unique had to find new ways of drawing those artists out of the pack. In the early days of the growing corporate trend, advertising companies had been eager to associate their product with music-related enterprises such as festivals, and record and artist campaigns, in an attempt to market their product to the ever-expanding youth market. It was becoming mutually beneficial to both record companies (and their artists) and corporate America to align their efforts for maximum exposure and profit. Artists began to 'package' themselves—or allow their record companies to do it for them—in an effort to gain wider exposure and sell more records. The festivals provided the advertisers a forum that was usually spread across multi-genre lines, thereby allowing a maximum exposure for a minimum investment. Whether or not this association affected the 'purity' of the music or not is a subject best left for another time, but corporate sponsorship of festivals was on the rise and the passionate debate between those who were affected—the musicians and the fans—had begun. Music presentation, whether in concert or at festivals, was definitely changing.

"Having come from the sixties generation (and not as a musician but as a 'head' as we called ourselves), and entered into the fray professionally in the late sixties/early seventies, I naively thought that the trend of the sixties would continue unabated, that the message would grow and the art form would thrive," says Frank Marino. "But it was not to be. So, as I made my way through the seventies, I was placed by my handlers and managers into these same 'scenes,' which were becoming the norm. And I began to feel very uncomfortable with it all. You see, I still valued the art. And I still valued the message. But as I said, these were becoming less and less important to others. They were 'minor details.' The 'big picture' was where did you play? How many people were there? How did you [go]over? Did you 'blow the others away'? Were you loud enough? What effects did you have? What wild clothes did you wear?

How did you respond to the interviewers? Did you act enough like a screwed-up, stoned-out freak to be able to 'get some ink?' How much merchandise did you sell? And on and on it went. And I became gradually more and more disgusted and disillusioned. 'What had they done to our dream?' I naively lamented. 'What happened to our idea?' I foolishly thought. But what I didn't realize at the time, was that some of the very people whom I thought were truly behind the original idea had sold out to the industry and were the new perpetrators of the demise of the message, and this simply for money. So I began to realize it was over. The true leaders of our 'movement' had long since died or faded away, to be replaced by a newer, colder version of themselves. And it all became about money, and only money."

Nowhere was this change more evident than at California Jam II. Any major item that could be marketed to the youth market seemed represented: from drinks and food to clothing and lifestyle items. Some of the musicians had signed on to perform not for the community atmosphere of the festival but to promote themselves. "Growing" a name and presence many times caused music artists to change their presentation, both of their music and of themselves. "When I played Cal Jam II, I had already done dozens of large festivals of this sort, and never felt really good at any of them, but it never really came home to me until I played that particular gig," Marino continues. "And this was because the very nature of this festival, namely its size, allowed more hubris into our industry than was there before. I observed another in a long line of huge get-togethers where the only thing important was the festival itself, rather than the music or the message. There were laser shows and sky-divers and air-shows, vendors and hawkers. There was music, but one could easily see, backstage at least, that the music was not exactly the main reason for being there. One particularly famous artist, who shall remain nameless, was having a brief conversation with me, talking perfectly normally, until the television crew spotted us and ran over to get some shots and talk. Then, to my utter amazement and disbelief, this person went from the personality that I had just talked about the weather with into the 'strange persona,' in the wink of an eye. That's the moment I'll always remember, that instant put-on of phoniness. But it wasn't just him, you see. It was the whole thing. It was the way we had built our system. It had become the dominant ruler over how we would act and interact."

By this point in time, it wasn't the music festival that was *changing* society but rather *reflecting* the sociological climate of the times much like Monterey Pop had done over a decade before. Transformation of the collective social order was nothing new to America—there had been flappers, teeny-boppers, beatniks, Beatlemaniacs, and flower children, after all. Yet it was hard to deny that the brotherhood of music festivals was being set aside for those who wanted to primarily enjoy *themselves*. The ever-evolving music festival scene was changing yet again.

1979
Back to the Garden

In U.S. news

The Three Mile Island nuclear power plant releases radiation; Chrysler asks the U.S. government for a $1 billion bailout from their financial problems; and the Iran hostage crisis rocks America.

In world news

The International Year of the Child is declared by the U.N.; the U.S. and China establish diplomatic relations; the Music for UNICEF concert is held; Ayatollah Khomeini creates the Council of the Islamic Revolution; Margaret Thatcher is elected Prime Minister of England; Jimmy Carter and Leonid Brezhnev sign Salt II; and China registers a population of one billion people.

In music news

The YMCA sues the Village People for libel; an anti-disco event is held at a Chicago baseball stadium; "Rapper's Delight" by the Sugarhill Gang launches hip hop; Winterland is closed; a stampede for seats at Riverfront Coliseum in Cincinnati during a Who concert kills eleven fans; and Sid Vicious overdoses.

Some of the year's most notable albums

Supertramp: *Breakfast in America*; the Cars: *Candy-O*; AC/DC: *Highway to Hell*; the Clash: *London Calling*; Ricki Lee Jones: *Ricki Lee Jones*; Pink Floyd: *The Wall*.

Rock's most popular songs

"Do Ya Think I'm Sexy"—Rod Stewart; "I Will Survive"—Gloria Gaynor; "What A Fool Believes"—Doobie Brothers; "Heart of Glass"—Blondie; "Bad Girls"—Donna Summer; "My Sharona"—the Knack; "Logical Song"—Supertramp; "Good Times Roll"—the Cars; "I Want You to Want Me"—Cheap Trick; "Is She Really Going Out With Him"—Joe Jackson; "London Calling"—the Clash; "Roxanne"—the Police; "Sultans of Swing"—Dire Straits.

Woodstock '79
August 14, 1979

> *"It wasn't really a 'festival' at all, it was really a concert."*
> —Barry Melton, Country Joe & the Fish

It was meant to celebrate the 10th anniversary of the legendary festival, but Woodstock '79 was instead a concert reuniting some of the musicians who had participated at the original event. They played not in a field of mud and humanity but at a "garden" of a different sort: Madison Square Garden in New York City. The Band, Richie Havens, Country Joe & the Fish, and Canned Heat would revisit those idyllic days in music history as well as Taj Mahal and Paul Butterfield.

"Woodstock '79 was a really crazy idea—it was held in Madison Square Garden in New York City," says Country Joe & the Fish's Barry Melton. "So, it wasn't really a 'festival' at all, it was really a concert. On the whole, the concert was a disappointment. And the promoters were so hung up in making a profit on a video of the event, they heated the stage to about 130 degrees Fahrenheit to facilitate the filming—which made it so hot, the event might as well have been held in Death Valley in mid-summer."

The idea of recapturing those distinctive days on a farm in Bethel, New York seemed to be more of a yearning than a realistic plan. The 1979 concert was no doubt enjoyable but it likely didn't transport those in attendance back in time the way they had hoped it would. It wouldn't be the last time the Woodstock Festival would be commemorated but there were now other festivals, other themes.

The Concert for Bangladesh, a one-evening event held by George Harrison and his friends in 1971, had demonstrated interest in humanitarian efforts and a series of five concerts held in September, 1973 called "No Nukes" would continue the tradition. This time focused on the issue of nuclear energy, the Musicians United for Safe Energy would also be held at Madison Square Garden. Led by founders Jackson Browne, Bonnie Raitt, Graham Nash, and Orleans' John Hall, the concerts also featured performances by Bruce Springsteen and the E Street Band, Crosby, Stills & Nash, James Taylor, Tom Petty & the Heartbreakers, Carly Simon, the Doobie Brothers, Jesse Colin Young, and Gil Scott-Heron. Awareness of the issue was raised, informed debate ensued, and a subsequent album and film raised money for groups advocating a "safer" environment.

1980–1981
I Wanna Be Sedated

In U.S. news

Jimmy Carter proclaims a grain embargo against the U.S.S.R.; the U.S. boycotts the Summer Olympics; the New York City Transportation Union goes on strike; Mount St. Helens erupts; and a bill is signed requiring nineteen- and twenty-year-olds to register for a peacetime military draft.

In world news

Yugoslavian President Tito dies and over 140 countries send delegates to his funeral; and the U.S.S.R. invades Afghanistan.

In music news

A benefit concert takes places for the people of Kampuchea; Paul McCartney is arrested in Tokyo for possession of marijuana; Bob Marley and the Wailers perform at Zimbabwe's Independence Festival; and John Lennon comes out of "retirement," releases an album, and is murdered.

Some of the year's most notable albums

Motorhead: *Ace of Spades*; Prince: *Dirty Mind*; Ozzy Osbourne: *Blizzard of Oz*; John Lennon & Yoko Ono: *Double Fantasy*; Blondie: *Eat to the Beat*; the Ramones: *End of the Century*; Elvis Costello: *Get Happy!*; Billy Joel: *Glass Houses*; Foreigner: *Head Games*; the Eagles: *Live*; Bruce Springsteen: *The River*.

Rock's most popular songs

"Crazy Train"—Ozzy Osbourne; "Don't Do Me Like That"—Tom Petty & the Heartbreakers; "Don't Stand So Close to Me"—the Police; "Heartbreaker" and "Hit Me With Your Best Shot"—Pat Benatar; "Hey Nineteen"—Steely Dan; "Hungry Heart"—Bruce Springsteen; "I Wanna Be Sedated"—the Ramones; "(Just Like) Starting Over"—John Lennon; "Running With the Devil"—Van Halen; "The Tide is High"—Blondie; "You Shook Me All Night Long"—AC/DC.

Heatwave
August 23, 1980

> *"I didn't really sense any politics at Heatwave. It was just a music thing in Canada."*
>
> —John "Mister Zero" Picard, the Kings

As the premise of the American rock festival found itself indoors at Madison Square Garden, in Canada there was another attempt to bring people together outside. This time it wasn't the established acts of festival rock that were being featured. This festival was something new. Called Heatwave, with alternating slogans that would advertise the music as "Punk Woodstock," "New Wave Woodstock," and "The 1980s Big Beat Rock and Roll Party," the latest music festival would take place at Mosport Park, in Bowmanville, Ontario, near Toronto.

While only 50,000 of the anticipated 100,000 attendees actually showed up and the promoter lost at least a million dollars, this festival was more important for the content of the music than for the size of the crowd. Again re-inventing itself, the music festival was ready to be introduced to a new generation—and that generation was most interested in a new and different rock sub-genre. This time the festival wouldn't feature singer/songwriters and psychedelic meanderings but rather an edgier, more eclectic music. Most of the people who came to participate were there just for the music. The feel-good booths of arts, crafts, and flower children paraphernalia were scarce. The major draw instead was for tee-shirts advertising a more intense, sometimes nihilistic mindset.

The headliners were Talking Heads and Elvis Costello and the Attractions (in their only North American appearance for that year), with performances by Rockpile (featuring Dave Edmunds and Nick Lowe). The Pretenders, the B-52s, the Kings, Teenage Head, Holly and the Italians, and the Rumour (although Graham Parker had recently left the band for a solo career) were on the bill. The Clash had been scheduled as one of the headliners but for some reason failed to appear. (Depending on whom you want to believe, the band had either changed their mind or were held up at customs.) The festival opened with punk rockers Teenage Head at 11 a.m. and closed a little after midnight with the Kings. Nona Hendryx, along with four other special musicians, joined the Talking Heads during their set.

As with many of the recent festivals, sometimes the event was remembered by the bands who participated as an opportunity lost. John "Mister Zero" Picard remembers Heatwave in such a way. "We closed the Heatwave show," recalls Picard. "We wanted the lights to be on. A lot of daytime shows lose energy with no light show to add to the event. Our drummer went in by helicopter. The rest in our singer's VW van. And of course this was before giant video screens, which really are great at big shows. It is hard to imagine life without them now. [Sometimes the bands were] tiny ants way in the distance. But you know the real story to me is about a lost opportunity. What I'm talking about is the Heatwave movie that never was. Somehow or other the promoters got a pro, mobile sound truck, and another company supplied a pro film crew ready to shoot with multiple 16mm cameras. The master audio tapes were recorded on 8-track, 7-audio, 1-SMPTE code. My memory of what happened is this: We were asked if it was okay to shoot our show. Hell, yeah! The deal I think was like this, 'look, let us shoot the bands, we'll put all the stuff in a vault and work out all the legal stuff later.' This made sense to us and Teenage Head. Everyone else's managers said no go. Sometime after the event, the fall maybe, some of us went to a small screening room and saw raw footage of our show without sound, or MOS if you've ever been on a movie set. And that was it. We never heard about it after that. But it was one of those things that stick in the back of your mind. 'What happened?' So, in the early nineties I decided to try and find out. I remembered the name of the mobile recording unit and knew it had evolved into something else, so I got in touch with the owner/operator/chief engineer and he said he still had the tapes and I could have them, no problem. I think he also gave me the name of the production company that handled the filming and after some digging I found them. The man in charge said that three weeks before they had been cleaning out their storage unit of unwanted film stock and other garbage and filled up more than one large dumpster with this stuff. He said when he came to the Heatwave shelf he went 'Ahh, I guess we should keep that,' and they did. It was that close to being lost forever. So, they gave me *all* of what they shot, which as I said, was the Kings on at night and Teenage Head in the morning. This is all in film cans, spools of negative and positive film. There are some crowd shots and helicopter views of the site but nothing of the other bands. However, there are audio tapes out there of the whole day. The unfortunate part is they only shot three or four songs of each band. But I have put together all of our stuff for my upcoming DVD about the band. There is about fourteen minutes of kick-ass rock and roll from the original Kings band. Anyway, that is, to me, the main memory of Heatwave. How some short-sighted managers prevented the documentation of a great event, which, while no *Woodstock*, could have had its own place in cool rock and roll movies."

In retrospect, the filming of the event may or may not have been the most important aspect of participating in the festival. "In the end, it was just another gig," says Picard. "If those dummies had let them make the movie, it would have changed all of our careers for the better. Society/youth wise I think things were so different then. I didn't really sense any politics at Heatwave; it was just a music thing in Canada. Even Atlantic City was mostly about the music. I don't remember any anti-war stuff. Today's festivals are really about one thing: money. All the bands are corporations, as are the events. Back in the day, so much was word of mouth. There was purity to it, and bands were different from each other, unlike the cookie-cutter flavors of the week we get now."

Heatwave was the latest of the festival evolution, with a different atmosphere. Alternate music was on the rise. Coming along was a massive festival that would fuse in an idiosyncratic way the new music with the festival disposition of years past.

Glastonbury Fayre
Relaunch 1981

Taking his cue from the Isle of Wight Festival and an outdoor appearance of Led Zeppelin at the Bath Showground, English farmer Michael Eavis decided to launch the Pilton Festival on the Worthy Farm, six miles outside of the town of Glastonbury. It was a small event attended only by about 1,500 people who came out primarily to see T. Rex, but the Glastonbury Fayre has grown to become one of the most popular of U.K. festivals. The festival does not take place every year and many years when it did occur there were copious amounts of rain, mud, and gatecrashers, but people turnout in great numbers to experience "Glasto."

In 1971, Eavis decided not to be involved and left the running of the festival to Andrew Kerr and Arabella Churchill. The event was held in June during the summer solstice and featured David Bowie, Fairport Convention, Traffic, and other engaging acts. That year's festival drew greater interest and was filmed for a documentary entitled *Glastonbury Fayre*. In 1980, the children's area of the festival was designated to benefit the charity Children's World.

The idea of the festival was abandoned for many years, but Eavis decided to re-launch it in conjunction with the Campaign for Nuclear Disarmament in 1981. The newly designed Pyramid Stage was built employing scrap materials from the Ministry of Defense. The Glastonbury festival by now featured contemporary music, traditional and environmental crafts, demonstrations on alternative lifestyles, and even a megalith circle. By 1985, the festival had grown so large that the adjacent Cockmill Farm was purchased to expand the event.

With upwards of 100,000 people now attending Glasto, the all-too-familiar sense of entitlement resulted in extensive gate-crashing and security issues. One incident, the so-called "Battle of Yeoman's Bridge," resulted in the festival organizers decision to forego the festival the following year. Returning in 1992 with a more durable fence and less-inclusive admission policies, Glasto was back. In 1994, the festival experienced the destruction of the main stage due to a fire just weeks before opening day. A 150-kw wind turbine was featured that year to provide some of the power and a world record was recorded when 826 people, juggling at least three objects, kept 2,478 objects in the air at one time. By 1998, the size of the festival had grown to include an estimated 250,000 people. The gate-crashing continued throughout the next few years but eventually security was established to discourage entry to those who had not paid.

In 2002, the Mean Fiddler Music Group was managing the logistics and Glastonbury Festivals Ltd. was donating most of their profits to various charities. There are many elements of the festival that are managed independently by entities such as Greenpeace, Radio Avalon, and Carlsberg Beer. The staff of the event is mainly composed of volunteers.

Over the years the festival has featured diverse artists such as David Bowie, the Who, Bjork, Modest Mouse, Iggy Pop & the Stooges, John Fogerty, Nick Lowe, Paul McCartney, and many other exciting and established or up-and-coming acts. By 2007, Glastonbury was one of Britain's premier location festivals.

1982
Don't Stop Believin'

In U.S. news

The Vietnam Veterans Memorial is dedicated in Washington, D.C.; the Equal Rights Amendment fails to pass; the "Freeway Killer" is convicted; U.S. Brigadier General James Dozier is held hostage by the Red Brigades; Atlanta child murderer Wayne Williams is convicted; ground is broken in Washington, D.C. for the Vietnam Veterans Memorial; and the Tylenol scare puts U.S. consumers on alert.

In world news

War erupts between Great Britain and Argentina in the Falkland Islands; Canada patriates its Constitution; the World's Fair is held in Tennessee; and the Lebanon War continues as Lebanon President Bachir Gemayel is assassinated.

In music news

Ozzy Osborne bites the head off a bat thrown to him in concert; someone steals the headstone of Lynyrd Skynyrd's Ronnie Van Zant; Ronnie James Dio leaves Black Sabbath; Randy Rhodes is killed in an airplane accident; and Germany begins the first mass production of the compact disc.

Some of the year's most notable albums

Michael Jackson: *Thriller*; Laura Branigan: *Branigan*; Men at Work: *Business As Usual*; the Cure: *Pornography*; the Clash: *Combat Rock*; Led Zeppelin: *Coda*; Bad Religion: *How Could Hell Be Any Worse?*; John Cougar Mellencamp: *American Fool*.

Rock's most popular songs

"Bad to the Bone"—George Thorogood and the Destroyers; "Do You Really Want to Hurt Me"—Culture Club; "Don't Stop Believin'" and "Open Arms"— Journey; "Gloria"—Laura Branigan; "Hungry Like the Wolf"—Duran Duran; "Hurts So Good"—John Mellancamp; "Eye of the Tiger"—Survivor; "We Got the Beat"—the Go-Gos.

US Festival
September 3–5, 1982

"I think I wanted a lot of people who didn't know each other getting together, gathering, meeting, and discussing a lot of ideas, things of life that come out in certain types of music."

—Steve Wozniak

Entrepreneur Steve Wozniak had an idea. As it turned out, it was an idea worth sharing. Wozniak had already made his mark in the world of business and innovation by leading the personal computer revolution that occurred during the seventies. Wozniak was the creator of the Apple I and Apple II computers and co-founder of the Apple Corporation. Possessing a creative mind, Wozniak envisioned a celebration of, in his words, "all the aspects of life; like art, technology, education." Together with a group of very dedicated people, Steve Wozniak's idea would result in a more organized, West Coast version of Woodstock: the US Festival.

Although altruistic in spirit, the US Festival, which was held over the Labor Day weekend of September 3–5 of 1982, was not originally intended as a free or charity event. And there was nothing necessarily wrong with that: the organizers intended to spend huge amounts of money to make their festival an important celebration of some of the good things that were occurring in the world. Though many in the "love generation" were by now jaded and felt that the objectives of their youth had not been actualized, that age group was now firmly entrenched in the various mechanisms of American business and society. The hopes and dreams of the once idealistic flower children gave way to the reality of jobs, careers, homes, and children. That isn't to say that the concerns of people less fortunate or those denied basic human rights were not of a concern to them; it was merely a fact of life that earning a living and providing decent lifestyles for loved ones became more of a priority for many, if not most. Those responsibilities did not mean, however, that they still couldn't enjoy their music.

Yet rock music itself had changed. The mind-captivating psychedelia of the sixties had evolved into the power chords of the seventies. In the eighties, rock was shifting yet again to a predominately less-structured but more intense (some believe the word "frantic" to be more descriptive) beat and delivery. Punk and new wave were now popular; albeit a good measure of lyrical pop artists and songs were tossed into the mix. The music of the festival, which had begun with an assorted combination of rock, r & b, and soul, was returning to include various blends of that music. There was a little bit of everything heard on the airwaves and everyone seemed able to find at least something they liked. With this in mind, Steve Wozniak turned his attention to a festival that could embrace the music and remind those who attended that they too could make a difference in society and in the world.

The US Festival was scheduled to be held at the Glen Helen Regional Park in San Bernardino, California. The talent brought together for the event would be reflective of popular artists of the day but also legendary bands as well: the Ramones, Talking Heads, the Police, Eddie Money, Santana, the Cars, the Kinks, Pat Benatar, Tom Petty & the Heartbreakers, the Grateful Dead, Jimmy Buffet, and Fleetwood Mac would perform.

But before the first notes of the music could ring out, much had to be done in the way of preparation for the large audience that was anticipated. The bulldozing and construction of a huge state-of-the-art stage, and a festival area that could accommodate half-a-million people if need be, were the first things accomplished in preparation for the festival. Despite the challenges of creating an inclusive environment from scratch, things came together quicker than Steve Wozniak had thought they would. "I thought it would take me maybe five years to ten years to get the wherewithal, the abilities, [to] run into people that knew how to manage such a huge project," Wozniak reflects. "It only wound up taking one year."

Wozniak's concept of the event was not based on re-creating Woodstock but would certainly reflect the origins of that festival. "Around 1974, before I started Apple, I encountered a station called KFAT and they were playing a different type of singer, songwriter, a cross between country and folk and comedy," remembers Wozniak. "It was just a lot of music and songs and words that just touched you deeper inside. It wasn't the normal pop music of the radio stations of the day. I think that started my thinking, 'Boy, it would be great to have just a huge, Woodstock-style festival based on this kind of music.' We wound up having a different kind of music. [The KFAT music] just wouldn't have attracted that many people."

The idea of a music festival continued to appeal to Wozniak. "I kinda thought of the idea in the summer of '81 driving in my car, and I mentioned it to a friend of mine because he ran a night club. He was in the music business and he liked [the idea], Jim Valentine. So it was probably about September or October when I was at Berkeley that he brought Pete Ellis up to meet me. I liked Pete Ellis."

Peter Ellis, a Ph.D. in Community Education and Administration from the University of Michigan, was already involved in community affairs and youth development and enhancement. (Ellis was the co-founder of the University of Phoenix and would become a founding partner of Community Crime Prevention Associates.) After their first meeting, Wozniak decided that he liked Pete Ellis enough to make a commitment. "The next time Pete Ellis came up, I think I handed him a two million dollar check and hey, he set up the office in San Jose and I could visit on weekends . . . I was a student [at Berkeley]," remembers Wozniak.

The organization that would launch the music festival had their seed money and now they needed to develop Wozniak's idea. Wozniak also wanted to commemorate the current advances in technology. "Pete Ellis brought a lot of management expertise and friends from the past," says Wozniak. "I think we were discussing what we should celebrate; you know you kind of want to celebrate *something*. And technology was the biggest thing kickin' around right then. But we not only had technology tents and shows [planned], we also had a speaker program, futurist and science fiction speakers, musicians, artists, that sort of thing. I think I wanted a lot of people who didn't know each other getting together, gathering, meeting, and discussing a lot of ideas, things of life that come out in certain types of music. Technology was not at first a part of the plan. That came about later."

Pete Ellis had been involved with liberal politics at San Jose State University in the sixties. He was part of a group that launched a "survival fair," where one of the activities was the burying of a Ford Pinto. Wozniak remembers Ellis speaking of a philosophy that would shift "me" thinking back to "us" thinking. Ellis and Wozniak developed ideas that would reflect the "US attitude." "The US philosophy was more specific," says Wozniak. "It kind of stemmed from a lot of things that Pete Ellis had been working on with his group, developing programs for schools to teach children how to work together instead of against each other to get things accomplished. I think he'd already, in his literature, created and prepared things along the lines of this US thinking. I was extremely amenable to it. It agreed with my own way of thinking. Basically getting to 'yes,' working together. When we got down and started talking about what we agreed, and what we liked, and what we felt, these were the sort of themes that came out of it. I was already closely attached, both mentally and in acts I had done, to youth, to music, to technology, to education, and to cooperation, working together. Being kind of a nice guy, that sort of thing. Charitable. It all melded, gelled very well."

Wozniak is a creative thinker but also a businessman. An entity Wozniak and his fellow planners called UNUSON (Unite Us in Song) was established. "I absolutely felt that if it was going to lose money I wouldn't have done it," Wozniak remembers. "I felt we're going to put on a good festival and I just . . . had a feeling that it was the time for such a thing and if we did it, we would either break even or make money."

No matter how altruistic the concept of a music festival might be, a lot of detailed work is involved in accommodating a large group of people and it's ultimately the talent that draws the crowd. "I was actually attending Berkeley for my last year of college under a fake name, anonymously, so I did not work full time on this," remembers Wozniak. (He was enrolled under the name Rocky Clark.) "We set up offices in San Jose. We first proceeded on trying to get a site and once we had a site agreed on we started working on a lot of the planning and logistics: what would have to be built, what companies [would be involved], how much it would cost."

The organizers employed real estate agents to search for an appropriate site. The first acceptable piece of land was off of California's Highway 5 near Bakersfield's Grapevine. At first look it was agreed that the site was large enough but, because the piece of property spanned three counties, the paperwork involved with filing requests for various permits was massive. Additionally, the local press speculated that over one million people would attend the festival and the locals, as usual, got nervous. The organizers decided to look elsewhere and the next site they considered was a State park in Riverside County. Things looked good until the county officials realized that a Labor Day event would be too great a fire danger, something that was always a concern in Southern California during the summer months. Finally, something unprecedented happened. San Bernardino County contacted the organizers to inform them that the County was interested in hosting the event at Glen Haven Regional Park. The County officials were looking for an opportunity to stimulate their economy and thought the festival may be a great prospect for them. And in another shocker, no one opposed the permit at the requisite approval meeting.

With the community apparently on their side, the organizers offered local organizations such as the Rotary and Kiwanis Clubs an opportunity to run their own concessions at the festival. The California Highway Patrol (CHP) made the decision to cooperate with the organizers. The promoters set their minds to the bulldozing of the large mound of dirt that was the original site, and the grading and creation of a large amphitheater. Meanwhile, the CHP studied traffic scenarios and devised a plan to inform those who attended the festival of their parking options. The organizers of the festival paid to construct their own interstate off-ramp (with full approval by the powers that be). Shuttle buses would be used to bring people from outlaying parking lots. Pancho Rodriquez, Stanley Kephart, Craig Tocher, and Otis Swanson each headed teams critical to the design, development, production, and construction of the physical aspects of the festival.

"We worked it all out ahead of time," says Wozniak. "We were not going to be the sort of people who would make promises or deceive politicians or just go off and do what we wanted to do. No, every step of the way they were just tightly in with us. In our main office we had the top guys in the Highway Patrol and the County Sheriffs were well behind us. We worked with them; we went down to their office. I [later] got an Honorary Sheriff's badge. . . . We totally, totally worked with the local communities. And didn't tell some lies just to pull something off behind their backs. I've heard of that happening a lot. And that's probably normal for most people but we were a little more upstanding than that."

The logistical plans were moving along but the performers, without whom such plans would be unnecessary, had yet to be contacted. "It was actually very late in the game that we actually got to 'Oh, we've got to start booking some groups, how do we do that?'" says Wozniak. "And we looked to [promoter] Bill Graham's people to help do the booking. Bill Graham was just an icon, who meant a lot in my own life. We didn't choose him for that reason. We just chose him because we needed somebody who was professional in the business. We pretty much hired Bill Graham, who had a big reputation as a promoter, to book the groups and you wind up getting the big groups. I wanted pretty high-level, well-known names, at least as headliners. Pretty much you get the ones that are touring that time of year. It's not like you have a lot of choice. You can pick and choose the music you've heard, pick groups, that sort of thing. But it turned out not to be the case. If I had one selection of my own it might have been Emmylou Harris and she couldn't make it because of a conflict. So you start booking a few groups and you consider others and turn some down and that's how it goes. Basically we needed somebody who knew how to put together a huge music festival."

Bill Graham attempted to dissuade Wozniak from featuring just country acts as Graham felt the revenue would come from the stronger rock acts. Wozniak liked various types of music and had little problem with that. As the artists began to be approached, many found Wozniak's attachment to the project intriguing. Ric Ocasek of the Cars was a fan of Apple so that band was happy to sign on. Pat Benatar said that when her husband Neil Giraldo heard about the "Techno Fair" they were in. Soon the bill began to fill.

While things were running well, the usual glitches did cause concern. For one, veteran promoter Bill Graham had his own way of doing things that didn't necessarily fit into the plans of the festival organizers. "There was kind of an ego conflict, kind of a pride thing," Wozniak remembers. "Bill had been on tour with the Rolling Stones [who Graham was currently managing] and really hadn't been on our site. I think when he got there he realized that we had done huge amounts of engineering, preparation, thinking, in areas that he normally does and he was sort of relegated to not being in charge of the whole thing, but just the stage. He had his ideas, 'This should be done, my friend so-and-so handles parking, and we should do this and we should do that.' I kind of got [involved] as more of an "us"-type compromiser. I said, 'Hey, we'll just draw the parking lines the way Bill wants and just appease him. We can be happy. It's not going to hurt anything.' Actually, the funny thing is, our people had done kind of a professional engineering job and Bill's ideas didn't work too well."

Wozniak certainly was interested in technological advances and something huge along that line was going to make its American festival debut at the US Festival: the massive Diamond Vision video screen, which would become an appreciated staple for future big festivals and concerts. "Bill Graham had been working in Europe," remembers Wozniak. "He was aware that the Diamond Vision was the new big screen. It hadn't been used in a concert in the United States yet so as soon as [he] mentioned that, we had to have that screen because we were going to have the hugest amphitheater ever. We had to do a lot of technology. We had delayed speaker systems put out into the audience. Just unbelievable size of scale. So we were the first to use the Diamond Vision at a concert in the United States. I mean, it just fit. Everything had to be kind of big, on a world-size scale, for the US Festival."

Embracing the stage were two, fifty-feet high Eidaphor screens with the twenty by thirty feet Diamond Vision screen over the 300 by 67 feet stage area. Using a font generation program that Janek Kaliczak and Apple had been developing for over one and one-half years, brief messages would be displayed on the screen between sets throughout the festival.

Wozniak and his wife, Olympic kayaker Candi Clark, were expecting their first child at this time. As the day of the event drew near, Wozniak had his wife flown down to Southern California, where he was on-site and extremely busy. The couple's son Jesse was born two weeks prematurely less than two days before the festival in

Culver City. "I, one of the key people, was totally running on no sleep and that was not the plan," says Wozniak. Nonetheless, the new dad was on hand to watch the first fans arrive.

It was September 3 and things were in place. The 500-acre festival grounds featured over 100,000 campsites. Thousands of fans began to arrive. California weather is fairly predictable and temperatures in September are usually hot, but the 115-degree heat that arrived on that day was extraordinary. There was nothing the organizers could do about that but, since they anticipated hot weather, they had in place water trucks, 800 water fountains, shower areas, and water cannons to spray the audience. The festival continued to be attendee-friendly by including a large pool placed in a beer garden, which also featured a large sound system to allow those away from the stage to hear the music. The crowd came dressed in casual or beachwear attire, ready to sit in the sun, visit with their friends or meet new ones, and, of course, listen to some great music.

What was also of importance, especially to those who attended, was the extremely well-organized availability of clean portable toilets and accessibility to the food and drink concessions. In addition to the refreshment stands, booths were set up demonstrating new technology in music and communication. Lecturers and speakers sharing knowledge on a variety of subjects in booths and tents held the attention of those who were interested or with time on their hands. Beach balls bounced through the crowd and Frisbees sailed. It was a California experience and on the first day of the festival people were already having fun.

Techies and those with imagination enjoyed the various booths. There were five different tech tents. Microcomputers were of course well-represented and music displays captured the interest of weekend musicians with electronic drums and keyboards. Robert Moog even participated in a demonstration of his creation. There were displays by the L-5 Society promoting grassroots space development, a satellite television system featuring over fifty channels, an interactive Atari tent that highlighted the latest video games, and Scientology representatives explaining the fundaments and prophesy of L. Ron Hubbard. Skywriting displayed messages over the heads of the crowd and those who arrived were delighted at the level of entertainment and information.

As the festival got underway, Steve Wozniak and Bill Graham held a press conference to discuss the festival and where Wozniak announced that the first direct television broadcast between the U.S. and the Soviet Union would occur that evening.

Many of those who heard the announcement failed to note its significance. The broadcast would later cause considerable controversy.

It had been decided that punk and new wave would be featured on the opening day of the festival and the bill didn't disappoint. The music portion of the festival was kicked off by the English new wave band Gang of Four. The Ramones represented hard core punk and didn't seem to mind performing in leather jackets amid the scorching heat. The English Beat, Oingo Boingo, the B-52's, and Talking Heads were well presented and enjoyed by those in the audience. When the band the Police, who's *Ghost in the Machine* album was currently popular, took the stage, lead singer Sting noted that the festival was the largest crowd the band had ever played to but cautioned that "it doesn't mean anything unless we all act together. We must have cohesion."

Hundreds of thousands of people *were* acting together. The turnout for the event was remarkable. The organizers were not just promoting a concert but a community spirit and people came from all over to take part and participate. "We had it promoted on Westwood One, a radio network that reached all over the country, so we had people from all fifty states," says Wozniak. "[They stayed] in huge camping areas and had a great, festive time. I think a lot of people just wanted to do that. You know, everybody's always looking for the new thing and where's the world going, and technology was really it then. We had a great technology fair, too."

The Moscow broadcast was featured in between the appearance of Talking Heads and the Police. Thousands watched a short travelogue of the city of Moscow and a personalized greeting from representatives of the Soviet Union. More from Moscow would follow the next day. The project was expensive, difficult, and ground-breaking, but Wozniak and his organizers were no doubt disappointed at the reception of the event or the controversy that developed. "Somebody in Pete Ellis' list of contacts, or Jim Valentine, had a contact in Russia," Wozniak remembers. "Technical people who were interested in peace. And there was some equipment that the United States had taken over to Moscow for an Olympics that we pulled out of, but the broadcasting equipment from ABC or NBC or whomever, was left there in a warehouse. So they pulled this equipment out, with dish antennas, and set it up to basically do video through satellite. We figured out how to make all the payments to satellite companies and get a phone line. Back then you had to reserve a phone line maybe a week in advance to Russia so we had to get special permission to have a radio call just to do the set-ups. And we didn't know if the video was going to pop-up on our screen or not from the Soviet Union. This was common technology for a lot of country-to-country. You could do video through satellites, but the Soviet Union was almost cut off back then. It was very difficult."

The broadcast was big news in the USSR. "They publicized it real big," remembers Wozniak. "Three minutes on their national news that goes to 800 million Soviets or whatever. I was a well-known name in the Soviet Union, but we got no publicity in the United States." For some reason the U.S. press refused to be impressed. "I just think it was a topic, kind of related to peace that U.S. papers won't cover. Not enough interest. I don't know why. We'd hold a press conference, nobody would show up. Nobody was interested in all this Soviet stuff. I mean we had cosmonauts talking to astronauts. It really, really changed my life a lot, realizing that we're the same people once you can really talk face-to-face."

Despite the importance of the broadcast, even Bill Graham was unimpressed. "I remember just taking my scooter out and riding around in the amphitheater, above the crowds of people during the shows," says Wozniak. "It was almost like an enjoyable time for [me]. I had it easy and I had special places on the stage to watch it. My friends and family did [also]. Well, the group Berlin played and I had been on a radio station saying that I was going to come hear [their] show, but I was caught up in one of our tents where we did the first three space bridges to the Soviet Union. And this is back during the Cold War. The Soviet Union was kinda like Al Queda is now. So when I announced that we had live music going to the Soviet Union and they were sending back live music of theirs to our screen, some of the people booed. I had to announce it because Bill Graham thought it was a fake. He wouldn't go up and announce it on the microphone. He was looking at the monitors and he said, 'Steve, this is a fake. It's coming from a studio in Southern California.' He was even in Herb Caen's column in the *San Francisco Chronicle* for weeks after that saying it's a fake and he'd give ten thousand dollars if I could prove it was real. And I actually got the PAL Video tapes from Russia. It was real. And he told Herb Caen that he donated ten thousand dollars to a charity for me. Huh, right! I never knew anything about it. But, it was real."

Wozniak and his organizers had accomplished something significant. Perhaps if the crowd had heard about the broadcast from Sting, or some other entertainer, they would have paid more attention and understood its historical significance. "When I announced it, they booed," remembers Wozniak. "Pretty much they watched it. I don't know the general reaction. I haven't heard people comment on it that it was a big, important part of their life. I think it was more important to us to present it than it was for them to see it."

On Saturday the Joe Sharino Band kicked off the music. Managed by Jim Valentine, the band had played at Wozniak's wedding. Wozniak was no doubt pleased to introduce their music to a broader audience. "For me personally, there was the awe of this huge event, and the absolute fear that we were performing there among a bunch of rock icons," remembers Joe Sharino. "We actually discussed that as the only unsigned band performing, that we'd consider it a victory to just get through our set without any problems or anyone booing. And, of course, it turned out wonderfully and people sang along with us at the end. The song "Get Together" became the theme song for the [US] movie, which was very cool. It was about 95 degrees when we went on, which just added to the stress, but in the first few minutes we could tell it was going to go well. The crowd was great, very up."

The crowd was already at 200,000 and growing by Saturday. "I think we built the site to where it could hold half a million," says Wozniak. "Maybe my first idea was to have a site that could hold a million people. Our site, where the fences were, I don't think could have fit more than a half a million in. I think that was our planning, but I could be wrong. Maybe a million could have fit. I think we would not have had the facilities to handle that many. You need a lot of food, water, whatever . . . fortunately people could have left."

"I remember the good vibes there," says Joe Sharino. "People were peaceful, friendly. It was a special environment. There really was a kind of "us" feeling there." Sharino also had the opportunity to meet other artists. "Santana was very friendly and warm," remembers Sharino. "I talked to him and to Eddie Money the longest. Pat Benatar was also very friendly and just a New York girl, it seemed to me. Everyone was excited to play at this behemoth festival and I think they could sense the vibe was a positive one. Wozniak was his usual friendly, jovial self, and I wished I could find the words to tell him how much I appreciated him having us there. He introduced us by saying "These are real people . . . the Joe Sharino Band."

It wasn't surprising that with all the talent involved there would be a few personality problems backstage. "I was so excited to meet Bill Graham and he walks up and starts yelling at me!" says Sharino. "I thought, well, I'm dead. Turns out he made a mistake and then someone told him 'It wasn't this guy. . . .' So then he apologizes and we're buddies. Very strange. The whole day was like a dream in some ways."

The dust rising from the parched ground was sometimes uncomfortable but it didn't diminish the enthusiasm of the crowd. Also appearing that day were Dave Edmunds, Eddie Money, the Cars, the Kinks, Pat Benatar, and Tom Petty & the Heartbreakers.

Eddie Money had an interesting experience coming into the festival. "All of the acts were in a long convoy of limos on the way to the show," recalls Money. "I spotted a hot dog vendor and the craving hit me! I had my driver stop so I could go score a hot dog, but of course the entire convoy had to stop for me as I was in the second limo. So now you've got the Police, the Cars, and God only knows who else having to wait for me to get my hot dog. Fantastic!"

That wasn't Money's only memory. "It was like 110 degrees," he remembers. "My manager, the late Bill Graham, suggested that I include my song "Gimme Some Water" into the set and arranged for me to have a fire hose onstage and spray down the audience who absolutely loved me for it."

The crowd likely remembered him, but Money would also remember the crowd. "For me personally, it was the first big show that I did after going through some personal problems and issues," Money says. "And to perform in front of like 650,000 people, I felt that I was completely healed! To see that the fans still wanted me and my music touched me deeply." During Money's set the Diamond Vision showed teens in Moscow dancing live.

But there was a small tiff between Bill Graham and the Kinks. Evidently the Kinks showed up late and when they dragged their time onstage longer than was scheduled, Graham pulled the plug on them saying, "If Mr. Davies wants to play a full set; he should show up on time."

Between Benatar and Petty's sets a magnificent laser display was enthusiastically received by the crowd. The platform for the laser-light stood on a nearby hill and shot beams across the desert.

The festival opened Sunday with "Breakfast with the Dead" as the Grateful Dead performed their feel-good music to an appreciative audience. The music continued with Jerry Jeff Walker, Jimmy Buffett, Jackson Browne, and Fleetwood Mac. By this point in his career Browne was also known as a political activist and his music inspired a group of people to carry an American flag through the audience as the crowd cheered.

Stevie Nicks remembers being awed, looking down at the crowd as her helicopter circled over them. Those who attended seemed appreciative of the efforts and consideration of the organizers. As they were leaving the festival after every show, many even helped pick up trash along their way.

Yet despite the extraordinarily successful organization and the massive number of people in attendance, the organizers of the US Festival lost money. A lot of money. It was unclear to those who had worked so hard how this could have happened. "It was hard to tell at the time," says Steve Wozniak. "I wasn't sure [why] so I hired a Big Eight accounting firm because the press reported a lot more people there than we had sold tickets to. If we had sold that many tickets, we would have made money. So the Big Eight accounting firm came in and their super-high-priced accountants and lawyers said all the people had a whole ton of ways to get in for free and that's why we lost money."

Although it wasn't a pleasant factor, the loss of money didn't ruin the experience for Steve Wozniak. He had a good time. The performers enjoyed themselves as well. For many it was a landmark experience. "I gained a lot of confidence as a performer," Joe Sharino says. "We'd done shows for 5,000 people or so, but never 250,000. We came away feeling we could play for anybody, anywhere, and entertain them. We were scared, but a friend said to me just before we went on 'Just put the love out there. . . .' and we did. Professionally, we got tons of press and interviews in California, but also we ended up in *Rolling Stone* and on the national news on ABC and NBC."

Although Steve Wozniak says that his US experience was very important to him personally, he reminds us that "it's just entertainment." "Once you have enough food and you have some friends, well, its time for entertainment," Wozniak says. "There are lots of varieties. Rock concerts, it's a huge mass of people getting together, a lot of strangers meeting. That's very different than going to a musical, where you go with a person you know and a few friends you know, [or] you go to the ballet. Even when you go to a movie you're in the dark and you're alone. Whereas at a music festival you're with thousands of people. I don't know what else relates to that; maybe sports events are much closer. I think with a rock concert, [you are] in this atmosphere with other people enjoying the same thing at the same time. Sometimes you listen to a sort of music, you think, 'Oh, I wish I had the girlfriend here,' or something. Well, when you both listen together it's a more meaningful thing. And I think that's true in rock concerts. There are a lot of people around me enjoying the same thing I'm enjoying."

There were over two dozen arrests and twelve drug overdoses, but all were relatively minor. That's not a bad statistic with over 400,000 people in attendance. The organizers had done a good job, yet despite Wozniak's success, his first estimates of the monetary loss was two to three million dollars. Weeks later it was obvious that the total loss was substantially greater. Still, to many, if not most of the people who attended or participated, the US Festival was an awesome success.

"[The US Festival] proved a lot of things," says Joe Sharino. "A festival can be peaceful, loving, organized, and big acts can come together and put aside their egos to just play their music as a part of the festival, a movement almost. [US] was important because there weren't as many festivals at that time, certainly not that size, and people really came out and supported the idea. It also brought together technology and music, which is now kind of a marriage. What's strange is that the eighties were supposed to be a decade of greed, the 'me' decade, and the US Festival was counter to all of that." Or as Homer Simpson said on *The Simpsons*, "There can only be one truly great festival in a lifetime, and it's the US Festival!"

1983
Rock the Casbah

In U.S. news

A riot occurs at Sing Sing Prison; Ronald Reagan proclaims it the "Year of the Bible"; the EPA evacuates Times Beach, Missouri; Sally Ride becomes the first woman in space; Nintendo goes on sale; Guion Bluford is the first African-American in space; Vanessa Williams is crowned the first African-American Miss America; Microsoft Word is released; and Martin Luther King, Jr. Day is established.

In world news

Nazi Klaus Barbi is arrested in Bolivia and charged with war crimes; Reagan calls the U.S.S.R. an "evil empire" and proposes the "Star Wars" program; the U.S. embassy in Beirut is bombed; the U.S.S.R. shoots down a Korean Airliner; and U.S. troops invade Grenada.

In music news

Diana Ross performs in Central Park; and heavy metal grabs the public's attention.

Some of the year's most notable albums

Quiet Riot: *Mental Health*; Iron Maiden: *Piece of Mind*; Metallica: *Kill 'em All*; Def Leppard: *Pyromania*; Mötley Crüe: *Shout at the Devil*; David Bowie: *Let's Dance*; Phil Collins: *Hello, I Must Be Going*; the Police: *Synchronicity*.

Rock's most popular songs

"1999" and "Little Red Corvette"—Prince; "Beat It"—Michael Jackson; "Burning Down the House"—Talking Heads; "China Girl" and "Let's Dance"—David Bowie; "Do You Really Want to Hurt Me" and "Karma Chameleon"—Culture Club; "Down Under"—Men at Work; "Every Breath You Take"—the Police; "Hungry Like the Wolf"—Duran Duran; "Love is a Battlefield"—Pat Benatar; "Owner of a Lonely Heart"—Yes; "Rock the Casbah"—the Clash.

US Festival II
May 28–30, 1983

"I hear great stories. Very seldom do I hear somebody say, 'Yeah, it was just so-so.'"
—Steve Wozniak

Although the US Festival held on Labor Day Weekend 1982 was meant to be a one-time celebration, when Steve Wozniak began to hear the feedback of those who had attended he started to consider bringing the festival back for an encore. Wozniak was moved when he heard from people that their experience at the US Festival was an important moment in their lives. Wozniak enjoyed bringing happiness to others and the thought of launching another festival appealed to him.

Everything had gone according to plan for the first festival, with the exception of the financial aspect. Wozniak's friends and advisers discouraged him from organizing a second festival as the first had lost money. Not to be deterred, Wozniak investigated the problem. "The second festival only came about after the Big Eight accounting firm gave their auditing of why we lost money," says Wozniak. "I just realized I could cut the holes where we lost money and we'd make money. It was partly inspired because boy, we had such an incredible [experience]. During the first night [of the first festival] the Police were playing under a full moon and the crowd was mesmerized. Bill Graham was in one of the best moods I'd ever seen him in. He said to me, 'There's going to be a lot of people doing this now. This is really going to be a go.' He saw the promise with this type of event, [one that could] make money."

This time the construction of a site would be not be necessary, and the publicity surrounding the uniqueness of the event would be less than before. So many people had taken the time to express their gratitude for the original US Festival that the organizers felt a return to the event would be welcomed. If the organizers were to top the last festival, an even bigger roster of star acts was necessary. Even though he was trying to make a profit this time, Wozniak knew that the best way to secure top acts was by paying big bucks. A date was established, Memorial Day Weekend 1983, and the search for name performers began.

This time the securing of the talent wouldn't be left to Bill Graham. At one point in the previous year's US Festival there had been a problem with Graham's crew not honoring the backstage credentials of Wozniak's crew. Woz' guys went to a local store and bought the colored stickers that Graham's people were using and solved that little problem.

Yet the thought of butting heads with Graham again was not appealing. "I actually liked Bill Graham," says Wozniak. "I was pushing so hard with my staff [for the first festival], but I won't run them over and be a one-person, run everything dictator. They all had such bad run-ins with Bill Graham's people. Bill Graham's people came in and took over their jobs, more or less. So they wouldn't work with him and I finally had to agree with my staff and tell the press my staff just didn't go along with Bill Graham, he didn't do things well, didn't work with them. But the next year it left us without a good booking party and we were getting a little desperate."

At this point, established promoter Barry Fey and his bookers were called in. "He had that instant, infinite money and over-paid groups," says Wozniak. Still, Wozniak took it upon himself to sample California students to see who they would like to see at the festival. With the combination of these elements, the resulting bill was top-notch.

An attempt was made to reunite one of America's top groups, the Eagles. That didn't pan out but there was no dearth of other exciting talent. Saturday's bill would feature Flock of Seagulls, INXS, Divinyls, Wall of Voodoo, Oingo Boingo, the English Beat, Stray Cats, Men at Work, and the Clash. Sunday would be Heavy Metal Day with Mötley Crüe, Ozzy Osbourne, Judas Priest, Triumph, the Scorpions, Quiet Riot, and Van Halen. (Motley's Vince Neil would famously gloat over the success of Heavy Metal Day by proclaiming it, "the day new wave died and rock 'n' roll took over.") Appearing on Monday were Los Lobos, Little Steven & the Disciples of Soul, Berlin, Quarterflash, Missing Persons, Joe Walsh, U2, the Pretenders, Stevie Nicks, and David Bowie.

A fourth day was added. On the following Saturday, June 4, there would be a Country Day. Wozniak would at last have his wish granted by having Emmylou Harris appear at the festival. Willie Nelson, Alabama, Waylon Jennings, Hank Williams, Jr., Ricky Skaggs, the Thrasher Brothers, and Riders in the Sky would also perform that day. No one could say there wasn't a little something for everybody throughout the four days of the US Festival. Over 650,000 would ultimately attend.

Wozniak relied on mostly the same people who had worked together so successfully on the first festival to bring the second to fruition. "I think I had an excellent staff that really pulled off some incredible stuff," he says. The only major differences in the second festival would be upgrades. The sound and stage systems remained state-of-the-art. Arrangements with concessions were simplified to eliminate mass amounts of paperwork, but everything that had worked so successfully in the past remained intact.

This time the performances were sometimes more dramatic than in the previous year. U2's Bono climbed the rope ladder of a lighting tower—about fifty feet high— and threw a white flag into the crowd. David Bowie's act was a full-blown theatrical production.

And this time some controversy was thrown into the mix. The Clash took issue to Van Halen being paid a reported one million dollars and demanded that Wozniak donate that much to charity. (Wozniak had already been donating large amounts of money to charity so the Clash's demand was a non-issue.) But the band wanted to fly banners that read "Sex, Style, Subversion." They didn't seem to "get" what the US Festival was about. The issue of some acts receiving large amounts of money to appear didn't seem to deter Joe Strummer and company from performing at the festival. The Clash ranted against commercialism but they apparently readily accepted their paycheck. There was an altercation between stage coordinator Patrick Stansfield and Strummer when the band made the audience wait an extended time for an encore. Stansfield cut the mike. Strummer punched Stansfield, the stage manager hit Strummer, the Clash was ordered off the stage, and their manager called the stage crew fascists.

The Clash did have their fans and when, later that evening, those fans found themselves faced with the arrival of heavy metal fans anxious to participate in the next day's concert there were some squabbles. Some of the portable toilets were overturned but cooler heads stepped in and a grudging peace was restored.

"The second festival had a huge day where we actually did have, according to the press, 400,000, according to reality 300,000 people," says Wozniak. The crowd that showed up to hear their metal favorites was impressive. Tommy Lee of Mötley Crüe was so nervous that he says he felt like puking. Judas Priest came onstage riding motorcycles. Ozzy Osbourne noted that it was like being in the middle of a forest fire. Members of Van Halen allegedly took the stage so drunk that even their fans weren't happy.

The response of the crowd to what was happening on stage was sometimes intense. "It was scary," says Wozniak. "That day had all the normal things of a huge concert, people getting pressed and having to be pulled over the fence near the stage and treated, but that's normal at concerts. Stuff we expected. All the logistics of handling the events, both years, just ran pretty smoothly."

Both US Festivals remain a respected contribution to rock festival history. "I still get tons of e-mail to this day," says Wozniak. "I got two letters yesterday from people just telling me their experience. You know, 'of all the concerts they've gone to in their life, it was the best one,' or 'a life-changing experience,' or 'they'll never forget what it took to just get there,' even. I hear great stories. Very seldom do I hear somebody say, 'Yeah, it was just so-so.'"

Although the US Festivals have yet to be repeated, another is not out of the question. "Our reputation, in the right places, is immaculate," says Wozniak. "We would be welcomed, in a lot of places you wouldn't even expect. We would still never deviate from our theme of before, the whole principal of speaking to [the concept of] working together and celebrating the arts, the technology, education, as well as music."

The US Festival stage remains in use . . . at Disneyland. Steve Wozniak continues to be involved in the creative aspects of the business world and in his community. His CL 9 venture developed the first universal remote control. Wozniak is involved with education both as a teacher and a philanthropist. He received the National Medal of Technology in 1985, was inducted into the National Inventors Hall of Fame in 2000, and founded the Wheels of Zeus to create wireless GPS technology. (On a lighter note, Wozniak is known as a prankster, started Dial-a-Joke in San Francisco, and was the first consumer to buy a Segway PT.) Wozniak had set out to create an amiable gathering of young people in music and technology and his US Festival was successful in almost every way, albeit not financially. The rock festival was back but could it be sustained?

In 1977 when Warner Communications System's Quebec television cable system launched *Sight on Sound*, no one could have foreseen what that moment in time would mean to the future of rock music. Music Television would become a force of music entertainment on par with FM radio formatting. It would literally change the world of music.

Future MTV president and CEO Bob Pittman produced the fifteen-minute WNBC television show *Album Tracks* in the late seventies. At that same time, John Lack was executive-producing a television series of music videos titled *Pop Clips*, a creation of the former Monkees band member Michael Nesmith. HBO was getting ready to launch its thirty-minute music video show "Video Jukebox." Bob Pittman had the idea that a cable channel modeled after Top Forty radio and featuring music video exclusively would appeal to teenagers and young adults in a way that network television could not. It would be *theirs*. Rather than personalities like aging television and radio legends such as Dick Clark and Casey Kasem, Music Television would feature young and hip "video jockeys" who would introduce the videos provided by record labels in promotion of their artists. At 12:01 a.m. on August 1, 1981, MTV launched with John Lack intoning "Ladies and Gentleman, rock and roll." Original music by John Petersen and Jonathan Ellis played over a montage of the Apollo 11 moon landing. In a prophecy of the future of the music industry, the first video to be played was the Buggles' "Video Killed the Radio Star."

When MTV debuted, most of the music videos being produced were concert clips or short promotional videos. The number of households tuned in during the early days of MTV was over 500,000. It was clear to all involved that the idea was a major national hit. The record companies quickly realized the promotional potential of music videos and began to budget money to produce videos of their artists for MTV. The amount of money spent on videos sky-rocketed and soon exceptionally creative filmmakers were producing and directing videos that went far beyond the "in-concert" themes of years past and some now included storylines and elaborate production elements.

As name artists provided identification spots stating "I want my MTV," the power of the new enterprise grew exponentially. Where some acts were sometimes "just another song on the radio," their appearance in videos identified them as a performing entity to new fans. Duran Duran, Culture Club, Van Halen, the Police, Eurythmics, Madonna, and Bon Jovi experienced great success through their initial MTV exposure. In 1984, MTV even launched its own "MTV Video Music Awards" show, which was a music industry showcase like no other.

Despite its success, MTV was not without its detractors. Many felt that the video was made more important than the music, which is undeniably a valid point. Especially in the early days, MTV catered to the more established acts or those artists fortunate enough to have the backing of big bucks by their record labels. Regardless of what the cynics thought, MTV was now a major element of the music industry and would soon be host of a festival that would not only be the first of its kind but would offer an opportunity for people all over the world to participate.

1985–1987
Glory Days

In U.S. news

A blood test for AIDs is approved; Ronald Reagan attends a funeral service at a site that includes the graves of SS troops; and John Gotti becomes head of the powerful Gambino crime family.

In world news

Mikhail Gorbachev comes into power in the U.S.S.R.; AP reporter Terry Anderson is taken hostage in Beirut; South Africa ends its ban on interracial marriages; the Greenpeace vessel Rainbow Warrior is sunk by French officials; the cruise ship Achille Lauro is hijacked by Palestinian terrorists; and terrorists from the Middle East open fire on airports in Rome and Vienna.

In music news

David Lee Roth leaves Van Halen; Michael Jackson purchases the Beatles publishing; and hearings on behalf of the Parents Music Resource Center are held.

Some of the year's most notable albums

Dire Straits: *Brothers in Arms*; John Fogarty: *Centerfield*; David Lee Roth: *Crazy from the Heat*; Heart: *Heart*; Phil Collins: *No Jacket Required*; Stevie Ray Vaughn & Double Trouble: *Soul to Soul*; Bruce Springsteen: *Born in the USA*.

Rock's most popular songs

"Born in the USA," "Glory Days," and "I'm On Fire"—Bruce Springsteen; "The Boys of Summer"—Don Henley; "Broken Wings"—Mister Mister; "Can't Fight this Feeling"—REO Speedwagon; "Don't Come Around Here No More"—Tom Petty & the Heartbreakers; "Don't You (Forget About Me)"—Simple Minds; "Everybody Wants to Rule the World"—Tears for Fears; "I Want to Know What Love Is"—Foreigner; "Legs"—ZZ Top; "Material Girl"—Madonna; "Money for Nothing"—Dire Straits; "Private Dancer"—Tina Turner.

Live Aid
July 13, 1985

"I was all too horribly aware that when it came to playing the solo *introduction to the* very first song of the day *I would be performing to some 150 million people."*
—Andy Bown, Status Quo

Like John Phillips before him, Bob Geldof was a rock star. Although Phillips was living out his dream in California and the Irish Geldof resided in London, each man had a vision. Phillips' dream had been to bring people together to form a community of brotherhood and music, and he had succeeded in accomplishing that in ways no one expected with Monterey Pop. Geldof, the son of a Dublin merchant, had worked as a truck driver, busker, English language teacher, and factory worker, and had once relocated to Vancouver, Canada to work as a music journalist. He returned to Dublin in 1975 to try his luck at publishing, but also took time to perform with his band the Boomtown Rats. The Rats experienced number one hits with "Rat Trap" and "I Don't Like Mondays," and life was good. One evening while relaxing in his London home, Geldof watched a documentary that horrified him. He felt strongly compelled to move outside the comfort level of his music career to become intimately involved in an issue far more important than entertainment: starving people.

VISNEWS cameraman Mohamed Amin and BBC correspondent Michael Buerk had recorded the dire famine in Ethiopia that was caused by, among other things, a lack of much-needed rainfall for the sixth consecutive season. The BBC aired the first of Buerk's report on October 24, 1984. The segment brought to the forefront a situation that was shocking and certainly unacceptable to anyone who cared about their fellow man. Bob Geldof decided to investigate the Ethiopian situation first-hand. He flew to that country and found the condition to be as alarming as Amin and Buerk had depicted in their news documentary. Upon his return Geldof told his friend Midge Ure of Ultravox that he wanted to do something to help the people so miserably afflicted. According to Ure, the pair felt that the way they were most qualified to help would be by producing a record and donating the proceeds to the cause. When Geldof ran into Spandau Ballet's Gary Kemp, he mentioned the news segment and asked if Kemp might be interested in getting together with their friends to record a song. Acting on their desire to personally address the issue, Geldof and Ure wrote the song "Do They Know It's Christmas?" Thinking that the more star power the record featured may result in a greater number of records being sold, Geldof called several of his fellow rock stars to ask if they would participate in recording the song. The money earned from their efforts would be donated to Ethiopia to help provide for food. Using a pun, they would call their venture Band Aid. Geldof was adamant that every penny go to Ethiopia and not to real or padded "administrative costs."

On November 25, 1984, Geldof, Ure, and some of the biggest names in British rock music contributed to the record, which was produced by Trevor Horn. Included were members of Genesis, the Boomtown Rats, Spandau Ballet, Ultravox, Duran Duran, Heaven 17, Bananarama, U2, the Style Council, Kool & the Gang, Wham, the Police, Status Quo, Culture Club, Frankie Goes to Hollywood, and Big Country as well as Madonna, Paul Young, and Boy George, who was flown to the recording studio via Concord. (Paul McCartney and David Bowie recorded separately and their voices were dubbed onto the record—with Bowie's on the B-side: "Feed the World.") Video of the artists recording the song was sent to air on London's evening newscast even as the artists continued to record. The following morning, Geldof appeared on Mike Reid's Radio 1 breakfast show to talk about the record and pledge all proceeds from the endeavor to the cause of African famine relief.

On December 3 the record was released and it went straight to number one, where it remained for five weeks. Becoming the biggest-selling single in Britain for its time, "Do They Know It's Christmas" sold over 3 million copies. (A problem arose when the British government refused to waive the Value Added Tax attached to the record but when Geldof stood up to Prime Minister Margaret Thatcher through the press, the government made the decision to donate the tax to the charity.)

Actor and political activist Harry Belafonte and his manager Ken Kragen had heard of the Band Aid effort and thought Americans should be involved to help to curb the famine also. Kragen knew that many artists would be in Los Angeles to attend the American Music Awards. Kragen got busy making calls and sending written invitations from Quincy Jones, who would produce the record. The invitation asked that all those who may potentially be involved to "check your egos at the door." Not to be outdone, and to demonstrate that they too were concerned with worldwide human rights issues, rock musicians in the United States recorded the song "We Are the World," written by Michael Jackson and Lionel Richie, on January 28, 1985. Over forty artists came together, including Stevie Wonder, Ray Charles, Bob Dylan, Michael Jackson (with his brothers Randy, Tito, Jackie, and Marlon, and sister LaToya), Willie Nelson, Waylon Jennings, Diana Ross, Tina Turner, Billy Joel, Paul

Simon, Cyndi Lauper, Bruce Springsteen, George Michael, Smokey Robinson, Kim Carnes, Dionne Warwick, Lindsey Buckingham, Sheila E., Kenny Rogers, Daryl Hall, John Oates, Lionel Richie, James Ingram, the Pointer Sisters, Al Jarreau, Steve Perry, Huey Lewis and the News, Jeffrey Osborne, Kenny Loggins, Bette Midler, Harry Belafonte, and Dan Aykroyd. Bob Geldof wanted to be part of the project also and traveled to the United States to participate. Released on March 7, the song became the number one song in America by April 13 and went on to sell 7.5 million copies and win Grammy Awards for Record of the Year, Song of the Year, and Best Pop Performance by a Duo or Group. Musicians in Canada, Austria, and Norway also released records featuring the involvement of multiple artists with the proceeds donated to battle the famine of the African people.

Bob Geldof said that the idea of a full-blown concert dedicated to the issue of Ethiopia famine came to him while he was in Sudan. While he was in that country, it was confirmed to him that reports of food being held up at the ports due to a trucking cartel were accurate. Geldof surmised that if opposition to the cartel could be funded and mounted, the cartel could be broken and the food could be delivered to the people who needed it. Geldof asked his friend Ure to help him mount a massive worldwide appeal for funds. A man named Mike Mitchell, who had worked as financial chief under the leadership of Peter Uberroth and Harry Uscher for the 1984 Los Angeles Olympics, also saw famine in Africa as an issue that needed to be addressed. Through an Indonesian businessman living in London, Mitchell became aware of Geldof's efforts.

Meeting in New York, Geldof discussed with Mitchell his idea to platform the largest international festival yet: two "sister concerts"—with one held in London and one in the United States—that would be broadcast around the world to raise money for the cause. Mitchell met with producer Hal Uplinger the next day and it was decided that the BBC would produce the English concert which would, hopefully, be held in London's most famous arena, Wembley Stadium. The BBC would own the right to broadcast in England. Hal Uplinger would produce the concerts for American television and distribute the program to the rest of the world. It was a massive plan. The idea of the sister concerts would require a tremendous amount of planning and coordination. There were a couple of other things to be considered. Geldof wanted the concerts to occur simultaneously and he wanted to bring the whole thing off on July 13, a date only ten weeks away. Geldof instilled urgency in all involved—people were dying and there was no time to lose. Geldof stated that the Band Aid release had kept millions of people alive, now it was important to give them *a life*.

Wembley was secured and the producers were pleased that equipment would already be in place due to a Bruce Springsteen concert that was to be held the previous week. Now a site in the U.S. had to be obtained. The first choice was a venue in New York City but that proved difficult. Yankee Stadium was unavailable because the Yankees were in town on the day of the event; Shea Stadium was undergoing minor scheduled renovations; and the Meadowlands was hosting a World Football Championship game. The powers-that-be at Philadelphia's JFK Stadium eventually said that they would be happy to be involved and the site was set. (It also didn't hurt that the Stadium had one of the largest backstage areas available.) Additionally, area police would donate their time and electronic equipment would be provided at cost.

Hal Uplinger brought together an outstanding team of technical people for the Philadelphia portion of the broadcast including directors Tony Verna, Lou Horowitz, and Sandy Fullerton, with Michael Mc Lees tapped to supervise the technical production. The involvement of Miro Valcheck, who was head of programming for the European Broadcast Union, was critical to the coordination of the European countries involved but also to involve some of the Eastern Bloc countries. (ABC would later comment that the main reason the broadcast was successful was that there were outstanding people in key production positions.) An equally talented production team was supplied by the BBC.

One of the major issues to be addressed was the foreign distribution. The purpose of the broadcast, after all, was to raise money to combat *world* hunger. The countries that bought into the broadcast would carry the concert for sixteen hours but would also hopefully provide a telethon to enable individuals to contribute. Post Newsweek TV, Taft Broadcasting, and Orbis Communications came onboard for the American syndication, and ABC agreed to telecast the last three hours of the show. (ABC would, at a later date, broadcast some of the acts that were omitted during their initial telecast.) MTV would broadcast the entire show. Brightstar and Intelsat would provide satellite transmission. In the end, thirteen satellites and twenty-two transponders were used to present the concert worldwide. Thirty-five trailers at the Philadelphia site would house the communication headquarters for both the JFK and Wembley concerts. Most of the broadcast entities could only broadcast in mono, but several radio entities provided simulcast sound. MTV already had stereo transmission in place but, although the station broadcasted in stereo, there were not many people who owned television sets capable of stereo reception.

In England Harvey Goldsmith, who had already worked on a charity concert called Concerts for Kampuchea, and in the United States Bill Graham and Larry Magid, were brought in to help coordinate talent, although many of the musicians who agreed to perform were first contacted directly by Geldof working out of his home. It was Geldof's idea to try to include the most significant artists of the past twenty-five years. Naturally some ego-hoops had to be navigated but the list of artists who were willing to commit grew quickly.

It was decided that each act would be allocated fourteen minutes, and that the concert would switch back and forth between the two locations after the completion of each performance. The logistics of pulling off such an intricate set of concerts were complicated and massive. Signs were posted on the artists' trailers noting the time they were to take the stage and each artist or band was requested to vacate the dressing trailers quickly so that the next performers could prepare. (Goldsmith would purchase over two dozen clocks that he set at strategic points backstage to encourage artists to be on time both in taking the stage and getting offstage.) On the stage, a green light would signify there were five minutes left to perform, while amber light would serve as a two-minute warning, and a red light made it clear that was all, folks.

In addition to the music, thirty one-minute interview inserts would be included in the broadcast. Featured were such dignitaries as President Jimmy Carter, Mrs. Coretta Scott King, Bishop Tutu, and celebrities such as Pele, Dionne Warwick, Charlton Heston, Sally Field, and Jeff Bridges. (It is interesting that while Madonna would perform, Michael Jackson, Prince, and Bruce Springsteen would not appear. Springsteen was in the middle of an eighteenth-month world tour and Prince had recently retired from performing, although he would soon "un-retire." Michael Jackson, allegedly for apparently unknown reasons, simply declined. In all fairness, re-arranging schedules was not always an easy thing to do and sometimes not possible. Many of the artists who may have wanted to appear were otherwise contracted for summer tours.)

The BBC, being a public channel without commercial content, had time to fill between the live acts and would conduct interviews from a backstage booth. The network would provide a clean feed (the performances without the commentary) to various European stations. Richard Skinner and Andy Kershaw were signed to anchor the Wembley proceedings.

ABC and MTV, of course, had to cater to the needs of their sponsors. (MTV would do a valiant job, but viewers were ultimately unhappy with the talking heads and the constant commercial cutaways that resulted in losing portions of some of the performances.)

By the morning of the event, everything was set and ready to go. The event kicked off with a royal salute by the Coldstream Guards and a rendition of "God Save the Queen." Prince Charles and Princess Diana, who was a huge rock fan, arrived at 11:30 a.m. to meet some of the artists backstage and take their seat in the Royal Box. (The band Queen, along with George Michael, Paula Yates, and Elton John would also sit in the box intermittently throughout the day.) Bob Geldof's girlfriend Paula Yates couldn't remember if flowers had been provided for the Princess and stopped at a gas station on the way to the event to purchase a bouquet, which was presented by Yates and Geldof's daughter Fifi Trixibelle. Over in America, Congress proclaimed "Live Aid Day."

The program was billed as a "Global Jukebox" and didn't disappoint. Giant Diamond Vision screens—the same in both venues—and revolving stages would provide those in the audience a good view. It had been a rainy summer in England but this day was bright with sunshine.

Although Status Quo had said that they were finished performing live, Geldof had talked them into appearing. They were the first to perform and opened with their occasion-appropriate song "Rockin' All Over the World." Andy Bown remembers that moment. "I like to think it was a sunny day," says Bown. "We arrived quite early, around 9 a.m. I suppose, and even at that hour the atmosphere was electric. Soon the place was crawling with artists, a few of whom were obviously nervous. I know I was. By eleven o'clock, Wembley Stadium was heaving with glamour and style. I remember one of the Spandau [Ballet] boys had the very latest mobile phone. It was about the size of a Smartcar. I was impressed. And Paul and Linda performed an official drive-past on the back of a jeep, holding up two fingers to all and sundry. Exciting times. We went up to check the stage and Bob Geldof emerged from the bowels in a very bleary state, having just grabbed a couple of hours sleep. Poor sod was absolutely knackered. I thanked him for coming (I can't help it) and then seemed to slip into a quiet, dream-like trance."

Performing to a world-wide audience must have been a daunting experience. "I once read a Paul Simon interview in which he said he didn't ever really get nervous but just lapsed into a state of acute weariness and I felt that this, or something very similar, was possibly happening to me," remembers Bown. "I was all too horribly aware that when it came to playing the *solo* introduction to the *very first song of the day* I would be performing to some 150 million people, and my command of the piano was frankly, appalling. So I chose not to think about it. I concentrated on filing my nails. I concentrated on drinking tea. I counted the blades of grass on the pitch. I invented Sudoku. In the event, whatever mind games I played worked like a charm for me, because everything went spectacularly to plan for us—we tore it up—and the next thing I remember is sitting way up in the grandstand with Fish, consuming worrying amounts of Scottish liquids as we thoroughly enjoyed the rest of the show. Fantastic day."

Style Council was next, followed by Bob Geldof and his Boomtown Rats. The Rats' set included their hit song "I Don't Like Mondays" and provided an incredible moment for the man who worked so hard to bring Ethiopia's famine to the attention of a worldwide audience. There is a line in the song that states "The lesson today is how to die." The singing of that line was not meant to be particularly meaningful but as Geldof sang it, the enormity of the event and the seriousness of what those onstage were attempting to accomplish overwhelmed Geldof and he stopped singing. While the line washed over the audience, Geldof looked around the stadium in awe and raised his fist. The audience united in a deafening cheer and the Rats continued their performance. Geldof called the moment "cathartic" as it seemed to define his life. (Gary Kemp would later say that because of Geldof's charisma he would "make a frightening politician.") At the end of the set the audience sang "For He's a Jolly Good Fellow" to Geldof.

Adam Ant and INXS, as well as Men at Work, performed in Melbourne. Ultravox followed at Wembley and it was the first time in a year that the band had performed live. Loudness, Off Cause, Eikichi Yazawa, and Motoharu Sano appeared in videos from Japan, and then Spandau Ballet performed live in London.

Bernard Watson, an eighteen-year-old non-professional musician from Miami Beach, had been hanging around JFK Stadium during the preparations trying to get Bill Graham to listen to his demo tape. On a whim, Graham told Watson he could launch the American concert by being the first to take the stage (eight minutes before the show was scheduled to start). The first professional to perform was Joan Baez, who was introduced by Jack Nicholson. Baez sang "Amazing Grace," telling the audience, "This is your Woodstock and it's long overdue." Elvis Costello took the stage in London to sing "All You Need Is Love." A tape was shown from Austria for Afrika, the Hooters appeared at JFK, and Nik Kershaw performed at Wembley. The Four Tops were next in Philadelphia. The legendary group was excited to be participating as they felt that anything involving a unity on this level was certainly worthwhile. B.B. King was seen performing at the Hague. Billy Ocean sang from the U.S., Sade from England, and then Chevy Chase introduced Black Sabbath. Yu Rock Mission performed in Belgrade, followed by Run-DMC from JFK, and Sting (with Branford Marsalis) in London. Phil Collins performed, and then Sting and Marsalis returned to the stage to join him. Rick Springfield took the stage in Philadelphia, and then REO Speedwagon performed their hit "Can't Fight This Feeling" before joining with the Beach Boys to sing "Roll with the Changes." Howard Jones appeared at Wembley, and then Autograph performed from Moscow. Bryan Ferry, with David Gilmour on guitar, performed as best they could while experiencing some of the day's few technical difficulties. The drummer put his stick through the drum skin, Gilmour had problems with his guitar, and the microphones cut out at one point but Ferry soldiered on and was well-received. Then came appearances by Crosby, Stills and Nash at JFK, Band Fur Afrika in Cologne, Judas Priest at JFK, Paul Young at Wembley, and a finish by Young and Alison Moyet singing "That's the Way Love Is."

Bryan Adams rocked out from Philadelphia, and then a relatively unknown U2 took the stage at Wembley. The performance they gave at Live Aid would result in U2 being recognized as one of the paramount acts in live entertainment. The audience was charmed when front man Bono jumped down into the crowd to "dance" with a young woman. It wasn't until years later that it came out that Bono wasn't dancing with the young lady but rather grabbing her to keep her from being crushed by the crowd. As people pushed forward, the young lady was trapped against the stage. Bono gestured frenetically to the stage crew to help her but when they didn't seem to understand, the singer took matters into his own hands and jumped down to grab her and act as if they were dancing.

The Beach Boys were introduced by Marilyn McCoo and performed several of their hits. Dire Straits appeared with Sting, and George Thorogood and the Destroyers appeared in the U.S. with guitar legends Bo Diddley and Albert Collins. Comedians Mel Smith and Griff Rhys Jones introduced Queen. Freddie Mercury was his usual energetic self and soon had the audience singing along with him. Mercury even danced with a cameraman during one of the band's numbers. (Although Brian May thinks that the band was perhaps over-excited, many thought that Queen's performance that day stole the show.) After Queen, a video of David Bowie and Mick

Jagger singing "Dancing in the Street" was shown. Simple Minds went on at JFK, followed by a solo Bowie with Thomas Dolby on keyboards.

"My most vivid memory of Live Aid was arriving at Wembley Stadium in a helicopter with David Bowie," remembers Thomas Dolby. "He has a well-documented fear of flying. He'd only recently started to fly over the Atlantic after taking the boat for years. This was his first trip in a helicopter. Up until that time, whenever we'd met he'd always been wonderfully kind and civil towards me. But for those fifteen minutes in the chopper he was the 'Cracked Actor'—fidgety, hat pulled down over his face, chain-smoking, demanding to know how soon we would touch down. I remember us banking over Wembley Stadium as Queen played. I could see Freddie Mercury's face projected massive on the jumbo screens. The moment we landed, Bowie's demeanor changed instantly. The chopper was encircled by hundreds of photographers. As he prepared to run the gauntlet, a broad grin spread across his face. 'This it is then!' he said, and exited the helicopter."

"A mere five minutes later, we were led onstage in front of 100,000 people and it was all down to me to kick off the set with the solo piano intro to 'TVC15,' continues Dolby. "The young band zoomed through four songs that we'd had only a couple of days to rehearse; we'd never actually played them back-to-back! I'd been worried I'd screw up the lead synth line in 'Heroes.' When we came to it though, I looked out over the hordes of people swaying together in the packed stadium as Bowie belted out his immortal rock anthem, seducing them with his smile and his suave presence. I was of the generation of English musicians that grew up with Bowie's music, we could play his songs in our sleep. I felt I was floating, and my fingers just knew where to go."

A poignant moment was experienced both onstage and off when Bowie dedicated his song 'Heroes,' which was being performed by an all-star group of musicians, to his son and all of the children in the world.

Problems naturally popped up during the day. Some of the artists announced to appear, such as Julian Lennon, Prince, Cat Stevens, Deep Purple, and Tears for Fears, for various reasons did not. Of course there were some technical difficulties and miscommunication but the spirit of the event prevailed and everything was somehow worked out. Unfortunately, a last minute snafu caused the BBC to omit the Philadelphia reunion of Crosby, Stills, Nash & Young when Young joined his former bandmates later in the day. Another problem arose when radio syndicator Westwood One served the production with a subpoena to stop the show because the producers had failed to recognize the company's radio performance rights to several of the artists appearing on the bill. Uplinger was able to pacify the syndicator by offering to have Bill Graham acknowledge their involvement onstage.

Another situation at first seemed beyond the control of the technicians but that was also worked out. Before September 11, 2001, it was not unusual to have helicopters hovering over major U.S. events. Such was the case in Philadelphia and one helicopter in particular was interfering with the satellite transmission dishes. When Uplinger put in a call to Federal Aviation Control he was told that there was nothing they could do about the matter. Uplinger was not deterred and put in a call to a contact he had made with people from the Assistance International Development Office at the White House and they cleared the airspace of helicopters and small planes.

Three hundred telephone lines were provided by the BBC to handle the viewer donations, which were solicited on air. Pleas for financial participation were aired every twenty minutes. Although the initial goal had been to raise one million pounds, seven hours into the broadcast Geldof realized that much more could be raised. He appeared on camera and in his typically direct manner told the viewing audience "People are dying, *now*. Give us the money, *now*." (Geldof had previously stated that if even 10 percent of those tuning in to watch contributed, the number and amount would be substantial.) Additional donations began to pore in almost instantly, especially when a brief video produced by the CBC about famine and the innocent children it effected (while the Cars' song "Drive" played over the haunting images) was shown. David Bowie had seen this footage earlier and had insisted it be played; even offering his final song in exchange for the time it would take to air it.

The Pretenders took the stage. The Who performed at a raucous pace at Wembley. Including Kenney Jones on drums, the band's set was thrown a bit off-kilter by some minor technical problems and the members of the band seemed to be having some personal difficulties as well. A generator exploded as Roger Daltry sang "My Generation," causing his last words in the line "Why don't you all just fade away" to be left a bit ambiguous. Santana and Pat Metheny appeared at JFK.

Various celebrities continued to hang out backstage in Philadelphia while the crowd out front was periodically misted with water to help keep them cool. There were only a handful of arrests at either venue. Everything went off amazingly well. The stars of the show walked through the crowd to greet fans, or hung out in the replica diner the Hard Rock Café had built, where refreshments were provided for free and the Café asked only for donations.

ABC specified that only six artists would appear on their prime time broadcast, which was hosted by Dick Clark. This was difficult for two reasons: many of the acts wanted to be featured at that time and also because the more popular artists were appearing at various other times throughout the sixteen-hour concert. One of the major challenges was the fact that ABC had asked that Phil Collins, who had already appeared on the Wembley stage earlier in the day, begin the American broadcast at precisely 8 p.m. With all the logistics involved throughout the day this seemed like an impossible feat but Collins, who had been interviewed on the Concorde as he made his way to the United States for his second appearance of the day, miraculously appeared at the piano at 8 p.m. on the dot. (British Airways had provided free use of a Concorde for the day of the event.) Duran Duran had been asked to make dual appearances as well, but decided against it. While on the Concorde, Phil Collins ran into Cher, who didn't know about the concert. Collins filled her in as to the importance of the day and Cher surprised Collins by "dropping by" to participate in Philadelphia's finale.

A video of "All of Us" from Norway was shown, and then Elton John performed. Ashford & Simpson sang, and they were joined by Teddy Pendergast for "Reach Out and Touch (Somebody's Hand)." It was Pendergast's first public appearance since a car accident in 1982 had left him paralyzed and, as the crowd cheered him, tears rolled down his face. In London, Elton John was joined by Kiki Dee, then Wham. Kool & the Gang appeared in a pre-recorded video, then Madonna. Wembley began its wrap up with Freddie Mercury and Brian May performing "Is This the World We Created?"

It had been important to Geldof and Ure to include at least one of the remaining Beatles in the concert. Not only was this a nod of respect to the Fabs but it was thought that participation by a Beatle would bring an extra measure of legitimacy to the endeavor. George Harrison and Ringo Starr wavered on appearing for some reason, but Paul McCartney was convinced by his children—who he referred to as his "management"—to perform. (Yoko Ono came to the event in Philadelphia to represent the slain John Lennon.) Paul McCartney sat at a piano to sing "Let It Be." Unfortunately, McCartney's microphone was turned off for the first few minutes but the audience hardly noticed as they were just thrilled to see the rock legend. McCartney later said that he considered changing the lyrics to "There shall be some feedback, let it be."

Finally an all-star cast united to sing "Do They Know It's Christmas?" Geldof was raised onto the shoulders of Paul McCartney and Pete Townshend to uproarious applause and cheering.

The British concert had gone off spectacularly. It also had an immediate impact on those not able to get into Wembley. Midge Ure remembers leaving Wembley and being shocked and thrilled that people in the streets were listening to the broadcast, hanging out in bars, partying to the event, and showing vast amounts of brotherly love.

The JFK concert continued with Tom Petty, who had decided to perform "American Girl" right before taking the stage; Kenny Loggins; the Cars; Neil Young, who claimed he was doing the most laid-back act in the show; Power Station; the Thompson Twins first solo and then with Madonna; Eric Clapton, who chose to highlight songs from both his past and current work; and Phil Collins in his second appearance (singing the same songs on both continents). Led Zeppelin's Robert Plant, Jimmy Page, and John Paul Jones reunited to perform "Whole Lotta Love" and "Stairway to Heaven." (Plant had to write down the words to the latter on a cheat sheet as it had been so long since he had sung the rock anthem.) Then Crosby, Stills, Nash & Young followed suit, reuniting to sing "Only Love Can Break Your Heart," "Daylight Again," and "Find the Cost of Freedom." It would be the last performance of Duran Duran for some time to come, then Cliff Richard sang, and Patti LaBelle performed. Hall & Oates performed their set and were then joined by Eddie Kendricks and David Ruffin for a medley of Temptations hits. Mick Jagger (who said he was there not only for the cause but to enjoy himself) joined in, and then sang "State of Shock," and "It's Only Rock and Roll" with Tina Turner, who would initiate the staged "wardrobe malfunction" as Jagger ripped away part of her dress and left her to perform in a leotard. She also accidentally stabbed Jagger in the foot with her stiletto heel.

The Philadelphia show came to a close with Bob Dylan, Keith Richards, and Ron Wood taking the stage. In a striking moment of unity, when Dylan broke a guitar string, Ron Wood simply handed the legend *his* guitar. Wood then played air guitar until he was handed a replacement. Dylan caused a bit of controversy when he mentioned that he hoped that a little of the money raised would be used to pay the mortgages on the farms of some American farmers. Geldof would later say that Dylan's comment demonstrated a lack of understanding about the purpose of the event. Geldof pointed out that there is a difference between losing one's livelihood and losing one's life. Geldof considered Dylan's comment crass. (Willie Nelson, Neil Young, and John Mellencamp would be inspired by Dylan's remarks to later launch

Farm Aid.) In another controversy, the opinionated band Chumbawamba questioned the altruistic intent of those who performed at the concerts and the following year released an album titled "Pictures of Starving Children Sell Records."

Lionel Richie took to the stage to lead a star-studded sing-a-long of "We Are the World" and close the concert. Richie was extremely popular but certainly not of the caliber of many of the legendary performers who had preceded him both in America and in London. The climax was a bit of an anti-climax.

A total of 72,000 people attended the Wembley concert with 90,000 in attendance at JFK. An estimated 1.5 billion viewers from over 100 countries watched the broadcast that started at noon at Wembley and three hours later in Philadelphia. The worldwide reception of the broadcast was unbelievable. One estimate of those tuning in was said to be 95 percent of the number of televisions around the world.

While the initial hope was that Live Aid would raise one million pounds, the final figure was close to 284 million dollars. The largest donation came from the ruling family of Dubai who donated 1 million pounds. Geldof later mentioned that the Republic of Ireland donated the most of any country per capita even though that country was experiencing a serious economic depression at the time. Critics such as television pundit Bill O'Reilly questioned how much of the money raised by the event actually made it to the most-needy people. Many informed individuals have noted that the corrupt governments who are most often involved in such circumstances acutely obstruct charity donations and use the money instead for their own nefarious activities. While that all may be true, a massive amount of money was raised and donated but also British Parliament allowed the RAF to continue Ethiopian airlifts and the U.S. Congress formed a commission to address the problem of the trucking cartel and transportation issues. Tons of milk powder, oil, sugar, grain, and biscuits were transported to those in need in Africa. A great amount of cash was also given to agencies that could help them.

Midge Ure says that not only is it the money raised that counts but the awareness and involvement of the rock audience. Participating in the world's first global concert festival as viewers, many people realized that they could make a difference in the lives of others they would never even meet. Bob Geldof would remember that day in music history succinctly. He would say that "on that day, for once in our bloody lives, we won."

In July, 1995 BBC and VH1 aired a ten-hour retrospective of the Live Aid concert with current artist interviews, performances from the original broadcast, and footage of Bob Geldof returning to Africa. Although there had been no initial plans for a commercial release of the concert footage, in 2004 the Warner Music Group released a four-disc DVD. In 2005, the entire BBC broadcast of the event was video-streamed on the internet through a fan site.

The music festival had now been expanded to play out on the world stage of television. What had begun at Monterey Pop was being redeveloped to fit the times. The traditional music festival would not be abandoned by any means, but promoters began to realize that festivals could be organized in a variety of completely different ways. The music festival had changed and evolved once again, but its roots would not be forgotten or abandoned.

South by Southwest
1987

In 1987, Austin, Texas, was not a major market for music but it was a town that knew how to party. After the War Between the States, many of the troops of General George Armstrong Custer settled in the city and frequented the numerous bars that sprung up at that location to offer them a place to congregate. With the competition between establishments came various forms of music entertainment. Many contemporary nightspots remained located in this same area some one hundred years later and the people of Austin continued to enjoy the community of music entertainment.

In 1982, Roland Swenson attended the New Music Seminar in New York. Swenson returned to his home base of Austin with the thought that a music event held in that city would benefit the growing music industry of the area. Tucked away deep in Texas, Austin musicians were somewhat isolated and they were ready to reach out to the rest of the country, and internationally, to play (and share) their music.

With the sponsorship of *Austin Chronicle* publisher Nick Barbaro, Swenson, *Chronicle* editor Louis Black, and booking agent Louis Jay Meyers created the first South by Southwest Music Conference. The quartet was unsure of how the conference would be received, but when 700 people turned out they realized that they were onto something that could boost their local industry and establish Austin as a destination music location. Over two hundred bands played in twelve clubs over the course of that first event. Blues and punk scenes flourished in Austin and when those in the Los Angeles and New York music industry were offered the opportunity to see firsthand what was happening in Texas, they were intrigued and jumped at the invitation. South by Southwest had the support of the Austin community at large but it also brought in millions of tourist dollars for area businesses.

Now considered one of the most important annual music festivals, South by Southwest is currently a private company with a year-round staff that organizes the South by Southwest Music and Media Conference. The event is held every spring over four days, centered around the Austin Convention Center and nearby clubs. Artists from all over the country play at SBSW, where record labels sign deals, venues and tours are booked, and European distribution is offered. In 1994, South by Southwest added both a film and interactive (primarily web-based) conference. Workshops, meetings, and panels are well-attended and well-received. In 2006 over 1,400 acts performed before 8,000 attendees and showed that South by Southwest is growing as one of the premier events for those in the music industry to see and be seen.

But not every band that wants to play at South by Southwest is given the opportunity. Artists and bands that apply for a showcase are judged and graded by a committee that listens to their demos, at least twice, and selects those who they feel have the most potential. Expanding the festival, North by Northeast was established in Toronto and is now an annual three-day music festival held on the second weekend in June.

1989–1990
What I Am

In U.S. news

George H. W. Bush is elected President; Los Angeles City Council bans sale or possession of semi-automatic weapons; Time, Inc., and Warner Communications merge; the junk bond market collapses; the "Night Stalker" is convicted; and *Seinfeld* and *The Simpsons* premier.

In world news

The first global positioning system satellite is placed into orbit; the Soviets withdraw from Afghanistan; Ayatollah Khomeini places a bounty on author Salman Rushdie; the Exxon Valdez spills 11 million gallons of oil; students protest in China's Tiananmen Square resulting in a massacre; Game Boy debuts; Gorbachev visits China; Khomeini dies; the Velvet Revolution takes place in Czechoslovakia; and the Berlin Wall comes down.

In music news

James Brown is sentenced to six years in jail; Tiny Tim campaigns for mayor of New York City; and the Madonna video "Like a Prayer" causes controversy.

Some of the year's most notable albums

Shawn Colvin: *Steady On*; Green Day: *1,000 Hours*; Jane's Addiction: *Nothing's Shocking*; Milli Vanilli: *Girl You Know It's True*; N.W.A.: *Straight Outta Compton*; Nine Inch Nails: *Pretty Hate Machine*; Bonnie Raitt: *Nick of Time*; Red Hot Chili Peppers: *Mother's Milk*; Skid Row: *Skid Row*.

Rock's most popular songs

"Another Day in Paradise"—Phil Collins; "Love Shack"—The B52s; "Eternal Flame"—the Bangles; "Monsters of Rock"—Judas Priest; "Ring My Bell"—Colette; "She Drives Me Crazy"—Fine Young Cannibals; "If I Could Turn Back Time"—Cher; "Straight Up"—Paula Abdul; "What I Am"—Edie Brickell & the New Bohemians; "You Got It"—Roy Orbison.

Woodstock '89
August 16–17, 1989

"It feels older."
    —Michael Lang

After the lack of enthusiasm for the tenth anniversary of the Woodstock festival one would think that the twentieth anniversary of Woodstock would be a big deal. It was to the media, which remembered the event with newspaper stories and magazine articles. CBS radio even broadcasted "Woodstock Moments." Yet the original event apparently wasn't noteworthy enough at this point in time for someone to organize a formal remembrance. Even so, to thousands of people it was an important enough anniversary date that they traveled to the site of the original festival even if nothing dramatically official had been planned.

Although the commemorative date fell in the middle of the week that year, people began to arrive at the site of the '69 festival to either remember their own previous experiences or attempt to tap into the consciousness of a three-day moment in time that they had either somehow missed or been too young to participate. There was no stage, no bands scheduled, no food or drink, and no portable toilets.

Max Yasgur had died eleven years before and his farm was now owned by others. A monument to the original festival had been erected with a list of those who performed and the event's trademark guitar and bird. Michael Lang, one of the original festival producers, showed up to remember one of the most important days of his life and was recognized by many who wanted to shake his hand. Lang was inevitably asked how it felt to be on the site again and he replied, fittingly, "It feels older."

This time there was no miles-long line of abandoned vehicles. Anyone wishing to enter the site could drive right up, park on the field, and create their own campsite if the mood struck them. At least at first. Close to 30,000 people would appear on Friday and over 50,000 would sign the guest book located at the memorial (still it was a far, far cry from the over 500,000 present at the first Woodstock). Some people quickly erected a stage and musicians and instruments began to appear. Some hot dog and souvenir tables were brought in. In a suitable throw-back to the earlier event, it rained a little. People sat strumming guitars and singing sixties songs. Tourists from various parts of the world showed up to gawk at the hippies but instead found more yuppies and families with children who came to the site for a quick look. Nobody knew if anything had been planned or not—they simply wanted to be there for their own reasons.

Wavy Gravy walked through the crowd, enjoying the recognition. Many of the people there were now middle-aged and entrenched in lives far removed from what they had dreamed during those long-ago days in the mud. The negative elements of the festival seemed to have been conveniently forgotten in place of fonder memories of comradery and great music. The younger people who came to pay tribute realized that events such as the one they missed twenty years ago would likely be impossible to replicate these days. The world had changed and so had the music.

A three-day concert—not festival—had been planned at the nearby Imperial Hotel at Swan Lake but, although some of those who played at the original festival returned to entertain, the tickets this time were seventy-five dollars. Not too many people showed up—those in town were mostly there to see what was happening at the original site. Melanie sang again and Jimi Hendrix's father Al addressed the crowd. Lisa Best played and Savoy Brown appreciated the opportunity to perform at the site where they had been previously unable to play.

Several of the performers who played at the Imperial found themselves drawn to return to Yasgur's farm themselves. There were a lot of memories no doubt, but things had definitely changed in ways they perhaps didn't consider. There was an attention to ecology now and those who were there this time . . . even cleaned up after themselves.

Moscow Peace Festival
1989

Called a festival, although technically a concert, an event occurred in 1989 that was an interesting twist on events past. Heavy metal rock producer and manger Doc McGhee joined forces with other promoters, and the Make a Difference Foundation, to stage a concert for the people of Moscow that would emphasize world peace and also, in an interesting twist of irony, help Russia in its war against drugs. Communism was collapsing and the people of the almost extinct USSR were focused on the future. Whether or not their focus was on what the promoters of the Moscow Peace Festival were peddling is debatable.

The concert was held over two days at Lenin Stadium and was attended by upwards of 100,000 people. Some of the performances were also shown on television.

Appearing on the bill were Cinderella, the Scorpions, Gorky Park, Mötley Crüe, Skid Row, Ozzy Osbourne, and Bon Jovi. Each band was scheduled to perform a six-song set. The premise of the show seemed straight-forward but things went on backstage that were counter-intuitive to the fellowship of man and the war on drugs that was being addressed onstage.

Egos clashed when some members of other bands saw or heard that headliner Bon Jovi was planning a theatrical stage production as well as a longer time on the stage than the others. Ozzy Osbourne wanted to call off his appearance and Jon Bon Jovi responded to that news by saying Osbourne could have the headlining spot if it meant that much to him. Mötley Crüe were unhappy with McGhee, who was also their manager. Punches were thrown and McGhee was fired by the band. Members of Skid Row clashed with many of the other bands. Peace, love, and resistance to drugs didn't seem to apply backstage.

The Make a Difference Foundation released a compilation album that year that featured each band performing a song originally recorded by a rock icon that had died due to drugs or alcohol. The rock festival had been redefined under another interesting premise that featured a good cause and some stellar performances, but the Moscow Peace Festival marked a very disconcerting time for altruistic concerts and festivals. Charity festivals were temporarily on the downswing. Many of the people who were interested in attending a festival didn't want to be bothered with all that. They wanted to party. Still, there were one or two important awareness festivals to come.

A Gathering of the Tribes
October 6–7, 1990

Promoter Bill Graham continued to be involved in rock festivals on several levels. The idea for what would develop into A Gathering of the Tribes was presented to Graham by the Cult's singer Ian Astbury. During a national tour, Astbury had experienced vehicle problems in North Dakota. After a Native American man fixed the vehicle, he invited Astbury to his home for dinner. The ensuing conversation included the man telling Astbury that he would soon leave for college where he intended to study resource management so that he could learn how to purify the drinking water for his tribe. When the man casually asked what Astbury was doing to help *his* community, the singer was shocked to realize that he was doing little at all. Upon further reflection, Astbury decided to team with Bill Graham to launch a two-day, two-location festival that would both raise money and make people aware of some of the most basic of Native American needs.

Astbury and Graham decided to make the music bill reflective of the times and contracted to hold the California concerts at the Shoreline Amphitheater in San Francisco and the Pacific Amphitheater in Costa Mesa. They would feature rock, rap, grunge, folk, and acts that transverse many of rock's sub-genres including Soundgarden, Iggy Pop, Steve Jones of the Sex Pistols, Joan Baez, the Indigo Girls, Ice T, Queen Latifa, and Public Enemy. The concerts quickly sold out.

The eventual appearance of Public Enemy became questionable in San Francisco due to violence that had been erupting at the rappers' recent concerts. The media was fueling the fire of controversy and the decision was made that Public Enemy would not appear. The San Francisco festival, which was more of an outdoor concert than festival, featured mesmerizing performances. In his usual attention-grabbing manner, Iggy Pop cut himself with a bottle and bled all over the stage.

Despite the success of the music, Astbury says that he finished the weekend in the red. Hopefully Astbury's desire to have great numbers of people focus on the needs of Native Americans was successful, but that may be doubtful. A Gathering of the Tribes, however, would make way for a new and unique concept: a long-running mobile festival that would take place all over the United States.

1991
Smells Like Teen Spirit

In U.S. news

Michigan court bars Dr. Jack Kevorkian from assisted suicide; the Rodney King video tape hits the media; William Kennedy Smith and Mike Tyson are charged with sexual assault; Jeffrey Dahmer is arrested for multiple murders; the Clarence Thomas hearings take place; and Magic Johnson announces he has HIV.

In world news

The Gulf War rages; the PIRA bombs 10 Downing Street and Victoria Station in London; Germany gains independence from WWII Allied countries; 138,000 people are killed during a cyclone in Bangladesh; and Boris Yeltsin is elected President of Russia as the U.S.S.R. collapses.

In music news

Grunge music becomes popular; Christian music is on the upswing; Garth Brooks' country popularity crosses over to the pop charts; three people are crushed during an AC/DC concert; Michael Jackson signs a 1 billion dollar contract with Sony; and a wrongful death suit against Ozzy Osbourne and his music's influence on the death of a teenager is dismissed.

Some of the year's most notable albums

DJ Jeff & the Fresh Prince: *Homebase*; Guns N' Roses: *Use Your Illusion I & II*; Metallica: *Metallica*; Sarah McLachlan: *Solace*; Morrissey: *Kill Uncle*; R.E.M.: *Out of Time*; Skid Row: *Slave to the Grind*; Smashing Pumpkins: *Gish*; U2: *Achtung Baby*; Van Halen: *For Unlawful Carnal Knowledge*; Widespread Panic: *Widespread Panic*.

Rock's most popular songs

"Bohemian Rhapsody"—Queen; "I Can't Make You Love Me" and "Something to Talk About"—Bonnie Raitt; "Losin' My Religion"—R.E.M.; "Smells Like Teen Spirit"—Nirvana; "Top of the World"—Van Halen.

Lollapalooza
1991

"It was the original hybrid of live music."
—Peter DiStefano, Porno for Pyros

Live Aid had driven the music festival to an international stage and the local festival, to many, just didn't seem exciting anymore. The state of music festivals in general was one of uncertainty. The few attempts at returning to a less expansive state of mind had been only moderately successful. Even so, people continued to be interested in sharing music and partying. In the early eighties a trend had started which was called "raves." Rave parties were primarily centered on electronic dance music. Instead of live performances, DJs provided the music. NRG in Houston and The Music Institute in Detroit were major rave venues and the craze was also prominent throughout the United Kingdom and Europe. By the late eighties the music had grown to include psychedelic sound experimentation. The music was central to the events, but an important element of the rave was drugs. Ecstasy was the chemical of choice with methamphetamine, speed, and other drugs also a featured part of the rave experience.

When it became apparent what their children were doing behind the closed doors of their parties, some parents began to pressure authorities to put an end to the gatherings. Public pressure drove the rave party underground, to be held in secret locations such as warehouses and private clubs. These parties were pronounced "illegal" by law enforcement and politicians, but they continued to thrive throughout the nineties. The rave society created a social network that was reflected by those-in-the-know, using the acronym PLUR, which stood for Peace, Love, Unity, and Respect. There seemed to be little respect as drugs continued to be the main focus of most raves and with the introduction of date rape tablets a serious criminal element hung like a contaminated cloud over the parties. By the end of the nineties, raves started to fall out of fashion. They just weren't novel anymore, and suspicion and foreboding impacted the enjoyment of attending such an event. Young people began to look to satisfy their desire for music and their need for a social scene in clubs and, instead of calling themselves "ravers" they were now "clubbers." Raves remain popular with some these days, but the feeling of fellowship sought by the mainstream would center back on the traditional rock festival . . . with a twist.

By 1991, it was time yet again to redefine the rock festival. Younger generations continued to rebel against the establishment, but in a much less involved way. Young people may not have liked the way the world was going—but then again, they may have—but making a statement about world affairs wasn't usually their foremost thought. The mindset of the majority of those under twenty-one was to retreat into their own youth-based society and live their lives outside of the mainstream, except when necessary for education and employment. Grunge music was beginning its popularity with the advent of bands such as Nirvana and "alternative" was the buzz word of those currently foremost on the music scene. Hip hop music was coming into play on the radio and the punk element continued to thrive. Rather than power ballads or pop music of the eighties, young people were now looking to a variety of sounds.

Musician Perry Ferrell had attended A Gathering of Tribes and was struck by its unique music bill. There was definitely something for everybody and the festival had been a terrific opportunity to expose different types of music to new listeners. Farrell, lead singer of the popular band Jane's Addiction, was looking for a grand way for his band to say farewell.

Farrell had heard the word "lollapalooza" in a Three Stooges short film and understood the word to mean unusual and remarkable. Farrell felt that it would be fun to launch a traveling festival that would feature Jane's Addiction, but also offer a variety of the new music and other elements that would make attendance an enjoyable and involving experience. Farrell's Lollapalooza would also include comedy and dance performances and craft booths. Circus acts, monks, art, virtual reality games, and tables and booths featuring political and environmental issues of the day developed Lollapalooza from just another big concert into a cultural festival much like the US Festival had done a decade before.

An effective new twist was the decision that Lollapalooza would travel throughout the United States and Canada. The traveling festival was an opportunity to not only represent new music and new artists but also to expose the music and artists to a geographically wide variety of audiences. The bill would reflect that of A Gathering of the Tribes in that it would be diverse and representative of the sub-genres of the day. Jane's Addiction would headline the first tour but also performing would be Nine Inch Nails, Butthole Surfers, the Rollins Band, Siouxsie & the Banshees, Violent Femmes, Living Colour, and Ice T and Body Count.

The first Lollapalooza would prove so successful that those involved decided to make it an annual event. The festival-on-wheels kicked off the next season with an additional stage for up-and-coming and local bands. When grunge became the music du jour, those bands were the featured performers. Mosh pits and crowd surfing brought an additional element to audience involvement. Attendees could also participate by playing on giant jungle gyms, giving readings at open-microphone booths, getting a tattoo or a body piercing, and communing with their fellow fans in a variety of other ways.

Before the advent of on-line ticketing, people would line-up for days to purchase tickets to Lollapalooza. In the beginning, the ticket prices were low and almost anybody looking for a good time could afford them. As the higher prices of the nineties became a reality, many people accused the festival of selling out to corporate interests by raising the admittance and charging increasing prices for food and drink. There was a mini-protest in Detroit that had some in the crowd ripping up sods of ground to throw at each other (and bands). Respect for the festival by some of those who initially attended began to wane as climbing on seats and scaffolds and the destruction of property and bonfires increased.

"Oooo, in the past I really didn't like the outdoor shows," remembers Nathan Larson of Shudder to Think. "Festivals. There's nowhere to sit. There's a fair amount of mud. Heat rash sets in. My wife loves them, but she's European and I think it's in the blood over there. But growing up I never once did the "wake-up -where-you-fell the night before" in some overcrowded field, dehydrated, shelterless and ill in the merciless sun. I just never saw the appeal. I liked a proper bathroom. Oh, I did the wake-up-where-you fell thing mind you, just never in the context of an outdoor concert. I always awoke on concrete, in a large city. My perspective has changed a bit now that I'm not in one of the bands, and it's a bit ironic that next week my wife and I will celebrate our sixth anniversary at Hultsfred, an outdoor festival in Sweden where, tragically, a number of kids were killed during a Pearl Jam set several years ago. See what I mean? These events are dangerous, kids!"

Despite its inherent problems, the overwhelming excellence and number of bands can make for a memorable experience. "Lollapalooza '95 in Pittsburgh ruled," remembers Greg Gillis of Girl Talk. "I was thirteen-years-old and that was my first festival. My dad took my best friend and I. The line-up was insane: Sonic Youth, Cypress Hill, Hole, Beck, Elastica, Jesus Lizard, Pavement, Superchunk, and so on. I wasn't familiar with the Jesus Lizard prior to that festival, and their performance pretty much blew my mind. We spent our time during Cypress Hill and Hole sneaking up front and by the time Sonic Youth went on, we were leaning against the stage. They were amazing. That festival's line-up was the first time I saw normal-looking people making somewhat non-traditional music and being very successful at it. It seemed like a real movement to my young, teenage mind. That was very influential in me starting my own musical projects."

"I have a bunch of glorious, cherished, and squalid memories of Lollapalooza, what was it '95?" says Craig Wedren of Shudder to Think. "Amazing lineup that included Boredoms, Nick Cave, Beastie Boys, Breeders, Stereolab, Pharcide, Smashing Pumpkins, P-Funk, Green Day—damn! We sure took that shit for granted, but in retrospect it was kind of a high-water mark, the crest of some sort of unwitting wave. Every day we were on at the same time as the [Nick Cave and the] Bad Seeds, who were one of our favorite, all-time bands, and who we never once got to actually see. So we would take extended breaks between songs (alterna-macho festival-goers were usually freaked out and angry at our sets anyway, so we had little to lose) and catch waves of their set wafting over from the main stage. I think they had much the same challenge we did, reception-wise, and we flattered ourselves by imagining a kinship that, in reality, went precisely one way, because they didn't know we existed. In the middle of this beer-sweaty, teenaged sunfest, the Bad Seeds looked impeccable *at all times*, emerging from the men's room, by the mist tent, ghost-gods from a completely different world. I don't think I had the balls to say 'hello,' didn't really want to humanize my heroes, needed them more as apparitions than men."

Not only does Lollapalooza provide music by professional bands and musicians but it is a good networking tool for those who would like to *become* involved with music. "Also at that same festival, I met a local promoter named Manny Thiener," says Greg Gillis. "He was passing out a pamphlet about local music. I read it and then found out abut Pittsburgh college radio stations and many underground/experimental bands. Since then, Manny has put on almost all of my local shows and has been extremely helpful in my musical development."

Lollapalooza can be a great opportunity for artist exposure. Having people hear a band for the first time or see a band whose song they may have heard on the radio is an important part of artist development. "For some new bands, where they just have their first song on the radio, the festival can be great at putting together all the pieces that lead to breaking them around the country," says the Tea Party/the Art Decay's Stuart Chatwood.

While being asked to join Lollapalooza is sometimes an honor and usually a good thing for a band to do, it sometimes comes with complications. "The band I was with,

Artificial Joy Club, had just signed with Interscope Records in January of 1997, after a few months of U.S. record labels flying up to Canada to see us," remembers Drew Lamarche. "We were traveling back and forth between Ottawa and Los Angeles for a few months while our album was being set to be released. From what I recall, we were in L.A. doing our first video for the album and our manager, Doug Goldstein, had contacted us and asked if we wanted to do the first leg of the Lollapalooza '97 tour. Our album was set to come out in early July and we were going to start the tour a few weeks before the CD hit the shelves. We had to go from L.A. back to Ottawa a few days after the video shoot, play at the Universal Music Conference in Canada, and then get home and leave for the second date of the tour in Atlanta. I think it was about a twenty-hour drive that we had to do. Unfortunately we had to miss the first date due to the travel time. We had to pull everything together in a very short amount of time. We had no crew, just the band. I was excited to be on the tour since I actually had attended the first three Lollapalooza tour shows around Toronto. I never actually imagined that I would be playing at Lollapalooza! We had a good time slot; I think we were on at around 6 p.m. on the second stage in between KoRn and Snoop Dogg on the main stage. We did make a lot of fans and friends on the tour."

All this is not to say there aren't complications. "It was so fucking hot that day we played," remembers Zia McCabe of the Dandy Warhols. "I had baby Matilda with me the whole day and by the time we got to the interview in the trailer with the fluorescent lights I knew I was going to get a migraine. I was sick back at the hotel. Tildy wanted me to hold her so I had to throw up in the dark bathroom holding her. It was awful! It was pretty great having the Brian Jonestown Massacre onstage with us for the gig though. [And] the Pixies, so cool to see them."

Backstage, business goes on as usual. "Meeting up with other bands is always a bit strange," says Stuart Chatwood. "Everyone is a bit hungover and tired, so by the time everyone is feeling better and moved beyond the basic 'Hey . . . what's up?' dialogue, it's time to play. Socially, I think the tone is set by the biggest band. If they hang out with other acts, the smaller acts see how lame it is to put on airs of exclusivity, when the band they are trying to emulate is hanging out with everyone. We have met some great people over the years, but lasting friendship made backstage on a multi-band festival is rare."

But many times the bands and artists do have a good time while on the Lollapalooza tour. In addition to playing, there are sometimes enjoyable diversions. "The New Orleans gig in 1993 . . ." remembers Porno for Pyros guitarist Peter DiStefano. "It was so fun to slide in the mud after the set. The San Francisco gig was fun, too. I bungee jumped right after my set." DiStefano was pleased to be on the Lollapalooza tour. "I was very grateful for Perry," he says. "He picked me up and I have had a great ride."

"Some of the memories that have stayed in my mind from Lollapalooza were all the shows and hanging out with the other bands and the tour crew," recalls Drew Lamarche. "Catering was always great as well, everyone shared the catering area, so aside from the food being great you would be having lunch or dinner with Tool, Snoop, Devo, KoRn, and all the other artists. I recall a few times that there was a day off [and] we would end up with a lot of other bands at some hotel bar. I seem to remember some karaoke action by some people!"

At the peak of grunge in 1994, Nirvana was asked to headline Lollapalooza but Kurt Cobain sent his regrets. Within weeks the singer/songwriter committed suicide. Cobain's widow Courtney Love used the festival as an outlet for her grief and anger, and addressed the crowd at various stops along the tour. Lollapalooza continued to travel throughout the country every summer, featuring name acts and those on the rise. The festival was something that thousands looked forward to: to enjoy good music and connect with friends, old and new.

As much as it was an opportunity for sharing music though, being on such a long tour with other bands and artists can be stressful to a musician. "On the road" is not an easy place to be. "My old band Shudder to Think did Lollapalooza in 1994, I think," remembers Nathan Larson. "I was a sniffy little bastard: I hated it. The rest of my band would be out basking like lizards and I would be on somebody's bus watching *Blade Runner* or *Spinal Tap*, pale as pale could be. I don't remember exactly, but it was me and James Iha, slumping there in the air-conditioned darkness while joyful and terrible and sexy and life-changing dramas played out among the multitudes of kids outside the bus. I remember being concerned about the lack of an ironing board . . . or at least some kind of steamer! You do get wrinkly. Of course hindsight is twenty-twenty, but if I'd only taken a moment out of my pissy, half-drunken heat-struck fugue for ten seconds to glance around I would have maybe gotten a chance to appreciate the unbelievable lineup that year. Included [were] some of the best bands to come out of that decade, as well as some truly legendary figures. I truly envy the kids who attended and hope they could *dig* this: the Breeders, George Clinton and P-Funk, Tribe Called Quest, Luscious Jackson, Nick *Cave* for God's sake! The Smashing Pumpkins (we were there by their good grace), Guided by Voices, the Flaming Lips, the Pharcyde, the Beastie Boys, Green Day, L7, the Black Crowes,

Porno for Pyros, Cypress Hill, and that's just what I remember and I don't remember much! As I mentioned I was drunk most of the time . . . but in a private, expensive 'on-somebody's-bus-on-somebody-else's-liquor' kind of way. I've since quit drinking and for some reason I feel much better about everything."

This isn't to say that Larson didn't experience any of the behind-the-scenes drama. "I mentioned wrinkles," continues Larson. "That didn't deter the Bad Seeds from slinking around in suits in 108 degree weather. I remember Nick Cave carrying around a briefcase and I would wonder what the hell was in it. It was hot! We played about four, five p.m. The sun would be *right smack in your face* and there was nothing to be done about it. I recall coming off stage every day looking like somebody had just dumped several gallons of Gatorade over my head, and knowing that a shower was days away. That's tough . . . that's tough. Porta-johns. A washcloth. Ah, the humanity. Where was the Gold Bond powder? I recall standing on the main stage and watching Courtney Love, just offstage, doing some impressive gymnastics on the stage rigging. She was wearing a tiny dress, and spending a lot of time upside-down. Oh, and she wasn't wearing any underwear; the latter fact was what I think really intrigued the stage staff. I wonder if perhaps she was trying to get attention somehow, a cry for help. We'll never know."

There were some meaningful memories as well. "I remember the [Tibetan] Monks in the morning," recalls Larson. "The Tibetan Monks would chant and that was lovely, a lovely thing in the morning. I loved that. I remember a Tribe Called Quest being one of the finest hip-hop outfits of all time. I *still* love them so much. When I'm in L.A. I drive around and *only* listen to Tribe. I remember P-Funk playing forever, then coming back and playing more. Then back at the hotel, all night, chanting 'ain't no party like a P-Funk party cause a P-Funk party don't stop,' over and over. And as amazing as it was, you sometimes wished a P-Funk party *would* stop, maybe for like five minutes? With all respect though, seriously, total genius. I remember being in a really scary part of Houston, Texas, and watching Bushwick Bill, the dwarf from the Ghetto Boys, playing basketball."

Craig Wedren has lots of memories of Lollapalooza. "Hanging out, bonding with the brilliant and sweet Stereolab and Pharcyde . . . Mind-blowing Pharcyde extended freestyle sets . . . a heartbreaking, night of the living dead, end-of-the-tour party at the Chateau Marmont where half of the attendees (musicians all) were pathetically smacked out and the other half were shooting video. Yuck. We were so excited to hang out with some of our friends and heroes, but that shit was dark and we bailed early. Truly, it felt like the end of something, and not just a tour . . . Vineyards at the Gorge in Washington . . . People yelling "faggots" during our *kick-ass* sets . . . staying in like a Super 8 or something down South, where the P-Funk posse (they must've had thirty to fifty people with them, band, families, entourage, it was an entire planet of freaks) had *taken over*. We were walking to our rooms and Bushwick Bill from Ghetto Boys tumbles out of one of the rooms. We felt we had made it then . . . *Killing* in the sun. Shudder to Think, like Lollapalooza itself, was at some kind of weird peak but didn't even know it. It didn't cause any riffs or fissures that weren't already well on their way to pulling the band apart, and I don't remember it effecting our personal lives too dramatically."

By the late nineties Perry Farrell had made his mark on music society and decided to take a break from Lollapalooza. Evidently he, like many others, had not been happy when the festival's co-owners booked the mainstream band Metallica. The festival seemed to be moving away from the cutting-edge "indie band" vibe. "When we did Lollapalooza, Metallica was the big dog and it was a bite with little teeth," says Mark De Gli Antoni of Soul Coughing. "They cracked me up. Every night exactly scripted as the night before, even using the identical stage patter. James would be up there giving the impression of raucous spontaneity. I recorded a bunch of his jokes and would play them back through my sampler during our set. It was Soundgarden who rocked that tour. Fantastic band."

There were still lots of positive aspects for those who came to the festival and for those who participated on stage. "My observations at Lollapalooza were the various types of people who attended," says Drew Lamarche. "You could always see the fans of the bands who were playing, always wearing band shirts and stuff. I think a lot of people actually go [to the festival] just to say they went. I think people who attended didn't have to worry about violence and lack of feeling safe. I would say that everyone on the tour was personable. There didn't seem to be any bad attitudes. Everyone I saw seemed to be having a good time. Every night when we got off stage, we would always talk to the fans who would gather at the side of the stage and yell at us for autographs and just to talk."

"The year we did it was the 'rock' year, so the mood and atmosphere was different from those that preceded it," remembers Stuart Chatwood. "At any given festival, backstage there is always a hierarchy. Who gets to hang with who, which sticker do you have to get side-stage, what level of VIP are you . . . That year Metallica was headlining what started off as an 'alternative' festival, so the real alternative, I guess, was Metallica. They were not mixing well with the other artists, due to a large area of the backstage being police-taped off by their crew. I always find that the bigger the band, the nicer the band, but the worse [their] crew is. So I don't know if this was a band or crew directive to seal them off from the 'philistines' playing before them. On a different and much cooler note, we shared a dressing room area with the Ramones and Soundgarden. Love them or hate them, the Ramones are legends, or to put it better, coolness personified."

There were some drawbacks for the bands performing. "I love playing in the sunshine, so I loved playing that tour," says Craig Wedren. "The flipside though, is that rock and roll is kind of a night thing, best enjoyed in the dark (shadowier shades being better/more forgiving for the requisite fantasy/suspension of disbelief of rock or anything theatrical and fantastic), which I can appreciate. I don't love seeing bands in those situations (i.e., broad daylight). There's also a fundamental lack of control over your environment on a festival tour; you sort of have to surrender to its weird rhythms (very different than an autonomous, club tour)—the heat, a lot of waiting, traffic and human congestion, et cetera, none of which I particularly minded. I'm a summer-loving Leo and so was in kind of a sun-drenched dream-state a lot of the time but other members of the band loathed it."

In the meantime, Perry Farrell created a festival dubbed ENIT to showcase Porno for Pyros. This festival would appear in remote locations and have music, drum circles, tree plantings and . . . attempts to contact aliens. Only four shows ultimately launched.

The 1996 Lollapalooza was not without its problems but those involved both on and off the stage played the hand they were dealt. "My band Satchel joined the festival on its second leg in Southern Florida," remembers Shawn Smith. "Rage Against the Machine was starting a three-show run playing with Soundgarden. All three Rage performances were mind-blowing, to say the least, but the last two were something I will never forget. After Florida, the show played at a drag strip in North Carolina. The local authorities had tried to ban the festival but were unsuccessful, so they brought in troopers from all over the state and surrounded the grounds with law enforcement. They were on the ground and in towers and even had air support."

"So Rage goes on in the middle of this," continues Smith. "You can imagine how great it was. The defining moment was the crowd flipping off the cops in the towers and in the helicopter: 'Fuck you. I won't do what you tell me.' I thought it was an incredible moment. The next day the show was in a big rolling farm in Tennessee. It was the complete opposite of the night before. This time there was not a cop in sight. Word was the local sheriff kept the money his county got to pay for police presence so it was just regular concert security. It's hard to describe the feeling of freedom this show had. Rage in this environment was equally as powerful as the night before but . . . I just can't describe it. It was like seeing a vision of hope for the future of this planet and its people. There are so many reasons that festivals are corporate bullshit but it's moments like these that make them worth it. The music and the energy of the mass of people can take us out of the illusion and give is a glimpse into what really matters in life. For some of us at least."

When the William Morris Agency became involved, various attempts at resurrecting the once-popular festival were attempted. But by 1998, the festival seemed only a shimmering moment of summers past and it was decided that for the time being, Lollapalooza was over. "I saw the end of Lollapalooza at the Metallica show," says Stuart Chatwood. "In the early history of the festival, it was all about belonging to something together, but by this time the tastes had diverged too much to hold the whole thing together."

When a reformed Jane's Addiction band set out on a summer tour in 2003, Lollapalooza was revived. The prices were even stiffer than before, however, and turnout wasn't all it could have been. A two-day expansion of the 2003 tour was announced in 2004, but then cancelled due to low ticket sales. Perry Farrell decided that he didn't want to abandon Lollapalooza and teamed with Capital Sports & Entertainment and Charles Attal Presents to bring the festival new life by bringing it back as a two-day "destination festival." In 2005, Lollapalooza was held in Grant Park, Chicago featuring seventy acts on five stages. Over 65,000 people attended despite record heat. In 2006, a five-year, five million dollar commitment was made to have the festival return to the park annually.

In 2007 Lollapalooza was very well-received. Pearl Jam headlined, and Amy Winehouse and LCD Soundsystem were outstanding. The atmosphere of the festival may not have been exactly like the first one, but for most, it was still Lollapalooza.

1994
Welcome to Paradise

In U.S. news

Al Gore presides over UCLA's Superhighway Summit; O. J. Simpson is charged with murder; major league baseball strikes and the World Series is cancelled; Clinton signs the Assault Weapons Ban; Ronald Reagan announces he has Alzheimer's disease; Republicans secure both Houses of Congress; and the Whitewater investigation begins.

In world news

Boris Yeltsin and Bill Clinton sign the Kremlin Accords; the Church of England ordains its first female priests; U.S. troops withdraw from Somalia; hundreds of thousands are murdered in Rwanda; Nelson Mandela becomes South Africa's first black President; Israel and Jordan sign a peace treaty; and Iraq removes troops from Kuwait border.

In music news

Kurt Cobain commits suicide; Pink Floyd tours for the last time; the Fillmore re-opens in San Francisco; and Pearl Jam files suit against Ticketmaster saying the company has a monopoly on tickets.

Some of the year's most notable albums

Barenaked Ladies: *Maybe You Should Drive*; Beck: *One Foot in the Grave*; Mary J. Blige: *My Life*; Jeff Buckley: *Grace*; Ani DiFranco: *Out of Range*; Green Day: *Dookie*; Hole: *Live through This*; KoRn: *KoRn*; the Notorious B.I.G.: *Ready to Die*; the Offspring: *Smash*; Pearl Jam: *Vitology*; the Prodigy: *Music for the Jilted Generation*; Smashing Pumpkins: *Pisces Iscariot*; Stone Temple Pilots: *Purple*; Weezer: *Weezer*.

Rock's most popular songs

"All I Want to Do"—Sheryl Crow; "Better Man"—Pearl Jam; "Closer"—Nine Inch Nails; "Crazy"—Aerosmith; "Loser"—Beck; "Mary Jane's Last Dance"—Tom Petty & the Heartbreakers; "Mr. Jones"—Counting Crows; "Rape Me"—Nirvana; "Welcome to Paradise"—Green Day.

Woodstock '94
August 12–14

> *"Music festivals provide a much-needed place to feed the soul and spirit."*
> —Melissa Etheridge

The granddaddy of festivals was finally getting its due. To commemorate the twenty-fifth anniversary of the original Woodstock, it was decided to hold a three-day concert and festival in Saugerties, New York—a site a mere 10 miles from the town of Woodstock—on August 12–14. (The event was at first scheduled for only two days, but as interest grew it was expanded another day.) The festival was promoted as "2 More Days of Peace and Music." (Where was the Love?) The field that was once denied to the promoters of the original festival would serve as the location by which Woodstock '69 would be remembered. Two stages were featured and over fifty musicians and bands were on hand to remember. (Some missed Lollapalooza concert dates to take part.) The acts included some who had performed at the original: Santana, The Band, Country Joe McDonald (with the Fugs), Crosby, Stills & Nash (without Young), Joe Cocker, and John Sebastian. Wavy Gravy was tapped to serve as the emcee. These legendary artists would be joined by other veteran rockers such as Bob Dylan (who was late for his set and did not say a word to the audience while he was on stage); Aerosmith (whose front man and drummer had attended the original as part of the appreciative crowd); the Allman Brothers Band; and Traffic. Mainstream rock was represented by Sheryl Crow, Melissa Etheridge, Del Amitri, Peacebomb, Spin Doctors (whose act included dancers with an aversion to clothing), Orleans, Zucchero, Kings X, and Bob Weir with Rob Wasserman.

"I remember standing backstage when Joe Cocker began "With A Little Help from My Friends," recalls Melissa Etheridge. "The organ shook the entire stage. I loved it. I had recently 'come out' that year and when I was performing, a rainbow flag kept waving high and strong. It was very powerful and the first time I had seen any outward gay pride in my audience."

Peter Gabriel headlined (his set included an impressive light show). Hip hop artists such as Cypress Hill, Arrested Development, and Salt-N-Pepa were on hand along with r & b, blues, and soul's Neville Brothers, Blues Traveler, and the Sisters of Glory (Thelma Houston, Phoebe Snow, Mavis Staples, CeCe Peniston, and Lois

Walden). Metal music was a part of the festival with bands such as Jackyl (whose lead singer Jesse James Dupree removed all his clothes), 3, and Metallica, and electronic acts such as Todd Rundgren, Aphex Twin (whose performance was cut short because of a contract dispute), and the Orb. Post Grunge bands included Blind Melon, Live, Candlebox, and Collective Soul.

"I remember walking on stage to watch another band that was playing before us," recalls Will Turpin of Collective Soul. "Kings X was a big influence on me and I wanted to see them perform. When I walked up on the stage from the backstage I was absolutely floored at the size of the crowd and the fact that I was to play on the same stage as one of my heroes in a couple of hours. It was a sea of humanity in front of the stage. I couldn't see where the crowd ended. I was feeling insecure and intimidated. Soon the music and the energy from the crowd were turning insecurities into a confidence and a determination to kick some rock 'n' roll ass. We played later on Friday night to a roaring crowd and left it all out on the stage."

The experience was beneficial to those attendees who were looking to enjoy the music of artists new to them but also to the newer artists. "I think our experience at Woodstock '99 solidified Collective Soul as a solid rock band," continues Turpin. "The crowd loved us and you can tell when you listen to the audio recording. People have told me that the crowd sang "Heaven Let Your Light Shine Down" louder than any other song the rest of the weekend."

Punk and alternative music was well represented by Green Day, Porno for Pyros, James, Primus, Rollins Band, Violent Femmes, the Cranberries, Red Hot Chili Peppers (who first appeared dressed as light bulbs and returned mid-set dressed as Jimi Hendrix), Nine Inch Nails (who, according to lead singer Trent Reznor, were only appearing to finance their upcoming tour), Blind Melon, and Orbital. Rounding out the bill were percussionist Youssou N'Dour, Paul Rodgers' Rock and Blues Revue (with Slash, Jason Bonham, Neal Schon, and Andy Fraser), and Jimmy Cliff's All-Star Reggae Jam (with Rita Marley, Eek-A-Mouse, and Shabba Ranks). It was quite a bill and certainly one that supported the premise of three days of music. Even so, there were some popular acts of the day that were missed. Members of KISS were approached with a million dollar offer to reunite but they passed.

The attendance wasn't quite as significant as that of the '69 festival, but it was impressive coming in at about 300,000 to 400,000. It was expected that gate-crashing would be a problem and sure enough by Friday night the gates were down and the concert was . . . "free." The planning of the event was, however, more successful this time out. The portable toilets were cleaned regularly, although it was a scramble to keep them available. There were plenty of food and drink booths. (It helped that the Pepsi-Cola Company was one of the sponsors and no alcohol was sold. At various times, plastic bottles of water were distributed from the towers and the available food was shared by thousands).

Even with the community spirit, the fact that music had become a business was very much evident. "The downside [of the festival] was a shameless marketing orgy," says Orleans' Larry Hoppen. "Three dollars for a can of soda and the like. Corporate greed on display. Not a shock, but a stark reminder of the way things have gotten, even in rock 'n' roll. Woodstock '94 was positive, for sure, but the commercial greed was a drag, even while the crowds braved the rain, mud, and lack of working sanitary facilities as the weekend wore on, just as the audience of 1969 had done. Everyone got along, but everyone also got ripped off to one degree or another, including the small local vendors who were treated, in my opinion, unfairly relative to what they were promised."

After passing through metal detectors, people camped on the site with sleeping bags and blankets, and everyone seemed to get along. The Peace Patrol, mostly comprised of young people who agreed to act as mediators in exchange for free admission, provided effective security. Large video screens showed the action onstage, the sound was crisp and clear, music was almost nonstop, and the set changes were managed well. Mosh pits and crowd surfing were part of the action and, although the slamming occasionally got too enthusiastic, it was handled as were any problems having to do with drugs (which were, of course, in abundance).

Those who now lived in the Woodstock area complained little about any inconvenience *this* festival brought to them. "Orleans had lived and rehearsed in Saugerties, New York since 1972," reflects Larry Hoppen. "John Hall's house, and later mine, were right there. In fact, my house was just over the hill from the concert grounds, so I could smell the garbage the week following the festival. Seriously, Woodstock '94 was a very big deal to me—us, as Orleans was playing as a local band *and* a national band. We were excited. We played on the Friday [with] really beautiful weather, which didn't last. Our slot was late afternoon/early evening, bridging the gap between the local bands that played while the crowds formed, and the national bands of the night, which got the weekend off in earnest. I remember that an unknown Blues Traveler was the next band after us."

Appearing at Woodstock '94 was not just an interesting new experience for those who attended but also for the performers. "I also remember that our whole twenty-five or thirty-minute set went by so fast," remembers Hoppen. "Somewhere I have a pro tape of it. It was *really* loud onstage, and really exciting, a huge rush. You don't play in front of 350,000 people every day. Also, most of the times we play "Dance With Me," nobody's in a mosh pit, but at '94 the area in front of the stage was completely about moshing so that's indelible as a mind's image. I remember floating around backstage the whole rest of the night, checking out sets from other artists, talking to friends, fans, reporters, and going home really tired but really satisfied. For the rest of the weekend, I just stuck my head out my living room window to hear who was playing. Professionally, of course it's good to have that kind of event on your resume and as a performance experience. Personally, this was just on the heels of coming back from Orleans' second tour of Japan, which was also a great thrill and experience, so it was one fantastic summer that I'll always have."

As often happens at festivals, the artists had an opportunity to socialize in a way they normally could not. "The artist compound was cool," says Will Turpin. "It was the first time I had been around so many of our peers. It was a circle of trailers that surrounded a catering tent and lots of tables. Live, Sheryl Crow, Kings X, Violent Femmes . . . . All musicians I respected and was proud to be performing with."

The weather had been pleasant until Mother Nature threw a surprise party. It rained. Hard. The ground turned to mud and all bets were off. This was, after all, Woodstock.

The performers known as WOMAD gave an inspirational performance, but the crowd was impatient to see Green Day, and had to be asked to show respect by Wavy Gravy and Peter Gabriel, who briefly joined the entity. Green Day's performance was as energetic as always but a surprise came when someone in the crowd threw a slab of mud at singer Billy Joe Armstrong. Apparently not offended, Armstrong caught the mud and put it in his mouth. Soon others were throwing pieces of the soggy dirt and the band's crew started to toss them back. Wavy Grave stuck a chunk in *his* mouth and tossed some back for good measure. Things started to get out of hand and people began to swarm the stage. When bass player Mike Dirnt was mistaken for a fan, security tackled him, and in the fracas Dirnt lost several of his teeth.

The band Primus ironically had a song titled "My Name is Mud" but singer Les Claypool let it be known that tossing mud at him would not be appreciated. He received some anyway and told the crowd that throwing items on stage demonstrated that those that tossed them had "small and insignificant genitalia." Nine Inch Nails took the stage already covered in mud so as to put an end to the mud tossing. The festival was now known as "Mudstock."

"When I was playing "Like the Way I Do" I saw a section of the crowd get muddier and muddier," remembers Melissa Etheridge. "I called to them, calling them the mud people. I said 'Come to me' [and] they formed a large line and made their way to the front. Way cool."

Aerosmith took the stage to play in the rain and fireworks ended their set. Next comedian Tom Arnold introduced his "friend—Arnold Schwarzenegger," but it was, in fact, comedian Chris Farley.

The Band was expanded to include Jefferson Airplane's Jack Casady and Jorma Kaukonen, the Grateful Dead's Bob Weir, the Byrds' Roger McGuinn, Country Joe McDonald, John Sebastian, and Bruce Hornsby. Peter Gabriel would acknowledge the mud, but his set was more noted for the thousands of brightly lit candles throughout the crowd.

"Musically, there were some *fine* performances," says Hoppen. "I think you can never 'go back', nothing will ever recapture the original Woodstock Festival in 1969 and Woodstock '94 is no exception to that. '94 did, however, showcase Generation X pretty well in terms of culture—moshing, the bands reflecting Gen X musical taste— Nine Inch Nails, Primus, Collective Soul, et cetera. In that sense it was reflective of the times socially, but not, in my opinion, a developmental moment, certainly not in the many ways the original festival was."

"I don't think there is much social development you could associate with the [Woodstock] anniversary festivals," says Will Turpin. "The motivation for Woodstock '94 and '99 was much more financial than anything social or political. The original Woodstock was about a sociopolitical movement that the youth were trying to define at that moment. [But] I feel that Woodstock '94 played out in a positive way. People from different backgrounds got together and had a great time. Everybody talked about how much fun they had."

Music festivals are supposed to be fun. When the crowd rises above inconveniences like rain, mud, and exorbitant prices for concessions, they can turn their minds to why they are there: for the entertainment. The original Woodstock was about the music but also about the community. The world was growing somewhat detached but the people who attended Woodstock '94 at least gave it a shot.

Music Midtown
1994

While music promoters and fans were celebrating what *had been* up North, down South they were looking to the future. Alex Cooley had experienced a great deal of success with the Atlanta Pop Festivals and by now, partnered with Peter Conlon, was the South's premier music promoter. Cooley and Conlon attended the New Orleans Jazz & Heritage Festival and decided to launch an Atlanta-based festival atmosphere that would reflect the wide variety of music they both enjoyed. In 1994, the partners leased a parcel of undeveloped land in Atlanta's Midtown section at Peachtree and Tenth Streets.

The three-day festival was usually scheduled on the first weekend in May, and was an event that drew music fans from all over the country. The premise of the festival was simple: music, and lots of it. Classic rock, alternative, blues and soul, hip hop, funk—you name it and it was represented. Santana, Incubus, Bonnie Raitt, Ja Rule, Earth, Wind & Fire, Cheap Trick, Stone Temple Pilots, Counting Crows, Joan Jett & the Blackhearts, Bush, Hoobastank, Kid Rock, the Steve Miller Band, ZZ Top, No Doubt, Los Lobos, and Pete Yorn were just a handful of the hundreds of performers who appeared over the years. Six stages kept the music flowing and local dee jays, whose stations sponsored the event, kept attendees involved in the mix.

The number of people the festival attracted grew each year until it was commonplace to expect thousands over the three days of each festival. When it was decided to build a Federal Reserve Bank on the site where the festival was held, Music Midtown was moved first to the Underground area of the city, and then to a forty-two acre location adjacent to the SciTrek Museum. By this time, as many as 300,000 would attend the festival each year. Music Midtown was an exciting place to be, although sometimes those in attendance could get a bit rowdy.

In 1998, Cooley and Conlon sold their Southern Promotions company to SFX Entertainment, a subsidiary of Clear Channel Communications. In 2005, the date of Music Midtown was changed to June and the festival was affected by rain from Tropical Storm Arlene. In an effort to avoid a quagmire of mud, the promoters laid outdoor tile in front of the stages. The budget for the festival had by this time doubled. The ticket prices were raised to allow the promoters to pay the increasing cost of talent. Moving the festival to June also placed Music Midtown in the position of having to compete with summer tours, Bonnaroo, and other music festivals. The number of attendees went down.

Peter Conlon announced in 2006 that, because of the cost of producing the festival in its traditional form, Music Midtown was cancelled. Unlike Bonnaroo (which is held in the country), holding such a massive group of concerts in a city the size of Atlanta must be problematic. Although the festival did not return in 2007, many are hopeful that another site will be obtained and the festival will return.

1995
This Ain't a Love Song

In U.S. news

The first Republican-controlled Congress since 1954 takes office; the O. J. Simpson murder trial consumes the airwaves; terrorists bomb a government office building in Oklahoma City; and the Million Man March takes place.

In world news

A U.N. tribunal charges Bosnian Serb leaders with genocide; for the first time in decades no British soldiers are on patrol in the streets of Belfast; the Nuclear Non-Proliferation Treaty is extended indefinitely; Iraq admits possession of biological weapons; and it is the fiftieth anniversary of the bombing of Hiroshima.

In music news

R.E.M.'s Bill Berry suffers a brain aneurysm; Selena is shot and killed; Jimmy Page is unsuccessfully attacked by a man with a knife while onstage; Phillip Taylor Kramer of Iron Butterfly disappears from Highway 101; *The Beatles Anthology* airs on network television; and the Rock and Roll Hall of Fame opens.

Some of the year's most notable albums

Alanis Morissette: *Jagged Little Pill*; Alice in Chains: *Alice in Chains*; the Beatles: *The Beatles Anthology*; Blink 182: *Cheshire Cat*; Bon Jovi: *These Days*; Foo Fighters: *Foo Fighters*; Green Day: *Insomniac*; Hootie & the Blowfish: *Cracked Rear View*; the Ramones: *Adios Amigos*; Kenny Wayne Shepard: *Ledbetter Heights*.

Rock's most popular songs

"Name"—Goo Goo Dolls; "Buddy Holly"—Weezer; "Freak Like Me"—Adina Howard; "Hand in My Pocket"—Alanis Morissette; "Have You Ever Really Loved a Woman"—Bryan Adams; "Kiss From a Rose"—Seal; "Only Wanna Be with You"—Hootie & the Blowfish; "This Ain't a Love Song"—Bon Jovi.

Vans Warped Tour
1995

"Warped Tour is hands down a festival that every kid knows about or looks forward to attending because of its large roster of musical acts and sponsors that help make it one of the best festivals of the year."

—Tommy Guindon, Halifax.

The celebration that was Woodstock '94 came off fairly well. Yet it was considered by some to be "just another" festival or an attempt by the older generation to force a dated state-of-mind on young people who loved music. Entrepreneur Kevin Lyman had been to several of the Lollapalooza shows and he thought there might be a festival audience for some of his favorite Southern California punk and ska bands. But first Lyman wanted to test the water. Lyman, who booked the venues, traveled throughout the summer with the bands, they drew well, and everyone enjoyed themselves. But the enterprise didn't make those who participated any real money—expenses of travel were more than the group of musicians really pulled in for profit—but it had been an adventure for those involved and they had a good time. Lyman wasn't sure if he wanted to do it again the next summer, but in 1995 when he was approached by representatives of the Vans shoe company to put together a skateboarding festival that would travel all over the country, he responded with the idea of including live music. (Lyman had experience through promoting events such as "Holiday Havoc," which featured skateboarding contests and music.) The Vans business people found the idea intriguing and thought it could work. The Vans Warped Tour was born and it is now known as "The Tour That Won't Die" and is the longest running annual music tour in the country. (The Warped name is said to have come from *Warped* magazine, which is published in Japan and features extreme sports as well as music.)

The Warped Tour very much represents the moment. The Tour holds its festivals in venues that are large enough to feature both demonstrations of extreme sports and music stages. Dozens of bands are presented in thirty-minute sets on as many as ten stages. Timing is everything and while bands often play simultaneously, the disruption of the music of the other acts usually doesn't occur. There are two main stages that feature the better-known, headlining bands, and a "talent board" directs the members of the crowd to the location of the bands and artists they most want to see and hear. Some of the exceptional aspects of the Tour include the "fan vote," which allows an act to play an additional ten minutes, and the "BBQ Band" who, while appointed a slot on the bill, must also prepare food for the bands and crews backstage. "One of the most unique aspects of the Warped Tour is the post-show BBQ," says Jonas Kleiner of Buck-O-Nine. "Every evening the "Barbecue Band" hosts a huge bbq for all the musicians and crew. It's a great way for everyone to meet each other and relax for a couple hours."

"I remember with great fondness the barbeques we used to have on the '97 Warped Tour at the end of each day before the buses would roll out," says Daniel Glass of Royal Crown Revue. "One of the bands towed a huge grill behind their Tour van and every night after the fans had gone home and the stages were broken down, we'd throw burgers on the grill and wind down for a few hours before moving on to the next town. The barbeques were a necessity, because the official Tour catering was still very primitive (okay, downright horrible) on the '97 Tour, and we were often stuck out in vacant fields or parking lots of stadiums and arenas that were in the middle of nowhere. But the barbeques also served as a gathering place, since we had no hotel rooms and basically lived on busses and at the venues. They were a chance for the bands to hang out, talk shop, and generally enjoy a bit of quiet among the blaring punk rock, the roar of motocross bikes, and the rumbling of bus generators. It was a real family atmosphere and I made a lot of close friendships that have endured to this day. Some of the highlights of the nightly barbeques included a dice game called 'C-Lo' that was run by Social D (which tended to empty the pockets of many a young fan bold enough to join in). Pennywise guitarist Fletcher Dragge's famous 'hot dog milkshakes' also became the stuff of legend, and Social D's bassist Johnny Maurer was a licensed barber who would give haircuts to all the musicians who wanted 'em. Unfortunately, by the time we did the Tour again in 1999, the barbeques were long gone and so was the family atmosphere."

The sponsored barbeque idea has apparently not been a feature of all Tours but many of the performers continue to gather at the end of the night. With participation by so many, both on and off the stage, the atmosphere of the festival is usually one of kinship and like interests. That doesn't mean that some people aren't working very hard. "It's a real cake walk for the actual band members," says Matt Kelly of Dropkick Murphys. "The people who deserve most of the credit are the people who make the Tour happen: the crew, the stagehands, the caterers, and the kids who attend. The bands have a half-hour a day to 'work' (I use the term loosely), and the rest of the time is pretty relaxed. The crew, and especially the stagehands and caterers, work morning, noon, and night. The actual attendees have to hang out of doors all day and brave the elements."

While the bands certainly have a lot to gain from appearing on the bill, touring throughout summer does have some negative elements. "When you're away from home for that long, you're bound to miss things at home, but that's one of the cons to touring," says Kelly. "I suppose the half-hour set times ruin my stamina, as we [would] normally play for an hour-and-fifteen minutes or more."

And if you think that bands playing on the Warped Tour are all living the rock star life, think again. "The other incredible memory I have of Warped is from the first Australian tour of 1998, in which we pulled up to the first venue (a field about a mile from the beach) and were informed that our accommodation for the entire tour would be tents that we'd have to set up ourselves," remembers Daniel Glass. "Interesting how our management neglected to inform us of that small fact before we got on the plane!"

"Something that sticks out to me is our day in South Carolina," says Kyle Castellani of Nural. "We drove through the night and got there around 4 a.m. and immediately tried to get some rest for the long day coming. Because our van was so packed, me and our guitarist Doug slept outside under some trees. We woke up at 9 a.m. to rain pouring on us and a Fuse camera man in our faces! Apparently, Fuse was so intrigued by our grungy lifestyle that they decided to spend the next three days filming our day-to-day routine."

"Be humble and respectful to everyone you deal with, especially all the people behind the scenes running the Tour," says Jonas Kleiner. "An unwritten rule of my band is we all act with humility and respect toward others. It's the best way to conduct yourself. Some bands forget that, or never learn it to begin with. I saw first-hand bands on the Tour acting like 'rock stars' or prima donnas that got ridiculed by other bands, and lost the respect of many on the Tour. The Warped Tour is tough work, out in the summer heat. Its best to think of the big picture before letting the heat and your ego boil over."

With so many people involved, there are bound to be personal conflicts and controversy from time to time. On the 2004 Tour, the band Guttermouth had problems with some of the other bands and left the Tour after, they say, being threatened with violence. The Vandals were said to have been asked to leave the Tour after their bass player, a devout Catholic, allegedly called members of Good Charlotte "faggots" and there was a physical altercation. Some of the bands find the corporate sponsorship of Vans distasteful and others think the quality of the other bands is lacking. There have been complaints about some of the band members having a prayer group and complaints about the Tour ruining the businesses of small clubs that would otherwise feature the up-and-coming talent. You can't please everybody and there will always be egos and issues, but for the most part, the Tour works.

The deluge of music and people surrounding a Warped Tour is a given. The quality of the music varies to taste and it's impossible to please all people with all variety of bands featured on the Tour. "In 2003 it was damned near impossible to escape the terrible music that surrounded the entire outdoor shopping mall once you were inside the Vans Warped Tour," says Corporal Joebot Twopointoh of the Phenomenauts. "It wasn't completely impossible, however, because at that time there were brave crusaders that quietly snuck their way in and found a spot on the grass where they could set up their own music and attempt to help passersby escape the chode-rock sounds from the main stages. This group of bands was soon granted their own stage in 2004 called The Space Station."

The Warped Tour also includes booths and tents, and representation by independent record companies, publishing entities, and music and sports equipment vendors. Because there are so many vendors and sponsors, the ticket prices for the Tour are kept relatively low, allowing for a larger audience to attend. Despite the planning and preparation by the organizers, it is still possible to have a festival deceit. "I realized that anybody could pull a sneaky maneuver and set their stuff up for the Warped Tour crowd, and lots of bands did, but they weren't getting the same recognition," says Corporal Joebot Twopointoh. "They sounded like every band on the main stages, and in this day a lot of bands try to claim they have an original sound, but they're missing the point as to what "original" means. They think an unconventional guitar chord or off-timely drum beat switch is going to sound different because they haven't heard anything so shitty before. Well guess what? That's what *everyone* is trying to do and that's why you failed, because it sounds shitty. The Tour impacted my life, because I realized that bands are striving for "original" music over playing "good" music. The Space Station bands received tons of recognition because they weren't spewing radio-schlock looking for the next big genre. They were playing well-written songs."

The bands themselves often set up tents and will sign autographs, give away swag, and sell CDs after their performance. This practice not only cultivates fans and earns the bands some extra cash but gives the musicians something to do. It gets lonely and boring on the road.

Contrary to what the fans might think, the Tour can be grueling and isn't always one big party. Yet forming or renewing friendships are possible. "We [interact with others on the bill] as little as possible, unless they're friends of ours," says Matt Kelly. "We actually had a little Boston enclave last time we did Warped Tour. Luckily there were other bands from Boston on the tour, as well as bands and crew members we're friendly with, so we typically had a good time."

Unlike most festivals, the Warped Tour does have its pecking order. "We tried to meet bands whenever we had the chance but because we were following the Tour and only playing select dates we were given the "Not So VIP" pass and couldn't go backstage, eat the catering food, et cetera, and that's where you'd usually find most bands on the bill," says Kyle Castellani. "Although we met hundreds of bands that were in the same situation as us."

"Though the majority of bands were making me sick enough to puke, there were some good bands that we quickly became friends with because we had to go through these months together and find some music we liked," says Corporal Joebot Twopointoh. "I was actually extremely excited to meet Andrew WK and his great band who came to nearly every single performance of my band TreePhort. I also met the L.A.-based Kids of Whitney High and a hilarious band called Beret, who dressed like French stereotypes and went crazy for every show. Most importantly, I met six good friends that live in the San Francisco Bay area called the Phenomenauts and I was compelled to move to their town when they asked me to become Joebot Twopointoh."

"The Warped Tours were great and I have a lot of fun memories from them," says Jonas Kleiner. "The memories that stand out the most are that I was able to meet some of my music heroes on the tour. From a young age, two of my favorite bands were Social Distortion and the Descendents. One summer on the Warped Tour I was fortunate enough to meet Mike Ness (Social Distortion) and Milo [Aukerman] (Descendents). They were both really cool and down to earth. Milo told me that a few months earlier he had purchased a copy of our CD *Twenty Eight Teeth* and really liked it, especially our cover of the Joe Jackson song "I'm the Man." Hearing that made the whole tour for me! Meeting people from other bands and developing new friendships was huge for us."

The Warped Tour has extended internationally and that provides yet another opportunity for the artists to grow their fan base. Additionally, there comes a certain sense of self-affirmation that sometimes comes with participating in the Tour. "In those first few years, the Warped Tour was all about integrity—providing a wide variety of great music at an affordable price to kids who weren't going to hear it on mainstream radio," says Daniel Glass. "It was a hot, loud, dirty way to spend the month of July—we all referred to it as "Punk Rock Summer Camp," but everyone involved believed in the cause and was willing to go the extra mile to make the Tour a success. We especially felt that way in places like Europe and Australia, where we were kind of like "ambassadors" of a certain lifestyle and belief system. I believe that those tours really helped to shape our band ethic, which although it wasn't "punk" per se, was just as outside the mainstream by popular music standards. Being on the Warped Tour really reinforced that belief that we could do things "our way" and not have to compromise when it came to presenting ourselves to the world."

The Warped Tour is a great opportunity for lesser-known bands to establish themselves. Now SideOneDummy Records releases a yearly Warped Tour compilation CD with over twenty-five songs performed by artists on the upcoming Tour. In 1998, the Warped Tour expanded to Canada, Australia, Japan, and Europe. Over 500,000 tickets are sold each year. "Thousands of sweaty, screaming teenagers and twenty-somethings having a great time," says Jonas Kleiner. "Listening to their favorite bands and discovering new bands they may have never heard before."

Every year of the Tour has that little bit of a different flavor. "Honestly, it's strange for a band like us on the Tour because after talking to thousands of people and listening to all the different bands, we kinda felt out of place," says Kyle Castellani. "We sold thousands of CDs and people liked our music, but we felt like the '06 Warped Tour had mostly bands that catered to a specific genre. The kids know who they like and who they don't like: everyone in between better make a damn good impression."

Yes, there is a variety of music and an astonishing number of bands and, yes, there are some things that happen that can take a band totally by surprise. "With all of this you can only imagine how many stories have been accumulated throughout the years," says Tommy Guindon of Halifax. "One specific one I remember was not exactly a heartwarming memory, but yet one of sheer principal. I believe we were in D.C. about two years ago and it was getting towards the end of the day and the wind was picking up. As I was walking to the stage, a huge gust of wind came from nowhere and blew a fence into a large group of people, injuring many. I immediately rushed over and helped as many people as I could. To me it was a memorable moment because without even thinking, my whole mindset changed from getting ready to play a show to helping as many people as possible while they sat crying or overwhelmed by the fact that a fence just hit them. To hear kids who normally play the role of an emo/trendy kid, say thank you and actually mean it (well I guess in that moment they were really acting emo), but they meant it and were extremely grateful."

"I think overall [the Tour] is positive," says Jonas Kleiner. "Kids are exposed to music that they might not get to hear all the time. Plus, it's an outdoor event. It's a fun and memorable way to spend a day with your friends. Some bands have been critical of the Warped Tour and its corporate sponsors, but in reality, it takes that kind of backing to properly put on this type of event that travels from city to city all summer. I think people genuinely look forward to the Warped Tour coming every summer in the same way people in Europe look forward to summer festivals over there."

"The Tour had a strong impact on all us both personally and professionally," says Kyle Castellani. "It rekindled that fire we need and reminded us of what we're trying to achieve. We've never lost site of what we're after, but it's easy to become comfortable with where you are in life until a humbling experience like the Warped Tour comes along and shows you that you haven't made it yet, but [encourages you] to keep pushing."

"I think [whether or not the rock festival is a positive or negative experience] depends on the intent of the organizer," says Daniel Glass. "In the case of Warped tour founder Kevin Lyman, he was all about giving the fans an authentic, affordable experience and giving the bands (many of them non-mainstream) a national platform on which to be seen and heard. It was inspiring to get to know Kevin and to observe him in the thick of things right alongside the musicians, willing to take risks and get his hands dirty in the name of 'art.' I'm pretty sure that it took quite a few years before the Tour started turning a profit, but because he stuck with his principles, Kevin's baby is still going strong thirteen years later. On the downside, I also saw Warped become progressively more corporate and lose much of the family environment that made those early years so special. As the Tour got bigger, people cared less, superstar attitudes entered the picture, and Warped seem to become kind of like every other big concert. I heard that this year's Tour, however, included a big push toward environmentally friendly practices, something that is desperately needed in the filthy world of the rock 'n' roll road show!"

1996
Until It Sleeps

In U.S. news

Lyle and Erik Menendez are found guilty of the murder of their parents; suspected Unabomber Ted Kaczynski is arrested; a bomb goes off during the Summer Olympics in Atlanta; Fox News debuts; Jon Benet Ramsey is found murdered; President Clinton signs the Electronic Freedom of Information Act Amendments; and Operation Desert Strike begins in Iraq.

In world news

France announces an end to nuclear testing; the Iraq disarmament crisis commences; Yeltsin meets with Chechnyan rebels to negotiate cease-fire; Dolly the Sheep is cloned; and Osama bin Laden writes "The Declaration of Jihad on the Americans Occupying the Country of the Two Sacred Places," his first open call for war.

In music news

The Prince's Trust concert features the Who in their first appearance since 1989; the Ramones play their last gig at Lollapalooza; Tupac Shakur is shot in Las Vegas and dies six days later; Snoop Dogg is acquitted of murder; the Beatles' "Real Love" song is released; and the Sex Pistols reunite.

Some of the year's most notable albums

Outkast: *ATLiens*; Dave Matthews Band: *Crash*; Tupac Shakur: *All Eyez on Me*; Soundgarden: *Down on the Upside*; the Wallflowers: *Bringing Down the House*; Prince: *Emancipation*; Rage Against the Machine: *Evil Empire*; Porno for Pyros: *Good God's Urge*; Bad Religion: *The Gray Race*.

Rock's most popular songs

"Free as a Bird"—the Beatles; "Hero Of The Day"—Metallica; "Smells Like Teen Spirit"—Nirvana; "Zero"—the Smashing Pumpkins; "People of the Sun"—Rage Against the Machine; "I Want To Come Over"—Melissa Etheridge.

Ozzfest
1996

"Sharon and Ozzie could be credited with helping save metal with the Ozzfest tours, as they were the only bright hope of banding us all together to pillage the earth as a dark, pierced, and tattooed tribe."

—David Ellefson, Megadeth

The touring festival scene that stemmed from Lollapalooza had been successful, but not without its controversy. Alternative music was the focus of both Lollapalooza and Van's Warped Tour, but heavy metal had been included almost as an after-thought. Metal acts had toured with the festivals, but sometimes the line between alternative and metal is blurred. When Sharon Osbourne asked to have her husband, heavy metal icon Ozzy Osbourne, included in one of the tours, Osbourne was allegedly denied a spot. In her usual assertive manner, Sharon talked it over with Ozzie and decided that they should launch their own festival that would feature primarily, if not all, metal bands and artists.

Named after Ozzy, Ozzfest was initiated in 1996. The Osbournes designed the festival to allow established metal bands to experience a broader audience and the opportunity for new bands to receive exposure. Ozzy, of course, would headline. The event would do nothing if not bring the head of the metal family back into the public eye. "I remember the first time that I heard the idea of the first Ozzfest some years ago," says Michael Ehre of Metalium. "I thought 'Wow, that's really cool! Ozzy has his own festival! Can it get much better?' It must be a dream come true to make your own very special festival, give it your name, and go on tour with that!"

Sharon Osbourne is known for her hard-driving business sense and, after the success of the first festival, the Osbournes decided to launch a traveling summer festival to equal Lollapalooza's influence on the summer landscape. The first Ozzfest was held over two days on October 25th in Phoenix, Arizona and October 26th in Devore, California. Slayer, Biohazard, Sepultura, Danzig, Fear Factory, and Narcotic Gypsy were featured on the main stage along with Ozzy, while Powerman 5000, Earth Crisis, Neurosis, Cellophane, and Coal Chamber took the smaller second stage. "In hindsight, Ozzfest became metal's first major backlash to alternative music of that day, a music style which has always been the antithesis of all things metal," says Megadeth's David Ellefson. "In fact, Sharon and Ozzie could be credited with helping save metal with the Ozzfest tours as they were the only bright hope of banding us all together to pillage the earth as a dark, pierced and tattooed tribe. As usual, metal thrives through its own brothers in arms."

By 1998, Ozzfest was even traveling to Great Britain and by 2002 had expanded into Europe. Ozzfest as we know it today, usually features twenty bands or so over a time frame of twelve hours. The competition to find placement on the bill is fierce but because of the exposure it guarantees, apparently well worth the effort. The festival has launched the careers of bands such as Slipknot and Limp Bizkit. The main stage headliners, bands such as Iron Maiden and System of a Down, are sometimes paid extremely well to appear. The second stage is for the up-and-coming bands although the metal favorite Black Label Society sometimes headlines the second stage.

The festival operates on the basis of rotating time spots so that no one band—excluding the headliners—has a monopoly on a receptive audience. "[I have] many memories and many moments of confusion and delight," says Andrew W.K. "The rotating time slots meant that every day, each group played at a different time. One day we were scheduled to play first thing in the morning—9 a.m., I think. However, the festival was using a special schedule called "Ozzfest Time," which had everyone push their clocks and watches back thirty minutes. In addition, the Ozzfest stage managers liked to keep ahead of schedule, just in case things ran late during the course of the day. So most days, set times would be thirty to forty-five minutes earlier than "real" time. That meant when we were going on at 9 a.m., it was actually 8:15 a.m. or so. Nine a.m. is early as it is, but 8:15 a.m.? Wow! I thought it was just amazingly intense to roll out of bed and right onto the stage. We could see people lined up in the parking lot, still waiting for the gates to open. However, this was one of the most fun sets we played. I sang most of our show while running around the lawn in front of the stage, taking advantage of all the open space where the crowd normally would've been. Due to the rotating lineup, every band had a chance to experience this early morning, dream-like scenario. Truly unique!"

"[Appearing with Ozzfest] definitely did a lot for our band on the professional end," says Throwdown's Dave Peters. "We played to a *lot* of people that had never even heard of us and are now diehard fans. I don't know that [Ozzfest] impacted my personal life any more than any other long tour, but it sure did for our bass player Matt. He met his wife during that tour! I met mine at a bowling alley. Pretty white trash."

The memories collected on the Ozzfest tour can sometimes be of a chaotic atmosphere but are noteworthy nonetheless. "One was the day before the first show, when we got to do sound check in Chicago," recalls Godhead's Jason Miller. "The confusion and pandemonium was just overwhelming. Realizing that we couldn't go one minute over our set time or we'd be cut off. Five-minute changeovers between bands. Playing in Minneapolis to what seemed like an endless crowd. Having to have security escort me away from an endless sea of autograph seekers after I stayed much longer than I had time to. Playing St. Louis in the rain with people throwing mud everywhere. Making *so* many friends that I still talk to today."

"Ozzfest was a turning point in my career since the second I found out we were booked on it," says Dustin Tooker of Grade 8. "To be part of the festival is a great honor and I am very proud to be a part of its alumni. The moment that meant the most to me on the tour was when we got to share the stage at Alpine Valley, Wisconsin with the band Disturbed and the late Darrell "Dimebag" Abbott and his brother Vinnie. The lead singer of my band is my little brother, so for us to get requested to go on stage with another set of metal brothers was amazing, especially because Dime had such an influence on me. I remember being onstage in front of 50,000 with them and Dime, being the fun guy he was, would keep trying to pass off his guitar to my little brother (who can't play a lick). It was a great moment in time to see them together. We almost forgot about the audience and it turned into just a bunch of great friends playing together."

Friendships made on the tour sometimes remain long after the festival is over. "I think that is the most important thing I got out of the tour were friendships," says Tooker. "And to me that's what the festival should be about. Great bands having a great time together. But as we know, there are outside forces that always make it about money. And that's the last reason why I started to play music. So I think in some ways, it sucked as well. The Ozzfest put a lot of pressure on people. I am thankful to still be playing after the tour. A lot of bands on our year have broken up since then."

Metal bands from locations other than the United States appreciate the opportunities offered by performing at Ozzfest. "[I have] lots of great memories from Ozzfest," says Silenoz from Norway's Dimmu Borgir. "A lot of sweaty people! We're not used to playing under those kinds of heat conditions and in the sun, so we understood pretty much straight away that drinking a lot of water was the key, even if our set time was only thirty minutes. We played on the main stage and we performed in front of a lot of people every night, which was great of course, albeit a bit weird at times since the pavilions have seating and you could tell a lot of people weren't too familiar with our music and the way we looked. But I knew that every night we won over new fans and from our point of view Ozzfest seemed like a very professionally organized festival with well-oiled machinery. Oh and yes, Sharon's dogs were running around backstage so we had to be careful so they wouldn't get too close to our leg spikes."

"The most impressive memory [I have] is that I could perform a show on the main stage of the fantastic festival called Ozzfest!" says singer Kyoko of the Mad Capsule Markets. "I feel it's great bands and the audience, from kids to adults, enjoy the festival. It's very important for me and [my] band to perform at the huge festival. It's good experience for my life, work and music. I'll never forget the beautiful scene I saw on the stage. I remembered it was raining, with huge clouds, while Slipknot performed, and after that [there was] a big rainbow. That's very impactive. It's awesome [that a] band can control the weather itself!"

In the end, it doesn't really matter where you're from. Ozzfest more than likely will be a unique experience. "Beer, boobs, crazy-ass motherfuckers and a lot of great bands and great people," says Dustin Schoenhofer of Walls of Jericho. "I don't remember shit 'cause it was two months of straight party, but it was the best tour I've ever been on, for sure."

"Ozzfest was a chance to play in front of a particular audience that we may not have been exposed to otherwise," says Andrew W.K. "I enjoyed the challenge of confronting potential hostile reactions head-on and changing people's opinions. There was one day where I jumped into the crowd and a guy in the crowd tried repeatedly to punch me. He landed one solid punch, although, much like a boxer, my face was slick with my own sweat and mucus, so his hand sort of slid around and mushed up my mouth. Initially I wanted to punch him back, but instead I looked into his eyes and tried my best to smile. I cuddled him and he became gleeful."

"I think [appearing at Ozzfest] puts you on the map as an artist and [places you] in a special, elite club," says Jason Miller. "I also became friends with the Osbourne family, a relationship that will always be very special to me. I tried to make as many friends as I could. It's like summer camp for bands!"

Ozzfest not only has a history of offering traditional metal bands an audience but has also featured nu-metal. "Ozzfest '98 was an interesting time in the history of metal," says David Ellefson. "Nu-metal was thriving, thrash metal was dying. My generation planted our feet and head banged while nu-metal guys jumped up and down pogo style. We tuned our guitars to standard pitch and held true to the "old school" riffs while the nu guys used seven-string guitars and experimented with alternate dark tunings and spastic drumming. So, there I was sandwiched between two of MTV's darlings, Limp Bizket and Tool. Talk about culture shock! I knew times were changing, but to where?"

Yet with all things music, tastes often change. "Everything was redeemed later that year on "New Year's Evil" at Phoenix, Arizona's brand new Bank One Ballpark baseball stadium," says Ellefson. "The newly reformed Black Sabbath, featuring all original members, was the headliner as they played their first live set together in years. With Slayer, Pantera, and Soulfly as the other three bands on the five-band bill, it was clear that old-school metal was going to rule once again. Black Sabbath then went on to become the main attraction of Ozzfest tours for many years to follow which confirmed that dark, evil riffs of the past still ruled!"

"I have to say a favorite moment of mine was at the last date of Ozzfest '98 in the U.S., which I was visiting, not playing," says Aimee Echo. "It was a particularly good year for the tour, in my opinion, with a really diverse line-up, my favorite being Tool, the Melvins, and Motorhead. Sharon Osbourne asked if I wanted to get up and sing "Paranoid" with Ozzy. I, of course, said yes quickly and then realized I might be in over my head. So I said, 'What if I forget the words?' A very young Kelly, who was by her mother's side, said 'Just read the teleprompter like dad does!'"

As with any festival, the bands on the bill either make friends with each other or keep to themselves. "Pretty much all the bands (minus a couple bad apples) were awesome to hang out with," says Dave Peters. "When we weren't being real ignorant and running around shirtless, we played Scrabble. Most nights were Scrabble nights, though. We started a gang on Ozzfest with some of the other bands. White dudes that listen to metal don't really get to be in a gang growing up, so we felt like it was time. We called it S.O.C. (Shirts Off Crew). We had a mostly voluntary membership, but we jumped a lotta fat guys in too. Didn't beat 'em up or anything, but just took their shirts off and then made them circle pit on strangers' busses with us at odd hours of the night. We really didn't *do* anything except just have our shirts off and eat BBQ and make noise. Except one night about thirty of us stormed the pit during Sabbath. We had members and crew of our band, Every Time I Die, Bleeding Through, Lamb of God, Slipknot, Unearth, Alreyu, and a bunch of others, too. We did the wall of death and then got Ozzy and the whole crowd of 30,000 people or so chanting the "Ole" song that you always hear at soccer matches. After that we left and I think we sort of disbanded because it's downhill from there."

Ozzfest 2002 was marked by tragedy when Dave Williams of Drowning Pool was found dead of a heart condition on the band's tour bus. Another interesting year for Ozzfest was in 2004. Onstage footage from the tour was shown on MTV and the network also hosted "Battle for Ozzfest," in order to have bands compete for a slot on the next year's bill. Eight bands were chosen and then had to "earn" favor from Sharon and Ozzy by tagging along on the festival tour to perform various tasks (some of which were unpleasant, which made for good television).

In the beginning years of Ozzfest, Ozzie claimed that he was mostly unfamiliar with any of the acts that share his Ozzfest bill as he didn't listen to radio and didn't keep up with the current crop of metal bands. He left the task of deciding who should perform to Sharon and she was later joined in the process by the Osbourne's son Jack. The family aspect of the festival extended beyond the Osbournes to the acts on tour with them. It was all one big happy family for the most part, barring any individual troubles and spats.

"To even be able to tour with bands like Sabbath, Priest, and Slayer on the same bill in the first place is a dream come true," says Silonoz. "So we were off to a good start! But one memory in particular remains: a couple of days after we had the radio incident in Cleveland where the DJ kicked us out after asking us about Rob Halford's sexual orientation and whatnot. Upon [which] we responded with swearing and cursing live on the radio about why the fuck that was so important and why did the DJ even make an issue about it at all? So what if he's gay, like that's gonna change the fact that he's the Metal God, right! The news about us behaving badly at the radio station must have spread to the Priest camp, as a couple of nights after the incident, several crates of imported English ale and beer suddenly appeared in our dressing room with a note saying 'Thanks for defending the Metal God! —Rob' We still have that note up in our practice room!"

In 2006, Ozzy said that it would no longer be a given that he would make an appearance at Ozzfest. The road was getting long for the aging rocker. Also in 2006, an incident that occurred on the main stage brought national attention. Iron Maiden was onstage when their sound was cut-off. Lead singer Bruce Dickinson believed it to have been on purpose as he was at odds with Sharon Osbourne. After the band left the stage, Sharon went onstage to say that she loved Iron Maiden but that Dickenson had been unrespectful of the festival. It still isn't clear what really happened that night. Other bands have complained over the year that they are underpaid and treated without respect by the Osbournes. As with anything, there are two sides to every story but with Ozzfest, in the end it's all about the exposure.

Ozzfest is known not only for the atmosphere but as a tour where anything can happen. "A lot of long, flat, airbrushed tits, a lot of dudes with wife-beater tans," remembers Dave Peters. "A dude going down on a chick in a grassy meadow and Matt's [Mentley] pants ripping on stage when he didn't have any underwear on. Straight up, balls in the wind. Unprecedented."

"[Playing at Ozzfest] was certainly a cathartic experience," says Aimee Echo. "The Ozzfest my former band Human Waste Project played was in the U.K. and it was amazing. We played for over 60,000 people, which is, to date, still the largest crowd I have played for. Black Sabbath headlined and Foo Fighters played. Great day. Seriously. I decided to quit my band that day! Strange, huh?"

In 2007, another big announcement was made: Ozzy would be back on the main stage and Ozzfest 2007 was going to be completely free of charge in order to encourage young people to attend. The tickets would only be available, however, through sponsor websites. Obtaining tickets wasn't necessarily easy. Potential attendees had to register, request their tickets, and wait several weeks to enter a code by which they would be issued tickets. VIP packages were available for purchase with a "Party Like a Rock Star" offer (a behind-the-scenes tour with a special host for $300), the "I'm Part of the Show" deal which cost $666 and featured all that plus a seat on the stage during Ozzy's set, or the Platinum package, which would be available only to ten people during any one night but included a personal meet-and-greet with Ozzy and his band (the bidding started at $1,000). All proceeds of these packages were tagged to be donated to the Sharon Osbourne Colon Cancer Program at Los Angeles' Cedars-Sinai Hospital.

Sharon Osbourne remarked that festivals have to "be creative, you have to keep evolving." Osbourne is concerned about the rising ticket prices of rock concerts and festivals and warns that if ticket prices don't better reflect the financial reality of the young people who want to attend a show, the industry will bankrupt itself.

Despite the ups and downs, crazy incidents and ticket hoopla, Ozzfest remains popular. While the festival atmosphere may be the same, the social community is less inclusive than the average rock festival. People attend Ozzfest to party with their own.

Steve Wozniak, US Festival, 1983

Photo by Dan Sokol

Ozzfest, 2004

Photo by Mick Huston/Redferns

Lollapalooza, 1992

Jewel, Woodstock, 1999

Photo by Henry Diltz/Corbis

Woodstock,1999

Mike Relm, Coachella, 2007

Rob Thomas, Live 8, Philadelphia, 2005

Slash, Live 8, London, 2003

Lilith Fair
1996

Just as Sharon Osbourne had seen the need to establish a traveling festival that would feature Ozzy's music, Sarah McLachlan also saw a issue in the music industry that needed to be addressed. McLachlan had finished recording her album *Surfacing* when she became frustrated that most promoters—and radio stations—had an aversion to featuring two female artists back-to-back. McLachlan made the decision to book her own tour with future Grammy-nominee Paula Cole.

On September 14, 1996, McLachlan and Cole played a gig in Nova Scotia that they titled the Lilith Fair. (Lilith appears in ancient mythology as many things, but most prominently as a goddess.) Also on the bill that evening were Lisa Loeb and Michelle McAdorey. The following year, McLachlan decided to mount a full-out Lilith Fair tour. The first tour featured only female artists and one dollar for each ticket sold was donated to a local women's charity. As well as McLachlan and Cole, Sheryl Crow, Indigo Girls, Lisa Loeb, Emmylou Harris, Shawn Colvin, Fiona Apple, Suzanne Vega, Jewel, Meredith Brooks, Patty Griffin, Dar Williams, Leah Andreone, and Juliana Hatfield were included. The touring festival would continue over the next two years, showcasing music's women and raising awareness for women's causes.

Gathering of the Vibes
1996

The year 1996 also marked the first Gathering of the Vibes, a "jam band" celebration of the life and music of Jerry Garcia of the Grateful Dead. Launched after the death of Garcia, the first festival was called "Deadhead Heaven." After changing the name of the festival to the Gathering of the Vibes, the yearly assembly brought an opportunity to honor the music icon and to celebrate the easy-going temperament of those who love jam bands. The festival continues to this day as a nature-based families party thrown yearly by Terrapin Presents at various points throughout the northeast. The official website for the Gathering advises those who attend to "respect everyone and we'll all have a wonderful time."

By 2007 the Gathering of the Vibes was a destination festival that had evolved almost to the status of a family reunion. It is held at Seaside Park in Bridgeport, Connecticut, which was one of the first parks in the United States and was designed by Frederick Law Olmsted and Calvert Vaux, and promoted by P.T. Barnum. The festival featured camping and playgrounds, handmade items for sale, baseball, soccer, volleyball, a skate park, and beaches. Sponsored by such entities as Ben & Jerry's Ice Cream, Nature's Gate, Guitar Hero II, and Texas Pete, Wavy Gravy emceed music from jam band favorites such as Bob Weir and Ratdog, Mickey Hart, Dickie Betts, Les Claypool, and George Clinton & P-Funk.

1999–2003
Bring It All Back

In U.S. news

The Columbine High School massacre occurs; Napster debuts; Stephen King is hit by a car; and John F. Kennedy, Jr., is killed in a plane crash.

In world news

The Y2K controversy begins; the Euro is introduced; the government of China restricts internet use; the Kosovo war rages; the music and culture Callatis Festival is held in Romania; Vladimir Putin takes office; and the population of the world reaches 6 billion.

In music news

George Harrison is stabbed in his home; Britney Spears releases her first album; KoRn is the first rock band to perform at the Apollo Theater; and a concert for animal rights is held in honor of Linda McCartney.

Some of the year's most notable albums

Britney Spears: *Baby One More Time*; Jimmy Eat World: *Clarity*; Collective Soul: *Dosage*; Eminem: *Slim Shady LP*; Staind: *Disfunction*; Blink-182: *Enema of the State*; the White Stripes: *The White Stripes*; Ja Rule: *Venni Vetti Vecci*; Red Hot Chili Peppers: *Californication*; Santana: *Supernatural*; Mary J. Blige: *Mary*; Foo Fighters: *There Is Nothing Left to Lose*; AFI: *Black Sails in the Sunset*.

Rock's most popular songs

"Pretty Fly (For a White Guy)"—the Offspring; "All Star"—Smash Mouth; "Smooth"—Santana with Rob Thomas; "American Woman"—Lenny Kravitz; "Last Kiss"—Pearl Jam; "Angel" and "I Will Remember You" —Sarah McLachlan; "Baby One More Time"—Britney Spears; "Livin la Vida Loca"—Ricky Martin; "Genie in a Bottle"—Christina Aguilera.

Woodstock '99
July 23–25, 1999

"I guess if you treat people like a bunch of animals, they will act like them.
The only thing that surprised me was that it wasn't worse than it ended up."
—Jim Bogios, Counting Crows

It was again time to celebrate the 1969 Woodstock Festival. By 1999, the thirtieth anniversary of that event, there were a lot of people who wanted society to return to the peace and love moment they believed the festival represented. The twenty-fifth anniversary of the event had been enjoyed by thousands and there was really no reason to believe that this gathering would be any less than what had been celebrated just five years before. But Woodstock '99 wasn't quite what they expected.

Michael Lang, one of the promoters of the original Woodstock festival, joined forces with promoters John Scher and Ossie Kilkenney to throw a three-day party in Rome, New York. Rather than the bucolic setting of Yasgur's farm, this celebration would be held at the Griffiss Air Force Base, which was said to be a hazardous waste site that was made available at a discounted price.

The music was inclusive, again offering something for everyone: pop, soul, rock (both hard and soft), hip hop, country, and heavy metal. The variety of music was, in fact, more reminiscent of the bill at the Monterey Pop Festival. Appearing were legendary artists like James Brown, Willie Nelson, Robby Keiger of the Doors, Mickey Hart and his Planet Drum (Hart was the only performer who had played at the original Woodstock Festival), and George Clinton & the P-Funk All-Stars. There were some of the hottest mainstream acts of the day such as Sheryl Crow, Bruce Hornsby, Elvis Costello, Jewel, Alanis Morissette, the Brian Setzer Orchestra, Erykah Badu, Dave Matthews Band, Moby, and Ice Cube. The bands were exciting: Red Hot Chili Peppers, Bush, Collective Soul, the Offspring, KoRn, Counting Crows, Kid Rock, Limp Bizkit, Creed, the Roots, Sevendust, Metallica, Megadeth, and Rage Against the Machine. Buckcherry, Reveille, Guster, Gigolo Aunts, Insane Clown Posse, Rusted Root, Djolba, Lit, Serial Joe, Everclear, Live, Spitfire, Everlast, Los Lobos, String Cheese Incident, Fat Boy Slim, Marty Friedman, the Chemical Brothers, G. Love and Special Sauce, Mike Ness, Partical, the Tragically Hip, Godsmack, moe, the Umbilical Brothers, Muse, Vertical Horizon, Oleander, Wyclef Jean, Our Lady Peace, and Pull rounded out a talented and contemporary bill.

The festival atmosphere once again encouraged and revitalized those who performed. "Collective Soul was scheduled to perform after Sevendust in '99," says Will Turpin, the band's bass player. "It was cool to hang and play with them since we were friends from the Atlanta music scene. There was no nervousness this time around. Collective Soul had released our fourth record, and at that point I guess you could say we were veterans. It was about throwing as much energy out there as you can and getting it thrown back from the crowd. There is an energy exchange with live music that can be amazing, especially with the festival crowds."

Some of the artists looked forward to the experience offered by celebrating Woodstock. "Every so often you get one of those 'this is surreal' moments, even in rock n' roll," says Megadeth's David Ellefson. "Woodstock '99 was one of them. Just the history alone from the 1969 Woodstock was nostalgic beyond belief and '99 was on track to top it with all the modern day media hype surrounding the event. The sheer enormity of it all, with the attendance and production, was like you were in the middle of a fantasy rock n' roll city built only for the weekend's extravagance."

Over 220,000 people would attend over July 23–25 and the music portion of the festival would be aired on pay-per-view television. John Scher would call it another gathering of the tribes, but this time it was to be the tribes from Ozzfest, Lollapalooza, and all the other "alternative" festivals. The promoters evidently figured that the "free" music of the sixties was an element of days long passed as they charged $160 for a three-day pass. One would think that amount would be conducive to a high-end experience but such was not necessarily the case.

This time the promoters would make sure they were not caught in the circumstances of an unplanned free concert. A twelve-foot plywood-and-steel fence had been erected to keep gate-crashers out. Over 500 New York State troopers were hired as security to discourage anyone from repeating the freebie mentality of years past. (At one point during the festival, part of the fence was knocked down but it was repaired before more than a handful dared sneak in for free.) The portable toilets issue was once again a problem and it wasn't long before many of them were up-ended and others overflowing. It was ninety degrees in the sun and the crowd was understandably thirsty. A lot of those people were out of luck. Food and beverage prices were much higher than those who were attending expected or were prepared to pay (although in the vendors defense, they were charging the same prices as at concerts and sporting events). There was free water coming out of a pipe near the sewage from the portable toilers—what more could you ask for? Several of the vendors requested that the promoters allow them to lower prices but they were encouraged to not do that as it could cause problems with competition. "My specific memory of Woodstock '99 was watching it on T.V. and wondering if it was going to be a totally corporate version of what happened in '69," says guitarist Matt Beck. "I'm not sure I ever got the answer to that question, but it was on my mind."

"I feel that the "festival" was a complete disaster, devoid of much redeeming value and should not have been produced, at least not the way it was," says Larry Hoppen of Orleans. The promoters claimed that over one thousand doctors, nurses, and EMTs, as well as a festival staff of thousands were working on-site. "I think that, well *hope* that, many lessons were learned about the running of a large festival like that," says Rusted Root's Liz Berlin. "I have heard since that the vendors were charging four dollars for a twelve-ounce bottle of water, that the people were not allowed to bring in their own food and drinks, and that the Porta-Potties were a disgusting mess by that time. There is a certain level of human consideration and cleanliness that is necessary as a course of basic respect for the concert-goer as a person that should be provided. And if the organizers were not able to provide that, then they were obviously overextended and had overreached their ability to provide a safe and healthy atmosphere."

Yet not all of those who performed found the various audiences who appeared in front of each stage united in their appreciation of the efforts of the talent. "The Umbilical Brothers have been performing together for over seventeen years," muses David Collins. "Over that time we have been asked many times what our best and worst gigs are. An easy question for us, as they both happened on the same day: at Woodstock '99. We were blown away to not only be part of this amazing venture, but to be one of the only non-musical acts on the bill. We arrived at the small airport to take a light plane down to Rome. There were flowers covering the cyclone fence of the airport, because only a short while before Kennedy and his wife had left this airport and crashed. Maybe that should have been a sign."

"We were to perform twice that day, within an hour of each other, separated by an interview with MTV," continues Collins. "We were driven from the trailer [and] in the distance we could see where we were heading—the East stage. It looked amazing, as Dave Mathews sang "The Space Between" just for us, and the 180,000 people in front of him. Backstage we waited for James Brown to finish his set. We were escorted up on stage to watch the last bits of his set. Jeff [Rowland] told us that every single move and expression was exactly the same as the last time he performed at Woodstock. Jeff introduced us to Wavy Gravy, who was apparently at the original Woodstock. I don't think he ever left. He was walking a fish on a leash as James finished up and we were introduced. 'Ladies and gentlemen, could we have your attention? Here with a very serious announcement about drugs are the Umbilical Brothers' (or something like that). My, how the crowd booed. That was really quite incredible. 180,000 people booing. Now that's comedy. In the comedy world, the technical term for how we went is called "killed." We killed. Talking to the crowd about the dangers of drugs, as we made time seem like it was going slower, faster than normal, dogs appearing out of nowhere, et cetera. We were on top of the world."

But one success does not necessarily a victory make and, unfortunately some of the "love" from the audience was captured for posterity. "We were quickly escorted to a tent with MTV," remembers Collins. "We were still flying. As soon as the interview was finished, we were driven to the West Stage for our second performance. Like before [when] we could see Dave Matthews, we could now see who was on the West Stage. And it was no Dave Matthews. It was a band called moe. Black wrap-around sunglasses, tattoos, heavy aggressive sound and matching audience. We weren't worried because we had gone so well on the East Stage. But this was a different story. [This] wasn't 180,000 in front of the stage, more like a couple thousand, if that. Just before we were introduced, the compere made some remark about women in the audience showing their breasts, and then introduced us. The audience was in no mood for anything but hard rock. In the comedy world, the technical term is we "died." We died the death of the Gods. A thousand deaths in a couple of minutes. We had been on stage for no longer than ten seconds before they started yelling for us to 'get off!' The worst thing about the whole venture was that they didn't telecast our first performance, but because we went so well, they did telecast the second."

Some of those attending or performing were uncomfortable from the get-go. "Woodstock '99 is the only festival I have been to or played at that had a bad vibe," remembers Counting Crow's Jim Bogios, who was playing with Sheryl Crow that day. "The moment I arrived and walked around, it just felt wrong. I guess if you treat people like a bunch of animals, they will act like them. The only thing that surprised me was that it wasn't worse than it ended up. You could feel the whole thing was wrong and could go off at any moment. Now that I think about it, we were right in the middle of the Lilith Fair and took a day off to play Woodstock. I can't tell you how happy we all were to get back to that tour."

The 500-foot-wide stage was designed by artist Peter Max who intended his work to create "an intergalactic consciousness." The festival kicked off with James Brown, who got everybody up and waving their hands over their head. The music portion of the festival was exhilarating and many of the performances were especially notable. KoRn drew a huge crowd and the Offspring amused the crowd by bringing out balloons of the Backstreet Boys and battering them with bats. Rage Against the Machine launched a particularly potent set while some of the more mild-mannered acts seemed almost to fade into the stage. Some people complained that the artists didn't deviate from their usual songs and offer unique-to-the-festival performances, but many of them did. And many of those performers not only had a good time, but a memorable one.

"When I was going on to the stage, with the rest of the band, there were all these people standing backstage along the way, kind of like a reception line," remembers Liz Berlin. "Press, musicians from other bands, old friends; it was very hard to focus on any one person. And we just kept walking on to the stage and started the show like we start any other show, and so all of a sudden I'm in the middle of a song and I look up and out into the biggest sea of people I had ever seen in my life, all focusing their energy on our music, dancing and screaming. And at that moment I felt I was almost physically lifted off of the ground from the inside. It was such an up-swell and rush of energy and astonishment and 'how did I get here?' "

This was "Woodstock" and what would a celebration of the original festival be without some rain and mud? "It was a blast," remembers Peter DiStefano. "What a danger jam that was for Porno for Pyros. It was great to have so many people in front of you. I loved it! I remember the helicopter ride in the thunderstorm and the pilot saying we might not make it and we will have to land if it gets any worse, the revolving stage and Perry [Ferrell] wearing my clothes for the gig. Carlos Santana blessed my pick before my performance. [The people in the audience] were great! They got the danger of it all. In rain and mud, the party must go on."

Not only was the audience present to see bands of renown but also up-and-comers who would make their mark that day and go on to become popular headliners. "I recall Godsmack's playing just before we went on and they were incredible," says David Ellefson of Megadeth. "Although they had toured the U.K. with us a few months prior, it was clear that they were now poised and ready to take over the world, which I'd say they certainly did thereafter."

Performers who had previous festival experience were nothing if not practical. "It was much less of a "Wow" situation in '99," says Will Turpin. "Experience and lots of touring had worn down the novelty. I do remember seeing lots of sunburned tits when we were performing. I think its fine to bare what God gave you if you feel the urge, but don't forget the sun block. It looked like some girls were going to be in pain the next day."

Good times, yet the mood of the festival suddenly began to darken and change. "I remember looking out at the crowd during the gig and it seemed to me I was staring in the face of hell," remembers Jim Bogios. "It was a scorching hot day; the sun was blaring in my face. My in-ear monitors had a loud high-pitched squeal to go along with the barely audible music we were playing in it. In front of me was a sea of frat boys with no shirts and khaki shorts all reaching out to grab a piece of flesh on the many girls being tossed around the audience. Then I saw two girls pinned in the front of the stage with several sets of hands grabbing them from all angles like a giant ravaging octopus. I struggled to cry out (as if they would hear me). Then thought about throwing my [drum] sticks at them, 'Duck, Sheryl!' Instead, I just sat there helpless trying to finish the gig, as I could feel the live MTV cameras focus in on my face to the left of me. Smile, sucker! Yes, this was indeed the closest to hell I ever want to be."

When Limp Bizkit played their song "Break Stuff" many down in front took them at their word and small scuffles of violence broke out. A sound-and-light barrier was torn down and used for crowd-surfing. On Sunday night Red Hot Chili Peppers took the stage (with a naked Flea). A group of people dedicated to peace had earlier handed out candles to be lit during the Chili Pepper's song "Under the Bridge." While most of the crowd lit the candles and held them aloft, others used them to light bonfires. A sound tower caught fire and the fire department made their way to extinguish the flames amid chants from the audience to let it burn. The show continued with an encore by the Chili Peppers, which ironically was to include Jimi Hendrix's song "Burn" as a tribute to Hendrix. But the song was not performed because of the fire.

As the Chili Peppers left the stage, all hell broke loose. The bonfires raged and people fueled them by tossing available objects into the flames. On-site ATMs were tipped over and looted, and many of the vendor booths were destroyed. The fence came down and was also thrown into the flames. Twelve refrigerator trailers, a bus, and portable toilets were also set afire. A light tower was brought down and a car was rolled over. MTV had been covering the event live and made the quick decision to bail. Host Kurt Loder would later say that the anger and "waves of hatred" on the scene were scary. The violence was eventually brought under control by the State Police, who were pelted with bottles. People were injured and people were enraged.

"We had to leave almost immediately after our set because we were scheduled to play in another city the next day," remembers Liz Berlin. "Our set was during the late afternoon and the crowd was very excited, very hot, and I imagine very exhausted from many days in that expansive festival environment. The sun was setting as were we driving away in our tour bus and we were watching the next performers on satellite TV. We were astonished to watch the demise of the once peaceful scene as the evening wore on and when it got to the point where people were tearing down scaffolding and setting bonfires in the middle of the field, it was hard to believe that that was the same place where we just played, to the same people. How can a situation turn so radically like that? It was reality-shaking for me and I think impressed upon me, maybe for the first time, the unpredictability of life in a mass public situation like that. We were very glad we weren't still there, but at the same time, it felt very odd to be driving away from a situation that was falling apart like that. Like a narrow escape, with a strong awareness of those left behind. Very surreal."

Other performers, such as Will Turpin, weren't that surprised at the way the festival concluded. "Woodstock '99 didn't have the positive energy flow that I felt in '94," Turpin says. "The festival was on a tarmac. It was hot and uncomfortable. In '94 the setting was green, rolling hills and fields of grass. There were shaded areas that had tent cities woven into the trees. It was much more accommodating at '94 compared to '99. After our performance we saw the riots at Woodstock on the TV in our bus. I wasn't surprised. People were not happy about the way they were being treated and an angry mob took over."

There were, naturally, injuries and arrests. Heatstroke was a big issue and people who stood too close to a sound tower were injured when moshers nearly knocked the tower down. There was said to be a birth and, unfortunately, a man who had recently undergone heart surgery died. At least four rapes were reported. By the end of the festival there were many arrests, yet only six of those people arrested were because of the violence on the final night. The promoters were out a lot of money in damages and, even when made aware that their audience was not happy about the financial aspects of the festival, were perplexed about why the destruction had taken place. The festival cost approximately $38 million to produce and the cost to the promoters would rise.

During the aftermath of the riot and the following morning, a chanting drummers circle sat beyond where State troopers stood in a line holding their batons. Ever optimistic, Michael Lang said he didn't think the damage done at the festival was a statement against Woodstock, but rather another Woodstock-era statement against the establishment. Only this time, Lang *was* the establishment.

"Woodstock '99 was a bit of a wreck," reflects Will Turpin. "You can't charge a premium for tickets and put people on a cement runway in the middle of the summer. Water and food were overpriced. People felt cheated and obviously they reacted in a negative way by the end of the weekend."

"[In] 1999 [it] was also a very different time in the Unites States than it is today," says Liz Berlin. "Pre-9-11, the music industry's diverse landscape included much more negative strains of music. There were a lot of songs across the genres with really negative and even violent content. When the attacks happened on 9-11, only two years later, all of that froze in time. Bands that were hugely popular whose focus was on violence kind of dropped off the charts and the whole landscape of the music industry changed to suit a massively changed nation. I know it sounds strange but for me, being a child of the eighties, having never really come into contact on a personal level with violence and the pandemonium of an unruly crowd like that, Woodstock '99, as amazing as it was to perform there and be a part of it, was a mild shattering of my peaceful reality that was completely shattered two years later with the terrorist attacks on the World Trade Center. The more I think about it, the more I think it changed everything for me, maybe like my generation's Altamont."

"We were the last band to play the three-day festival," says David Ellefson. "During our set I remember smelling smoke, like a huge bonfire was burning off in the distance somewhere. It wasn't until later that night back at the hotel that I found out a riot ensued during the Red Hot Chili Pepper's set, which started the fire. As the days rolled by, more and more reports of the damage poured in, detailing the looting and violence from an otherwise upbeat rock concert. These reports ultimately tainted Woodstock '99 from living fondly in the history books of rock as was originally planned. Unfortunately, the legacy of "peace and love" from yesteryear's Woodstock quickly eroded, as it became evident [Woodstock '99] voiced radical opinions, violence, disrespect and destruction."

Coachella Valley Music and Arts Festival
October 9–10, 1999

"It was hot, there were palm trees, and a lot of great haircuts and sunglasses. I can't wait to go back."

—Scott Avett, the Avett Brothers

The year 1999 was in many ways a tumultuous summer for music festivals but it also marked the beginning of an annual festival that would be viewed more much more positively than Woodstock '99. As in-your-face as Woodstock '99 had turned out, thousands of people continued to want to experience a community of music lovers who would attend a festival simply to kick back to enjoy the music and each other's company. The first Coachella Valley Music and Arts festival was molded to fit that need.

The first "Coachella" was held over October 9–10 at the Empire Polo Fields in the Colorado Desert town of Indio, California. Because Indio is a desert community, trees and shelter from the searing sun is at a premium and the primary negative aspect of the festival was the scorching desert heat. Having taken note of the hydration problem at Woodstock '99, the promoters of this festival made sure that water was not an issue for those who attended. The organizers even went so far as to supply each person entering the festival with a free bottle of water. (By 2007, a free bottle of water was exchanged for every 10 empty bottles returned for recycling.) On-site camping would not be allowed, thus likely nipping another problem in the bud. The festival organizers had initially intended a three-day event but finances seem to have gotten in the way of that plan.

Over 25,000 people attended the 1999 festival, at which Beck, Tool, and Rage Against the Machine headlined. Artists such as Jurassic 5, Modest Mouse, the Chemical Brothers, Morrissey, Ben Harper, Moby, and Perry Farrell performed as well as almost fifty other bands, dee jays, and electronic artists. As well as an excellent, multi-genre music bill, the festival featured various types of displays such as sculpture, interactive activities, and installation art. Set amid tents and booths, the event included several stages that kept the music flowing continuously. The bill was vastly entertaining but the heat was blistering and no doubt kept some people away. The first Coachella festival lost money.

Due to their lack of profit, the festival organizers decided not to repeat the festival the following year, but by 2001 Coachella was back on. Realizing that the summer heat had been a major problem and concern at the previous event, the festival was moved to April and would be held for only one day. When the promoters failed to sign a headlining act they turned to Perry Farrell for help. The reunion of Farrell's old band Jane's Addiction was a welcomed surprise and certainly their signing on drew a large audience.

By 2002, the festival had returned to a two-day event that featured a diverse bill as well as headliners Oasis and Bjork, and a reunited Siouxsie & the Banshees. The 2003 festival featured Red Hot Chili Peppers and the Beastie Boys, and another reunion:

this time the legendary Iggy Pop and the Stooges. In 2004, the festival "sold out" for the first time with over 50,000 people in attendance.

The extreme high summer temperatures of the region may have been avoided by the decision to move the festival from summer, but the climate at Coachella can still be quite warm in the spring. Even so, the desert can be a magical experience. "I think I'll never forget the heat and the amount of water I drank," says Blonde Redhead's Amedeo Pace. "It got quite stunning at sunset. I also love the fact that horses are usually populating the ground before us humans invade it."

In 2007, the festival would see its largest crowd yet with over 100,000 people in attendance for a reunited Rage Against the Machine. Coachella was, by now, known as the perfect place to reunite a band. Having started with Jane's Addiction, the festival was also the venue for reuniting Siouxsie & the Banshees, Iggy Pop and the Stooges, the Pixies, Gang of Four, Bauhaus, Tool (who hadn't appeared live in 3 years), Daft Punk, the Happy Mondays, the Jesus and Mary Chain, Crowded House, and Rage Against the Machine.

Coachella continued to provide elements beyond the outstanding music performances. Global interest and ecological issues remain pertinent to the festival. "The coolest thing I heard about the festival was a tent where you can go in, sit on an exercise bike and charge up your cell phone," says the Frames' Rob Bochnik. "I was so excited about this idea and the fact that the festival is showing people great ideas like this, and getting people to think along these lines. Imagine if, in every home in the U.S., there was an exercise room in which people would get on a bike or treadmill and crate electricity that could power their home, or at least certain appliances. A great way for people to work off the guilt they may experience after eating that extra hot dog, hamburger, donut, bucket of chicken. In Africa, people who live in areas without electricity were given radios that can be hand-cranked and require no electricity (from a wall plug) to operate. Therefore, someone who would otherwise have no access to the world outside his/her community could essentially hear about what is going on in the rest of the world, all at the expense of a few simple cranks. I am aware that exercise bikes that produce electricity can only produce enough power to charge a cell phone or laptop computer, but eventually people will figure out how to create more power output with less input, essentially doing more with less. America is in desperate need for ideas like these to be incorporated into people's everyday lives. Showing people ideas at a cool music festival [like Coachella] is a great way to get the ball rolling on cool ideas like this."

The musicians who participate seem to enjoy the laid-back feel of the festival but also enjoy the rejuvenation the festival can offer. "I felt like it was good for us to be a part of something of that size and importance," muses Amedeo Pace. "It did feel like it happened quite fast and [was] a bit like being thrown in cold water, which is always awakening."

"Our experiences are so fast and most times it's in and then out and we are off to the next drive or plane ride," says Scott Avett of the Avett brothers. "Coachella is obviously "big time" and a great opportunity for any independent artist like us. As far as a specific memory . . . it was hot, there were palm trees, and a lot of great haircuts and sunglasses. I can't wait to go back."

The festival atmosphere is sometimes so laid-back that the performers don't know what to expect. "Five minutes before I was scheduled to go on, my heart dove into my stomach when I saw about fifty people in the Gobi Tent," remembers dee jay/vee jay turntablist Mike Relm. "Fifty people is a good number in a small restaurant, not at a festival stage that could hold over 5,000. I thought I was going to be the laughing stock of the festival. I knew I was on during the Chili Pepper's set, but I thought there would be enough people who didn't like them to get me a decent audience by default. I had spent most of the day enjoying the festival, surrounded by tens of thousands of fans, which made it even worse for my self-esteem. I was imagining all the reviews that would pop up the next week: 'Mike Relm played to a near-empty tent at a sold-out Coachella.' I just stood at the side of the stage, staring at the floor trying to muster up any bit of confidence I could. Backstage was full of people I knew who had come to see me, which meant a lot, but I was so embarrassed. Then out of nowhere, I head a voice say, 'I don't give a fuck who else is here, I'm ready to see your show.' I turned around and it was Z-Trip. Bear in mind, we haven't seen each other in years so it was sort of a reunion under duress. But I'll never forget what he said next. 'Trust me, go up and do your thing. You'll get the place packed. They just gotta see you up there. Believe me, I've seen it happen.' This coming from a guy who brought out Beck and Chester Bennington onstage at these very grounds not long ago. He knows what he's talking about when it comes to this festival. So I took his word, sucked it up, and walked on stage. The next thing I remember doing was looking up about five minutes later. Lo and behold the tent was packed! It turned out to be quite possibly the best show I've done. It also helped that they provided a beautiful video wall for me. Plus there were palm trees in the background. Can't beat that. [Coachella] had a huge impact on my career. We're still getting calls for shows based on my performance there."

And there is the heat, which is a different experience for those who aren't use to it. "I can't get the heat off my mind," says Mando Diao's Mats Bjorke. "You know, coming from ice cold Sweden straight out in the desert . . . We got blisters on our feet while performing. Yes, we play barefoot."

Like other multi-genre festivals Coachella is a great place to gain recognition. "So many new acts are exposed to an audience who would not normally get to see them," says Mike Relm. "Just as record sales are taking a dip, tours aren't what they could be either. I think there's just too much out there in the world that people get overwhelmed and it takes a festival like Coachella to showcase musicians in an environment where people can experience multiple shows in one weekend. As crazy as the weekend might seem at first, it's really easy to make a nice schedule for yourself to see the bands you like and also get exposed to some that you didn't know you liked. You can't lose by going to these things."

"I saw the Teddybears, which was quite cool," says Mats Bjorke. "I know they are from Sweden, but they are like Mando Diao who almost don't play shows in Sweden. I saw the Roots, but it was too warm during the day. I had to save energy for our own show. You always feel that you grow as a person when you grow with your band. Playing Coachella is a step to be better known in the U.S."

Although the quality of the bill is probably worth any difficulties someone attending the festival may encounter, Coachella is not without its problems. "Palm trees . . . traffic . . . people . . . people . . . people . . . and more people," says Avett.

The traffic is heavy and the parking is somewhat unorganized. The sound bleed from the variety of stages sometimes interferes with the music from other stages. Yet Coachella maintains the festival feel with good music, political booths, the new age emphasis on ecological issues, and visual impressions that delight. A participant can now camp on-site and enjoy the festival to the fullest. Since Coachella remains an annual event, the festival has become one of the most popular destination festivals in the country.

Anger Management Tour
2000

While hip hop and rap acts had been included in Lollapalooza and other festivals, several artists of those genres felt it was time to throw a party that would feature *their* music. Ozzfest had become popular featuring metal acts and there certainly was a large audience for acts such as Eminem, Ludacris, Papa Roach, and other hip hop artists and rap acts. What the fans of the growing hip-hop scene got was the Anger Management Tour—a concert presentation that included montages of television clips showing Eminem being attacked by politicians, fans clamoring for the females present to bare their breasts, and some very short sets.

Touring on the success of the *Marshall Mathers* album, the first Anger Management Tour in 2000 featured Limp Bizkit, Eminem, with Papa Roach and Xzibit as the supporting acts. The tour was not greeted with favorable press as many reviewers felt those performing didn't have their heart in the show and might be appearing because of the money they were making. The more successful and promising up-and-coming hip hop and rap acts were included—likely with more peace of mind—in other touring festivals and that was that.

Bonnaroo
2002

"It's almost comical how many times, and at so many locations around the country, people have come up and said 'Man, I caught you guys at Bonnaroo.'"
— Andy "Padre" Miller, the Big Wu

Coachella had demonstrated that destination festivals could be well-organized and a lot of fun to attend. Festivals much like Coachella, although most on a much smaller scale, began to pop-up throughout the United States. If anyone wanted to have a festival experience during the summer, there were plenty of events from which to choose. By 2002, the rock festival had once again become central to the rock music experience.

The success of the Coachella festival was encouraging to promoters. It demonstrated that music festivals were still appealing to those who wanted to come out and enjoy a variety of music genres in a central location. Over June 13-15, 2002, an event would be held that would rival every other contemporary music festival as to its importance to twenty-first century rock music. *Rolling Stone* magazine would include the Bonnaroo experience as one of the fifty moments that changed the history of rock and roll, according to the festival's promoter Superfly Productions.

The word "bonnaroo" was made popular by boogie woogie legend Dr. John when he used it in the title of his 1974 album *Desitively Bonnaroo*. The word is a cajun slang word that references an especially good time. Superfly Productions, an independent music company that specializes in music production, talent booking, and creative services, along with Tennessee theater and club promotion enterprise AC Entertainment decided that a one-stop, destination festival would not only be an asset to the economy of Tennessee, but would truly reflect the original essence of the music festival. Located sixty miles southeast of Nashville in Manchester, Tennessee, Bonnaroo has done just that.

On June 21–23, 2002 the first Bonnaroo was held with an impressive bill that included Widespread Panic, Bela Fleck, Gov't Mule, Phil Lesh & Friends, Bob Weir, Ben Harper, String Cheese Incident, Jack Johnson, Ween, Norah Jones, the Big Wu, Umphrey's McGee, and many other artists. Seventy thousand tickets were sold through word-of-mouth in advance of the event. The people who came to enjoy the music and the festival experience evidently weren't impressed by the actions of many of those who attended Woodstock '99. Most everyone behaved and incidents were kept to a minimum. (That said, there has been an accidental death reported every year the festival has been held.)

The festival now runs four days and features multiple stages—two hosting headliners (the What Stage and the Which Stage)—and diverse performances by a variety of artists from all genres of music. At its inception, the festival's primary focus was on jam bands, but by 2007 the acts are primarily rock with alternative, hip hop, country, folk, gospel, electronica, reggae, and almost every other style of music known to man thrown into the mix. People travel from all over the country to see their favorite bands and to be exposed to music they may have never heard or experienced. Live music runs from noon to midnight (with music in separate tents featured through 5 a.m.). Artisans and craftsmen display their wares in the Bonnaroo Market. Large tents feature comedy, movies, and arcade games—continuously for twenty-four hours—at "Centeroo." The festival has become so popular that in 2003, Bonnaroo Northeast was planned to take place on Long Island. Unfortunately the event was canceled when permits were slow in being issued.

Most of the performers find the Bonnaroo experience different from their other live appearances. "When our manager at the time informed us that he strong-armed us a slot at the festival, he sounded rather apologetic: 'It's not a great slot . . . on a side stage' and so on," says Andy "Padre" Miller of the Big Wu. "Frankly, I thought we would be on a six-inch riser with a couple speakers on sticks for a sound system. But when I walked on stage and there were a few thousand people waiting, I just cracked up. Sometimes you know when the getting's gonna be good. Turned out that the time slot our manager was so sheepish about worked in our favor. Since we were a last-second addition, nobody else was scheduled to play, so we had the audience to ourselves."

Bonnaroo seems to affect performers in ways they didn't think it would. "Actually having a great time in the middle of Tennessee as a whole has stayed in my mind," says Steve Choi of RX Bandits. "I never thought it would. I observed the most respectful and mellow large festival audience I have ever seen. Bonnaroo in general was a shock because many touring bands are not used to large festivals being so nice and well-organized. In what we do, our personal life and our professional life are not very separate. It was a huge accomplishment for us musically and personally, and already has moved the band forward so much."

The people who attend Bonnaroo seem to enjoy the large crowd experience. "The second time we played Bonnaroo I asked the audience to scream as loud as they could at the end of a countdown," remembers JJ Gray from MOFRO. "It was one of the loudest, most energized things I've ever heard. I could have quit after that and still have been happy."

"The one thing that stood out to me at Bonnaroo was how electric the crowd felt," remembers Aesop Rock. "I have played a bunch of these large outdoor festivals over the years and it's difficult to find the feeling of intimacy when there are that many people standing around watching show after show. This was the first time that there was almost a venue-like vibe in the crowd. I found that really difficult to get at most festivals, even when the crowd is at maximum excitement."

The size of the crowd does sometimes challenge the performers in unexpected ways. "I observed that you shouldn't be in a hurry to drive a Ford (they're *all* Ford) tour van through a dense mass of humanity," says Padre Miller. "We were getting skinny on time to make load-in, yet we had to navigate goat paths through a sea of sweaty people to get to our stage. If somebody made an aftermarket cow-catcher for tour vans, we would've been the first to buy one. Perhaps modified for hippies; made out of Nerf and brightly colored to facilitate the joys of unintentional travel while tripping."

Performing for a hometown crowd is especially exciting for artists. Sharing that experience with others can be even more exhilarating. "Bonnaroo is only about an hour from where I live, so I have had the privilege of experiencing the festival four times so far (thrice as a performer and once as a spectator)," says Gabe Dixon of the Gabe Dixon Band. "I have many fond Bonnaroo memories, but one that I will never forget was from the first Bonnaroo in 2002. After playing a set with my band in one of the tents, I stuck around to see Norah Jones who was playing after us. She sounded great as always, but I had already seen her show several times that week because we had just finished opening for her on a run of dates. I left and headed over to the main stage. The ground was soggy and I nearly lost my shoe in the mud on my journey toward the music. As I got closer I realized that I was hearing the Dead. Just as I found a nice spot to plant myself among the people, the band kicked off the song "Tennessee Jed." The crowd let out a great roar of approval. A couple of verses went by and before I knew it I was singing the chorus along with tens of thousands of people. "Tennessee, Tennessee, there ain't no place I'd rather be. Baby won't you carry me back to Tennessee." I knew at that moment that this was no fleeting festival. I knew Bonnaroo was here to stay."

The make-up of the people who attend Bonnaroo is a variety of lifestyles and political preferences. There are hippies and people from the country. There are those who save all year for the Bonnaroo experience and others who attend on a whim. There are as many white collar workers as those employed in blue collared jobs. Everyone is welcome at Bonnaroo. "[I saw] some hard-working people letting off steam," says JJ Grey. "[And] some over-privileged rich kids spending Mama and Daddy's money and letting off steam. It felt great overall, but I'm nervous in a crowd so I had to chill."

Everyone has their own unique perspective. "I observed freedom, and a lot of it," says Gabe Dixon.

Bonnaroo is a place for performers to widen their audience but it is also an opportunity to *expand* their audience. "So much energy," says JJ Grey. "You could get drunk off it. That was great. Our show attendance nationwide definitely came up a notch after that."

"Every show affects me somehow," continues Aesop Rock. "Bonnaroo came at an odd time for me 'cause I [was] sort of between records. I [had] new material coming out in about two months, but it's difficult to do new songs for the first time at an event like this. That said, we got a great response and decided to split the set up between old and new. It's rare that we will perform songs for the first time at a festival, but it felt comfortable so we went for it. Getting a great response from never-before-done material is always a thrill."

Millions have poured into the local economy from Bonnaroo and the festival organizers have donated more than one million dollars directly to area charities. Bonnaroo is a festival that the locals don't mind, in fact, they welcome it. Well, maybe they didn't welcome the 2005 Bonnaroo strip club. Or they may not have been overwhelmed with the Grand Marshal of the annual Mardi Gras parade, American Idol's William Hung. And as always there are weather concerns. There was a torrential rain in 2005 and the residual mud caused problems with parking and mobility.

In 2006 the festival featured Tom Petty & the Heartbreakers, Beck, Radiohead, and Phil Lesh and Friends. Keeping up the "anything can happen at Bonnaroo" ideal, Stevie Nicks made a surprise appearance with Tom Petty, and Oysterhead reunited. The New Orleans Preservation Hall Jazz Band played in their own designated tent for three days and nights. Major League Baseball offered an exhibit, a broadband internet village operated on-site with wireless access, a disco powered by Xbox 360 was featured, and an on-site newspaper was published by *Relix* magazine and the *Bonnaroo Beacon*. There was a food drive to benefit the Good Samaritan Food Pantry of Manchester and a movie tent that showed the "mockumentary" *Electric Apricot: Quest for Festeroo* helmed by Primus' Les Claypool. New Line Cinema also offered a twenty-four-hour movie tent, there were daily yoga classes, and a comedy tent featured stand-up.

The festival is already rich with traditions. One exciting annual event is the Super Jam. Each year the Super Jam is comprised of a variety of musicians from a variety of bands. In 2007, Led Zeppelin's John Paul Jones played with Ben Harper, Gillian Welch, and Gov't Mule. Gov't Mule themselves played with Bob Weir, Lewis Black, Michael Franti, John Paul Jones, Jack Casady, Luther Dickenson, and Jorma Kaukonen; and Sting joined the Roots on "Roxanne."

Bonnaroo '07 was just as exhilarating as previous years and it was only a question of time before the media became even more involved. The festival swarmed with reporters and critics. That was not the only problem that year. Summer heat in the South can be brutal, even in June. Musician Ornette Coleman collapsed onstage due to heatstroke. Still, the memories of playing at Bonnaroo seem to outweigh any negative situations. Xavier Rudd remembers "good energy, *big* energy. It was interesting to see the Police. [It was] many people having much, *much* fun."

"The memory of seeing that many people gathered in one place to celebrate is a powerful image in itself," says Michael Kang of the String Cheese Incident. "I still remember listening to the Police, saying to myself that after all these years, Sting's voice still sounds pretty fucking good!"

For the most part, Bonnaroo is a positive experience for those who attend and for those who perform. "There's a lot of people everywhere," says Aesop Rock. "I am personally not the type that would attend a festival if I were not performing, as I don't do too good when walking around with 100,000 other people in a field, but there is a certain type of person that enjoys this, and when you stick them with 100,000 of their kind it really can get out of hand. [But] the vibe [at Bonnaroo] throughout was really positive." And the fans are typical. "I also saw a lot of weed being smoked and a couple pairs of tits."

"There are obvious professional benefits to performing [at Bonnaroo], but it was as a spectator that I felt the greatest personal impact," says Gabe Dixon. "Bonnaroo gives the concert-goer the opportunity to escape from the busyness of life for a few days. I think that is healthy."

"It's almost comical how many times, and at so many locations around the country, people have come up and said 'Man, I caught you guys at Bonnaroo,'" says Padre Miller. "For the record, I'm pretty sure Bonnaroo never paid us the promised money—*you* try and find the guy with [the] checkbook in a crowd of 80,000. But the experience itself couldn't be bought. Plus, said folks have bought a million cocktails as a result. As for me, I'll take a double Stoli Greyhound in lieu of straight cash, homie. Consider the tab paid."

In 2007, the organizers purchased 530 acres of the site, while leasing an additional 250 acres. The organizers of Bonnaroo intended to stick around a long time into the future. "[There were] lots of people dealing with heat and humidity," says Michael Kang. "[But] festivals such as Bonnaroo have changed the live music industry in a very profound way. Instead of fans going to see their favorite band in their hometown, they can now go see ten of their favorite bands and a bunch of new bands they have never seen. Festivals like Bonnaroo have their ups and downs. Sometimes it's harder to enjoy a mass experience if you want an intimate experience. Personally, it's just great to get to connect with so many artists and friends in the industry in one place. That's my favorite part of it. My least favorite part is the actual physical rigor of the experience . . . sweating your ass off during the middle of the day. I would say that everyone that has ever performed at Bonnaroo was probably affected in some way. It's still the biggest crowd we have ever performed in front of!"

Molson Canadian Rocks for Toronto
July 30, 2003

"It was like playing to a football stadium to your left, one to your right, and three in the middle."

—Stuart Chatwood, the Tea Party

Rock festivals were hot again, especially in the summer months where participants could enjoy sunny weather and the outdoor atmosphere. In addition to offering music, some festivals were now allocating profits for charitable or worldwide issues, much as Monterey Pop had done all those years ago. On July 30, 2003, this mindset would result in the one-day festival Molson Canadian Rocks for Toronto, which was held on July 30, 2003, at Downsview Park.

Estimates of 500,000 people attended the event, making it the largest outdoor ticketed event in Canadian history. The idea for the concert had been put forth by the Rolling Stones who said they wanted to participate in an event that would help the economy of Toronto after that year's SARS outbreak took its toll. (The Stones had no desire to re-live the Altamont festival and this event would be planned more extensively.) Alberta beef was also sold at the event to bring notice to the Canadian beef industry that had been targeted in the press because of a single case of mad cow disease. The festival would come to be referred to as SARSfest, SARSstock, and SARS-a-palooza.

The music wasn't as celebratory and open-ended as in festivals past: the opening bands were allowed only fifteen to twenty minutes to perform. Canadian Dan Ackroyd hosted the concert which included performances by Sam Roberts, the Isley Brothers, the Flaming Lips, Kathleen Edwards, the Tea Party, Sass Jordan, La Chicane, Blue Rodeo, and the Have Love Will Travel Revue with Ackroyd and Jim Belushi.

"SARS Fest was all about numbers," remembers the Tea Party's Stuart Chatwood. "490,000 people is like a large city, but one where there were no buildings. It was like playing to a football stadium to your left, one to your right, and three in the middle. You couldn't grasp the size until you saw the shot from the helicopter. With the numbers comes pressure, and I must say that our twenty-minute set was probably the shortest twenty minutes of my life."

Legendary acts were featured for the evening portion of the festival: Canadian favorites the Guess Who, Rush, and AC/DC. Surprisingly, Justin Timberlake was greeted by an onslaught of empty water bottles (which were given away free to concert-goers) and boos. During the Rolling Stones' headlining set, Keith Richards berated the crowd for their treatment of Timberlake and Timberlake returned to duet with Mick Jagger on "Miss You." That festival-loving feeling was back.

2005

Fix You

In U.S. news

The trial of Michael Jackson consumes television viewers; George W. Bush is reelected President; the BTK killer is apprehended; the Red Lake High School massacre occurs; and the New York City transit strike lasts three days.

In world news

The fight over the Gaza Strip rages; North Korea announces nuclear weapons capability; Prime Minister Rafik Hariri of Lebanon is assassinated; the number of suicide bombs in the Middle East rises; Pope John Paul II dies; 250,000 people attend a democracy demonstration in China; and a tsunami hits Indonesia.

In music news

Superstar concerts are held in Wales, the U.S., and Canada for tsunami relief; Cream briefly reunites; Audioslave is the first rock band to perform a free outdoor concert in Cuba; and Madonna ties with Elvis for the most singles to reach number one.

Some of the year's most notable albums

Alanis Morissette: *Jagged Little Pill Acoustic*; 50 Cent: *The Massacre*; Jet: *Radio Burst Party*; Bon Jovi: *Have a Nice Day*; Ben Folds: *Songs for Silverman*; Franz Ferdinand: *You Could Have It So Much Better*; the All-American Rejects: *Move Along*; Neil Young: *Prairie Wind*; Fall Out Boy: *From Under the Cork Tree*; Coldplay: *X & Y*; the White Stripes: *Get Behind Me Satan*; Madonna: *Confessions on a Dance Floor*.

Rock's most popular songs

"Hollaback Girl"—Gwen Stefani; "Wake Me Up When September Ends"—Green Day; "Breakaway"—Kelly Clarkson; "Fix You"—Coldplay; "Lonely No More"—Rob Thomas; "Don't Cha"—Pussycat Dolls.

Live 8
July 2, 2005

> *"Faced with such an overwhelming problem on such an inhuman scale, what you do is what you can."*
>
> —Murray Foster, Great Big Sea

Where Molson Canadian Rocks once again encouraged awareness and goodwill, an event on the scale of Live Aid was launched to follow two years later. It would be called Live 8. Although again not technically a festival, Live 8 was an undertaking of such proportion that it could easily be defined as a worldwide festival event. Harkening back to the "Summer of Love" and the social involvement that year represented, Live 8 would raise the bar. More than a charity event, Live 8 was created to influence world politics . . . at this place in time, right *now*.

Rocker Bob Geldof was once again involved as organizer but Geldof made it clear that he didn't consider Live 8 to be Live Aid II. In tandem with the organizations Make Poverty History and the Global Call for Action Against Poverty, Live 8 would be a series of simultaneous concerts that would take place in G8 countries and South Africa on July 2, 2005. Coinciding with the twentieth anniversary of Live Aid, the massive worldwide concert would focus on the issue of extreme poverty just days before the G8 conference that was to be held in Auchterarder, Scotland. The purpose of Live 8 was not to raise money but rather to raise awareness of the issue of world poverty, compel world leaders to drop the debt of the world's poorest countries, encourage governments to agree to negotiate fair trade rules, and increase and improve aid to those countries in greatest need. There would be ten concerts on July 2, with an eleventh on July 6 in Scotland itself. Also on board to help with the event were John Kennedy, Russell Simmons, Kevin Wall, Richard Curtis, Larry Magid, Ken Ehrlich, Tim Sexton, Harvey Goldsmith, and Greg Sills.

Geldof organized Live 8 much the same way he had put Live Aid together: by calling his friends and asking for their help. Over 1,000 musicians were set to perform at the concerts, which would be broadcast throughout the world on 182 television stations (and 2,000 radio stations). The event was announced on May 31, allowing just weeks to complete the organization of the largest event of its kind.

On June 1, Geldof extended the inclusiveness of the event by asking that one million people participate in the "Long Walk to Justice" by demonstrating in Edinburgh on the day of that concert. The area police and those who were providing security for the summit were not pleased with this idea as it would cause them crowd management and security problems. (The walk would go on as planned, but with 200,000 people instead of one million and in a mostly peaceful environment.)

By June 3 the momentum was beginning to propel the event forward. This time the British government came onboard almost immediately when British Chancellor Gordon Brown held a press conference to announce that the Valued Added Tax law would not be imposed on the cost of the London concert, saving promoters over one-half million dollars. On June 6 a text message lottery was held in Britain to launch ticket sales. Over 66,000 pairs of tickets were offered to those who "won" by answering a multiple choice question and whose names were then drawn at random. Each text message would earn about $1.50 for the cause. Over two million entries were sent, raising more than three million dollars. The money was divvied up between the Prince's Trust (which was cancelled that year because of Live 8), the Help a London Child charity, and other organizations with about $1.5 million applied to the cost of the event. A problem concerning the tickets for the concerts occurred when some of the tickets began to show up on eBay. Geldof demanded that eBay remove the auctions and, eventually, eBay complied.

The locations of the concerts were announced to be held in the cities of London (Hyde Park), Philadelphia (Museum of Art), Cornwall (The Eden Project), Rome (Circus Maximus), Paris (Palais de Versailles), Moscow (Red Square), Berlin (Siegessaule), Tokyo (Makuhari Messe), Barrie (Park Place), Johannesburg (Mary Fitzgerald Square), and later Edinburgh (Murrayfield Stadium). As major entertainers and legendary artists committed to the concerts, it became clear that Geldof and Midge Ure, who was once again actively involved, had achieved their goal of featuring most of rock music's notable and stellar acts. Included were Paul McCartney, Elton John, Madonna, U2, the Who, Coldplay, R.E.M., Snoop Dogg, Sting, Pink Floyd (playing together for the first time in twenty-four years), Robbie Williams, Mariah Carey, Bon Jovi, P. Diddy, Shakira, Brian Wilson, Crosby, Stills & Nash, Green Day, Faith Hill and Tim McGraw, Bryan Adams, Mötley Crüe, and the list went on and on. Introductions and guest appearances would be made by Nelson Mandela, Bill Gates, Kofi Annan, and many other prominent people.

Of course the stellar bill was not without criticism. There were cries (particularly from Blur's Damon Albarn and the Black Information Link) that although the event was said to draw attention to the plight of those in Africa, not many black performers were asked to appear. Geldof countered that he was trying to raise awareness by featuring the biggest names in music he could get and who those artists might be was not of foremost importance to him. In fact, many black artists *were* already on the bill, or were placed on the list of performers to fill this need. Even so, Peter Gabriel announced on June 15 that he would organize a concert on the same day called Africa Calling, which would feature all African artists and would be hosted by Youssou N'Dour. Damon Alburn further suggested that the record labels involved with the concerts donate a percentage of their profits from the resulting publicity of their artist's albums to humanitarian causes. (Pink Floyd's David Gilmour announced that he, for one, would do so.)

The artists would perform for free, and that was certainly a good thing considering the numbers involved. The concerts would not have been possible otherwise. (Still, some people complained when they heard, correctly or not, that some of the artists received gift bags with over $3,000 in merchandise.)

MTV, MTV2, VH1 and mtvU all jumped on board to broadcast the event. ABC announced they would air two hours of highlights the night of the concerts. Country Music Television and VH1 Classic would air highlights the day after. AOL Music would stream performances live and on-demand.

Each location offered an unbelievable list of performers. Tokyo kicked off with Rize, and that county's concert included Bjork, Good Charlotte, McFly, Def Tech, Do as Infinity, and Dreams Come True. The London bill included Geldof (who decided spontaneously to perform "I Don't Like Mondays," his show stopping song at Live Aid), Paul McCartney (who performed "Sgt. Pepper's Lonely Hearts Club Band" with U2, in a coat filched from Bono), George Michael (although Paul McCartney forgot to introduce him), Elton John (including the T-Rex hit "Children of the Revolution," which he performed with an allegedly drunk or high Pete Doherty), and Pink Floyd. Then before Madonna's set Geldof introduced Birhan Woldu, one of the starving children that had appeared in the news report that impelled Geldof to launch Live Aid, followed by performances by Mariah Carey (with the African Children's Choir), Coldplay (singing "Rockin' All Over the World," which was the song Status Quo opened Live Aid with), Annie Lennox, Joss Stone, Keane, R.E.M., Robbie Williams, Snoop Dogg, Sting, the Who (performing "Won't Get Fooled Again," a song they had performed at Live Aid), Scissor Sisters, Boomtown Rats, U2, Razorlight, Dido, Pete Doherty, Snow Patrol, Ms. Dynamite, Velvet Revolver, the Killers, Stereophonics, Travis, and UB40, with presentations by Dido Kofi Annan,

Brad Pitt, Bill Gates, David Beckman, Ricky Gervais, Birhan Woldu, Dawn French, Lenny Henry, Peter Kay, David Williams, and Matt Lucas.

The London show would run long, as many of the performers wanted to comment on the state of world affairs and the need for action. There was some panic when London starting running two hours behind. The gridlock that would be created in the city due to people missing their train home would be significant but cutting off the concert would mean that many fans would not be able to see legendary performers. It was decided to let the concert play out—it was just too important an event. Paul McCartney closed the London show with "Hey Jude" shortly after midnight.

Will Smith opened in the United States by asking the combined worldwide audiences to click their fingers every three seconds which signified the death of a child from hunger. In Philadelphia, the bill was equally impressive: Stevie Wonder (with Adam Levine), Maroon 5, Kayne West, Linkin Park, Alicia Keys, Black Eyed Peas (with Rita and Stephen Marley), Dave Matthews Band, Bon Jovi, Jars of Clay, Destiny's Child, Keith Urban, Slipknot, Rob Thomas, Def Leppard, Jay-Z, Lemon, Sarah McLachlan (with Josh Groban), Black Ice, DJ Green Lantern, Kaiser Chiefs, Toby Keith and Will Smith, and DJ Jazzy Jeff. Presenters were Chris Tucker, Richard Gere, Don Cheadle, Dhani Jones (with four other members of the Philadelphia Eagles football team), Jimmy Smits, Natalie Portman, Jennifer Connelly, Naomi Watts, and Kami.

"I was performing with Rob Thomas at the Philadelphia show," remembers Matt Beck. "My specific memory was being onstage before we started. (It was a rotating stage with a wall in the middle so bands could set up when the band on before was playing.) My memory is seeing the whole crowd of a million people for the first time as the stage rotated and just feeling like I was floating."

As with other events of its kind, Live 8 was something the performers would remember on both personal and professional levels. "My experience at Live 8 impacted me personally because I really wasn't aware of Third World debt and how these countries don't have a chance to get on their feet because they owe on grossly inflated and out-of-date debts," says Matt Beck.

Yet the severity of the issue didn't preclude the artists from enjoying the day. "I really noticed the comradery of the bands backstage," recalls Beck. "All our trailers were real close to each other and everyone was mingling. It was a very nice and positive atmosphere."

In Barrie, Canadians united to participate: Neil Young (with his wife Pegi), Bryan Adams, Celine Dion (via satellite from Las Vegas), Randy Bachman, Barenaked Ladies, Bruce Cockburn, Gordon Lightfoot, Great Big Sea, Jann Arden, Les Trois Accords, Sam Roberts, Our Lady Peace, Simple Plan, Tom Cochrane, Dobacaracol, Blue Rodeo, and the Tragically Hip. Dan Ackroyd and Tom Green hosted. Also performing were Deep Purple, Buckcherry, Jet, DMC, Mötley Crüe, and the African Guitar Summit.

Great Big Sea's Murray Foster remembers the day well. "The cliché that musicians get paid not to play music but for the other twenty-three hours in the day is true," says Foster. "After the stress of getting up at 4 a.m. in Regina and then almost missing what may have been the most important gig of our career because of a delayed flight, it was a relief to perform at Live 8 in Barrie, even if our first song was a tone too low and the second a tone too high. With no time for set-up, we played without instruments. Our drummer, Kris, doesn't sing a cappella stuff, and so liberated from his drums, he spent our ten minutes of fame running back and forth across the stage bawling non-existent harmonies into my ear. We finished our two songs, the crowd roared, and we left the stage."

Much like other events, what was going on backstage was almost as interesting as performing in front of thousands of people. "We wandered back to our trailer to drink a beer and commune with our exhaustion," continues Foster. "Then Kris and I headed to the musicians compound, a u-shaped arrangement of little one-room condos that served as dressing rooms. Each door had a band's name on it, and most of them were standing just outside their rooms. It made for an interesting visual: Blue Rodeo standing beside a sign that said "Blue Rodeo" and Mötley Crüe standing beside a sign that said "Mötley Crüe." It was a Simpsons moment, a museum of bands. What many would find extraordinary, musicians find just part of the gig."

"What's most striking visually about bands taken out of their context is their ordinariness," says Foster. "When you spend a lot of time around famous musicians you start to see past their fame. With the Tragically Hip, for example, once you get beyond stardom, what you're left with is just a bunch of fairly ordinary guys. The overall effect at Live 8 was that instead of looking at the cream of Canadian music, I could just as easily have been watching a beer ad shot at a cottage party where everyone's holding a Molson Canadian. There were two exceptions to this: the industry people and the non-Canadian bands. The non-Canadian bands stood out like Yao Ming at a jockey convention: Jet decked out in suede jackets and pointy boots, and

Mötley Crüe throwing off so much capital-F Fame that it wouldn't have mattered if they'd been in bathrobes. But the truly glamorous people backstage were the managers, promoters and publicists, who know that cool sunglasses, perfect breasts, and the ability to charm strangers are nothing more than the tools of the trade."

Backstage at Live 8 wasn't as notable as the fans might think. "What backstage at Live 8 felt like was closer to a high school reunion: a bunch of friends and acquaintances standing around catching up," says Foster. "You had the nerds, the posers, the artsies, the class clowns, the stoners, just like high school. You had people with wild reputations who you stared at wondering if it's all true. You had the popular people and the loners. Of course, at a certain point the high school metaphor breaks down. After all, Neil Young is still Neil Young."

For many it was just another day at the "office." "After the finale, people said goodbye and trickled off," remembers Foster. "There were no grand gestures and no big moments. Gord Downie didn't hop up on a cooler to deliver an impromptu poem about poverty. Steve Page didn't lead us in prayer. It was all very Canadian, like the Barrie Live 8 show itself."

Berlin featured an all-star bill as well: Brian Wilson, a-ha, Green Day (who would come under criticism for their inclusion of their political rant "Holiday"), Audioslave, Roxy Music, Chris de Burgh, Sasha, BAP, Daniel Powter, Faithless, Renee Olstead, Joana Zimmer, Juan Diego Florez, Katherine Jenkins, Reamonn, Juli, Herbert Gronemeyer, Otto, Silbermond, Sohne Mannheims and Wir sind Helden. Michael Mittermeier, Anne Will and Claudia Schiffer hosted.

The concerts were organized to raise awareness and they did, including for the artists involved. "One morning my cell rang and my product manager from my record label was on the other line," remembers Joana Zimmer. "'Hi Joana. Guess what?' He sounded very excited. 'What?' I asked curiously. It was June, 2005 and my first hit single 'I Believe' just came out. So everything was just exciting and everything was new to me. Lots of TV shows, interviews, and stage performances. 'Joana. You're one of the artists to perform at Live 8 in Berlin at the Brandenburg Gate.' 'Live who?' I asked. At first I didn't get it. 'Live 8! Remember, this happened twenty years ago already. It's a huge show and it'll take place in eight different cities all over the world with many different artists.' First I was speechless as he continued to read a list of the other performers like Herbert Gronemeyer, Shania Twain, Evanescence . . . . When the day came, I waited backstage with all the other bands and solo artists. It was very hot. I have to say that back then I wasn't too excited anymore. I felt part of this amazing show. I knew we were all here for a good cause. And I realized how perfect my song 'I Believe' would be for that purpose. It got a whole new political meaning for me. As I went out center stage I sang with all my heart and soul trying to touch this enormous crowd. 'For every little thing that we say or do . . . Give a little bit of love and it'll come back to you . . . .' It was one of the most touching moments so far. Today I would even say that this experience inspired me to become more active when it comes to charity concerts. A year later I traveled to Africa to visit hospitals and schools and for some charity concerts. Though it's only a little we can do, it's necessary not to give up. Bob Geldof and his projects are an excellent example."

The list of performers in Paris included Andrea Bocelli (with the Philarmonie der Nationen), Dido, Shakira, the Cure, Axelle Red, Cerrone & Nile Rodgers, Youssou N'Dour and Super Etoile de Dekar, David Hallyday, Magic System, Kyo, Alpha Blondy, Faudel, Amel Bent, Craig David, Ma Pokora, Calogero (with Passi), Muse, Placebo, Diam's, Florent Pagny (with Patricia Petitbon), Raphael, Louis Bertignac, Tina Arena, and Zucchero. Laurent Boyer, Yannick Noah, and Solidarite Sida presented.

The bill in Rome was extensive: Duran Duran, Faith Hill, Tim McGraw, Alex Britti, Elisa, Claudio Baglioni, Max Pezzali, Planet Funk, Irene Grandi, Articolo 31, Gemelli Diversi, Antonello Venditti, Cesare Cremonini, Noa, Biagio Antonacci, Ligabue (with Jonanotti and Piero Pelu), Negramaro, Fiorella Mannoia, Renato Zero, Negrita, Jovanotti, Pino Daniele, Povia, Francesco De Gregori, Laura Pausini, Nek, Francesco Renga, Le Vibrazioni, Meg, Tiromancino, Velvet, Zucchero, Stefano Senardi, Orchestra Piazza Vittorio, and Pagani & African Drum Collective. The Mayor of Lampedusa, Jane Alexander, and Paola Cortellesi presented.

"I remember that day in Rome as one of the most important moments in my professional career because it was clear to me that I was participating in something memorable," says Max Pezzali. "One of the main reasons why I started making music when I was a kid, was my dream of being on a huge stage with great artists, singing and playing for a noble cause. Listening to vinyl records of 'Concert for the People of Kampuchea' or 'The Secret Policeman's Concert' had been powerfully inspiring throughout my youth, giving me the firm belief that music could really change the world. On that unforgettable July 2 of 2005, my dream finally came true. I remember Faith Hill and Tim McGraw walking through the backstage of Circo Massimi with their beautiful daughter, just like any common family, enjoying the Roman summer air and having fun. I remember Duran Duran, legendary band of the eighties, playing with teenagers' 'punch,' and I remember the hospitality area filled with musicians and artists all having the same perfect knowledge of doing something important together. The crowd out there had the same kind of excitement: young kids and fifty-somethings, singing and dancing as one, feeling to be, at least for that day, at the very center of the universe."

Johannesburg was hosted by Nelson Mandela and included 4Peace Ensemble, Lucky Dube, Malaika, Zola, Jabu Khanyile & Bawete, Oumou Sangare, Mahotella Queens, Lindiwe, Vusi Mahlasela, Orchestra Baobab and Youssou N'Dour, and Super Etoile de Dakar, who also appeared at Cornwall and Paris. The state of the world was now such that Moscow could participate with Pet Shop Boys, Red Elvises, Spleen, Moral Code X, Bi-2, Jungo, Aliona Sviridova, Bravo, Linda, Dolphin Valery Sutkin, and Garik Sukachev.

"Our involvement with Live 8 happened as a pure coincidence," says Oleg Bernov of the Red Elvises. "Russia joined Live 8 at the last moment, so the organizers of the concert were actually struggling to find Russian bands to play that day, a Saturday. Not so many acts could donate their free performance in less than a week's time. The Red Elvises happened to be on tour in Russia. We happened to have a cancelled show in Moscow that evening. We just jumped at the possibility to play on the Red Square for a worldwide audience! When Live Aid was happening, I still lived in the Soviet Union and Russian TV broadcasted the concert, though it was not supposed to. I couldn't believe my eyes. And here I am twenty years later, participating in the same event!"

Peter Gabriel had made good on his promise to launch an all-Africa concert and hosted that event in Cornwall, with Goodwill Ambassadors Angelina Jolie and Johnny Kalsi presenting. Artists included Coco Mbassi, Dido (who appeared also in Paris and London), Akim El Sikameya, Daara J, Thomas Mapfumo & the Blacks Unlimited, Emmanuel Jal, Angelique Kidjo, Frititi, Modou Diouf & O Fogum, Geoffrey Oryema, Ayub Ogada, Uno, Siyaya, Maryam Mursal, Chartwell Dutiro, Mariza, Kanda Bongo Man, Shikisha, Tinariwen, and, once again, Youssou N'Dour and Super Etoile de Dakar.

The television broadcasts were not without their difficulties. The BBC had a small problem with the f-word being tossed about more freely than they would have wanted, especially by Madonna, Snoop Dogg, Razorlight, and Robbie Williams. But such is rock and roll. MTV and sister station VH1 met with the most criticism as they continuously cut from performances to commercials—even during the historically noteworthy performance of the reunited Pink Floyd. The Vee Jays came under fire for being too uninformed and sometimes inane. (MTV would later try to make up to viewers their less-than-stellar broadcast by broadcasting the performances without interruption the following week. Both MTV and VH1 aired six hours of the event commercial free.)

On July 2, during the concerts, a rally and protest march was held near the G8 conference site by the Make Poverty History coalition. Over 225,000 people, most wearing white, took part. "Edinburgh 50,000: The Final Push," the final Live 8 concert, took place in Edinburgh on July 6. Performers, many of whom had already appeared during the July 2 concerts, included James Bown, Annie Lennox, Bob Geldof, Midge Ure, Beverly Knight, Neneh Cherry, Chris Evans, Embrace, Herbert Gronemeyer, Feeder, Die Toten Hosen's Campino, Will Young, Katherine Jenkins, Jamie Culum, McFly, Natasha Bedingfield, Snow Patrol, Texas, the Corrs, Sugababes, Ronan Keating, the Thrills, the Proclaimers, Travis, Wet Wet Wet, 1 Giant Leap featuring Neneh Cherry, Maxi Jazz, Geoffrey Otyema, and Mahotella Queens. Nelson Mandella appeared in a pre-recorded speech and presenters included Bono, Eddie Izzard, George Clooney, Claudia Schiffer, Courni Nidu, Davina McCall, Peter Kay, Wangan Maathai, and Susan Sarandon.

"Opening the show at Murrayfield was one of the most nerve-wracking moments of my life," says Craig Reid of the Proclaimers. "The sound of the rapidly-filling stadium singing '[I'm Gonna Be] 500 Miles' back at us will never be forgotten."

The Live 8 List, compiled of the names of those who supported the call to action, was presented to the G8 Chairman, British Prime Minister Tony Blair. Only two days into their conference, G8 leaders pledged to double the amount of aid to poor countries and bring the number to $50 billion by 2010, with half of the amount going to Africa. Another announcement stated that the debt of eighteen of the poorest countries was being cancelled. Even though those who coordinated Live 8 initially claimed it was not a charity event, over $79 million dollars was raised and sent to countries in need.

A DVD was released in November of that year. In 2006, the BBC broadcasted *Live 8: What a Difference a Day Makes* while MTV, again obviously ignoring the significance of the event, ran a similar program off-prime hour.

It's hard to say what effect Live 8 had on the wide-spread issue of worldwide poverty but, unlike any event before it, it seems to have impacted the G8 Conference and brought food—and hope—to many. "Honestly, I can't say if we reached our goal, but I'm absolutely sure that music, once again, has showed that it's not a matter of bits and bytes, it's about sweat, soul, emotion, aggregation, it's about humanity and compassion, and it's still capable, just like decades ago, to stop the world and to draw its attention," says Max Pezzali. "It's a lesson we shouldn't forget again."

"I think it made many people think about world poverty, which was good," says Craig Reid. "It also put pressure on the G8 conference to take some positive action on Third World debt. People probably attended for many different reasons. Most of the audience at Murrayfield was soaking wet, but euphoric. [The event] impacted me personally by my being impressed by so many giving time and money for a very worthwhile cause. Professionally, it boosted the band's profile in a quite major way."

Murray Foster sums up the day nicely. "Even after taking part in such a massive event, it's still hard to say what our role in ending poverty actually was or is," says Foster. "We played Live 8 because it was fun, because we were asked to, and because it was the right thing to do. And maybe that's the way to think of it. Faced with such an overwhelming problem on such an inhuman scale, what you do is what you can."

2007
What Goes Around . . . Comes Around

In U.S. news

The war against terror divides Americans; the massacre of students at Virginia Tech takes place; the 35W Mississippi River Bridge collapses in Minneapolis; and Barry Bonds breaks Hank Aaron's home run record amid a baseball-wide investigation of players' use of steroids.

In world news

More American troops are sent to Iraq; Vietnam joins the World Trade Organization; suicide bombing rises; British Prime Minister Tony Blair resigns; abortion is legalized in Mexico City; and Nelson Mandela convenes a group of world leaders including Jimmy Carter, Desmond Tutu, Kofi Annan, and Li Zhaoxing to contribute their wisdom, independent leadership, and integrity to address the world's greatest problems.

In music news

The Concert for Diana is organized by Princes William and Harry; the Police reunite; and Jordan Sparks wins *American Idol*.

Some of the year's most notable albums

Amy Winehouse: *Back to Black*; Kanye West: *Graduation*; Foo Fighters: *Echoes, Silence, Patience & Grace*; Maroon 5: *It Won't Be Soon Before Long*; Daughtry: *Daughtry*; Linkin Park: *Minutes to Midnight*; Fergie: *Dutchess*; the Eagles: *Long Road Out of Eden*; Nickelback: *All the Right Reasons*; Akon: *Konvicted*.

Rock's most popular songs

"Girlfriend"—Avril Lavigne; "Makes Me Wonder"—Maroon 5; "Umbrella"—Rihanna; "Home"—Daughtry; "It Ends Tonight"—the All-American Rejects; "U + Ur Hand"—Pink; "Welcome to the Black Parade"—My Chemical Romance; "Big Girls Don't Cry"—Fergie; "What Goes Around . . . Comes Around"—Justin Timberlake; "Hey There Delilah"—Plain White T's.

Live Earth

July 7, 2007

"It was an incredible big festival with incredible great bands! I think nearly everyone in the Western world might have recognized it."

—Johannes Strate, Revolverheld

Former Vice-President Al Gore and Emmy-Award winning producer Kevin Wall are not your standard-issue music promoters. It had been two years since Live 8 had made its mark on history and the effect of that worldwide festival event was still being analyzed. There was no doubt, however, that Live 8 had garnered the attention of those who loved music all over the world for a world-impacting issue. The "formula" had been set. It was only a matter of time before a similar event would be launched to bring attention to another issue that effected the entire world population. That issue would be the environment and the event would be Live Earth.

Al Gore had been warning us for years of the threat of global warming through lectures, books, and his Academy Award-winning documentary *An Inconvenient Truth*. Whether one chose to believe those who championed the cause or not, the well-being of the environment is a topic which should be of concern to us all. Drawing on the premise of Live Aid and Live 8, and also on the "No Nukes" benefit concerts, Gore joined with Kevin Wall, a music concert producer and distributor, to bring Gore's passion of worldwide involvement in ecological issues to the television screens of those who would tune in to watch their favorite recording artists in concert. Gore and Wall invited over 150 artists and bands to perform in eight countries and eleven locations. The concerts would be televised on over 120 television outlets around the world.

The tickets to watch the concerts in person were sometimes steep; ranging in the United States and the United Kingdom from $53 to $348. (Those who could afford the more expensive tickets were usually in the front rows or backstage where they no doubt were often the guests of those who appeared onstage.) This time eBay was allowed to auction tickets and in the U.K. the tickets were available by online application.

Concerts were held in the United States (Giants Stadium), United Kingdom (Wembley Stadium), Australia (Aussie Stadium), South Africa (Coca Cola Dome), Japan (Makuhari Messe and To-ji), Germany (AOL Arena), Brazil (Copacabana Beach), and China (Oriental Pearl Tower). Music would be performed on seven continents and would play over the time span of twenty-four hours. Although not a part of the official program, 12,000 people attended a concert in Quebec and a portion of one of Toronto's busiest streets was closed for a Live Earth party. Hundreds of thousands of people attended the various concerts and concert-related festivals. Greenpeace organized information booths in major cities throughout the world.

The concert at Wembley Stadium in the U.K. featured performers such as Black Eyed Peas, Foo Fighters, Madonna, Red Hot Chili Peppers, Corinne Bailey Rae, John Legend, Beastie Boys, James Blunt, Metallica, and Keane among others. Such artists as Bon Jovi, Alicia Keyes, Kelly Clarkson, Ludacris, Kanye West, Fall Out Boy, Dave Matthews Band, AFI, John Mayer, Keith Urban (who performed a captivating version of "Gimme Shelter" with Alicia Keyes), Melissa Etheridge, Smashing Pumpkins, Roger Waters, and the Police (who were enjoying their reunion tour), appeared at Giants Stadium in New Jersey. (Sting has been active with environmental issues for some time and Melissa Etheridge won an Academy Award for her song "I Need to Wake Up," which was featured in Gore's film *An Inconvenient Truth*.) Crowded House, Jack Johnson, Toni Collette & the Finish, and Wolfmother performed in Aussie Stadium; Joss Stone and UB40 in South Africa; Linkin Park, Rihanna, and RIZE in Japan; Erique Iglesias, Shakira, Cat Stevens, and Snoop Dogg in Germany; Lenny Kravitz and Macy Gray in Brazil; Sarah Brightman in China; and the scientist-rockers Nunatak at the Rothera Research Station in Antarctica. And the list went on . . . . The concerts had star power to spare. "It was an incredible big festival with incredible great bands!" says Johannes Strate of Revolverheld. "I think nearly everyone in the Western world might have recognized it."

Many saw Live Earth as a gigantic infomercial for global warming and rejected the accuracy of its verbal content. Bob Geldof rejected the premise of the event, saying that people already were aware of global warming and that the event didn't have a final goal. Al Gore would respond by saying that the event would not be possible had it not been for the pioneering efforts of Geldof and those who helped him with Live Aid and Live 8. Roger Daltry didn't see how a giant concert would really help matters. Ironically, a few of those who performed were criticized by the media because they didn't seem devoted to the environmental issue. John Legend was featured in an SUV commercial and Sheryl Crow's song "Every Day is a Winding Road" plays during an ad for another SUV. Madonna was taken to task for the carbon emissions from her many houses, cars, and her private jet. The Black Eyed Peas' Fergie, however, vowed to sell her Hummer.

While Live Earth had no plans to raise money to combat the precarious ecology, viewers were invited to call in and commit to a seven-point pledge to demand a moratorium on building coal-powered plants, fighting for more renewable energy, and doing what they could personally to combat global warming. The names of some of those who called in were randomly displayed on a tickertape banner which scrolled across the stage at some venues and across the television screens. (Many people who made the call no doubt believed that a pledge was a small thing to give to have your name viewed by thousands and sometimes millions.)

The concert promoters did what they could backstage to emphasize their commitment to the environment. The tickets to the event were printed on recycled paper. In London, burger boxes were made of biodegradable reed and sugar cane pulp, and cooking oil from concession stands was to be converted into bio-diesel fuel. And often times the backstage talk, like that onstage between performances, was eco-friendly and serious.

NBC carried three hours of the concerts and the Bravo channel ran a continuous feed. There was no-host coverage on the Sundance channel and CNBC carried portions of the event. The level of talent was evident but the performances were sometimes predictable and well, boring. There were few of the big moments that defined Live Aid and Live 8. Many of the acts performing for Live Earth were repeating performances that viewers had seen only the week before at the Concert for Diana. Most of those who performed chose not to personalize their performance to the issue and performed their hits or current release. Keith Urban and Alicia Keyes generated at least some excitement and AFI covered "Ziggy Stardust." Roger Waters brought out Pink Floyd's famous dirigible pig during his set and that was fun. Over all, the excitement level for those who were watching at home was fairly low. *Entertainment Weekly*'s Leah Greenblatt said the band reunions felt "a little like AARP." Even so, it was reported that 27 million people watched, although for what length of time couldn't really be measured.

Alec Baldwin, Leonardo DiCaprio, Robert F. Kennedy, Jr., and Al Gore himself took the stage at various times to speak. Yet the festival feeling of Live Earth was subdued. The event seemed more like a parental lecture with some really good music, but was not all that innovative or attention-grabbing.

"I think there are more people now who think about our world and environment," says Johannes Strate. Perhaps he's right. The worldwide festival atmosphere, however, needs an event stronger than Live Earth to represent its power. Everything is done on a larger scale today but some things probably should remain the same. It's pretty hard to feel a sense of brotherhood over the airwaves but Live Aid and Live 8 had managed to bring off at least a semblance of unity. There is no template, really. An event that seeks to instill harmony on a worldwide basis needs to be able to not only embrace that brotherhood but make it their own. Maybe it really is "time to get back to the garden . . . ."

The Legacy of the Rock Festival

The rock festival, in all of its varying incarnations, has proven to be an enduring component of live rock music since the first chords of Monterey Pop rang out. The elements of the festival have changed and evolved from relatively small gatherings of like-minded youth to worldwide events that the entire family can participate in and enjoy. Today, those who want to experience a summer rock festival can pretty much attend an event made to order to suit their taste. The festival scene encompasses the destination experience, the traveling event, the televised charity or issue du jour, the large festival with several stages and arts and educational presentations, or a small hometown festival that includes rock music. There's something for everyone. Promoters bombard the media to ensure their event is well-publicized and attended and obtaining tickets is usually just a mouse click away. The rock festival has a rich history and a promising future. Festivals will no doubt reinvent themselves many times over before they fall out of fashion, if indeed they ever do.

Festivals past will not be forgotten. Hundreds of thousands of people remember their festival experience with a fond return to that moment in time when they were young and were not only discovering the music but a community of man like no other. Attending a music festival is usually, at the least, a memorable event and sometimes is a life-altering experience.

Even after forty years, the Monterey Pop Festival and the Summer of Love did not go unnoted. A traveling concert called the "Summer of Love 40th Anniversary" featured Jefferson Starship, Big Brother & the Holding Company, and Quicksilver Messenger Service, along with an appearance by Moby Grape, at the Monterey County Fairground, which was the site of the Monterey Pop Festival. *Rolling Stone* magazine presented a double issue dedicated to that very special moment in time. Articles and magazine covers featured a look back; and the festivals of 1967 and 1968 were all over the airwaves—both on television and radio. People of all ages continue to visit Max Yasgur's farm at Bethel, New York. A plaque has been placed on the site of the Woodstock Festival but a bigger draw is the Bethel Woods Center for the

Performing Arts, which was erected in 2006. Bethel Woods is an interpretive center dedicated to the festival that opened in 2007, almost forty years after the event.

Entertainment Weekly closed one if its July '07 issues with a commentary of the elements—good and bad—of the current festivals. The Van's Warped Tour and Bonnaroo continue to grow and prosper and new festivals pop up every summer. The music celebrations that are rock festivals are very much woven into the fabric of our times.

While those who attend have their own unique perspectives on the rock festival, so do those who perform. When asked if they felt the festivals were a positive or negative element of music and society, it isn't surprising that most music artists have a definite—if varied—opinion.

Melissa Etheridge:
"I think our society does not have enough ritual. Music festivals provide a much-needed place to feed the soul and spirit."

Barry Melton, Country Joe & the Fish:
"Looking back, I think the festivals of the sixties were a positive element. Monterey showed the world that large numbers of people could gather in peace to support a good cause, and Woodstock gave testament to the collective power of its generation."

Jack Casady, Jefferson Airplane:
"Now festivals are like a giant football or soccer game. The success of a festival has to do with the organizational skills and the people putting it on. You have to be organized whether you're putting on a festival or a marathon."

Frank Marino, Mahogany Rush:
"Well, [festivals] started out quite positive. But they became quite negative. Not only to the business and the art, but to the people as well. At one point I began to think of these shows as 'cheap psychiatry.' They were like giant scream-fests, where the fan could pay his twenty-five bucks and get to stand up and scream for a couple of hours, and perhaps get drunk in the bargain . . . rather like one who goes out to the train-yards and screams over the noise of the trains, into the wind. I think that the essence of the original festival idea was a great one, but when you introduce corporate ideas into art and try to marry them, well, it just never did work . . . and won't ever do so,

either. And it's not just music that has suffered this fate; it's many other things as well. Journalism, for instance. Where are the thinkers or the real social critics? The writers? When was the last time our nation had a real social or moral conscience? And where are the poets, writers, statesmen, et cetera? My goodness, even sports has fallen victim to the corporate drive for money, and the athletes now compete almost solely for the prizes encompassed in endorsements and fame."

Shawn Phillips:
"[The festival] was a positive element, as shown by its very niche in musical history."

Matt Kelly, Dropkick Murphys:
"It can be a double-edged sword. Look at the whole Woodstock thing a few years ago. It was an embarrassment to American festivals. I haven't heard of that sort of rioting/ looting/rape et cetera happening in recent memory in Europe. It seems that they really have the festival scene/culture dialed in."

Jim Bogios, Counting Crows:
"For the most part, festivals are fun and have a good vibe. People are excited and interested to listen to music and want to have a positive experience. You may be there to see a certain act, but then have the pleasure of discovering something new you wouldn't have done on your own. Watching something live can give you way more of an insight and understanding as well."

Tony McPhee, the Groundhogs:
"People attend festivals because it is the only way to see a number of bands in one place over a short period of time and the best way to see bands that you might not consider seeing at a one-off gig. It's good fun, especially if there's a real ale tent."

Zip Caplan, the Litter/White Lightning:
"Here was an event or an entity, if you will, that allowed a lot of people of the same beliefs (not religious—just ideals) to come together in one place and one setting and talk to each other—interact and exchange ideas—I think they were tremendously powerful in [earlier times]. I also think that most of the big get-togethers today are not anywhere near as profound for people as they were during that era. It seems to me that the present day counterparts are all about the money and party time and nothing else.

I don't know if the festivals really impacted my life as much as they were just a real lot of fun to play—met a lot of great people and got to party it up with other bands."

Liz Berlin, Rusted Root:
"Playing at Woodstock ['99] was a very expansive part of an already expansive time in my life. It's been a really crazy time with Rusted Root from the beginning and the opportunities we've been blessed with have been truly astonishing and have taken my life on a path I had never actually imagined for myself."

Leo Lyons, Ten Years After:
"Yes, historically festivals are important. I think as years go by they become milestones in peoples lives. A generation of people gathering together in one spot. They're also a great way for new bands to expose their music to a wider audience."

Kyoko, the Mad Capsule Markets:
"The music itself, for me, has the power to change people's lives, as I was changed by other great music I think. At the festival, [a] kind of power is gathered and there's a big [impact] around there. It will be something huge for society and for [each person]. It will keep [having] a big influence from [then] on."

Johnny Winter:
"It gets music to the fans on a greater scale. And sometimes festivals make a mark, like Woodstock."

Dave Peters, Throwdown:
"Ah, [festivals are] definitely positive. Sometimes fests can get a little out of control, but the way I look at it, there are 50,000 animals that are in a corral for a day instead of out roaming the streets."

Jason Miller, Godhead:
"I think [the music festival] has a great, positive effect. Anytime you can bring that many people together to just enjoy themselves, then it's a good thing!"

Scott Avett, the Avett Brothers:
"[The festival] is no doubt a positive thing, as long as big numbers of people don't get hurt or killed in mosh circles."

Larry Hoppen, Orleans:
"I'd go to a musically high-quality jazz/r & b/rock/pop fest if I knew one was accessible to me and my family and friends, and the price isn't the biggest factor. I believe that there are millions who'd agree with me. We just want to know that the music will be really good and the sound system will do it justice. Also that the 'seats' will be decent and that we won't get ripped off. Not too much to ask . . . ."

Peter DiStefano, Porno for Pyros:
"Sure [festivals are positive], if the person is there for the right intention."

John "Mister Zero" Picard, the Kings:
"I guess each generation has to live with the music they are given, but when you take the bands that have stood the test of time, from the classic era, one has to wonder if Nickelback will ever be in that league. Kids are now discovering Zep and Jimi and the Doors and are realizing that today's stuff is pretty shallow."

Steve Wozniak, US Festival organizer:
"[The US Festival] was more an important time in [the] life [of those who attended]. One of those times in life that cause them to think who they are and who they're going to be forever."

Drew Lamarche, Artificial Joy Club:
"I think that music festivals are all positive. Depending on the festival, it really can open someone up to different music and introduce them to artists that they may not have ever discovered. There are so many music festivals/tours all over the world and they seem to excite people. It's great for organizers to bundle as much entertainment as they can and it will multiply attendance for the tour and keep ticket costs at a reasonable price. Festival dates are my favorite shows to play; they are always a lot of fun and gratifying."

Joe Sharino, Joe Sharino Band:
"They're sort of mirrors of our culture."

Aesop Rock:
"I think [the festival] can be really positive, and while I personally wouldn't attend a festival if I were not performing, the types that do enjoy these events really make it

fun for the performers. There is something inherently cool about a lot of musicians getting together and playing a massive showcase for days. In theory, it sort of carries with it a feeling of the knocking down of walls between genres. A lot of these walls are put up by the media, and these festivals often allow artists to perform together without having to be sectioned off by some opinionated journalists. I think that's a really positive thing."

Chuck Negron, Three Dog Night:
"Festivals . . . I loved them and learned how to perform at these events. I met people I still know today and many of the musicians who attended these events still talk about them when we run into each other now. We changed the view of how important young people could be with these festivals and how our music was affecting the world."

Tony Joe White:
"I think music festivals are always good. I have played them all over the world and they all turned out cool."

Corporal Joebot Twopointoh, the Phenomenauts and TreePhort:
"Kids with money and idiots with guitars. [The festival experience can be] positive. It's bad, but so is everything else. Record sales are dropping due to mp3-mania, but there will always be kids with money and there will always be bands that can't write songs but get recognition because they're new. It will be sad that bands like the Briefs, One Man Army, Groovie Ghoulies, and the Teenage Harlets will break up before people realized how extremely great they were and their contribution is to music, but I guess that's the legacy (Van Gogh, et cetera). I think the mainstream music is pretty bad, but I'm glad that it's forcing the talented bands to work harder for those with good taste."

Eddie Money:
"The exposure to a wide audience of people is cool, and it's always a blast to perform in front of a giant audience."

Will Turpin, Collective Soul:
"I think festivals are cool. People can make a day of enjoying music and humanity. It's a great way to see some bands you may not otherwise go see."

Kyle Castellani, Nural:
"I believe anything involving music is a positive, with the obvious exception of Hillary Duff and Lindsay Lohan . . . and Paris Hilton."

Stuart Chatwood, the Tea Party/the Art Decay:
"A negative side appears when you are on tour with a festival, like some of the European weekends, where it's a bit disheartening to see the same artists act out the same stunts every night. It's something you'd expect from KISS but when you see some of the bands smashing equipment, pulling their pants down, having an audience member 'spontaneously' join them onstage and using the same banter onstage between songs, it really demystifies the whole thing and takes away the magic. I always remember a quote from Hendrix regretting that he lit his guitar on fire as he became somewhat of a circus performer, where people would expect the guitar arson."

Amedeo Pace, Blonde Redheads:
"[The festival] seems to have a positive effect on young people who have a thirst for music and desire to be exposed to as much as possible in the shortest amount of time. Conditions can sometimes be a bit unbearable, especially in unforgiving weather. It is, however, quite positive in the sense that it opens your eyes to new music or old music which you may not have been aware of."

Xavier Rudd:
"Especially at this time [in the world] anything that is a celebration of peace and good energy amongst people of different cultures is powerful and extremely necessary."

Silenoz, Dimmu Borgir:
"[Music festivals] are definitely a positive thing, without a doubt. I believe festivals, and shows in general, are good for people. They get to get away from the everyday misery. It's like they relax but at the same time go crazy as performances usually are a release for both the bands and the audience. Music is escapism really, and it's good to 'get away' some times, not having to worry too much about the day-to-day bullshit."

Nathan Larson, Shudder to Think:
"A couple of years back I saw the Pixies in Sweden and it was the first time I'd seen them since the late eighties when they blew my ass away at TT the Bears in Boston playing shit off of *Surfer Rosa*. Anyways, that night at Hultsfred, I think that's the

happiest I've ever been in such a context, standing outside watching a band amongst a sea of strangers, because it doesn't get much better than the Pixies. I remember looking around and thinking, 'Hey, this is alright.' The sun was hanging low, the weather was perfect, the vibe was altogether, the band launches into 'Debaser' . . . and somebody pukes on my shoes. Okay, that last part didn't happen but my point is, it's the kind of thing that goes down at these events, no? It's something one *aspires* to, right? It means you're having a *rocking time!*"

Alex Del Zoppo, Sweetwater:
"Personally, [music festivals] were positive for me. And we've spoken to thousands of others (many through e-mail) who say that one or another of these fests has changed their lives—and always in a positive way. Yes, there were the occasional kids who were grounded after telling their folks that they were going out for the day, then showing up at home a week later, but by and large, over 99 percent of the stories we've heard have been positive ones. Only Altamont was a blemish, but again that was a handful of people who caused the problem. Look at how many people are now becoming aware of starvation in the world, AIDS, and global warming through the more recent and widely televised festivals. It all began 'back then.'"

Greg Gillis, Girl Talk:
"I've been playing a few [festivals] this summer and sometimes it seems a little bit weird to have this 'more bang for your buck' mentality about music. I typically enjoy seeing any band at a club rather than a festival. But sometimes, with a giant audience, it can be an amazing experience. Fests definitely help people find out about new music as well, and it can sometimes blow your mind as a teenager."

Aimee Echo:
"I think rock festivals are fantastic, if they are well-organized. Some of my favorite rock moments have been at festivals. They definitely can be positive, transformative experiences for some, as they have been for me. I also understand there can be negative elements, you know, the kind of mob mentality stuff."

Fred Herrera, Sweetwater:
"For the most part, [the early festivals] made people aware that youth had something to say that was important, and they began a movement that eventually got us out of the Vietnam war and [influenced] many other positive things."

Mike Relm:
"I've observed [at festivals] the love for music that still exists. These days it's such a fashionable thing to say how the music industry is dying and how musicians are going to be out of work soon and no one is selling records anymore. The industry isn't going anywhere, it's just changing drastically. The love for music is as strong as it ever was and it's up to us to figure out ways to sustain careers."

Michael Kang, String Cheese Incident:
"I would say that music is inherently positive for society. However, I also believe that there is a much larger opportunity to have any large gathering become a much more meaningful harbinger of positive social change. I guess it ultimately depends on the people that are running the festival to see how far they want to go in making a festival a truly life-affirming, spiritual experience beyond what you usually get with mass media entertainment. I believe that the modern music festival could really be much more, but at the same time, it's still a good party, for most people."

Andy "Padre" Miller, the Big Wu:
"[A gathering of] 80,000 folks will have 80,000 stories. I had a positive experience [at Bonnaroo], but I didn't eat the brown acid. I'll let the other 79,999 be the judge."

✷ ✷ ✷ ✷ ✷

The artists also have given thought to the legacy of the rock festival. There's the negative side of festivals . . .

Frank Marino, Mahogany Rush:
"Today's festivals are even more of a sad joke than what was in the late seventies and eighties. And those festivals were to real music what the World Wrestling Federation was to real sports. To be fair, there is now at least the pretense of social criticism and moral message. But is it because the artists really care, or rather because it seems fashionable to imitate the sixties generation? We have artists like Bono, Geldof, and the like, getting involved in grandiose displays of 'art' for the sake of the world. But it isn't real. And because of that, it will never accomplish what they say they're setting out to accomplish. These festivals will make their initial splash, generate a bit of bandwagon

interest, and then move on into the dustbin of discarded ideas. Because if you want to really affect social change you need to persevere and to do it honestly. Having a SARS concert with the Rolling Stones, and fifteen-minute appearances by others, amounts to milking the public trough for whatever you can get. I mean, at that rate, why not just put fifty bands on that don't play at all? They can all just walk out and take bows so that fans can say, 'We paid. We were there . . . We saw them.' But where is the real message? Where is the real art? And where is the music? OzzFest is a whole other thing . . . a bunch of bands that want to make it so badly, sometimes paying to play on them . . . giving up all of their ideals just to be part of it . . . signing any ridiculous condition one can dream up. About the only light on the horizon is the Jam-Band festivals—at least they seem to want to really believe all of it, and they seem to still care about the music. But it won't be long, in fact it has already happened, before the corporate guys get a hold of that idea and milk it and ruin it as well. And now, after all of this, after thinking that it just couldn't get any worse—there's American Idol. Don't get me started."

Shawn Phillips:
"If by [festivals such as Live Aid and Live 8], by what's his face Mr. Geldof, then that's all for the good, as they are focusing on where it matters, i.e., the money, and the proper distribution thereof. I don't know what Vans Warped Tour is, and Ozzfest sounds like it has something to do with Ozzie Osbourne, who, as far as I'm concerned is not a musician of any note, just famous. Any festivals that take place today are going to have only the artists that are prominent on the corporate radio chains, and will only reflect whatever the powers that be consider music. That includes rap, which is simply an expression of powerlessness, and can't really be considered as music. Also there is the factor of vicariousness experienced by the listeners. If you hang a guitar around your knees and bang a few chords out at earsplitting volume, then they can identify with that, and say, 'Hey, I can do that,' but if you actually play intricate melodies on a guitar, which requires you to have the instrument at a comfortable position, then they feel it's way beyond anything they will ever be capable of, and let's face it, most people want to be famous just to be famous, without the years of work that's required to really earn it."

John "Mister Zero" Picaro, the Kings:
"Today's festivals are really about one thing: money. All the bands are corporations, as are the events. Back in the day, so much was word of mouth, there was a purity to it,

and bands were different from each other unlike the cookie-cutter flavors of the week we get now."

Tony McPhee, the Groundhogs:
"I only go to play smaller festivals [now, like] Farmer Phil's (local to us), Linton, and Pump-bottom Farm Blues Festival, Beautiful Days (Levellers) . . . . I don't know about the bigger ones, but I do think when festivals get too big they lose the original purpose and it all becomes too business-oriented."

Zia McCabe, Dandy Warhols:
"[Festivals are] positive, of course. I just think we have a lot of work to do stateside if we ever want to experience anything like all the fantastic festivals they have in Europe. Man, those are fun! We're getting closer with Coachella and Sasquatch. I would love to see more like that."

☆ ✷ ☆ ✷ ☆

And the positive . . .

Jack Casady, Jefferson Airplane:
"Events such as Live Aid and Live 8 are evolved from the festival. Regardless of how the music is used, [whether profits are] split by the musicians and the promoters, or used to raise awareness or for charity, it's all music."

Barry Melton, Country Joe & the Fish:
"I have enormous respect for the work of people like Bob Geldof, and I truly believe festivals such as Live Aid and Live 8 were magnificent events that demonstrate the remarkable power of music to bring people together to do good."

Stuart Chatwood: the Tea Party/the Art Decay:
"The music festival is a great venue for fans to dip their feet into other genres of music, and drift from stage to stage. From a band standpoint, this is great because it works inversely as well. Fans that would never listen to one station or go to the kind of website you'd be on would now have an opportunity to get into your music. Festivals also have a great motivating aspect, like Live Aid, amongst others."

Steve Choi, RX Bandits:
"Originally I would say [the festival experience was] negative, but our experience at Bonnaroo has made me question that."

Will Turpin, Collective Soul:
"I find a lot of pride when we are part of a festival that is about something bigger than music. Festivals that raise money or awareness for a need in society are a good reason for bands to get together and jam."

Andrew W.K.:
"I love music festivals! I think they're a great live music experience."

Rick Rose:
"I remember performing at a music festival in Burlington, Ontario with about fifteen bands. What they were doing then and still do now, is incorporate successful American bands with our country's top recording acts. On this show I performed alongside Mountain and the Joe Perry project. Having America so close to us, we had the pleasure of participating with these great American rock bands that brought a great attitude to the stage here in the Great White North!

Larry Hoppen, Orleans:
"I think it's important for people—of all ages—to be able to enjoy live music and new social interaction. When possible, it's also great to include other things—arts, crafts, worthy charitable causes and so on—as Woodstock '94 did. I also think it's important for promoters to produce their events with the audience in mind and a reasonable and genuine concern for safety, comfort, and value. When that happens, it's good for everyone—the crowd, the artists, the promoters, and everyone else involved."

Drew Lamarche, Artificial Joy Club:
"The impact [of appearing at Lollapalooza] for me was that it was a personal goal that I never thought I would achieve. Professionally, it did offer many chances to meet a lot of different people, a few who I tried to maintain contact with for a few years after. I think music festivals are great to perform at, since they usually offer many different types of music and artists, and can introduce new fans to the music. I've been lucky enough over the years to keep playing with various artists and still play various festivals every year."

Joe Sharino, the Joe Sharino Band:
"They're sort of mirrors of our culture. What's strange is that the eighties were supposed to be a decade of greed, the 'me' decade and the US Festival was counter to all of that."

JJ Grey, MOFRO:
"I don't really know what positive or negative is. To me life is so vast that trying to calculate the impact of all of humanity against the limited history we can comprehend is a fool's errand, never mind music or festivals. Especially since concepts of negative and positive ride the wave of public opinion, which changes by the minute."

Michael Ehre, Metalium:
"Like everything in the world, music festivals have positive and negative elements. I think for the fans it's great to see all your favorite bands on one weekend, for less money than it would cost if they would visit the concerts of each band. Also it's very cool to meet a lot of people from all over the world on these festivals. For younger bands, it's a cool chance to perform in front of a big audience. It is definitely more effective to play one festival like the Ozzfest or the German Wacken festival and reach maybe 20,000 or more people than to tour in small clubs for a month or longer and play in front of a few hundred fans each night. The negative element is that a lot of people don't go to club gigs anymore because they know that their bands will play one of the big festivals in summer. So they go there and don't spend their money for the club shows."

Matt Kelly, Dropkick Murphys:
"Aside from the Woodstock ['99] incident, I think it can be a great thing. It's a bit of a throwback to how things were in the days of old. Hundreds of thousands of people getting together to have a good time, hear music, sell their wares, et cetera. Man is a social animal, and festivals give that behavior the ability to thrive."

Peter DiStefano, Porno for Pyros:
"[Woodstock '99] made me grateful for the chance to play in front of that many people and it makes it hard to play a cave now."

Scott Avett, the Avett Brothers:
"It is so about the job for us and then having fun when it is over. We focus so much before a performance and if we are leaving directly after it, then the fun or perspective

on the place is sometimes lost in the mix. We live by advice that Tom T. Hall gave us a few years ago. He said, 'Have fun getting there but know that when you get there it's time to work.' We are rarely there for the party, but there to offer art as a vehicle for it and when it's over . . . we can enjoy it for the moment.''

Zip Caplan, the Litter/White Lightning:
"I will always have fond memories of these events but I can't think of any significant impact they had on my professional career—at that time they were nice to have as part of the bands venue resume but they were becoming pretty common for a while so after a period of time it wasn't like playing Woodstock or Shea Stadium or anything like that—just another gig—only a little better and definitely bigger."

Fred Herrera, Sweetwater:
"We always watch these [current festivals] with envy. If things worked out differently, mainly if Nancy hadn't been almost killed in a car accident four months after we played Woodstock, ruining her voice for decades and consequently sinking Sweetwater's ship, who knows what we'd be doing now. We'd probably be playing these things. Most of the bands of our ilk who hung together through thick and thin eventually won out and became perennial large-venue acts."

Aleksi Ahokas, Rapture:
"Things are usually happening after the actual gigs. [I remember] wandering around the area or the camping area seeing new people and colleagues . . . and the hotel parties. As a musician, even at concerts I'm always criticizing and analyzing things [so I can] learn. [So the festivals] are a pleasure for both performers and for the audience. It's either that or someone is in the wrong place. [How the] performers feel is really important. I guess the idea of a gig is that a band gives the audience something and then they give it back and it magnifies the energy. It's an endless loop where one plus one is more than two."

Gabe Dixon, Gabe Dixon Band:
"The music festival is an essential element of both music *and* society. I mean, 80,000 people assembled peaceably on this earth for any reason is a good thing but when you

consider that at [festivals like] Bonnaroo, they are there to celebrate good music and good times, well, to me, that is beautiful."

Mats Bjorke, Mando Diao:
"[The festival] is positive if it's talking about love and unity. In our hometown we got the Peace and Love Festival. It's a music festival with the mission to change Borlanges' bad [reputation] as a violent and criminal town. And it works!"

Alex Del Zoppo, Sweetwater:
"[I] actually attended a Lollapalooza event and had a wonderful time. Having only heard and read about Bonnaroo, that one seems as if it's the most organic one, having a lot in common with the ones we played back in the day, with great cross-sections of varied artists on their lists and in the way they organize their yearly events. When we folded as a band (the first time), we were a stadium act. So, of course, if we could all agree, it would be great to play one of these again, if they'd have us geezers!"

Nathan Larson, Shudder to Think:
"So here's what I would have done different: I would have a better attitude in general (well, I was twenty-four and a smartass who thought he was gonna be a rock star), I would have drunk less, I would have paid more attention to the music, I would have enjoyed the outdoors, and I would have found lots of girls to talk to. I would have slept under the stars, at least once. I would have picked out constellations. But I didn't and I can live with that, 'cause I got the chance to get around to all this stuff eventually."

Dustin Tooker, Grade 8:
"On the festival style tours you get to play for fans that you might not get in front of otherwise, so it's great to get exposed to different fans and appreciate different people. 'It's all rock 'n' roll to me,'—Billy Joel."

Craig Wedren, Shudder to Think:
"As for the fundamental good or badness of music festivals in general, I think history shows that it cuts both ways. I kind of love them—magic, freedom, hormones, *lots* of music and bodies—but they're gross. Births, deaths, hookups, breakups—festivals are

kind of a weird, souped-up, super-concentrated, but somehow totally divorced-from-reality version of . . . well . . . reality. Chemically enhanced reality minus the fat. I think 'Chill Out Tent' by the Hold Steady sort of nails it."

Andy "Padre" Miller, the Big Wu:
"Someone joked that there would be a Trivial Pursuit question: 'Who was the first band to play Bonnaroo?' a lá 'Who was the first act to play Woodstock?' It may be one that gets somebody the final piece of the pie during a high-stakes match. Hippies have the last laugh!"

Sources

Books

Graham, Bill and Robert Greenfield. *Bill Graham Presents My Life Inside Rock and Out.* New York: Dell, 1992.

Guiliano, Brenda and Geoffrey Guiliano. *The Lost Lennon Interviews.* Cincinnati: Adams Media Corporation, 1996.

Hillmore, Peter. *Live Aid: World Wide Concert Book.* New Jersey: Unicorn Publishing House, 1985.

Marsh, Dave. *Before I Get Old: The Story of the Who.* New Jersey: Plexus Publishing, 2003.

Phillips, John. *Papa John.* New York: Dell, 1987.

Shankar, Ravi. *Raga Mala: The Autobiography of Ravi Shankar.* New York: Welcome Rain, 2001.

Underwood, Lee. *Blue Melody: Tim Buckley Remembered.* New York: Backbeat Books, 2002.

Wenner, Jann S. *Lennon Remembers.* New York: W. W. Norton & Company, 2001.

Documentary Films

The Complete Monterey Pop Festival. Directed by D.A. Pennebaker & Chris Hegedus. Criterion Collection, 1967, 2002.

Isle of Wight Festival: Message to Love. Directed by Murray Lerner & Sony Wonder. 1970, 1997.

John Lennon and the Plastic Ono Band: Sweet Toronto. Geneon, 1969, 2002.

The Rolling Stones: Gimme Shelter. Directed by Albert Maysles & David Maysles & Charlotte Zwerin. Criterion Collection, 1969, 2000.

Woodstock: Three Days of Peace and Music. Directed by Michael Wadleigh. Warner Home Video, 1968, 1997.

Periodicals

Atlanta Journal Constitution, Arts and Entertainment, July 4, 1995: "What a Splash: Recalling Georgia's 'Woodstock'" by Richard L. Eldredge.

Atlanta Journal Constitution, January 5, 2006: "Music Midtown Canceled for '06; Promoters Cite Expense" by Nick Marino.

Beat Productions, November, 1969: "John and Yoko Ono, Live Peace in Toronto" by Johnny Dean.

Entertainment Weekly, June 22, 2007: "Summer of Love Revisited" by Clark Collins.

Entertainment Weekly, July 20, 2007: "Hot in Here" by Leah Greenblatt.

Entertainment Weekly, July 20, 2007: "Music to My Fears" by Dalton Ross.

Evansville Courier, October 21, 1995: " 'Bull Island' Rock Fest Shaky from Start to Finish."

Evansville Courier, October 22, 1995: "Food Shortage at Bull Island Triggered Edgy Crowd."

Evansville Courier, October 24, 1995: "Tumult Lived on After Bull Island Shut Down."

Freshwater (U.K.), August 26, 1970: "Town of Tents at Pop Festival" by David Wilsworth.

Freshwater (U.K.), August 27, 1970: "Gatecrasher Trouble at Festival" by David Wilsworth.

Freshwater (U.K.), August 31, 1970: "Art for Destitute as Pop Festival Ends."

Inland Valley Daily Bulletin, April 4, 2002: "One Day in 1974" by David Allen.

Ithaca Times, August 24, 1989: "Back to the Garden" by Stu Fox.

Marietta Daily Journal, Marietta, GA, August 20, 2007: "Sponsored Concert Great Deal for Fans, but Could Be Fad" by Mark Brown for Scripps Howard news service.

Metro, Silicon Valley, CA, June 14-20, 2001: "Pop Perfect: The Monterey Pop Festival Was the First and Still Is the Greatest of Rock Concerts" by Gina Arnold.

Minnesota Echoes, 2005: "Altamont" by Adam Stanley.

MTV News, May 25, 2007: "Ozzfest Not So Free After All: Organizers Offer VIP Ticket Plans" by Chris Harris.

People, July 23, 2007: "World Party" by Rennie Dyball.

The Providence Journal, August 13, 1989: "Woodstock II: Better than Ever" by Sheila Lennon.